CAMBRIDGE STUDIES IN INTERNATIONAL RELATIONS: 50

Africa and the international system

Cambridge Studies in International Relations is a joint initiative of Cambridge University Press and the British International Studies Association (BISA). The series will include a wide range of material, from undergraduate textbooks and surveys to research-based monographs and collaborative volumes. The aim of the series is to publish the best new scholarship in International Studies from Europe, North America and the rest of the world.

CAMBRIDGE STUDIES IN INTERNATIONAL RELATIONS 50

50 *Christopher Clapham*
Africa and the international system
The politics of state survival

49 *Susan Strange*
The retreat of the state
The diffusion of power in the world economy

48 *William I. Robinson*
Promoting polyarchy
Globalization, US intervention, and hegemony

47 *Roger D. Spegele*
Political realism in international theory

46 *Thomas J. Biersteker and Cynthia Weber (eds.)*
State sovereignty as social construct

45 *Mervyn Frost*
Ethics in international relations
A constitutive theory

44 *Mark W. Zacher with Brent A. Sutton*
Governing global networks
International regimes for transportation and communications

43 *Mark Neufeld*
The restructuring of international relations theory

42 *Thomas Risse-Kappan (ed.)*
Bringing transnational relations back in
Non-state actors, domestic structures and international institutions

41 *Hayward R. Alker*
Rediscoveries and reformulations
Humanistic methodologies for international studies

40 *Robert W. Cox with Timothy J. Sinclair*
Approaches to world order

39 *Jens Bartelson*
A genealogy of sovereignty

Series list continues after index.

Africa and the international system

The politics of state survival

Christopher Clapham
University of Lancaster

PUBLISHED BY THE PRESS SYNDICATE OF THE UNIVERSITY OF CAMBRIDGE
The Pitt Building, Trumpington Street, Cambridge, United Kingdom

CAMBRIDGE UNIVERSITY PRESS
The Edinburgh Building, Cambridge CB2 2RU, UK http://www.cup.cam.ac.uk
40 West 20th Street, New York, NY 10011–4211, USA http://www.cup.org
10 Stamford Road, Oakleigh, Melbourne 3166, Australia
Ruiz de Alarcón 13, 28014 Madrid, Spain

First published 1996
Reprinted 1997, 1998, 1999

Printed in the United Kingdom at the University Press, Cambridge

A catalogue record for this book is available from the British Library

Library of Congress Cataloguing in Publication data
Clapham, Christopher S.
Africa and the international system: the politics of state survival / Christopher Clapham.
p. cm. – (Cambridge studies in international relations: 50)
Includes bibliographical references and index.
ISBN 0 521 57207 X. – ISBN 0 521 57668 7 (pbk.)
1. Africa – Foreign relations – 1960–
2. Self-determination, National – Africa.
3. Sovereignty. I. Title. II. Series.
JX1582.C55 1966
327'.096'09045 – dc20 96–3882 CIP

ISBN 0 521 57207 X hardback
ISBN 0 521 57668 7 paperback

CE

Contents

Acknowledgements *page* xi
List of acronyms and abbreviations xiii

Part I African states and global politics **1**
1 Fragile states and the international system 3
Introduction 3
Statehood and global politics 8
Quasi-statehood and the negative sovereignty regime 15
Globalisation and sovereign statehood 24

2 The creation of an African international order 28
People and government in Africa 28
The colonial grid 30
Indigenising power 33
The waiting world 41

3 Domestic statehood and foreign policy 44
The idea of the African state 44
The monopoly state 56
The domestic politics of foreign policy management 62
Paying for the state 67
Conclusion 73

Part II Patterns of alliance **75**
4 The Foreign Policies of Post-Colonialism 77
The post-colonial relationship 77
The international politics of francophonie 88
Multilateral post-colonialism 98
Conclusion 103

5 The politics of solidarity 106
African states: allies or rivals? 106
The continental coalition 110
The politics of regionalism 117
The Afro-Arab relationship 125
Conclusion 131

6 The resort to the superpowers 134
Africa in the superpower world 134
The Soviet role 142
The militarisation of Africa's external relations 150
Africa in the post-Cold War world 158

Part III Struggling with decay 161

7 The international politics of economic failure 163
The failure of African economies 163
The externalisation of economic management 169
Responses to adjustment 176
The politics of aid dependence 181

8 The Externalisation of political accountability 187
The decline of sovereignty 187
The imposition of political conditionalities 192
The African state response 201

9 The International politics of insurgency 208
Insurgency and the African international order 208
The politics of the border 215
Insurgent diplomacy 222
The NGO connection 226
The insurgent international economy 230
Controlling insurgency 234
The post-insurgent state 239

10 The privatisation of diplomacy 244
African statehood and international relations 244
The shadow state 249
The 'de-stating' of external relations with Africa 256

11 Conclusion 267

Notes 275
Bibliography 311
Index 332

Acknowledgements

The University of Lancaster has employed and paid me, not only during the year that it took me to write this book, but for almost all of the much longer period during which I have been learning about international relations in Africa. While writing the book, I also benefited from a UK Economic & Social Research Council Senior Research Fellowship, which paid for another member of staff to carry out my teaching and other university duties for a year, and for my indispensable laptop computer. The Human Sciences Research Council of South Africa paid my air fare from London to Johannesburg, which also covered most of the cost of intermediate stops in Asmara, Addis Ababa, Nairobi, Kampala, Kigali and Harare, together with my subsistence costs for a month at the Africa Institute of South Africa in Pretoria; and the British Council met my subsistence costs for a further month at the South African Institute of International Affairs in Johannesburg. To all of these institutions I am most grateful.

I am also grateful for institutional and academic support to Denis Venter and the staff of the Africa Institute of South Africa in Pretoria; to Sara Pienaar, Greg Mills and the staff of the South African Institute of International Affairs in Johannesburg; and to Stephen Ellis and the librarians of the Afrika Studiecentrum at Leiden in the Netherlands.

While this book is written mostly from published sources, I also benefited greatly from the help and hospitality which I received while travelling to a number of African capitals early in 1995, to gather further material and absorb something of the flavour of international relations on the continent: from Bereket Habte-Selassie in Asmara; from Richard and Rita Pankhurst in Addis Ababa; from Daniel Davis and from Belinda Chesire in Nairobi; from Roger Tangri and Judy Butterman in Kampala; from Lillian Wong and from Pascal Ngoga in

Kigali; and from Rosaleen Duffy and from Eliphas Mukonoweshuro in Harare. None of these, needless to say, bears the slightest blame for anything I have written, except where this is acknowledged in the text.

Stephen Ellis, Sally Healy, Roy May, Douglas Rimmer and John Wiseman kindly read through all or part of drafts of this book, and made helpful suggestions and corrections, while bearing no responsibility for any errors or inanities that remain.

Caroline, Phoebe and Tom, finally, supported both my absence and my presence with equal equanimity.

CSC

Galgate, Lancaster
July 1995

Acronyms and abbreviations

ACP	African, Caribbean & Pacific States, associated with EC
ANC	African National Congress (South Africa)
BADEA	Banque Arabe pour le Developpement Economique en Afrique
CCCE	Caisse Centrale de Coopération Economique (France)
CFA	Communauté Financière Africaine (Franc Zone currency)
CMEA	Council for Mutual Economic Assistance (Comecon)
CPSU	Communist Party of the Soviet Union
EC/EU	European Community/European Union
ECOMOG	ECOWAS Monitoring Group (Liberia)
ECOWAS	Economic Community of West African States
ECU	European Currency Unit
ELF	Eritrean Liberation Front
ELF-PLF	ELF-Popular Liberation Forces
EPLF	Eritrean People's Liberation Front
EPRDF	Ethiopian Peoples' Revolutionary Democratic Front
ERA	Eritrean Relief Association
ERD	Emergency Relief Desk (Ethiopia/Eritrea)
EUA	European Unit of Account
FAO	Food & Agriculture Organisation of the United Nations
FF	French Franc
FLS	Front Line States
FNLA	Frente Nacional de Libertaçao de Angola
forex	foreign exchange
Frelimo	Frente de Libertaçao de Moçambique
GNP	Gross National Product
IGADD	Intergovernmental Authority on Drought & Development
IMF	International Monetary Fund
LAMCO	Liberian-American Mining Company
MNR	Mozambique National Resistance (Renamo)

MPLA	Movimento Popular de Libertaçao de Angola
NATO	North Atlantic Treaty Organisation
NGO	Non-Governmental Organisation
NPFL	National Patriotic Front of Liberia
NRA	National Resistance Army (Uganda)
OAU	Organisation of African Unity
ODA	Official Development Assistance
OPEC	Organisation of Petroleum Exporting Countries
opex	operational experts (Liberia)
OTRAG	Orbital Transport & Raketen AG (Germany)
PAC	Pan-African Congress (South Africa)
PTA	Preferential Trade Area of Eastern & Southern Africa
Renamo	Resistencia Nacional Moçambicana
REST	Relief Society of Tigray (Ethiopia)
RPF	Rwanda Patriotic Front
RUF	Revolutionary United Front (Sierra Leone)
SADC	Southern African Development Community
SALT	Strategic Arms Limitation Treaty
SNA	Somali National Alliance
SNM	Somali National Movement
SPLA	Sudan People's Liberation Army
Stabex	Stabilisation of Export Earnings scheme (EC)
SWAPO	South-West Africa People's Organisation (Namibia)
Sysmin	System for Mineral Products (EC)
TPLF	Tigray People's Liberation Front (Ethiopia)
UDEAC	Union Douanière des Etats de l'Afrique Centrale
UDI	Unilateral Declaration of Independence (Rhodesia)
UN	United Nations
UNDP	UN Development Programme
UNHCR	UN High Commission for Refugees
UNICEF	UN Children's Emergency Fund
Unita	Uniao Nacional para a Independencia Total de Angola
UNITAF	UN Transitional Assistance Force (Somalia)
UNOSOM	UN Operation in Somalia
US/USA	United States of America
USSR	Union of Soviet Socialist Republics
WFP	World Food Programme of the UN
ZANLA	Zimbabwe African National Liberation Army
ZANU	Zimbabwe African National Union
ZANU-PF	ZANU-Patriotic Front
ZAPU	Zimbabwe African People's Union

Part I
African states and global politics

1 Fragile states and the international system

Introduction

This book attempts to examine the workings of international politics from the viewpoint of a group of states – and in some degree their people – which are at the bottom of any conventional ordering of global power, importance and prestige. International relations has tended, understandably enough, to look at the world from the viewpoint of its most powerful states. It has been developed as a subject of study in the major capitalist states, and has been directed largely towards helping them to manage the demands of an increasingly complex international system – most obviously through the avoidance of war, but also through the management of the global economy and in other ways. Its dominant focus during the era of the Cold War was on the relationship between the superpowers, with a secondary but still important emphasis on relations between other industrial states such as those of Western Europe. Even the study of 'north–south' relations characteristically had a heavy emphasis on *north–south* relations, often within the context of superpower competition, rather than on south–north ones.

Yet most of the world's states – and in the context of this book, notably those of sub-Saharan Africa – are poor, weak and subordinate. Most of the people in them are poorer, weaker and more subordinate still. International politics affects these states and people in ways that often differ appreciably from the ways in which it affects the people and governments of more powerful states. In particular, even though states are central to the understanding of international relations in the 'Third World' as elsewhere, states themselves are often very different kinds of organisation from those that the conventional study of international relations tends to take for granted. Their interactions, both with their own populations and with other parts of the international system, correspondingly differ as well. And though the international relations of the Third World, Africa included, has attracted an increasing amount of attention, much of this have operated within assumptions about the nature of statehood and the international system which may be seriously misleading. A view of international politics from the bottom up may therefore help, not only to illuminate the impact of the global system on those who are least able to resist it, but to provide a perspective on that system, and hence on the study of international relations as a whole, which may complement and even correct the perspective gained by looking from the top downwards.

This view from below is especially apposite to sub-Saharan Africa – taken here to include all of the African continent and its adjacent islands apart from those states which border the Mediterranean – because its states are not only of very recent origin, and on the whole amongst the poorest in the world, but have also in the great majority of cases been created by international action in the form of European colonialism, and have been left with state frontiers which rarely correspond to pre-colonial social or geographical identities. The first question that needs to be asked is therefore how these states managed to survive – for a period of some thirty-five years, in most cases, after formal independence – within a global order dominated by states which were evidently vastly more powerful than they. This is not only a question about the nature of the international order which, in some measure, 'permitted' their survival, important though that obviously was. It is also a question about what African states – or more precisely, to make a very important distinction, the rulers who acted on their behalf – did in an attempt to help them to survive. The evident weakness of African states did not reduce them to a state of inertia, in which their fate was determined by external powers. On the contrary, it impelled them to take measures designed to ensure survival, or at least to improve their chances of it. This question of what African rulers did in an attempt to survive provides the primary focus for this book.

The issue of survival in turn, however, raises the question of *whose* survival: the state's, or the ruler's? In the great majority of cases, rulers seek to assure their personal survival by seeking the survival and indeed strengthening of their states. They can on the whole best protect their own security by preserving and enhancing the power of the states which they rule. But though the defence of statehood normally provides an essential element in personal survival strategies, these strategies none the less impose a particular view of statehood, which associates it with the welfare and security of the ruler. Since the security of African rulers was often particularly at risk, they felt the need to make use of their control over states in distinctive ways, the most characteristic of which was the construction of the 'monopoly states' referred to in later chapters. In some cases, and to an increasing extent, it even led to the development of the 'shadow states' discussed in the final chapter, in which rulers used formal statehood merely as a facade, behind which to conduct what became essentially personal survival strategies.

Survival is not, of course, the only goal of rulers, but it is none the less the precondition for pursuing any other goal. The less secure the rulers, the greater the prominence that it is likely to assume. The insecurity of many African rulers meant that for them, in Jackson and Rosberg's phrase, seamanship often mattered more than navigation: staying afloat was more important than going somewhere.[1] Since personal survival, however important it may be for individual politicians, is not normally regarded as a legitimate basis for political action, it is characteristically excluded in the rhetoric of international relations, in favour of goals which provide a more respectable rationale for their activities. In the case of African states, these most commonly consisted in domestic transformation goals, normally expressed in terms of 'development' and 'nationhood', and external transformation goals, normally expressed in terms of the 'liberation' either of African peoples from alien rule, or of African states from the domination of outside powers. This is turn led to a demand for 'unity' among African states and peoples. Studies which take as their starting point the formal goals of politicians therefore pay considerable attention to these essentially rhetorical appeals. Though rhetoric has a very significant role in politics, both domestic and international, as a way of trying to create solidarity and assure legitimacy for those who use it, these appeals are in this book given only subordinate attention, on the ground that they have been more than adequately covered elsewhere, at the expense of more fundamental issues in African international relations which have commonly been neglected. Other goals notably include aspects of the ruler's welfare apart from survival, such as self-enrichment, which in the case of a few African rulers reached manic proportions. These too on occasion affected Africa's international relations.

This view of the international system from the perspective of those who must use foreign policy essentially as a means of trying to assure their own survival raises issues in the study of international relations which may not be so obvious when it is viewed from the perspective of powerful states with reasonably stable domestic political systems. One of these is that the nature and role of the state itself, as the basic organising concept through which an understanding of the international system is conventionally put together, are far more ambivalent than they appear to be, at least, in those parts of the world which have historically given rise to the study of international relations. Alternative conceptions of statehood, and their application to the international politics especially of weak and fragile states, are examined in the next section. To anticipate: the less solid the state, the greater the need to look beyond it for an understanding of how the society that it claims to govern fits into the international system. Though African states and those who run them have assumed a critical importance in the external relations of the continent, they have done so not merely as the building blocks with which any study of the subject must be constructed, but rather as competitors in an often inchoate struggle for external resources. Africans have been deeply affected by the international system in many ways, some of which have been directly mediated by the state whereas others have not. Their varied engagement in activities which extend beyond the frontiers of their states may be said to constitute 'foreign policies' which are in part independent of those of their governments: smuggling, or going abroad for education, or fleeing as a refugee, can in this sense be regarded as foreign policy decisions, which may in turn affect (and sometimes subvert) the foreign policies of governments. Though a full investigation of these numerous linkages would go well beyond the limits of practicality in a book already conceived on an ambitious scale, they none the less need to be borne in mind, and are referred to at points where they have an important bearing on the policies of states. One particular kind of non-state foreign policy, that of guerrilla movements or insurgencies, has, however, been so important in the foreign relations of Africa that it is accorded a chapter of its own.

The foreign relations of Africa have moreover been far from static over the long period since independence which this book attempts to cover. Many of the most important changes during this period took place within African states themselves, especially in the decline of their economies at a time when most of the rest of the world was enjoying increasing prosperity, and in their failure in many if not most cases to create domestic political institutions that achieved the support of their populations. These failures in turn greatly intensified the problems of personal and state survival, and thus critically affected Africa's relations with the outside world. The outside world was likewise changing, from the relatively stable equilibrium between the great powers in the 1960s, to the stresses in superpower relations of the 'Second Cold War' of the 1970s, which were particularly marked in their effects on the Third World, the evident economic triumph of the capitalist states in the 1980s (with its knock-on effects on Africa in the form of structural adjustment programmes), and the collapse of the Soviet Union and its allies after 1989. The overall effect of these changes, both inside and outside Africa, was to make it increasingly difficult for African rulers to use international support as a means of maintaining both their states and their personal power, in the way that they had been able to do with considerable success during the decade and a half or so after independence.

Any study which seeks to appraise the relations between African states and their external environment must thus go some way beyond the confines of any narrow conception of international relations. The global system is certainly important, though here much must be taken as read. Equally important, and rather more in need of elucidation, is the nature of African states, which defines their approach to their external world. This most basically extends to 'nature' itself, in the form of the environmental base on which African societies are built – and nowhere in the world is the relationship between human beings and their immediate physical endowment more starkly and at times more tragically evident. It likewise includes the social values and identities which that physical endowment helps to define, often over a very long period, and which in turn help to shape the 'governmentalities', or attitudes to politics and authority, which characterise (often in different ways) the rulers and the ruled.[2] The specific mechanisms by which African states were created, and the peculiar emphasis which these placed on their relations with the external world, in both political and economic terms, provide another formative influence. Nor, finally, can Africa's external relations be divorced from post-independence trajectories which were not entirely determined by the pre-colonial and colonial inheritance and the influence of the outside world, but which were also affected by the actions of African rulers and peoples.

Statehood and global politics

However broadly the analysis of Africa's international politics must ultimately be conceived, the division of the world into states not only forms the basis for the conventional study of international relations, but also provides the single most important fact about the actual working of international politics in Africa. For the moment, therefore, states are where we need to start.

The first question that we have to ask is accordingly what 'states' *are*. Only the most innocent questioner, however, will expect this enquiry to lead to any clear and generally agreed answer. Politics is about conflict, and about the ability of people to devise power structures which, on the one hand, may work to the overall benefit or disadvantage of the individuals who are affected by them, but which, on the other hand, will invariably confer considerably greater benefits and costs on some people than on others. Not only is politics itself a contest, but the words and ideas which are used to describe it are contested too. States, as one of the most important constituents of the structure of global power, are themselves unavoidably part of the contested terrain which politics is about.[3] The definition of statehood is in particular contested because it combines (and, to a large extent, confuses) three different attributes which when taken together have the effect of giving some people power over others.

A first way of looking at statehood consists in equating states with governments which exercise claims to sovereign jurisdiction over a particular territory and population. States in this sense are coercive and administrative institutions, and their 'sovereignty' is the asserted right to act as the final arbiter of actions carried out within the territory which they control. In order to achieve sovereignty, the state requires an institutional structure, which in turn is expected to serve a number of functions. It has to identify a person or group of people who are deemed to 'represent' the state at the highest level, in that their actions and statements are deemed to carry the authority of the state as a whole. These people need to control subordinates, who in turn are charged with subsidiary but essential functions, the most important of which is the physical control of the national territory. The government which they form also needs to extract the money and other resources required to run the state, and may carry out a range of further functions, some of which are normally designed to improve the welfare of the state's population, through education, health care and other services. The state as government on the one hand serves (or at any rate claims to serve) as a mechanism for ensuring the welfare of its inhabitants, most basically through the provision of peace and order; while on the other hand it necessarily exercises power, which in turn implies the inequality of its citizens, and the ability of some of them to gain at the expense of others. The relative balance between the state as provider of welfare, and the state as source of exploitation, not only separates different theoretical conceptions of the state, but also has a powerful impact on its international relations.

A state in this sense may be more or less capable of imposing its control over the people whom it attempts to govern. No state, mercifully, has been able to exercise complete control over all of the population that is subordinated to it, as the failure of would-be 'totalitarian' states has made clear. Some states have none the less proved far more effective at regulating their populations and territories than others. Although African states have sometimes sought to implement ambitious programmes of social transformation, and have even for a while appeared to be successful in doing so, they have generally been amongst the weakest states in the global system, for reasons which will be explored in the next chapter. At times, they have been unable to maintain even the most exiguous control over much of the territory which they have claimed to govern. Only within the last century, after all, has the whole inhabited area of the globe (with a few exceptions, the most important of which is Antarctica) been divided between states, and statehood came later to much of Africa than to any other area of the inhabited world. The question of whether all of the continent and its inhabitants actually belong to states, which once appeared to have been settled beyond plausible dispute by colonial partition and independence, has been reopened by the evident disappearance of states from parts of the continent, and by the emergence in some of these of alternative authorities whose entitlement to statehood was contestable. The questions of whether international relations can exist without states, and if so what form such relations might take, are by no means empty ones, and the answers cannot be imposed from the outset by definitional sleight of hand.

A second way of approaching statehood is through what one may define, following Buzan, as the 'idea of the state'.[4] States in this sense must be 'constructed' in the minds of at least some of those who form them, including minimally those who run them. This construction is in particular required in order to provide the state with legitimacy, or in other words, with a basis in morality rather than merely force. It most significantly involves an attempt to find some answer to two questions: the first is why the state should exist in the form that it does, which may be defined as territorial legitimacy; the second is why the group of people who rule it should have any right to act on behalf of those who are merely its subjects or citizens, which may correspondingly be defined as governmental legitimacy. These questions are critical, in that they represent the only means by which the state can justify the claims that it makes on the people whom it seeks to control, and the support of other states and people outside it.

What is deemed to count as a satisfactory answer to the problem of legitimacy has varied very considerably over the course of human history, and still varies appreciably from one state to another. It characteristically draws on a complex of factors which help either to identify groups of people with one another, or to separate them from one another, such as language, religion, shared or unshared experiences and similar or different historical mythologies. In terms of the currently dominant value system of Western liberalism, a satisfactory answer to the question of territorial legitimacy requires that the population (or at least the great majority of it) should voluntarily agree to live within the state concerned, an agreement which in turn is ideally achieved through a sense of nationhood which binds members of the population to one another, and to the state to which they all belong; other claims to territorial legitimacy may rest on the asserted right of a state to control all of the territory which it has occupied at some point in the past; on its right to govern the area allocated to it by international agreements; or on revolutionary aspirations to liberation or even salvation.

The corresponding answer to the question of governmental legitimacy in Western liberal thought is that the government should have the right to act on behalf of its citizens, because they have chosen its leaders through some constitutional mechanism on which they are broadly agreed. At other times and in other places, this question has been answered in other ways, as for example through a widely shared belief that those in power derive their authority from God, or the claim that state authority expresses the dictatorship of the proletariat. In many cases, the question has not been satisfactorily answered at all; or else the 'idea of the state' has been shared (or indeed, it might be said, 'owned') by some of its members and not by others; it is then legitimate for those who own it, but not for those who don't. The ideas of the state espoused by the ruling group in any one state often differ significantly from those held either in other states, or else among other groups within their own state, and these differences account for (or sometimes just symbolise) many of the conflicts that inflame international politics.

The final way of defining a state is, in Northedge's words, as 'a territorial association of people recognized for purposes of law and diplomacy as a legally equal member of the system of states.'[5] Though a state may be able to control its territory, and even to achieve the loyalty of its population, it none the less needs this recognition in order to participate in the international transactions in which, in the modern interdependent world, a very large part of statehood consists. It may also, in practice, be central to the ability of states to control their own territories. The power of rulers derives not only from the material resources and ideological support of their own people, but equally from their ability to draw on the ideological and material resources provided by other states – and also non-states, such as transnational religious organisations or business corporations. The weaker the state, in terms of its size and capabilities, its level of physical control over its people and territory, and its ability or inability to embody an idea of the state shared by its people, the greater the extent to which it will need to call on external recognition and support. In the case of the African states with which we are concerned in this book, this recognition and support were often critical.

In the mythology of statehood, no significant problems arise from these alternative approaches, since states are deemed to satisfy all of them. State authorities exercise effective government over the territories which are ascribed to them. These territories are in turn legitimately governed by them, because their populations recognise their own identity as citizens of the state concerned, and the government of that state as their government. The recognition of their statehood, both internally by their populations and externally by other states, entitles the governments of states to act on behalf of the state in its internal and external transactions. International relations then consists in a dialogue between the governments of states, and through them, between their populations.

This is, however, a picture which derives at least as much from the self-serving claims of those who run states, and the conversion of these claims into a legitimating ideology for the international order of which as rulers they form part, as from any objective attributes of states themselves. From another perspective, states may be viewed as power structures, imposed on societies and physical endowments which they then seek to control in the interests of those who run them. Sometimes these power structures are relatively effective, and reasonably well integrated with their social and economic base. Sometimes they are merely perched on top of people and territories which they can do little to control, surviving if at all only by desperate efforts. States themselves, moreover, are no more than groupings of human beings, the relations between whom are structured in ways which may vary dramatically from one state to another. The use of a common title, with the ascription to them of a common international status, no more than thinly disguises the differences between them.

In practice, the attributes ascribed to states by the mythology of statehood very often do not actually coincide at all. There are few, perhaps no, states in which they are all realised in their entirety. Even in the United Kingdom, which satisfies the criteria for statehood better than most, there are substantial populations – most obviously in Northern Ireland, but also in Scotland and elsewhere – who do not accept their own membership of the state that claims them; the mechanisms which convert popular support into government power are open to serious question; and there have even been occasions, again most evidently in Northern Ireland, when the writ of the government over its territory did not run. In most states, and notably all of the African states with which this book is concerned, the gap between the myth and the reality of statehood is considerably greater.

In a sense, every failure of states to measure up to the ideal of statehood comes down to a failure in the idea of the state – though at the same time, the manifest impossibility of getting the entire population of virtually any state to share a common view of its identity, territory and constitution is such that this is only to be expected. The criterion that is most frequently not achieved is governmental legitimacy, which confers on the government of a state the moral right to act on behalf of its population. As already noted, this claim may be validated in a number of ways, but is most commonly expressed through election or other forms of consent. In quite a large number of states, as for example most of those ruled by military regimes, the requirement to rule with the consent of the population is formally recognised, but has none the less been discarded by a government which has actually seized power by force, and which claims a temporary right to rule in the name of some overriding value such as the maintenance of national unity or the extirpation of corruption. Such claims are often entirely bogus. Often, too, claims to rule by democratic principles are invalidated by the fraudulent conduct of elections, or by the imposition of constitutional systems which have little if any popular support. Non-democratic principles of legitimacy are even more open to abuse, and may well be accepted only by those who stand to gain from them. The failure of the principle of governmental legitimacy dissolves the moral relationship that is assumed by the myth of statehood to exist between the population of the state and the people who run it. It means that rulers do not govern on behalf of those people, however much they may claim to do so, but instead govern simply on their own behalf and that of their supporters. When, under such circumstances, one talks about 'the state', one is referring merely to the individuals who own it.

Claims to territorial legitimacy are likewise frequently contested, as for example when a government asserts its right to control part of the territory of the state, despite the absence of willing consent on the part of those who live within it. The immediate break-up of the Soviet Union after the collapse of Communist Party rule demonstrated all too clearly that the claims previously made that the USSR constituted a voluntary association of peoples were false. The unification of Germany likewise indicated that the claims previously made on behalf of the former German Democratic Republic had been equally fictitious. Given that a large number of territorial boundaries, including notably most of those assigned by colonialism to the states of Africa and Asia, were drawn up by means which paid little if any attention to the views of the people who were incorporated within them, it should be no surprise if the boundaries of states, or even their right to exist at all, were not generally accepted. In particular, these origins may well lead to a situation in which one part of the population – distinguished by its numerical strength, strategic location, or adherence to criteria (such as language or religion) in terms of which the idea of the state is implicitly defined – viewed itself as belonging to the state, whereas other sections of the population did not.

A third way in which the mythology of statehood may fail to apply, and one which has become increasingly important in recent years, is that the government of a state may simply be unable to exercise effective control over the territory which is nominally allocated to it. Over and above any fictitious claims to legitimacy which those who control the state may make on its behalf, their claims even to sovereignty may be equally fraudulent. On some occasions, people – such as the governments in exile of states under wartime enemy occupation – claim to constitute the government of a state, even when none of them is able safely to set foot inside it. More often, governments which control the capital city are unable to extend that control over the whole of the formal national territory, in the face of opposition from warlords, rebels or secessionists, or the collapse of their own administrative apparatus. In extreme cases, states may, as in the former Yugoslavia, split apart into entities which (with a greater or lesser degree of international acceptance) claim separate statehood, or else as in Somalia they may become so fragmented that no government exists at all.

International recognition, finally, characteristically corresponds, not to any consistent set of empirical criteria, but rather to the acceptability of the state concerned to current *international* mythologies of legitimate statehood. Several governments which controlled by far the greater part of their claimed territory, and even some which had plausible claims to the support of most of their populations, have been denied recognition, whereas others which had little or even no such control, and many which had no claim whatever to the support of their populations, have been accorded it without difficulty. The unilateral declaration of independence by white-ruled Rhodesia clearly infringed against the rules of acceptable statehood in post-colonial Africa and was not recognised even by South Africa, while the declaration of independence by Ojukwu's Biafra, which offended the principle of maintaining the territorial integrity of African states, regardless of any demand for 'self-determination', was eventually recognised only by five other states. Conversely, Western Saharan independence was recognised by a majority of African states, even though the main centres of its sparsely inhabited territory were claimed and occupied by Morocco.

These states which fail to meet the formal (or indeed mythical) requirements of statehood are of the greatest importance, both because they illustrate important features of the way in which the international system works, and equally because they affect a substantial number of states. This failure of reality to correspond to some often quite unattainable ideal is no more than the normal condition of humanity, and is not in itself any cause for concern. What matters is what people do when their ideals are not met, and in international politics this has mattered a great deal, because the lives of very large numbers of people have been directly affected by it. The lives of Africans have been especially at risk.

Quasi-statehood and the negative sovereignty regime

What effectively happened during much of the post-1945 era in international politics was that governments agreed among themselves to pretend in many cases that the criteria for legitimate statehood were met, regardless of how evidently fictitious this pretence may have been. This pretence in turn took the form of what Jackson has described as quasi-statehood.[6] Quasi-states, in Jackson's terms, are states which are recognised as sovereign and independent units by other states within the international system, but which cannot meet the demands of 'empirical' statehood, which requires the capacity to exercise effective power within their own territories, and be able to defend themselves against external attack. Such states have 'negative' or 'juridical' sovereignty, in that sovereignty is ascribed to them by other states, but do not possess the 'positive sovereignty' which derives from effective control.

This distinction epitomises the dichotomy which scholars in international relations (and especially Western ones) have been apt to make between 'real' states, or in other words developed industrial powers, and the doubtful or even fictitious states found in other parts of the world. As already noted, this dichotomy is misleading: the dramatic upheavals in European frontiers since the end of the Cold War have shown how fragile were the bases on which even some of the apparently most powerful states in the world depended. It would be more appropriate to place all states on a continuum, according not only to the level of effective government power over the state's territory (to which Jackson pays most attention), but also to the extent to which the 'idea' of each state is both shared and implemented. The idea of quasi-statehood, carrying with it the recognition that the approval or disapproval of the international system may well be more important to a state's prospects of survival than any criterion relating to its domestic power or legitimacy, is none the less a very useful one.

At the most general level, indeed, the idea that states either logically or historically precede the international system of which they form part is mistaken. As Halliday has pointed out, even the apparently most firmly rooted states, such as the United Kingdom or the United States, have been formed by their interactions with the international system, every bit as much as the international system has been formed by the interactions between states.[7] In practice, the existence of states within the international system has always been governed to an appreciable extent by the conventions of that system itself, which in turn have usually been established by tacit or explicit agreement between its currently leading states. The idea that states have a prior existence in their own right, derived from the identity of their peoples and the strength of their governments, so that diplomacy simply represents the relations between these states, has never been more than a very partial picture of the structure of global politics. In every age, states of an evidently artificial kind have been permitted to exist by the suffrance of the major powers. The Venetian Republic and the government of Malta by the Knights of St John continued in being for centuries, until the French Revolution and the changed strategic situation in Europe led to their abolition. The artificial state of Belgium was brought into existence in 1830, and its independence guaranteed by the great powers, not merely as a result of the revolt by its own peoples against its incorporation into the Netherlands, but equally because each of the regional powers was anxious that this strategically sensitive territory should not be controlled by any of the others. The states of north central Europe – Poland, Czechoslovakia and the Baltic Republics – were created (or re-established) after the First World War as a buffer zone between a defeated Germany and a revolutionary Russia, lost their independence once the resurgence first of Germany and then of Russia destroyed the international balance on which this independence rested, and then regained it with the end of the Cold War. The conventions of negative sovereignty applied during the Cold War extended the relative protection that buffer states had received from the balance of power between the major states in the international community to encompass the whole of Africa and much of the rest of the world as well.

At all events, the international rules of the game (or 'sovereignty regime', in Jackson's terms) devised after the end of the Second World War, and reinforced by the independence of numerous formerly colonial territories, profoundly influenced the structure of international politics during the period up to the end of the Cold War, and continued to have a considerable impact even after it. These rules defined both the membership of the international system, and the rights and obligations associated with membership. The conditions of membership were most precisely specified by United Nations General Assembly resolution 1514 of 1960, which called for the independence of colonial territories, coupled with resolution 1541 which applied the right of self-determination to 'a territory which is geographically separate and is distinct ethnically and/or culturally from the country administering it'.[8] This wording was designed to apply to the overseas empires of the European colonial powers, without threatening the integrity of states like the Soviet Union, or indeed many of the new African and Asian states themselves, which might be subject to demands for secession from groups within their territories. Admission to the international system on these terms necessarily implied that many of the new states thus included would be unable to defend themselves, or achieve the other criteria which had previously been associated with international viability. It carried with it, however, the protection of the United Nations Charter's guarantee against aggression by other states, and the right to engage in diplomatic relations with other existing states. This protection was tacitly refused to territories which, like South Africa under *apartheid* and Rhodesia after its unilateral declaration of independence, remained under white minority rule.

Although it came in time to have effects that were often damaging, the post-1945 negative sovereignty regime represented an understandable attempt to devise workable and generally acceptable principles of international management. The first of these, deriving from the experience of the two world wars, was the principle of non-aggression built into the charters first of the League of Nations, and subsequently of the United Nations. Both of those wars, and the suffering that resulted from them, had been unleashed through attacks by one state on the territory of another. The protection of state territories thus came to be seen as an indispensable requirement for the maintenance of global peace, in which the world as a whole had an interest – even if, as Hitler argued in the Nazi takeover of both Austria and parts of Czechoslovakia, existing frontiers were artificial and did not reflect the identities of the people on either side of them.

Even when the immediate legacy of the two world wars had faded away, the sovereignty principle was still required as a way to avert the terrifying dangers presented by the possibility of war between the superpowers. Since sovereignty is a mechanism through which weak states seek to protect themselves against strong ones, it is likely to have only limited appeal to the strongest states of all, which have had a pronounced tendency to justify their own intervention in the affairs of other peoples through such principles as the civilising mission, anti-communism, or proletarian internationalism. Both of the superpowers were willing to abandon or subvert the sovereignty principle when they felt that their own security required it – even when the 'threat' was presented by such evidently powerless states as Hungary or Nicaragua. This principle none the less helped them to establish lines of demarcation between their respective spheres of influence, and to reduce the danger that they might come into direct confrontation with one another. The importance of the negative sovereignty regime as a mechanism for regulating conflict between the superpowers was revealed when the end of the Cold War and the disappearance of the Soviet Union removed many of the previous constraints on external intervention.

A third function of the sovereignty principle was to provide guarantees which could enable formerly colonial territories to achieve independence under conditions of reasonable international security, despite their inability to defend themselves against serious military attack, or to meet other criteria which had previously been regarded as prerequisites of statehood. In this respect, international support for the independence of weak states was necessary to realise the principle of self-determination – broadly corresponding to territorial legitimacy – which had been introduced into public international morality after the First World War, and which gained greatly added force with decolonisation. The linkage between sovereignty, self-determination and decolonisation was obviously welcome to the new states which thereby gained support for their own independence. In addition, it inhibited conflicts between neighbouring post-colonial states which might have erupted with the removal of external domination, and helped the governments of these states to maintain their authority over their national territories. It was likewise welcome to the superpowers, as a mechanism for undermining the previously dominant Western European colonial powers, and bringing into existence a large number of new states over which they could seek to gain influence. It was even acceptable to most of the former colonial powers themselves, in providing a framework within which they could disengage relatively peacefully from empires which they were no longer able or willing to control.

Finally, then, the sovereignty principle provided a reasonably straightforward and generally acceptable rule which governments could use in order to regulate their relations with one another. The assumptions on which it ultimately rested may well, when closely examined, have proved to be mythical. But myths in political life can scarcely be avoided, and the myth of statehood could plausibly be regarded as serving, on the whole, the general interests of humanity. It was only when the gap between the myth and the reality started to have very damaging consequences for large numbers of people, and when the structure of international power which upheld that myth collapsed, that it came to be seriously questioned.

The effect of these provisions was to enhance the power of those individuals who gained the right to 'represent' states in the international community. Those who formed the government of an internationally recognised state were able to make alliances with other states, and to use their own domestic statehood as a bargaining counter with which to attract resources, such as weapons or development aid, which could enhance their ability to retain domestic control. They were also in some degree insulated against the danger of attack by their neighbours, and against the possibility that dissident groups within their own territories might gain international support. The principles of juridical statehood, however defensible they appeared to be, thus came to shape the international relations of fragile states in ways which eventually undermined the very goals of global peace and order which they had been intended to foster.

For one thing, the territorial legitimacy of many of the newly independent states rested more on the establishment of their frontiers by prior international agreement between the former colonial powers than on any sense of nationhood or common identity among the peoples of the territory themselves. In many cases, certainly, the success of nationalist movements formed to press for independence against the incumbent colonial power helped to generate a sense of identity which to a greater or lesser extent carried through into the post-independence period. The leaders of African states, as we shall see, likewise devised generally effective conventions in order to compensate for the artificiality of their frontiers. But the 'idea of the state' underlying the territorial integrity of most African states none the less rested much more on the maintenance of inherited colonial boundaries than on any internal rationale.

The governmental legitimacy of newly independent states was even more fragile. Though most of them reached independence under governments which had achieved popular support in reasonably fair elections, many of these governments lost much of their support over time, and were not subject to regular contested elections through which to re-establish their credentials. By far the commonest way of changing governments was through military *coup d'état*. Save for occasional and exceptional circumstances, the principles of juridical statehood excluded any scrutiny by international bodies of the credentials of governments, and in practice, the international community tacitly adopted the rule that the government of a state consisted of that group of people who controlled the most important buildings in the national capital. This may be described as 'letterbox sovereignty', in the sense that whoever opened the letters in the presidential palace received the invitation to represent the state concerned in the United Nations and other international bodies. At the time of Angolan independence in November 1975, when the Portuguese colonial regime withdrew without designating any successor, this principle gave a decisive advantage to the MPLA, as the claimant which controlled the capital city of Luanda, against the two rival claimants, the FNLA and Unita, which did not. A similar criterion was on various occasions the only practicable means of distinguishing between rival would-be governments of Chad.

Where a state comes into existence, or at the very least is able to survive, only as the result of international conventions, this has very significant consequences for that state itself. Even when there is a firm basis of indigenous nationalism to support its territorial and governmental legitimacy, its government needs to manoeuvre very carefully among those external powers on which its continued survival depends. Sometimes, as we will see in the case of African states, survival was best assured by a state firmly attaching itself to a great power ally or protector. At other times, the best strategy was to seek a balance – or in recent terminology 'non-alignment' – between the major exernal forces. Inevitably, however, the needs of state survival affected the structure of domestic politics as well as the government's external freedom of action. Nor did the relative protection that weak states received from the international system come free. Governments had to engage in a complex bargaining process, in which they sought to 'buy' external support by 'selling' what they had to offer, in terms of diplomatic clientage, strategic location, economic opportunity, or whatever else was available.

The weaker the internal legitimacy of the state, the greater was its external dependence, and the greater likewise was the price that the domestic regime had to pay for its external support. This in turn exacerbated the relationship between the government and the people whom it ruled. In all but the most exceptional cases, those people who constituted the government had an interest in their own survival, and thus in their continued control over the state's territory and population. If they could not achieve this end through the support of the population, they were likely to seek to achieve it through the support of outside powers, and their relations with the rest of the population were correspondingly altered. Those African rulers who, in the later years of the nineteenth century, signed protectorate treaties with intrusive colonial powers may well have been right to regard such treaties as essential for their own survival; but even those who had initially enjoyed the fullest legitimacy among their subjects came with time to act as the agents of colonial rule. A similar inexorable logic applied to the rulers of fragile independent states who found themselves looking for external resources to make good the deficiencies in their domestic authority. At its extreme, the quest for survival on the part of threatened governments could involve – and in several African cases did involve – a desperate search outside the state for the means required to kill people within it.

Once international recognition came to be a major factor in determining the powers of governments, and once these governments did not effectively control much of their formal territory, then the question even of who *was* the government was decided, at least to some degree, by outside states, rather than by people within the state itself. At one extreme, the government recognised by international institutions and the majority of outside states simply comprised that group of people who most closely approximated to external norms of legitimacy. The Khmer Rouge government of Cambodia continued to represent that country in the United Nations, even after being ejected from power at home, as a means by which outside states could express disapproval of the Vietnamese invasion, violating the rules of sovereignty, which had established the successor regime in power; the responsibility of the Khmer Rouge regime for killing very large numbers of Cambodians constituted, in the eyes of the international community, a less important disqualification. The government of the emir was likewise deemed to represent Kuwait after the complete takeover of the state by the Iraqis in August 1990. The decolonisation principle was also used as an external device for recognising governments: SWAPO was regarded by the United Nations as the 'sole and authentic representative of the Namibian people', during the latter part of the period when Namibia was governed by South Africa; and Polisario was recognised by the majority of African states as the government of an independent Western Sahara, even though the territory was to a large extent controlled by Morocco.

A world in which the government of a state simply consisted in whoever the majority of outside states said it was, and in which the state itself was only deemed to exist because other states said it did, had evidently moved quite some way from the myth of statehood outlined earlier in this chapter. Yet this myth, and the pretence that it was something more than a myth, continued to affect the people of the territories concerned, and those who sought to govern them. Recognition by the outside world was not merely an empty formula. It gave access, not only to seats in international organisations with high prestige but rather doubtful power, but to the ability to make real deals involving real resources. To be recognised as the ruler of a state was to be treated as a player in international politics; those who were not players, though they were able to operate on the margins of the international system, had a much more uncertain status. At the very least, even the purely nominal ruler of a state was in a position to buy whatever external resources he could get in exchange for selling his state's vote in the United Nations or other international fora. Equally important, the external state which supported him could do so, openly and legitimately, within the rules approved by the wider international system in which it too had to act; the potential costs of supporting an official government were appreciably less than those of supporting some non-state organisation which did not have the same recognition. Military aid could be provided on the basis that this was being used to uphold, rather than to subvert, the accepted structure of international statehood. Economic aid could be sought and provided within the generally recognised framework of bilateral relations and international financial institutions. To be able to sign a piece of paper on behalf of a state, and not merely on one's own personal behalf, was a real source of power.

It followed that the rulers and would-be rulers of weak and fragile states had a set of objectives which the logic of their own situation normally induced them to follow. First and most important, they had to establish themselves as the internationally recognised representatives of internationally recognised states. They could do this in various ways: by winning an election, by launching a military *coup d'état*, by leading an insurgent movement to victory against the incumbent government, even (and most difficult of all) by organising a secessionist movement which succeeded in splitting off part of the territory of an existing state in order to form a new one. They could get some external assistance in doing any of these things, but since they did not count as international players until after they had succeeded, this aid was likely to be secretive and limited. Having got there, they could start playing for real: they could use their role in the diplomatic game, together with their internal resources, in order to help keep themselves in power, to extend their control over their national territory, and to extract resources from their domestic environment with which to strike further bargains on the international scene. They could well have general moral goals such as the economic development and national unity of their states, or the achievement of independence or majority rule for territories still under colonial or minority control, which their foreign and domestic policies were intended to achieve. They almost certainly had personal goals, such as glory or perhaps merely self-enrichment. But all of these depended on their ability to keep themselves going through the effective management of their external as well as their domestic environment. This was what foreign policy in African (and indeed in most other) states was basically about.

For so long as statehood remained an important asset in bargaining with the international system, rulers could be expected to seek to consolidate the power of their own states, along with their own control over them. Their competitors, whether these were opposition leaders operating legitimately within those political systems that permitted it, or insurgents seeking to displace the incumbent regime by force, correspondingly sought to undermine the doctrine of state sovereignty in order to gain access to the external resources which this doctrine denied them. As the international advantages accruing to statehood declined, however, and as the costs of maintaining states increased – and both of these trends were evident in post-Cold War Africa – so the balance of advantage shifted. Not only were stateless competitors, and especially insurgent movements, able to improve their relative access to international resources, but even those who controlled states found it advantageous, on occasion, to operate in part outside the structures of formal statehood, and to undermine the very states which they governed. These shifts will in turn be examined in the latter part of this book.

Globalisation and sovereign statehood

The world in which quasi-states operate continues to change. The extent to which the environment of African statehood depended on the existence of a particular balance of forces in the international system was revealed by the end of the Cold War. The end of the Cold War may itself be seen, however, not simply as the collapse of a particular superpower or the failure of a particular system of economic and political management, but as the working through into the political sphere of changes in the global economy, and in the organisations and ideas which sustained it. Commonly lumped together under the heading of 'globalisation', these economic and related changes notably included a rapid increase in the mobility of capital; a resulting increase in levels of structural differentiation and functional integration in the global economy; a shift away from resources and towards human skills as the critical element in wealth creation, which in turn distinguished the regions which were (and were not) able to benefit from economic growth; a startling growth in information flows and the capacity to process information, encouraged by technical developments in mass communications; some corresponding emergence of a global culture, challenged though this was by a reaction towards particularist ideas; and consequent pressures on the governments of states, which were affected both by a need to manage their economies in accordance with a global search for comparative advantage, and by the impact of values derived from the global culture, in the form of demands both from external actors and from their own people.

The impact of these changes everywhere was complex and often contradictory, and their effect on Africa was in many ways peculiar. For a start, Africa had in a sense been 'globalised' in the late nineteenth century by European colonialism, which had imposed structures of economic production, systems of government, and cultural changes in language and education, which linked (and at the same time subordinated) them to the processes of global capitalist development. From this viewpoint, the increased external control exercised from the 1980s onwards, through the economic and political conditionalities discussed in chapters 7 and 8, represented a return to familiar conditions of subordination, after a period in which African governments had sought to use their political independence in order to establish autonomous (though at the same time often economically inefficient and politically autocratic) structures of their own. Due to its lack of economic development, moreover, Africa was probably less affected by most of the changes noted above than any other region of the world. The spread of global capital, in particular, scarcely affected it at all, because there were so few places where transnational corporations could find safe and potentially profitable investment opportunities. The increase in information flows, by contrast with much of the rest of the world, was likewise negligible. The shift from resources to skills did have a major (and damaging) direct impact, expressed in declining terms of trade, on a continent whose human capital was exceptionally poorly developed; and Africa was likewise involved in a number of other global developments, including environmental degradation and the drugs trade. For the most part, however, globalisation affected Africa at second remove, through the effect on it of changes in the external environment, notably in the major capitalist states, rather than through changes in Africa itself.

It was paradoxical but none the less understandable that the negative sovereignty regime which emerged after 1945 should have protected (and indeed magnified) the political leverage of newly independent post-colonial states, at the same time as their economies were becoming increasingly integrated into global structures of production, and their subordination to the most developed states was likewise becoming evident in terms not just of military technology, but of culture, information and ideology. With hindsight, the idea of negative sovereignty may be seen as a transitional stage in the process of globalisation. On the one hand, the recognition of formal statehood, protected by such international conventions as the Charter of the United Nations, conferred real power on the leaders of apparently powerless states. On the other hand, the power which these leaders exercised came to depend, as the discussion in the previous section has suggested, as much on the international system as on the support which they were able to derive from the people of the states which they governed. That the structures through which political power is exercised must ultimately achieve some kind of congruence with the structures of economic production is not mere Marxist dogma, but an enduring fact about political life, internationally as well as within individual states. For a relatively short period, aided by the division between capitalist and socialist superpowers, the process of globalisation enhanced the power of those who governed African states – in much the same way as the imposition of colonial rule, at least within many of the territories governed by the United Kingdom, enhanced the power of those indigenous princes who were able to establish an amicable relationship with the imperial regime. This power, however, rested on no more than an intermediary role. Indigenous politicians took over the government of states which colonial powers had to abandon under pressure from their local inhabitants on the one hand, and from the global superpowers on the other, but which the superpowers had no interest in governing directly themselves. To survive, they had to take a commission from their part in arranging deals between their domestic populations, and the external economy and political structure into which they were being integrated. As this integration proceeded, so the scope for arranging such deals, and the commission which the intermediary could extract from them, were progressively squeezed.

Where formerly underdeveloped states were able to achieve a breakthrough into export-led industrial production, as was the case with several east and south-east Asian states, these benefited from rapid economic growth, which in turn strengthened both the fiscal and the political autonomy of the state, even though (or because) the economy was increasingly integrated into global markets. Where, on the other hand, they were caught in a cycle of declining primary production, this reduced both the autonomy of the state *vis-à-vis* its external partners, and its authority *vis-à-vis* its domestic constituency. The pressures for structural adjustment of their economies and for political conditionality in their domestic governments, coupled with the growth of subnational identities and rural insurgent movements, thus reflected critical threats to African statehood which will be examined later in this volume.

For those states which occupied the lowest rungs in the hierarchy of international politics and the global economy, even statehood itself was thus not something which could be taken for granted. Though some of them incorporated indigenous concepts of statehood which predated the colonial era, for many the very idea of the state was of recent and external origin. Formal access to the international system through the recognition of independent sovereignty was little more than a generation old. Maintenance of that sovereignty, and the privileged position which it bestowed on those who managed states, was a constant struggle, success in which depended in part on the skill with which political elites were able to manage the relationships between their domestic and external environments, in part on developments in a global system in which their power was negligible. An examination of the forms which this struggle took, over the thirty-five years or so after the achievement of political independence, provides the subject matter of this book.

2 The creation of an African international order

People and government in Africa

In seeking to understand the international relations of Africa, it is helpful to start by looking at a map of the continent on which state boundaries do not appear, and which is coloured, not in a patchwork of blocks demarcating the formal territories of individual states, but in shades which correspond to population density and forms of economic activity, and to the patterns of altitude, rainfall and vegetation on which human life largely depends. What emerges is a continent which, despite rapid recent population growth, is still sparsely inhabited, with dense concentrations of people in relatively few places, including notably the West African coast and savannah, the Ethiopian highlands, the Great Lakes region of central Africa, and the central and southern highlands. These regions include large modern cities, founded for purposes of government (like Addis Ababa), mineral extraction (like Johannesburg), or foreign trade (like Lagos); but they still largely correspond to areas where local resources are sufficient to sustain relatively high populations, and which in turn have been able to maintain well-established structures of government.

Over much of the continent, both people and resources are thinly and precariously spread. Huge tracts of territory are suited only to animal husbandry, and require the people who inhabit them to move long distances with their flocks and herds to take advantage of seasonal conditions. Other areas have soils and rainfall which can sustain only temporary cultivation. Scattered and mobile people are likely to generate neither the resources on which permanent governmental institutions rely, nor the social structures and values needed to uphold them. African commentators, in particular, have often referred to the rich resources of the continent – largely in terms of minerals which acquire value only through their use within sophisticated industrial economies – and have contrasted this with the poverty in which most of its people live, inferring that Africans have been deprived of the wealth that is rightly theirs. This picture is misleading: in the resources that matter – people, earth and water – most of Africa is desperately poor.[1]

Governing Africa has therefore always been a struggle, and those who have sought to maintain some form of authority within the continent have had to make use of every possible resource in order to do so.[2] In much of the continent, including especially those zones suited only to nomadic pastoralism, there was before the imposition of colonial rule no overarching structure of territorial control corresponding to the criteria for statehood; instead, the maintenance of social order depended on lineage and clan structures, and on tacit conventions designed to limit conflict between them.[3] Though Africa has certainly sustained a number of impressive and long-lasting political systems which have as good a claim to statehood as their European equivalents at a similar stage of technological development, these have mostly been restricted to the population centres already noted. They have moreover tended to consist in a core, whose control over a progressively less governable periphery has expanded or contracted in accordance with its internal stability and economic and military strength: whereas European states defined themselves and fixed their boundaries in competition with neighbouring states much like themselves, African ones formed islands of relatively settled government, beyond which stretched deserts, forests or zones of progressively impoverished savannah which a strong ruler would seek to control but from which a weak one would retreat. Dissident or defeated groups could strike out into the borderlands to conquer or establish kingdoms of their own.[4]

Maintaining governments in these circumstances called for a determined use of available material and spiritual resources. Seldom did these resources permit the development of competing sources of authority within the core, some of the West African forest kingdoms providing the main exceptions; opposition was normally expressed in spatial terms, through the ability of regional rulers to gain a measure of autonomy which the central government had to respect, or as already noted by attempted secession. While it goes without saying that any structure of authority must depend on the beliefs and values of those who recognise it, spiritual power is especially important where material resources are weak, and this was maintained through Orthodox Christianity (in Ethiopia) or Islam (especially in the emirates of the Sahel), as well as through complex indigenous belief systems which for outsiders were readily dismissed as 'witchcraft'.[5] It is likewise striking that the most effective African insurgent movements, such as the NRA in southern Uganda or the EPLF and TPLF in Eritrea and northern Ethiopia, have drawn their support from regions with a long history of statehood, whereas insurgencies in historically stateless regions such as Somalia and Liberia have been much more prone to fragment. In material terms, settled agriculture was normally required in order to maintain the population density needed to support local-level authorities, but peasant societies are notoriously difficult to tax; state authorities, where these emerged, often therefore depended to a large extent on revenues derived from external trade. In its most intense and pathological form, this dependence is illustrated by the slave-trading kingdoms of both east and west African coasts; but the trans-Saharan caravan routes or the trade from the Red Sea into what is now southwestern Ethiopia likewise sustained the long-gone kingdoms of Timbuktu or Enarea.[6]

These origins continue to matter. Though both Africa's political structures and its economies have been drastically affected by European colonialism and its aftermath, neither human societies, nor Africa's unforgiving environment, are so readily transformed as the ideologies of the European enlightenment (transposed into 'nationalism' and 'development') have tended to assume. States are not the unbreakable monoliths which the Eurocentric (and, even then, very recent) study of international relations has taken them for, but continue to depend for their survival on their ability to derive both authority and material support from the world in which they exist. As the bases of the late twentieth-century African state system are increasingly called into question, so the patterns of the past become progressively more relevant.

The colonial grid

Western European colonialism has, on the face of it, transformed the map of Africa. It is of very recent origin. Extending (outside South Africa) little beyond a few coastal settlements until the last two decades of the nineteenth century, it then carved up the continent with astonishing speed into a collection of territories which by 1914 were recognisably the ancestors of the African state system as it existed eighty years later; a few adjustments apart, only the individual states of francophone west and central Africa remained to be demarcated.[7]

From the viewpoint of what was subsequently to become Africa's 'international relations', the colonial interlude, however short, was critical. The previously fuzzy borderlands between indigenous centres of government, together with the large areas which possessed no formalised government structures at all, were replaced (at least on the map, though only much later and more uncertainly on the ground) by precisely demarcated frontiers of the sort that European concepts of statehood deemed to be necessary. As has often been pointed out, these frontiers were rarely guided by any concern for the identity of indigenous states, societies or ecological units, though some pre-colonial monarchies were redefined as colonial territories; in some cases, such as the boundary between what are now Zaïre and Zambia, the process of demarcation reached an astonishing level of cartographical improbability. Within the territories thus defined, administrative hierarchies were established that radiated outwards from the newly established colonial capitals (or, very often, inwards, from the coast to the interior), and beyond those from the metropolitan capitals in Europe. These built up at least the rudiments of specialised administration, with functions that extended beyond simple law and order (always their main priority) to 'development' and social services. Controlled by foreigners, with Africans taking subordinate positions both at local level (where indigenous jurisdictions were to some extent maintained) and in the lower ranks of central administration, they none the less – in a way that pre-colonial political structures very rarely did – formed the basis for the states which independent Africans were later to rule.

How did these interloping Europeans come to establish such a grid of embryonic states in a continent where Africans, over countless generations, had not done so? To a large extent, of course, the colonisers simply established the kind of territorial structure which they assumed from their own experience to be a necessary and indispensable element of government. The boundaries which they demarcated, regardless of whether they meant anything to Africans, were essential in order to regulate competition between themselves. State-building resources not available within the continent were supplied from industrial Europe, in the form most obviously of military power, but also of communications technologies, bureaucratic organisation, and the capital needed to establish forms of economic production which were then expected to generate the revenues required to pay for local systems of government.

The sense remains, none the less, that colonial rule in Africa rested on a brilliant sleight of hand. Rarely has the confidence trick on which all government depends been pulled off so effectively and with such slight resources, a success which can only have conveyed to the leaders of newly independent states a sense of the solidity and permanence of the states which they inherited which was to prove misleading. Paradoxically – given that a broad correspondence of values between governors and governed is normally regarded as an essential component of legitimacy – the very alienness of the new regimes was an immense advantage. Since the military technology at the disposal of the conquerors was so evidently superior to that available locally, the colonialists were able to present a facade of overwhelming power which they rarely had to back up by a major commitment of resources. The actual resources at their disposal were small, and had to be spread extremely thinly.[8] In practice, too, much of the administrative capacity especially of British colonial regimes was derived from making deals with local-level actors who counted for something in their own right, and who were consequently able to bolster their own position by establishing a clientelist relationship with the colonial regime.[9] As soon as these regimes came to be challenged, even by the slight resources at the disposal of the leaders of anti-colonial nationalist movements, it became obvious how little the colonialists (with the sole exception of the Portuguese) were prepared to spend on trying to keep them.

Revolutionary as the colonial state was in the African context, it intensified a dependence of political authority on external resources which was already one of the common features of pre-colonial state systems in the continent. This 'extraversion', moreover, related every bit as much to the morality or legitimacy of power as to its economic base and its use of military force.[10] External religions, whether Christian or Moslem, acquired an official status not accorded to indigenous belief systems,[11] even though these continued to exercise considerable influence both within and alongside the new official cults. Education in an alien language, which itself became the language of rule throughout the colonial territory, was the essential vehicle for acquiring the skills that were needed to operate within the modern colonial state; more intangibly, it helped a very limited number of Africans to gain both the confidence to rule, and the recognition of their right to do so by the indigenous population, as well as by the outside world.[12]

The material basis of the state was still more evidently externalised. In place of the relatively meagre revenues that could be extracted by indigenous pre-colonial rulers from passing caravans or slave-traders, the colonial state could organise the thoroughgoing incorporation of their new territories into global markets, by bringing in metropolitan companies to exploit local mineral resources, or more often by encouraging (or forcing) their subjects to produce tropical crops for export. External trade thus became not merely a relatively minor adjunct to local subsistence production, but in many areas led to a radical shift in the basic structure of the economy. Regardless of whether this transformation should be treated from an economic viewpoint as a desirable process of 'development' or a damaging one of 'dependence', the intensified external economic underpinnings of government necessarily affected the nature of political power.

A final consequence of colonialism, of obvious importance to Africa's subsequent international relations, was that it not only divided the continent into state-like territories, but did so under the aegis of eight different colonial powers.[13] This created three main external languages of rule – French, English and Portuguese – which divided independent Africa into its major linguistic and cultural blocs, and also left African states with different internal structures and external linkages. Several of the legacies of differing systems of colonial rule turned out to be very important indeed; these included the Portuguese refusal to decolonise and the Belgian failure to develop indigenous institutions which they could decolonise to; the imposition of white settlement in anglophone southern Africa; and the peculiar relationships which France established with her former colonies. They should none the less be seen as variants on the common theme that colonialism, by creating African states of a kind that had never existed before, and endowing them with economies and structures of government which were inherently external, gave the subsequent international relations of the continent a distinctive centrality and form.

Indigenising power

Despite its apparently overwhelming dominance, the timespan of European colonialism in Africa proved to be extremely short. Only a couple of generations, in most cases, separated the imposition of effective colonial rule in the late nineteenth and early twentieth centuries from the achievement of independence, which for the great majority of colonies came in the decade between the independence of Sudan in 1956 and that of Botswana in 1966. The major exceptions were the Portuguese colonies which did not become independent until 1974/75, and the settler-governed colonies of southern Africa which eventually achieved internationally recognised independence in 1980 (Zimbabwe) and 1990 (Namibia). Three sub-Saharan states, Ethiopia, Liberia and South Africa, had been independent for varying periods before 1945, though not until 1994 did South Africa gain the African majority government which placed it on a footing with the other states of the continent.

The changes in the global system which encouraged the rapid accession to independence of a large number of African states which plainly did not meet what had hitherto been the normally accepted criteria for statehood are briefly assessed in the next section. This section is concerned with the internal elements in the transition, and their implications for independent Africa's external relations. The most important of these elements, which dominated everything else, was the continuation into independence of the territorial units and rudimentary state structures established by colonial rule, regardless of their frequent artificiality, their alienness, and the recentness of their creation. One distinguished observer has seen this imposition of an alien statehood on Africa, by contrast with the possible creation of indigenous structures of rule corresponding to local power centres and conceptions of government, as the major determinant of Africa's subsequent crises.[14] Though the record of the one African state which did follow this pattern of development, Ethiopia, and that of other states such as Liberia, Rwanda and Somalia which partially did so, does not altogether bear out this assessment, the post-colonial state none the less remains at the centre of Africa's foreign relations.

The survival of these colonial creations provides a clear illustration of the combination of internal and external factors which were to shape their subsequent foreign relations. For a start, the lines on maps created by colonial partition defined entities which were recognisable by outside states – and most critically by the departing colonial states – as appropriate candidates for sovereign statehood. The post-1945 international order has been extremely reluctant to accept any challenge to the frontiers which it inherited, regardless of their origins. When, for example, the three Baltic states of Estonia, Latvia and Lithuania emerged from the Soviet Union to resume the sovereign statehood which they had possessed between 1918 and 1940, they did so within the boundaries which they had been allocated as Union Republics of the USSR, rather than those that they had enjoyed before 1940. A similar logic prescribed the break-up of Yugoslavia along the boundaries laid down by the previous internal division of the country. For African territories, independence within their existing boundaries was internationally unproblematic, whereas any attempt to alter them (except by voluntary union, as in the case of British Somaliland and formerly Italian Somalia) would have raised virtually insuperable difficulties.

Secondly, however, the indigenous elites who led the movements for independence were themselves strongly committed to maintaining the states created under colonial rule. They needed to take over a machinery of government in working order, rather than seek to create one from scratch within the unimaginable confusion produced by a simultaneous achievement of independence and reordering of the entire political structure. Many Africans were, by the time of independence, already working within the bureaucracies that colonial officialdom had established, as central and regional administrators and junior army officers, and thereby acquired an interest in their preservation. Both models of administration and languages of rule followed the colonial pattern. There was, in short, no alternative.

But onto these practical considerations was grafted the ideology of self-rule articulated by the anti-colonial party leaders who expected at independence to graduate into the rulers of the newly sovereign states. So far from rejecting the basis of colonial statehood, they adopted and indeed glorified it, turning it into the foundation for a 'nationalism' which was presented as authentically African, and which simultaneously redefined pre-colonial identities and political structures as the source of a divisive and illegitimate 'tribalism'. These 'nationalist' leaders varied in their commitment to sub-national political identities on the one hand, and to supra-national identities on the other. Quite a number of them, most evidently in Nigeria, drew on regional bases for electoral support which were implicitly or explicitly defined in terms of a sub-national ethnicity. Others, most obviously Kwame Nkrumah in Ghana, pressed at least rhetorically for an African unity which would bridge over the divisions established by colonialism and eventually lead to the establishment of a United States of Africa. In some parts of the continent, notably French West and Equatorial Africa but also

British East and Central Africa, inter-territorial arrangements linked neighbouring colonies under the control of the same colonial power. Regardless of these variations, the former colony converted into post-colonial state became the indispensable territorial basis for participation in the international system.[15]

The nationalist leaders themselves were usually perfectly equipped to play the bridging role between domestic and international politics which the structure of their states thrust on them. On the one hand, they needed to build an electoral base within their own societies, and this required the mobilisation of support down to the lowest level. This could generally be achieved through the articulation of indigenous resentment at alien rule, presented with a greater or lesser degree of intensity in keeping with the level of violence or consensuality with which colonialism had been imposed, coupled with the construction of the clientele network needed in order to organise local support. The degree of hostility with which nationalist leaders opposed colonial government in turn became a major determinant of their attitudes towards the outside world as a whole, and the relationships which they sought after independence. In some cases, such as Botswana and Côte d'Ivoire, the successor elites were so closely associated with the former colonial government that an almost seamless transition took place, but this could only be achieved where these elites retained sufficient authority to carry the electorate with them. Ghana (then the Gold Coast) provided the classic case of an elite group which too readily presumed on its right to govern the country after independence, and found itself undercut by a more radical party with a stridently anti-colonial message.

Even the most radical of nationalist leaders, however, generally possessed attributes which linked them to the outside world. The most obvious of these was university education, normally though not always in the colonial metropole, which helped to endow Africans with the breadth of vision, the self-confidence, and the technical skills which were needed in order to lead the opposition to colonial rule and manage the independent state thereafter. Territorial political leaders within the French colonies gained the much more intensive political training and range of international contacts provided by election to the National Assembly in Paris. Once nationalist leaders were in many states displaced by *coups d'état* from the mid-1960s onwards, the first generation of military rulers usually possessed the equivalent background provided by officer training establishments in the metropole.

A further aspect of nationalist leadership which was to have a pronounced effect on post-independence external relations was its extremely personal character. It is normal for any movement which seeks to mobilise the identity of some previously excluded political community to coalesce around a single leader, who thus comes to embody the struggle to an extent that is hard to recapture in routinised and well-established political systems. Both revolutionary and nationalist movements provide a host of examples. In the case of African nationalist movements, which often progressed from foundation to full independence within a single decade, this effect was especially marked. Almost all of them were identified with a leader who acquired immense prestige, and whose right to make policy on behalf of the movement was virtually unchallenged. Though there were, as will be argued, good structural reasons for the personalisation of foreign policy-making in fragile and newly independent states, this tendency was also inherent in the nationalist movements themselves. It made itself evident, both in the nature of the foreign policy-making process, with its emphasis on summit diplomacy conducted by national leaders in person, and also in the latitude open to leaders in choosing the substance of their foreign policies, with negligible internal accountability.

The colonial authorities, too, generally acted in such a way as to maintain the external linkages which they had established. As already noted, the resources which these had been prepared to devote to the maintenance of their African empires were generally small, and once their rule came to be challenged, they did not (apart from Portugal, and the South African administration in Namibia) think it worth increasing the stakes and costs to the level that would have been required to cling on by force. The most sensible solution, adopted by both British and French, was therefore to leave with every appearance of willingness, while establishing as good a relationship as circumstances allowed with the successor regimes – many of which were in any event led by politicians who were closely associated with the colonial power. The French had already made unsuccessful attempts to defeat nationalist movements in both Indochina and Algeria, and were not inclined to repeat the experience south of the Sahara, even though their potential opponents in Africa were much more weakly organised, and possessed much slighter access to external military support, than their Asian and North African equivalents. The British had established a pattern of withdrawal from south Asia, which could be adapted to

Africa. Though the contrasting patterns of Belgian and Portuguese decolonisation raised severe difficulties, both of the two major colonial powers in the continent managed the process in such a way as to leave the existing linkages largely undisturbed.

This 'normal' pattern of relatively painless decolonisation was severely disrupted in a limited number of cases, which were none the less extremely important, because by their very failure they created many of the crises to which African states had to respond, not merely in the early years of independence but right through to the achievement of majority rule in South Africa in 1994. In chronological order, the first crisis of decolonisation was the failure of the French in Guinea to devise an appropriate formula which would reconcile the domestic position of the nationalist leader, Sekou Touré, with continued association with France. This failure resulted partly from the impact of French colonialism on the internal structure of power in Guinea, but partly also from the breakdown of personal relations between two particularly prickly characters, Sekou Touré and Charles de Gaulle. It led to Guinea being forced into independence in 1958, stripped of the security which the post-colonial relationship provided in other formerly French colonies.[16] Guinea's brutal caesarean birth required Sekou Touré to look for external aid, and led to an act of union with Nkrumah's Ghana (which effectively provided for Ghanaian assistance and diplomatic support, without affecting Guinea's actual independence or Sekou Touré's control over domestic politics) and to attempts to build an alliance with the Soviet Union and later with the United States. Relations with France remained hostile right up until Sekou Touré's death in 1984, and also embittered relations with neighbouring francophone states, notably Côte d'Ivoire, which remained within the post-colonial fold. Guinea thus provides a peculiarly acute example of the international relations of post-colonialism.

The failure of Belgian decolonisation in what is now Zaïre was of a rather different kind. Despite establishing (after an initial period of ruthless exploitation), a model if paternalist system of colonial rule, the Belgians did nothing to create the political conditions conducive to a transfer of power. The provision of primary education, which fostered demands for independence, was exceptionally high, whereas the creation of an indigenous university-educated elite, necessary to produce the leadership required to channel those demands into a manageable political order, was virtually non-existent; nor were there any effective means through which Africans in different parts of the vast and roadless territory could establish the contacts with one another which might have led to a sense of common identity. Once independence was achieved in June 1960, the whole structure of statehood almost immediately collapsed, prompting the attempted secession of the mineral-producing Katanga region, Belgian military intervention, and a desperate appeal by the new government to the United Nations for the troops that were needed to maintain basic order and the integrity of the state. This crisis traumatised the continent in the year in which the largest number of its states became independent.

If the failures of French and Belgian decolonisation sprang from the overcentralisation of colonial rule, those of the British derived, rather, from excessive devolution. In Nigeria and Sudan, and also to some extent Uganda, devolved forms of government within the territory helped to promote internal divisions which eventually led to civil war. In Southern Rhodesia (now Zimbabwe) and indeed South Africa, the transfer of power in the early twentieth century to the representatives of the white settler community created obstacles to African majority rule which could only be resolved by force, and which preoccupied the energies of the international community to a greater degree than any other African issue, until the achievement of majority rule in South Africa in 1994.

An analogous but rather different linkage between decolonisation and the international system followed from the refusal of the Portuguese government to concede any devolution at all. It continued to regard its African possessions, right up to independence in 1974/75, as constitutionally part of the metropolitan state – a formula which the French had also applied in Algeria. In this case, the nationalist movements established their foreign policies before independence, in the search for diplomatic support and military aid, and the legacies of these policies continued into the independence period – most dangerously in Angola, where the rivalry between different would-be nationalist movements, each with its own external alliances, carried through into a civil war which was still raging nearly two decades after independence in 1975. The major difference between British over-devolution and Portuguese non-devolution was that the British model created the structure for an indigenous state which a ruling African elite could subsequently take over, whereas the Portuguese model left very little behind indeed.

The significance of these failed decolonisations, from the viewpoint of the continent's international relations, lay not only in the rupture of the normal post-colonial relationship between the territory and colonial power concerned, but equally in the fact that – given the level of dependence inherent in the African situation – this relationship had urgently to be replaced by others. The option of an 'autonomous' independent state, not heavily reliant on any significant external relationship, was simply not available. Both the search for new relationships, and the forms which such relationships took, made them more likely to generate international conflict than the maintenance of the old connection with the former colonial regime. Alliance with one or other of the superpowers, for example, almost automatically brought the African state concerned, and also very often its neighbours, into global structures of competition. Armed conflicts resulting from the failure of decolonisation required the warring parties to seek help from outside allies, and often induced a level of militarisation which was extremely difficult to reverse. Such conflicts often extended across artificial frontiers, into the territories of neighbouring states. Though the decolonisation settlements might plausibly be regarded as bringing African states into the global order under the subordinate status established by colonial rule, the absence of a post-colonial settlement created still more problematic relationships between newly independent states and the international system.

One group of African states, finally, was independent already. Each of them – Ethiopia under Emperor Haile-Selassie, Liberia under the True Whig Party oligarchy, and South Africa under the National Party's *apartheid* regime – had an elitist and exploitative domestic power structure, which was threatened by the surge in political participation among its neighbours, and the installation of regimes which depended on popular suffrage. The two northern governments, most notably Ethiopia, sought by swift diplomatic footwork to establish good relations with the emerging independent states, on terms which insulated them so far as possible from demands to apply to their own territories the principles of self-determination which were being implemented elsewhere. No such option was open to the South African government, no matter how hard it tried to claim that the principle of non-intervention in the internal affairs of other states should apply as much to it as to other African states. Though domestic autocracy could readily be reconciled with African nationalism, the exclusive domination of a white settler regime could not. Eventually, however, demands for participation in all three states were to challenge the incumbent oligarchies, and lead to domestic conflicts which in turn helped to destabilise the region as a whole. Prior independence exacerbated rather than resolved the problems of creating a viable political order.

The waiting world

The international system into which the newly independent African states emerged during the late 1950s and 1960s seemed in many ways to be a threatening one. Then at the height of the Cold War, the world was divided between two superpowers, which possessed terrifying levels of military force, and which in the Cuban missile crisis of 1962 had come close to mutual destruction. These superpowers were not only the leaders of military alliances, but also dominated competing structures of international production and trade, and defined their role in terms of ideological principles which in turn they sought to export to every other country in the world. African states, abruptly (though not unwillingly) propelled into global politics, without most of the empirical attributes of statehood which had previously been regarded as essential to sustain the right to international sovereignty, had to find their feet in an unfamiliar environment, within which a highly unequal division of global power and wealth placed them at the very bottom of the heap. The international order created after 1945, which set the scene for African foreign policies, was one which Africans had virtually no hand in establishing, and which they were almost powerless to alter.

Despite these initial impressions, however, the world which African states found awaiting them proved in many ways to be extraordinarily supportive. As has been discussed in the previous chapter, the experience of the Second World War, and the recognition that the 'grand alliance' of the victorious powers was no more than an alliance of convenience, had led to the establishment in 1945 of the formalised system of global conflict management embodied in the United Nations and its satellite organisations. The Charter of the United Nations was in turn founded on the sovereignty of states, an essentially defensive principle which sought to limit conflict by giving each of the superpowers some security in holding onto the territories which it and its allies already controlled. It was at the same time a principle which could only enhance the security and bargaining power of the smallest and weakest states, and one which the leaders of African states would eagerly adopt.

Whereas in many parts of the world, moreover, the formal recognition of state sovereignty was in practice deeply compromised by superpower competition, and the resulting need for weak states to seek external protection, African states were relatively free. They did not form part of that 'backyard' or reserved domain, as in Eastern and Central Europe, or Central America and the Caribbean, over which each of the superpowers claimed an exclusive jurisdiction. Nor did they fall into the still more dangerous regions, such as the Middle East or south-east Asia, in which the superpowers competed for dominance by supporting regional clients against the local rivals who were sustained by their global opponents. The only part of sub-Saharan Africa which was dragged into superpower confrontation before the mid-1970s was the Horn, where intense regional conflicts combined with a strategic location on the southern edge of the Middle East to provide an irresistible formula for superpower intervention. Put simply, African states were accorded an international freedom of action which largely reflected the fact that they did not matter very much. Though superpower competition in the continent certainly occurred, it was for the most part restricted to diplomatic rivalries which enhanced rather than undermined the bargaining power of the leaders of African states.

As relative latecomers on the international scene, African states could also benefit from the supportive ethos which had already been established by other formerly colonial states, especially in Asia. The decade after 1945, before any sub-Saharan African colony had gained its independence, saw the withdrawal of the European imperial powers from all of their former possessions in south and east Asia, save only for the British in Malaysia/Singapore and Hong Kong. This led to the emergence of massive Asian states, notably India and Indonesia, which were anxious to establish their own autonomy from either of the superpowers, and which were to take a leading role in the establishment of the Non-Aligned Movement; though the movement itself was not to be formally founded until 1961, the Asian and African (but very largely Asian) summit held at Bandung in Indonesia in 1955 had already articulated the principles on which it was to be based. These principles, including especially the insistence on state sovereignty and on the right to separate independence of each and every colonial territory, undermined and eventually displaced the earlier assumption that independent statehood required the achievement of objective criteria of power, wealth and governmental effectiveness.[17]

Supported by the superpowers, which (once the United States had given independence to the Philippines, and regularised the status of Hawaii and Puerto Rico) had no overseas colonies of their own to lose, they permitted the decolonisation even of such microstates as The Gambia.

Even the colonial powers, which on the face of it had most to lose from decolonisation, for the most part accepted it with grace. As already noted, they were not (apart from Portugal) interested in fighting for continued domination, and could usually establish friendly relations with the incoming regimes; and when push came to shove, their relations with the United States and their rapidly developing economic and political links with other states in Western Europe, mattered far more to them than clinging on to empire. In those cases where independence was delayed, especially in the Portuguese colonies and the settler territories of southern Africa, the sympathy and increasingly the tangible support of the vast majority of the world's states were overwhelmingly on the side of independent black African statehood.

International sympathy could not rectify the endemic weaknesses of many of the African states which gained independence after 1956. Development aid did little if anything to compensate for their poverty, while diplomatic support and even military assistance could at best only paper over their internal divisions. Formal sovereignty notwithstanding, much of the structure of the international system was – at least as they saw it – skewed to the benefit of the older and richer states, especially in the area of the international economy. None the less, if there was ever a moment for poor, divided and defenceless states to take their bow on the international stage, the fifteen years or so after 1956 provided it.

3 Domestic statehood and foreign policy

The idea of the African state

At independence, the great majority of African states appeared to possess all of the attributes of statehood outlined in chapter 1. Their territories were, with few exceptions, clearly demarcated, and there were few disputes about who was to count as a citizen of one state rather than another. Though the range of functions performed by their governments was often modest, and the machinery of government was correspondingly slight, there was little doubt about their capacity to exercise their responsibilities over the whole of their national territories. Save for one or two of the largest and most disparate states, notably Sudan and Congo/Zaïre, their territorial integrity did not seem to be threatened; and even when, as in Nigeria and Uganda, political parties with rival regional and ethnic bases had competed for power, these had been induced to accept a constitutional settlement which maintained the existing territory. The new regimes usually enjoyed the governmental legitimacy conferred by elections, which in several cases had bestowed on them virtually unanimous popular support. Save again for a few exceptional cases, such as the challenge to Mauritania's existence posed by a Moroccan claim on the whole of its territory, or the Somali Republic's demand for self-determination on behalf of ethnic Somalis living in north-east Kenya, their relations with their neighbours were usually correct if not necessarily cordial; and in any event, these neighbours were in no position to threaten them. The global power structure was, as already noted, much more a source of support than a threat to weak and newly emergent states.

Over time, the African international order was to be threatened most fundamentally by the weakness of its economic base, and the progressively declining ability of African rulers to extract from their economies the resources which they needed to maintain the state structures which they had inherited from colonialism, and subsequently greatly expanded. This economic failure was to be accompanied by a pervasive crisis of political authority, and by changes in the global power structure which reduced the bargaining capacity of African rulers. At the outset, however, the external relations of African states were largely defined by the 'ideas of the state' which were held by their leaders, and to a very varying degree shared by their populations.

In the most general sense, as already discussed, the foreign policy of any state reflects the way in which its government defines its own mission, and the extent to which that mission is shared by the population as a whole. Such a mission, or 'idea of the state', encompasses not only its explicit institutions and goals, but also the often unarticulated collection of assumptions, identities and traditions which shape its behaviour, and at the same time confer on its government such legitimacy as it possesses. In cases where the idea of the state is almost universally shared, any threat to the security of the incumbent government, by other than legitimate constitutional means, can come only from outside, and the state's foreign policy can be regarded as representing the domestic political community as a whole. Such threats as it has to contend with will then largely be determined by the extent to which its national mission is congruent with those of its neighbours and the major global powers. Insofar as the idea of the state is 'owned' by particular sections of the population – which may be defined in terms of ethnicity, class, ideology, institutional vested interest, or indeed the personal connections of an individual ruler – its foreign (and also domestic) policies will correspondingly reflect the interests of its owners, and be directed against those members of the population who contest the idea of the state, as much as (or instead of) towards the achievement of any authentically national goals. The subordination of South African foreign policy, prior to the transition to majority rule in 1990–4, to the overriding goal of securing white minority rule provides a particularly clear example.

The foreign policies which African states followed after independence therefore depended most basically on the extent to which their ideas of the state were shared, firstly among their own populations, secondly with their neighbours and African states as a whole, and finally with the dominant states of the international system. Any significant challenge to those ideas, either domestic or external, in turn defined the threats which rulers faced, and the options open to them in attempting to counter them. Such a challenge could arise from any of the three basic questions to which the idea of the state had to posit an answer: the question of territory, or what the extent of the state should be; the question of government, or who should control it; and the question of policy, or what it should try to do.

The question of territory was the simplest, since in almost every case the legacies of nationalism and colonial statehood, combined with international acceptability and practical convenience, ensured that the existing colonial frontiers should be maintained. This was the case, not merely despite the artificiality of the frontiers bequeathed to African states by colonial rule, but even because of it. Touval has rightly pointed out that frontiers are frequently, throughout the world, imposed as the result of wars and other mechanisms which pay scant attention to the opinions of the people affected.[1] But what matters is not so much the nature of the frontiers themselves, as the nature of the states which those frontiers are used to define. The determination with which the frontiers between African states were maintained after independence resulted not simply from continuing colonial influence, nor even from the global conventions of respect for sovereign statehood, important though these were, but rather from the relationship between the state and the territory in the particular conditions of post-colonial Africa.

This relationship may broadly be conceived in either of two ways: there are territories which are created by states, and there are states which are created by territories. In the first case, the state is founded on the association of a group of people, who may or may not constitute a 'nation', and the development of means for governing these people which eventually constitute a state. Where the jurisdiction of this state comes up against the jurisdiction of other states which control neighbouring territories, a territory is created and a frontier is formed around it. These frontiers may be adjusted in one direction or the other, without affecting the identity of the state which lies within them. This has been the common experience, not merely of the major European states, but equally of parts of Asia such as Iran, Thailand, Cambodia or Vietnam, where the state was founded on a core community which sought to impose its control on peripheral groups, and to maintain its independence against neighbours strong enough to threaten it. As noted below, it also distinguished a number of states in Africa.

In the second case, which has been the common (though not universal) experience of modern African states, the territories came first, and the state was then established inside them. The Ghanaian or Ivoirian state was the organisation which had been created in order to govern a territory already identified as Ghana (or Gold Coast, in its colonial form) or Côte d'Ivoire. In this second case, the frontiers were usually more 'artificial' than in the first, but they were for that very reason more, and not less, central to the identity of the state that lay within them. There was, to put it another way, no 'idea' of Mali or of Zambia which preceded its frontiers and which could be used to challenge them. African rulers were therefore generally able to agree on the mutual recognition of their frontiers, because these frontiers constituted the basis for their own title to rule. Having done so, they could then call in aid the international conventions of juridical statehood and non-aggression which ensured that whenever the integrity of their territory was threatened, by either internal or external opponents, the overwhelming weight of international support would favour the status quo. This support was clearly demonstrated in the two cases during the post-independence period when serious secessionist movements sought to separate Katanga from Congo/Zaïre, and Biafra from Nigeria. It also inhibited territorial claims made by the Somali Republic and Morocco against their neighbours.

Not all African states, however, depended on their frontiers for their identities. Some of them embodied an idea of the state which made it possible to conceive of the state in terms separate from its frontiers, and thus potentially called its territorial structure into question. Touval identified four states – Ghana, Morocco, the Somali Republic and Togo – as challenging the principle that the colonial boundaries between African states should be retained.[2] Nkrumah's Ghana was the most quixotic, since the legitimacy of its boundaries was in this case denied in the name of a Pan-Africanism which would sweep away all of the imposed colonial frontiers of Africa, and establish a continental 'union government' in their place. There was, however, no suggestion that this principle might justify any challenge to Nkrumah's own control over Ghana's territory, and with his demise the idea was forgotten, and Ghana reverted to the normal conventions of African statehood. The Togolese unionist movement sought to restore the former German colony of Togo, divided in 1919 between France and Britain, and in the process to unite the Ewe people who were thus split between Togo and what became Ghana.[3] In time Togo too came to accept the frontiers inherited from French trusteeship. The 'idea' of Morocco derived from the alleged territory of the pre-colonial Moroccan kingdom, and was used by King Hassan II in order to associate his monarchy with a historic Moroccan mission which could be used to claim territory allocated under colonial rule to Algeria, Mauritania, and Spanish Sahara – and in the process to strengthen his own political authority within Morocco. The Somali claim was explicitly nationalist, and sought to bring all of the Somali peoples within a single state through a union of Italian Somalia, British Somaliland, and the Somali-inhabited areas of Djibouti, Ethiopia and Kenya. These last two cases posed a much more serious challenge to the inherited colonial frontiers than those of Ghana and Togo, but – save for Western Sahara, which Morocco continued to occupy – the Moroccans and the Somalis were obliged to accept the continental consensus.

A number of other African states had conceptions of statehood which preceded the demarcation of their boundaries and which could be used to challenge them, but none the less found it convenient to side with the majority. Some, like Rwanda and Burundi in central Africa, and Lesotho and Swaziland in southern Africa, were either broadly satisfied with their frontiers, or else recognised the imprudence of challenging neighbours much more powerful than themselves; the proposed transfer of South African territory inhabited by ethnic Swazis to Swaziland by the *apartheid* regime then in power in South Africa was abandoned in the face of opposition from the people who were to have been transferred. Though some Liberians resented the theft (as they saw it) by British and French colonialists of large areas of Liberian territory which became part of Sierra Leone, Guinea and Côte d'Ivoire, the Liberian government forbore to pursue claims which would have embittered its relations with all of its neighbours. The two states whose boundaries were much more seriously contested than any others in Africa, Ethiopia and Sudan, were guided by an idea of the state which implicitly ascribed a dominating role to some people within it at the expense of others: in Ethiopia to Christian Amharic speakers, especially from the central region of Shoa; in Sudan to Arabic-speaking Moslems, especially from the Nile valleys around Khartoum. In each case, adherence to the principle of respect for existing boundaries helped to protect the central government against secessionist claims. These governments none the less had to seek international alliances through which to obtain the arms and diplomatic support needed to maintain their conceptions of statehood.

The overwhelming support both of African states and of the major powers for the maintenance of existing frontiers helped to inhibit, but did not entirely prevent, challenges to the territoriality of African states arising from inside them. The danger was particularly acute when, as in Sudan or Nigeria, the opposition enjoyed widespread support in large and relatively clearly defined regions which possessed at least some of the attributes required for separate independent statehood; or when, as in north eastern Kenya or eastern Ghana, a region bordered a neighbouring state governed by fellow members of the locally predominant ethnic group. In Nigeria, a process of progressive political breakdown led eventually to the attempted secession of Biafra and to the civil war of 1967–70, while Sudan suffered continuously from civil war, save only for the period from 1972 until 1983, from 1964 onwards. In the most acute case of all, and the only one in which the demand for a redefinition of state frontiers was successful, the Eritrean secessionist challenge to the idea of the Ethiopian state was posed in the name of an alternative Eritrean statehood which derived from Italian colonial rule, and which far more closely resembled the territoriality of other post-colonial states than did the post-imperial Ethiopian one. Indeed, the great majority of the challenges to the territoriality of existing African states were articulated in the name of a territory demarcated under colonial rule, whether as a separate colony or else as a distinct subdivision within a colony. Katanga, Togoland, Biafra, Southern Sudan, and Eritrea were all multiethnic territories, the boundaries of which were created by colonialism, and the demands posed for their separate independence, for their transfer from one state to another, or for some autonomous political status within an existing state, all drew on the same principles of territoriality as did most post-colonial independent African states.

One critical effect of the idea of territoriality in the definition of African statehood was thus to help insulate ethnic conflict from the international system. It rendered illegitimate the assumption – which had, for example, assumed overriding importance in the idea of European statehood – that peoples with a common language, culture and historical identity were entitled to be governed as part of a single state, and that international frontiers should be demarcated in order to allow for this. Only the Somali claim to ethnic nationhood explicitly sought to apply this principle to Africa. Even where ethnicity in practice provided much of the impetus behind demands for a separate political status – as for example in Togoland, Biafra, or indeed the secession of Somaliland from the Somali Republic – the territorial principle prevailed. Though ethnic differences of one kind or another were central to the domestic politics of virtually all African states, and were managed internally in widely differing ways, their impact on Africa's international relations – though by no means negligible – was relatively muted.

One consequence of this emphasis on the territoriality of artificial African states was to reinforce the principle of 'negative sovereignty' – characteristically defined in terms of respect for existing frontiers, and non-interference in the internal affairs of other states – which has already been identified as a critical element in the relationship between African states and the international system. This in turn helped to insulate the second ingredient of the idea of the state, the structure of domestic government or the question of who should rule, from international scrutiny. The great majority of post-colonial African states came to independence under the leadership of the nationalist politicians who had organised opposition to colonial rule, and who had in most cases demonstrated their popular support through reasonably fair elections. These might have been expected to insist on nationalist and even democratic credentials similar to their own, as prerequisites for the acceptance of legitimate African governments. This did not happen. The domestic structure of government, however unequal and conflictual it may have been internally, was not regarded as presenting any particular challenge to the African state system externally. The government of Ethiopia by an emperor, whose power (according to the constitution in force until 1974) derived directly from God, in no way diminished Ethiopia's capacity to play a prominent role in continental diplomacy: indeed, Ethiopia's status as the one truly historic independent African state, and the personal prestige of emperor Haile-Selassie, were of enormous value to pre-1974 Ethiopia in conducting its foreign relations. Even the government of Liberia by an elite drawn disproportionately from Americo-Liberian immigrants, at the expense of the indigenous African inhabitants, was a matter of no great concern to other African states. Only in Zanzibar, where the overthrow of the sultanate immediately after independence in 1964 led to the country's union with Tanganyika to form Tanzania, did an independent African state's domestic system of government have any significant bearing on its international status. Even the overthrow of nationalist governments by military *coups d'état*, which became a fairly regular occurrence from the mid-1960s onwards, did not call into question the international acceptability of the new regimes. Not until after the end of the Cold War, under the impetus of economic decline, domestic political protest, and the greatly increased self-confidence of Western states, was the internal structure of African governments to become a source of major international concern; and even then, this concern came almost entirely from outside the continent rather than from within it.

It was very different when the governing community was of white European origin, as in Rhodesia/Zimbabwe, Namibia and South Africa, since this posed a moral (as well as, often, a military) challenge to other African states. Such regimes not only oppressed the great majority of their own citizens – which was not a problem when such oppression was imposed by African governments – but denied the status of African peoples and the idea of the government of Africa by Africans. They were therefore readily identified with colonial regimes, which offended the idea of African government in the same way. For so long as white minority rule continued, its maintenance remained the critical priority of the white regimes, and its overthrow of the black ones. This necessarily created conflictual relationships across the 'front line' between white and black ruled parts of Africa, and with the African (and, eventually, global) international community as a whole. In these cases, the internal structure of statehood had a determining effect on external relations, in a way that it did not in other African states.

The idea of the state could not, however, be insulated from domestic politics, and it was in this indirect fashion that the structure of government largely came to affect international relations. In some cases, the ownership of the state was defined in class, elite or racial terms, creating a level of domestic conflict with profound international implications. The imperial mission of the Ethiopian state, expressed in its territorial expansion in the later nineteenth century, meant that the preservation of its territorial integrity – coupled until 1974 with the maintenance of its imperial system of government – became the overriding goal of its foreign policy. The 1974 revolution changed the structure of government, but exacerbated the relationship between the central government and ethnic or regional identities. In both Rwanda and Burundi, the division of the population between the historically dominant Tutsi and the much more numerous Hutu was to provide the basis for appalling levels of bloodshed; although the outcome was different in the two cases, since a Tutsi-dominated regime retained control in Burundi while a Hutu one took over in Rwanda, the maintenance of the domestic power structure in both countries was central to the management of external relations. In Liberia, the violent overthrow of the Americo-Liberian regime in 1980 led to a brief period of upheaval, before the historically close relationship with the United States was restored – only to be cast into question again by the brutality, incompetence, corruption and ethnic favouritism of the subsequent regime.

Where domestic political conflict took a broadly ideological form, this invariably turned on the degree of accommodation with (or hostility to) the former colonial power displayed by the governing party on the one hand, and its opponents on the other. This in turn usually closely reflected the class structure of the party system: patron parties, built on a clientele structure controlled by established elites who had normally enjoyed close relations with the colonial regime, generally favoured the maintenance of continued links after independence; parties which drew their strength from radicalised urban populations were correspondingly opposed, both to internal elites and to their colonial connections. In some states, such as Nigeria and Cameroon, a ruling party at independence which favoured accommodation with the former coloniser was challenged by more radical opposition movements, and looked to its colonial patron for support. In Ghana and Mali it was the other way round, and a radical ruling party felt threatened by opponents which it regarded as the internal agents of neocolonialism. This variant aroused much greater strains in the state's relations with the international system, since the leadership needed to find new sources of external support in order to displace the former colonial ruler, and consequently looked to alternative patrons such as the Soviet Union.

Given the pre-eminence of the leader within the nationalist parties, however, these could to an appreciable extent define their foreign policies by personal choice. Jomo Kenyatta had been imprisoned for many years by the colonial regime, one of whose representatives had memorably described him as 'a leader unto darkness and to death', but none the less maintained a close association with the United Kingdom once he became the ruler of an independent Kenya. In Malawi, the elderly Dr Hastings Kamuzu Banda had been installed as party leader by a group of younger and more radical colleagues, but launched a drastic and successful purge immediately after independence – in which he received the support of the former British governor, who had just exchanged the position for that of high commissioner. Julius Nyerere in neighbouring Tanzania, who had enjoyed a trouble-free passage to independence in close association with the British colonial regime, none the less emerged as one of the most articulate spokesmen of anti-colonial nationalism.

The multiparty electoral systems which in most African states were introduced by the departing colonial regime in the last few years before independence could not be expected to provide a viable framework for the allocation of political power once independence had been achieved, even though they often retained a residual legitimacy which was called upon when a new constitution was needed. Insofar as the regime sought to establish a new form of governmental legitimacy, this was more likely to be based on the personality of the leader that on the constitutional structure of the state. Underlying the leadership there was often a tacit ethnic or regional alliance: Kikuyu with support from the Rift Valley peoples in Kenyatta's Kenya; Hausa-Fulani in alliance first with Ibos and subsequently with a section of the Yoruba in the first Nigerian republic; northerners in association with some southern groups in Ahidjo's Cameroon. If this alliance was capable of incorporating the most powerful factions within the state, it might well prove enduring. If not, there could be trouble. The options open to such governments in the foreign policy sphere, and their relationship to the domestic power structure, are examined in the next section.

The third element in the idea of the state, that of policy or what the government should try to do, turned essentially in the African case on a choice between alternative approaches to the problems of political disunity and economic underdevelopment which at independence confronted virtually all African regimes. The issue of political disunity most directly affected international relations when governments sought to strengthen the domestic basis of government through measures designed to enhance the sense of national unity among the people comprising the state. Conventionally described as 'nation-building', this enterprise involved an attempt to extend the idea of the state as widely as possible through the population, and especially among the most influential members of all of its constituent ethnic groups. In states which were themselves externally created, however, fostering a sense of domestic nationhood almost necessarily involved an attempt to cut off those contacts which some sections at least of the population already had with the outside world. This was most evident when nation-building drew on the support already fostered by anti-colonial nationalism, since it then threatened both the interests which the former colonial power retained within the territory, and those sections of the domestic population who were most closely associated with the colonial regime. The clearest example was provided by Guinea under Sekou Touré, where the bitterness of the breach with France reflected both Sekou Toure's hostility to the system of administrative chieftaincy through which French rule within the country had been maintained, and his fears that ethnic divisions within Guinea might be used by the French to undermine his rule.[4] Given the level of penetration of African states by the former colonial power, in social and economic as well as in directly political terms, nationalism and anti-colonialism were organically linked. During the later 1970s in Nigeria, when a self-confident military regime, boosted by victory in the civil war of 1967–70 and by the massive revenues generated by the oil boom, was attempting to foster a sense of Nigerian identity, this in turn was reflected in a series of clashes with the United Kingdom: over its alleged involvement in an attempted *coup d'état* which led to the assassination of the Nigerian head of state, over the nationalisation of British Petroleum assets in Nigeria, and over British policy towards the then white minority regime in Rhodesia/Zimbabwe.

Since the major social and economic linkages of African states were with the industrial states (and notably the former colonial metropoles), rather than with their own neighbours, the nation-building project did not have such marked effects on regional relationships as on south–north ones. In this respect again, the African experience differed from that of Europe, where nationalism almost necessarily led to regional conflict. None the less, the juxtaposition of a radical nationalist state with moderate or conservative neighbours frequently soured relations: between Guinea and both Senegal and Côte d'Ivoire; between Ghana and all its francophone neighbours including notably Côte d'Ivoire and Togo; or between Tanzania and Kenya. Nor did the pursuit of a relatively modest and unambitious policy of conciliation, both with different groups within the national territory and with external powers, remove the construction of domestic statehood from the realm of foreign policy. On the contrary, it involved the maintenance within the domestic economy and political structure of the existing external linkages established notably by colonialism, and reinforced the structures of dependence which these linkages involved.

Within the bipolar global order which existed until 1989, the most evident linkage between economic development programmes and the international order was provided by the association of capitalist states with the United States and its allies on the one hand, and of socialist ones with the Soviet Union and its allies on the other. This division probably had a less important impact on sub-Saharan Africa than on any other major region of the world, partly – as already noted – because African states were not on the whole important enough to the superpowers for these to invest a great deal in the attempt to control them, but partly also because the social and economic structures of African states were insufficiently developed to pose a significant choice between socialist and capitalist strategies of economic development. Though state control of the economy provided an attractive means through which rulers could increase their access to resources, and in the process claim the support of socialist states within the global order, it was scarcely possible for any African state to disengage from the capitalist world economy; nor was the domestic class structure sufficiently articulated to offer opportunities for a revolution in Marxist terms. The one exception was Ethiopia, where the overthrow of the imperial regime did lead to a revolutionary reign of terror and to a drastic reallocation of the means of production, notably agricultural land. Though other factors, and especially Ethiopia's strategic situation, influenced the subsequent switch in alliance from the United States to the Soviet Union, this remains the one African case where domestic revolution evidently affected foreign policy alignment.

The foreign policies of African states were, in short, most basically determined by the kind of states that they were. Created in large measure by the international system, they continued to need access to it as the condition for their own survival. The form which that access took in turn depended, in part on the structure of domestic statehood imposed by relatively unchanging features of their internal composition, in part on options open to their rulers, in part on their linkages with the international economy. Many African states became relatively comfortable with their own identities, which were not to any great extent threatened either internally or externally, and their external relations were accordingly unproblematic. Despite frequent changes of regime, for example, the identity of Ghana was fairly effectively established;[5] the same might be said of Benin, which likewise had a succession of unstable governments, or of Botswana, which was governed by the same regime for three decades after independence.

Those African states where the idea of the state was most basically challenged in turn had the greatest need for external support, in order to maintain their territorial integrity or to keep their existing regime in power. However, even in those states which met the conventional norms of African statehood, and whose boundaries and domestic structures of government were not seriously threatened, the idea of the state still had a critical influence on external relations.

The monopoly state

Within an often astonishingly short period after independence, the nationalist parties formed to mobilise popular support against the colonial regime, and at the same time to launch their leaders into positions of state power, declined from their previous position of apparently unchallengeable strength. In the process, the imposition of control from the top, rather than the mobilisation of support from below, became the predominant relationship between African rulers and those who had now become their subjects. There is some room for dispute over whether this was a necessary and inevitable transformation, determined by the structures of African statehood, or whether it derived from the choice of those who enjoyed the power to decide. There is, however, no doubt about its virtual universality. In the initial phase, opposition parties were permitted to remain in being only where the government lacked the resources to crush them, or where they were in any event so feeble that they presented no challenge to its tenure of power. In the first case, as in Nigeria and Sierra Leone, the opposition was able to contest elections after independence, but was not permitted to win them; in Sierra Leone, the opposition All People's Congress actually won the 1967 election, and its leader was sworn in as prime minister, only to be instantly ousted by a military putsch orchestrated by the leader of the governing party. In a very small number of cases, notably Botswana and The Gambia, opposition parties were permitted to compete in regular elections but never had any plausible prospect of winning. In no state on the African mainland, from independence through to 1990, did any opposition party gain power as the result of winning a general election against an incumbent government.

In a second phase, even the governing parties atrophied as their mobilising functions were removed, their electoral organisation became redundant, and their leaders were appointed to governmental positions which depended on the favour of the head of state rather than the support of their constituents.[6] The rhetoric of party rule, even in cases where the party was ostensibly awarded a key role in nation-building and development, became almost entirely devoid of content, its emptiness revealed when military *coups d'état* from the mid-1960s onwards were not only unopposed by party organisations, but scarcely even needed to abolish them; they had effectively already abolished themselves.

Once political parties were removed as effective participants from the African scene, states emerged as the sole viable mechanisms through which African leaders could maintain their power and seek their other goals. The preservation and if possible strengthening of the state became the overriding priority of government, not only within domestic politics but equally in foreign policy. The kind of state which Africa possessed, and the role of statehood in mediating between the domestic and external environments, thus became the critical determinants of African international relations.

Within a very few years of independence, these states were turned into organisations of a broadly similar kind, which may be characterised as 'monopoly states'. Confronted by weak administrative structures, fragile economies, and in some cases dangerous sources of domestic opposition, political leaders sought to entrench themselves in power by using the machinery of the state to suppress or co-opt any rival organisation – be it an opposition political party, a trades union, or even a major corporation. Rather than acknowledging the weakness of their position, and accepting the limitations on their power which this imposed, they chose to up the stakes and go for broke. There were, of course, variations in the level of monopoly. Even though the vast majority of African states, between the mid-1960s and the early 1990s, had either single-party governments or military regimes, in a few cases, as already noted, opposition parties were permitted to survive. Within the monopoly framework, some rulers (broadly corresponding to those whom Jackson and Rosberg characterise as 'princes') chose to govern by co-opting potential opponents into the system of rewards, whereas others ('autocrats', in Jackson and Rosberg's terms) employed a much higher level of direct coercion.[7] Often, the difference depended not so much on the personality of the ruler concerned, as on the structure of domestic politics and the availability of rewards. Rulers differed, too, in the extent to which they sought to use their position in order to achieve more general goals, over and above the maintenance of their own power: in terms of their willingness to use coercion, there was little to choose between Samuel Doe of Liberia and Mengistu Haile-Mariam of Ethiopia, but whereas Doe's was merely a personal dictatorship, Mengistu sought through Marxism–Leninism (however counter-productively) to establish a powerful and centralised Ethiopian state, and a planned economy.[8]

The monopoly state none the less exhibited many of the same characteristics across sub-Saharan Africa as a whole. The first was a high dependence on personal leadership. Indeed, the entire system revolved around the leader, and depended on his retention of power. In a sense, the leader was omnipotent, in that there was nothing which he (they were all male) could not decide to do. At the same time, he was extremely insecure, in that the impossibility of removing him through any agreed constitutional mechanism had to be balanced against the possibility that he might at any time be removed by a *coup d'état* launched from within the state apparatus, or (over rather a longer period) by a rebellion organised in the countryside. Two African leaders, Haile-Selassie of Ethiopia and Felix Houphouet-Boigny of Côte d'Ivoire, remained continuously in power for just over thirty-three years, while several others managed more than two decades. In very few cases before the upheavals of the early 1990s did African leaders voluntarily abandon power, or accept any political structure which might oblige them to do so: the only examples were a few nationalist politicians who eventually retired – Senghor in Senegal, Ahidjo in Cameroon, Stevens in Sierra Leone, Nyerere in Tanzania – and an equally small number of military regimes which eventually honoured their commitment to hand over to an elected government – as in Ghana in 1969 and 1979, and Nigeria in 1979. The rest chose to stick it out, until death, a military *coup d'état*, or some other upheaval overthrew them. The price of failure was, however, high, and well over half of leading African politicians between independence and 1991 were assassinated, executed, imprisoned, or forced into exile.[9]

This personalism directly affected the conduct of foreign policy. African leaders characteristically conducted much of their foreign relations themselves, not merely because of the personal gratification afforded by foreign travel and summit diplomacy, but because their own regimes and even their own lives often depended on it. While some studies have sought to demonstrate the institutionalisation of the foreign policy-making process, especially with respect to large states and relatively uncontentious issues,[10] the management of sensitive issues was highly personalised. Nor did the conduct of diplomacy appear to become increasingly routinised as the years passed since independence and the bureaucracy expanded. Indeed, the growing insecurity of African regimes, and the shrinking of their freedom of action in the face of political weakness and economic collapse, may well have had the opposite effect.

In managing his regime, the leader depended on his ability to retain the obedience of the major sources of power within the country. Some of these, such as the military, were immediately threatening but readily identifiable. Others, such as the urban mob or potentially disaffected regional interests, did not present such an immediate danger, but neither did they have such identifiable and co-optable leaders. Organised political opposition was not a factor, except in the form of a rural insurgency, but neither was organised political support. Even the astonishingly throughgoing process by which Mengistu Haile-Mariam sought to establish a Leninist vanguard party in Ethiopia proved to be wasted, since the party collapsed at the moment when Mengistu himself lost power.

As the monopoly state was established in the years after independence, not only did the range of people with the capacity to influence the political process and gain access to political benefits shrink,[11] but the means through which they had to seek this access and influence changed. The possibility of organising a domestic constituency was removed, except insofar as this could be co-opted into the governing structure. Leaders gained the power to decide which groups or interests they would incorporate into the political process, and which they would exclude; in the process, politics turned into a patronage operation, governed by the need for control on the part of the ruler, and the need for access to state benefits on the part of the subordinates and those whom, in however tenuous a manner, they sought to represent.

A state which is managed in this way makes distinctive demands on the international system. Clientelist systems lack the capacity to create any sense of moral community amongst those who participate in them, let alone among those who are excluded.[12] Nor do they encourage production, by giving incentives in the form of economic benefits or political participation to those who create wealth. It is a peculiarly consumption-oriented form of political management, which depends on the diversion of consumption opportunities to those groups which offer most help, or pose most danger, to people in power. Characteristically, these are urban groups, and notably those most dependent on state employment and other benefits conferred by the state. Foreign policies, in their broadest sense, therefore became a means through which leaders attempted to gain access to the resources required to maintain the domestic political structure. These resources included both those needed to meet the expectations of the governing coalition, and those needed to suppress the demands of the excluded. Beneath a veneer of rhetoric designed to maintain the appearance of commitment to moral principles – a function for which the remaining white minority regimes provided an excellent target – a clientelist domestic political structure entailed a clientelist foreign policy.

The effects of this form of management on the relations between the state and the international economy are examined in a later section. In the political sphere, the impact of monopoly statehood on external relations was most clearly illustrated by the military regimes which seized power from the mid-1960s onwards. Military coups reflected both the decline in political participation which permitted the capture of the state by its own employees, and the strains on patronage resources which led to intensified conflict between those who were in a position to compete for them. The military regime was in effect the monopoly state personified.

Unlike Latin America, where the military was closely associated with right-wing political groupings and in turn with the United States, African militaries as a whole did not have any in-built bias towards any particular external alliance. Specific military regimes, however, were often closely associated with different external patrons. Many of the first generation of African military regimes, in both francophone and anglophone states, were led by officers trained in colonial military establishments, who retained a sometimes embarrassing subservience to their colonial mentors.[13] An important group of francophone military rulers, including Eyadema of Togo and Bokassa of the Central African Republic, had served with the French army in Indochina. In the Horn of Africa, where post-colonial connections were weak and the need for weapons was high, military rulers were more likely to seek alliance with one of the superpowers: the Soviet Union had already been training the Somali army for several years before the coup in October 1969, and (until the Ogaden war of 1977) General Siyad Barre established a close relationship with the Russians. For Colonel Mengistu Haile-Mariam, who led the revolutionary regime in Ethiopia, a Soviet alliance (as well as counteracting Russian support for the

Somalis) provided an appealing alternative to the preceding imperial government's dependence on the Americans.

In few cases were outside states unambiguously involved in fomenting military coups against African regimes.[14] Despite the attractiveness of the externally manipulated coup, as a quick and painless device for removing a hostile head of state, major powers rarely had either the interest or the opportunity to make it worthwhile. The overthrow of the self-proclaimed emperor Bokassa in 1979 was not merely engineered but implemented by the French, under the guise of a domestic *coup d'état*;[15] and a plausible case has been made for Soviet involvement in the Somali coup of 1969,[16] and in an attempted coup in Sudan two years later. I am aware of no plausible case for either United States or British involvement in African coups, though claims have been made, and a number of African military regimes, after seizing power, established close relations with both the United States and the United Kingdom.

The external impact of African military regimes followed not so much from their ideological leanings, or from the involvement of outside states in bringing them to power, as from the military's need to call for external assistance in order to make good its lack of domestic legitimacy. The Murtala regime in Nigeria was exceptional, in that the massive increase in government revenues resulting from the oil boom of the mid-1970s enabled it to pursue nationalist policies at home, and to exercise considerable influence abroad. On the whole, military regimes were in any event likely to take over at a time when the incumbent government was weakened by the decay of its patronage base; and a change of regime aroused the expectations of those who had been excluded from the previous government, without creating any enhanced capacity to meet them. The military itself became a major source of additional demands on the new regime, since it provided not only its power base but the readiest means of overthrowing it. Military regimes were therefore particularly in need of financial or – if that failed – repressive aid.

Though a few African military regimes succeeded in developing a political programme which generated a measure of popular support, and even on rare occasions (such as the Rawlings victory in Ghana in November 1992) managed to win reasonably fair elections,[17] they were also responsible for by far the greatest number of cases of political collapse. As time went by, even patronage systems were displaced, in countries such as Doe's Liberia, Siyad Barre's Somalia, Mobutu's Zaïre, or (in a rare civilian case) Obote's second government in Uganda, by what Lemarchand has referred to as prebendal alliances.[18] Rural patrons, who acted as the essential (if self-interested) intermediaries between national leadership elites and rural constituencies, were replaced by bands of soldiers and officials who had no connections with the areas which they pillaged. Prebendal alliances rapidly destroyed any sense of common identity and governmental legitimacy that had previously existed among the peoples of the affected state: Liberia under the rapacious rule first of Samuel Doe, and later of Charles Taylor and other predatory factions, provided one of the clearest examples of how a peaceful and relatively wealthy state could be destroyed by such means.

The domestic politics of foreign policy management

The search for outside resources to maintain domestic power structures was central to the foreign policies of the great majority of African states. The way in which this search was conducted, however, varied appreciably according to the nature of the governments concerned, and the domestic and external threats which they faced. Subsequent chapters will examine the benefits and costs of seeking alliances with each of the major external actors – the former colonial powers, the superpowers, and fellow African and other Third World states – which constituted the external universe of African foreign policies. The internal universe of domestic politics, however, also helped to define the possible options, and the factors which were likely to influence the choice of one rather than another.

As a general rule, it may be assumed that African leaders sought to maximise their own security and freedom of action within the setting in which they had to act. Even this cannot be taken as axiomatic: freedom and security may in some respects be competing goals, and the pursuit of each is subject to personal judgements which are sometimes hard for an outsider to follow; other goals, including a genuine ideological commitment to ends which do not necessarily coincide with the leader's own welfare, cannot be excluded. Nonetheless, this simple rule provides a place to start. The framework for action comprised the major sources of pressure on the policy-maker from both domestic and external settings – two categories which were on occasion difficult to distinguish from one another. In choosing a general policy orientation, and where necessary a set of specific alliances, the leader then needed to balance these pressures against one another in such a way as to achieve his own goals. This balancing act has been awkwardly but helpfully defined by Steven David as 'omni-balancing', to distinguish it from the maintenance of a balance within the external environment alone, which has been used by international relations theorists to explain foreign policy behaviour in coherent and united nation-states.[19]

For all but a minority of African leaders, this process was likely to start with an assessment of the domestic situation, since their security was usually much more directly threatened by domestic than by external considerations. Those leaders who enjoyed unchallenged control over their domestic environments started with an enormous advantage, and were much more likely than threatened rulers to be able to set the agenda in their dealings with outside states. Even an apparently unchallenged domestic base sometimes, as already noted in the previous section, tacitly depended on the recognition of existing external interests, such as those of the former colonial power. It did, however, enable the leader to start with a set of useful bargaining chips, including the ability to decide how he would allocate his support in global disputes and continental alliances, and the selective disposition of opportunities to gain access to resources within his personal gift; these included the right to establish military bases or other facilities on his territory, or economic privileges such as fishing rights or investment opportunities. He would certainly want something in exchange, be it diplomatic support, development or military aid, or possibly personal kickbacks or privileges for himself and his associates. The stronger his domestic position, and the greater the resources at the disposal of his state – in terms of its economic resources, strategic situation, or leadership role among a group of neighbouring states – the better the bargain he could strike.

At this point, one of the more important choices facing a relatively secure leader was whether to opt for alignment or non-alignment: whether to balance rival external powers against one another, or to seek the relative security but potential dependence implied by a close and lasting relationship with a single major ally. Non-alignment was the more gratifying choice; it asserted the leader's independence, and opened the way for him to build up his own position among other African or Third World states, and thus to establish alliances which would not be open to the client of a major power. Even in dealing with major powers, it might pay the leader to play these off against one another; client states easily gain the impression that they are being taken for granted – or in other words, that their patron does not pay them as much as they are worth, because he does not need to – and so an expression of independence can be used to maximise rewards. Though the non-aligned option was most readily adopted by a leader with a secure home base, it could equally be used to deter external powers from making common cause with his domestic rivals. Emperor Haile-Selassie of Ethiopia was firmly aligned for all essential purposes with the West and notably with the United States, but none the less used contacts with the USSR in order to inhibit Soviet support for the secessionist movement in Eritrea; he likewise used his relations with Nasser in an attempt to neutralise Arab support.

The choice of a regular alliance with a major power was often predetermined by elements in the leader's position which appeared to fall outside the sphere of foreign relations altogether. Just as Haile-Selassie could not plausibly present himself as an ally of the Soviet Union, so other conservative leaders such as Felix Houphouet-Boigny were held within the Western (and in this case, post-colonial) alliance system by a domestic political structure which offered little scope for experiment. For some leaders, a close alliance with the West offered a measure of security, which they may well have felt worth exchanging for the potentially higher but none the less riskier rewards of non-alignment. The leaders of small states who, regardless of domestic opposition, felt more vulnerable, and who in any event had little prospect of becoming regional leaders in their own right, were more likely to opt for a client role than the leaders of large ones. The fact that the francophone states of West Africa were all much smaller in population than the two large anglophone ones of Nigeria and Ghana can only have encouraged the great majority of them to remain in close association with France. To be the client of a major state outside the continent was a way of protecting oneself against the ambitions of a regional leader within it.

Under some circumstances, the very weakness of a client provided him with the ability to manipulate his patron. If the client was heavily dependent on the patron, then the patron might well also depend on the client, whose domestic and regional opponents were associated with rival patrons. The United States for example sought to reduce its commitment to the Haile-Selassie regime in Ethiopia during the early 1970s, since the ageing emperor was clearly reaching the end of his reign, and too close an association could subsequently prove a liability; Haile-Selassie was none the less able to induce a reluctant United States to provide him with sophisticated F5–E aircraft, to counter the threat presented by Soviet arms supplies to Somalia.[20] In the late 1980s, Mengistu Haile-Mariam was able to persuade an equally reluctant Soviet Union to keep supplying the arms required to prop up his failing regime. The French faced a similar dilemma, especially in Chad, where any failure to protect an incumbent regime against Libyan intervention aroused intense concern in neighbouring francophone states in which French interests were much greater, and enabled even Hissene Habre, despite the hostility towards him in the French political establishment, to call on French aid against President Qadhafi.[21]

The relative pay-off between the goals of economic development and personal prestige or security also influenced the choice between a non-aligned or a clientelist strategy. While non-alignment was a good mechanism for maximising one's diplomatic status, it was counter-productive as a means of attracting commercial investment. From the viewpoint of rulers such as Houphouet-Boigny in Côte d'Ivoire or Kamuzu Banda in Malawi, the search for economic support dictated a clientelist approach, in contrast to the priority given to political goals and non-aligned strategies by their neighbours, Nkrumah in Ghana and Kaunda in Zambia. Once the inadequacies of the USSR as a source of economic development aid became apparent from the 1970s onwards, any foreign policy concerned with economic advantage had to look towards the West.

When leaders faced appreciable domestic threats, the demands of omnibalancing became considerably more intricate, and their scope for independent action was correspondingly reduced. Many such threats were almost inherently associated with external alliances and enmities. Within a Cold War context, a right-wing or capitalist regime which faced a threat from a left-wing or socialist opposition was ineluctably pressed towards closer association with its capitalist patron: though a posture of non-alignment might have led to a formal undertaking on the part of the opposition's external backers not to become involved in the state's domestic affairs, these backers knew that they could only gain from a change of regime. In those parts of the continent, notably the Horn, where the conventions of territoriality never fully applied, internal ethnic or religious divisions were still harder to insulate from the structure of regional or global alliances. Where an ethnic group straddled a national border, or where a group which was out of power within one state could make common cause with its fellows who controlled a neighbouring state, domestic and regional policies were no more than parts of the same equation. Where the states involved were in turn associated with rival superpowers (or even former colonial powers), the structure of competition was raised from the regional to the global level. Such was the relationship in the period up to 1977 between the Ethiopian government and its protector the United States on the one hand, and Somalis living within Ethiopia, the government of the Somali Republic, and the Soviet Union on the other. Only the most explicit commitment to the USSR, coupled with its ability to offer appreciably greater resources to the Russians than its rival, reinforced by a far more convincing adherence to Marxism-Leninism, enabled the Mengistu Haile-Mariam regime to reverse the superpower alliance structure and gain the support of the Soviet Union (militarily, at that point, vastly more valuable than that of the United States) in the Ogaden war of 1977–8.

Sudan provided a particularly clear example of the changes in external alliances which followed from changes in the domestic structure of power, and from the conceptions of Sudanese nationhood espoused by the government in Khartoum. Any Sudanese government faced a fundamental choice between strategies designed to conciliate the Christian communities of the south on the one hand, or to control or conquer them on the other; as part of either strategy, it also needed to manage complex divisions, both within the south of the country and within the Moslem and largely Arabic speaking north. A strategy of control called for a reliable external source of arms, and hence for an ideology of domestic government which (regardless of the genuineness of the regime's commitment to it) fostered close relations between the regime and its main suppliers. Such an ideology was provided in the early years of the Nimairi regime between 1969 and 1971 by communism, and in the period after the al-Bashir government's seizure of power in 1989 by militant Islam. This strategy was also liable to exacerbate relations with Ethiopia and other neighbouring states, thus encouraging Ethiopian support for the southern opposition; it likewise strained Sudan's relations with the West. An alternative strategy, followed by Nimairi after the 1972 Addis Ababa agreement and briefly attempted in the later 1980s, sought reconciliation with the south and association with the West, with an emphasis on economic development rather than armaments as the most sought-after external resource. This also carried the benefit of encouraging amicable relations with Sudan's neighbours, but aroused potentially fatal opposition among Arabist and Islamist groups which were in a position to threaten the central government in Khartoum. In short, foreign policy management was intricately linked with domestic political control.

Paying for the state

States do not come free. They have to be paid for. African states were paid for through their engagement in the international economy. Whereas at one time, during the heyday of dependency theories of Third World underdevelopment, this engagement was regarded, at least by some observers, as inherently damaging to any prospect of African development (and in many other ways as well), it may now be treated as an inevitable fate, and in some respects even a beneficial one. There was certainly no other way in which African states and peoples could gain access to the numerous products which they needed but could not create themselves. Despite the success with which some Third World states were able to profit from their integration into the international economy to achieve remarkable levels of growth, however, for the great majority of African states this association with the global economy was an ambivalent one. In particular, the financial demands of state maintenance and expansion, coupled with the structure of the state itself, both exacerbated the problems of African economic development, and critically affected the continent's external relations. This book is not concerned with the highly disputed issues of economic development, though some reference to them will be inevitable. It must, however, pay attention to the peculiar effects of the interactions between Africa's states, their revenue base, and their international relations. A subsequent chapter will look in greater detail at the impact on African states of the debt crisis of the 1980s and the 'structural adjustment programmes' imposed on them by international financial institutions. For the moment, at least some outline of the economic basis of African statehood is required.

As was noted in the previous chapter, permanent political institutions in Africa have, over a very long period, depended to a large extent on the revenues exacted from long-distance trade. With the advent of colonial rule, this dependence was deliberately fostered and intensified. The colonialists, after all, sought the profits that were, so they hoped, to be made from access to African resources, and they likewise expected to use some of these profits in order to pay for the framework of territorial government which the efficient extraction of resources required. Money was to be made out of Africa in two main ways. The first of them, mineral extraction, initially aroused the greatest hopes from entrepreneurs who hoped to make their fortunes in Africa; but the investment costs were massive, and outside parts of southern Africa, the returns were generally disappointing.[22] The second was by inducing Africans (and, to some extent, immigrants) to produce tropical crops for export. The extent to which this required coercion varied considerably: the British forced Africans into the monetary economy by imposing taxes which they could only pay by growing cash crops or seeking employment, a device which led to such upheavals as the Sierra Leone Hut Tax War of 1898; the rapid spread of cocoa-growing in Gold Coast/Ghana, on the other hand, was largely due to the readiness of the local population to take advantage of the economic opportunities which it offered. There was little plantation agriculture outside southern Africa, and the impact of other forms of production, notably industry, was slight. The proportion of Africa's export production accounted for by primary products remained virtually unchanged after independence, and amounted to 92 per cent in both 1970 and 1991.[23] Within this total, there was, however, an appreciable shift over that period from agricultural produce (51 per cent of exports in 1970, 34 per cent in 1991) to minerals (which, including oil, rose from 41 per cent to 58 per cent).

A great advantage of international trade, from a government's point of view, was that it was relatively easy to tax. You put tax officials on the frontier (preferably at the ports, which were the easiest frontiers to control), and collected the money as the goods went past. All African governments depended for a very high proportion of their revenues on taxes raised in one way or another from international trade.[24] Tariffs on imported goods were one way of doing it. Royalties from mineral-exporting companies were another. A third, devised by the colonial regimes but enthusiastically adopted by independent governments, was to require farmers to sell their crops to a government-managed marketing board, which normally payed them substantially less than these crops were worth on the international market, and then profited from their resale. Further mechanisms devised by African states after independence included nationalisation, which enabled the government to keep the profits itself (and also pay its supporters by appointing them to jobs in the nationalised corporations), and the maintenance of domestic currencies at an overvalued exchange rate, which enabled (and indeed obliged) governments still further to depress real prices paid to farmers, while also reducing the local currency price of imports.

The demands on these revenues increased sharply with independence. African nationalist movements had sought to raise support for independence, not simply by mobilising the identities of the colonised against external rule, but equally by the promise of tangible benefits once self-government was achieved. These benefits, generally described as 'development projects', in essence amounted to a combination of long-term infrastructural investments, immediate consumption goods, and straightforward patronage pay-offs: such goods as education, roads, and health and welfare provision may be classified under all three of these heads, though there was also an increase in elite consumption, prestige spending (on diplomatic representation, among other things) and corruption. These goods invariably increased demands on state revenues, rarely generated any new revenues of their own, and led in particular to a dramatic increase in state employment. They required a corresponding increase in the share of national product, and especially of export revenues, which was extracted by the state.[25]

These revenues were, however, inherently insecure.[26] The prices of primary products traded on world markets were liable to fluctuate wildly and unpredictably, in response partly to supply factors (bad weather in Brazil, the world's major coffee producer, instantly raised the revenues of African coffee-exporting states), and partly to demand ones (the price of copper, which was used largely for electric cable, was highly sensitive to boom and recession in Western industrial economies). Over a longer period, and more insidiously, the importance of material resources in the creation of wealth declined in relation to the importance of human skills. States with negligible physical resources but industrious and well-qualified populations, such as Japan, Singapore and South Korea, rose rapidly up the global league tables of per capita wealth, whereas states with a high dependence on exporting primary produce, including not only African states but also previously wealthy societies such as Argentina and Australia, slipped down. This, rather than any manipulation of global prices by capitalist industrial states, explained the declining terms of trade (the decline in the unit price of exports, relative to the unit price of imports) from which African states suffered from the mid-1950s onwards. This decline was masked by fluctuations, such as the short-lived commodity boom of the early 1970s, and the ability of global oil producers to maintain an artificially high price for a decade or so after 1973; despite controversy among economists over whether a continuing decline is the inevitable fate of primary producers, it was one from which most African producers suffered during the two decades to the mid-1990s.[27] The rate of decline, like the level of year-to-year fluctuation, varied for different primary products, and this in turn exacerbated the revenue insecurity of African states because of the high dependence of quite a number of them on a very small number of crops or minerals. In 1987, for example, there were eleven states in sub-Saharan Africa which derived more than 75 per cent of their export earnings from a single product, and a further ten which did so from only two products. Nigeria gained nearly 95 per cent of its earnings from petroleum, while Congo earned 87 per cent from coffee. The ability of African states to spread their risks was very limited.[28]

This dependence on export revenues, especially when these were derived from royalties and other exactions from mineral-exporting multinational corporations, led to the emergence of what has been termed the 'rentier state'.[29] The rentier state is an organisation which maintains itself by appropriating the income in excess of the costs of production, or rents, derived from production for a global market. These states are not reponsible for generating the conditions under which economic enterprise can flourish, nor do they directly depend on their own citizens to raise the money needed to produce the social goods which those citizens desire. Instead, the state receives a cheque from the corporation which extracts the goods, the size of which depends on the difference between production costs and the price prevailing in the world market.

This is a form of incorporation into the global market that places enormous obstacles in the way of effective and accountable government. It is inherently open to corruption, both in the relationship between the corporation and the state, and in the spending of money by agents of the state, since very large sums of money are involved in transactions which are not open to public inspection. Since control of government provides the opportunity to cream off sums of money vastly greater than any that could be gained through economically productive activity, the pressure to control the state – and the disincentive to relinquish that control – is overwhelming. Those who control the state in turn have the means to protect themselves against opposition: at its most benign, as in the case of some of the Gulf monarchies, by providing the public services required to purchase the acquiescence of the citizenry; alternatively, by co-opting potential opposition leaders through the offer of a share in state resources; or ultimately, by purchasing the weapons (and if need be, direct military assistance) required to retain power by force. It was symptomatic of the relationship between the rentier state and its population that despite the wave of democratisation sweeping Africa in the early 1990s, no African oil-producing state – from Algeria south through Nigeria and Gabon to Angola – achieved a successful democratic transition.

African rentier states, except for Botswana, were in no position to keep themselves going for more than short periods through the relatively benign mechanism of using mineral revenues to buy popular acquiescence. The level of population in relation to resources, coupled – as in the case of oil-boom Nigeria – with levels of elite discretionary consumption that rapidly became unsustainable, obliged them to concentrate their efforts on those sections of the population that were most important to them. These were, firstly, the ruling groups themselves and their associates; secondly, other sections of the state bureaucracy, and especially the military; thirdly, urban groups which, because of their concentration at the centres of power, were better placed than rural ones to bring pressure on the rulers. The economic effects of this process have been classically analysed by Bates.[30] Discriminatory pricing policies designed to extract cash from export producers drove farmers out of cash crop production, with the result that not only did African states suffer from declining terms of trade: they produced less as well. The maintenance of low food prices, designed to meet the demands of urban groups, correspondingly led to a reduction in marketed food production and to increased dependence on imported food; in the great majority of African states, per capita food production declined.[31] Protected industrial sectors and overvalued exchange rates created ample opportunities for patronage and corruption, while diverting resources to uneconomic uses.[32] This analysis broadly coincided with that of the World Bank's Berg Report,[33] which in turn provided much of the conceptual basis for the imposition of structural adjustment programmes on African states by international financial institutions in the 1980s.

Meanwhile, the decay of their resource base pressed African rulers into ever more urgent measures to gain revenues, and this in turn forced them into the international arena. For those relatively creditworthy states, such as Côte d'Ivoire, Kenya or Nigeria, which could raise money on world markets, or borrow it from industrial states or international institutions, it led to a rapid increase in indebtedness, the results of which are examined in a later chapter. As the oil boom ended in the early 1980s, even previously prosperous oil-producing states found themselves obliged to mortgage their revenues in advance, in order to meet obligations which they had undertaken in the belief that high oil prices would continue for ever. Less creditworthy states had to rely on aid, which became an increasingly important constituent, not merely of state revenues but of national GNP: by 1991, it amounted to over 10 per cent of the GNP of the great majority of sub-Saharan African states, and in the exceptional case of Mozambique to 69 per cent of GNP.[34] The effects of the dependence which this created are likewise examined in a later chapter.

As farmers and traders retreated from state-controlled markets, they sought alternative economic and political outlets which in turn increased the pressures on the state, both domestically and internationally. What was termed the 'informal sector' became the major growth area within African economies. This term encompassed a wide variety of economic activities, the common feature of which was that they either subverted or evaded the control of the state; they included parallel markets in which food, for example, was sold at prices determined by supply and demand, rather than those fixed by the state; illegal dealings in foreign currencies, where confidence in the national currency had collapsed; and, especially, export and import markets which operated across state borders by bribing or evading officials. The informal sector demonstrated levels of economic enterprise and market-oriented rationality which delighted the *laissez-faire* economist, and revealed the incapacity of African states to police their economic frontiers. It had a very significant role in the failure of the monopoly state, even though many of the activities which it encompassed were organised by politically influential individuals who thus sought to profit from evasion of the regulations which they imposed on others. As markets evaded the control of the state, moreover, so also did political movements. The growth of cross-border insurgency, by people for whom the state had become a threat rather than a source of security, precisely mirrored the growth of cross-border trade by people for whom it had become a source of exploitation rather than development.

Conclusion

The security which African states had appeared to possess at independence turned out to be misleading. It rested in part on conventions of international statehood that derived from a global power structure which, however immutable it seemed for the forty years after 1945, was eventually like other such power structures to pass away; in part on conceptions of the state within Africa which had, on the whole, the effect of insulating domestic politics from the international system – or rather, more precisely, of giving governments a highly privileged position as intermediaries between their own societies and external sources of power; in part on the continuation into the post-colonial era of the structures of the colonial state and the habits of acceptance which upheld them. None of these state-enhancing mythologies could, however, alter the underlying weaknesses of African states: the artificiality not just of their frontiers but more importantly of their identities, which resulted from the generally haphazard character of their colonial creation; the weakness of their governing structures, and the extreme difficulty of devising generally acceptable mechanisms for regulating the tenure and exercise of power; and the inadequacy of their economic base, and their dependence on an international economy which, though indispensable and in some respects supportive, was none the less the source of damaging and unpredictable fluctuations and distortions.

The measures taken by African rulers in an attempt to compensate for their weaknesses ultimately exacerbated rather than resolved their problems. These essentially rested on the use of the power of the state in order to rectify a lack of power in other respects. Much of this enterprise was directed towards the domestic arena, and in the process strained to breaking point the relationships between African states and the societies which they sought to govern.[35] Much of it also turned, however, on relationships between African states and the international system, since these states – which were, as already noted, for the most part created by the international system in the first place – had to look beyond their own frontiers in order to generate the resources that they needed in order to keep themselves going at home. In this quest, they could seek support from each of three international arenas which, though obviously interlinked, none the less offered rather different resources and operated in rather different ways. These arenas were formed by the former colonising states and their associates; by the African state system and, in some degree, the 'Third World' as a whole; and by the global confrontation between the two superpowers. The next three chapters will look at each in turn.

Part II

Patterns of alliance

4 The foreign policies of post-colonialism

The post-colonial relationship

The peculiar character of Africa's relations with the outside world is strikingly illustrated by the fact that the first and most obvious source of external support which African rulers could look to for the maintenance of their newly acquired statehood was the very colonial power from which they had just gained independence. The relationship with the former colonial power was the only substantial external relationship which African states possessed at independence, and it was therefore bound to be central to their diplomacy; there was much to be said for trying to ensure that it would be a supportive rather than a threatening one. At the same time, it was potentially a difficult relationship, not just because of its inherent inequality – a problem which equally applied to African relations with the superpowers – but because it reached deep into the domestic structure and identity of the new state itself. It carried with it a constant reminder of the colonial past, and could never be entirely divorced from a sense of subordination. In defining their relations with the former metropole, African leaders were thus defining their relations with their own history. In the process, they also necessarily defined the point at which they sought to position themselves in relation both to the global power structure, and to the different interests and identities within their own societies which were closely associated, in one way or another, with the colonial experience.

The most important feature of the post-colonial relationship was its depth and complexity. From the viewpoint of African leaders, this was the relationship over which they could exercise least control. Whereas other contacts, even with superpowers, were ones which they could make (and even break) themselves, those with the former colonial power were expressed through myriad linkages and connections, which extended well beyond the sphere of formal government. Almost anyone of any importance had their own links with the former metropole. Many of the leading members of the state bureaucracy had been trained there – including, most sensitively, the senior indigenous officers in the armed forces. Trading networks were routed through the coloniser's capital, and major companies operating within the country were usually based there. The cultural and educational life of the country was heavily influenced by the colonial experience. Most pervasively of all, the very language through which the new state engaged in its transactions with the outside world, and through which it usually had to conduct its own domestic business, was the language of the coloniser. For African leaders bent on the project of monopoly statehood, for whom any challenge to their own power was suspect, the continued shadow of colonialism could be a perennial irritant, and indeed a potential threat. Given that it had links with the great majority of those who were in a position to exercise state power, the former metropole could afford to look beyond the current ruler, and might well regard itself as standing to benefit from his departure. The ruler's goal of seeking to monopolise exchanges between the domestic political system and the outside world was compromised from the start.

The former metropole, none the less, continued to have interests within the African state, which in turn were closely associated with the maintenance of that state, and which could generally be best pursued through a supportive relationship with its government. Its dominant economic role continued after independence, and could be protected by friendly connections with the new regime; African rulers could expect to receive something in exchange for the maintenance of existing economic ties, and were normally – in one way or another – brought into a partnership which assured them a share in the profits and sometimes in the management of the import–export economy. Expatriate workers from the former metropole frequently increased in number after independence, especially in the francophone states, and provided a strong inducement for their home governments to help guarantee peaceful conditions and friendly relations with the African state. Metropolitan companies with significant African interests likewise sought favourable business conditions, and could often influence their own domestic governments, not least through financial contributions to the ruling party.

The former metropoles also had less tangible reasons for support. They continued to look on the territories which they had once ruled as 'their' part of Africa, and retained an inclination to protect them. The success or failure of decolonisation reflected well or badly on them – most traumatically for the Belgians, who saw a territory in which they had invested a vast amount of effort collapse into anarchy within days of independence. A successful relationship with viable African former colonies enabled the European state to carry through into the post-colonial era some of the diplomatic clout which it had previously gained from empire; for France in particular, the presence of a train of ex-colonial client states provided an indispensable element of national grandeur.[1] The post-colonial associations, notably the Commonwealth and the francophone community, helped to sustain a continuing sense of obligation. All this meant that once independence had been achieved, there were common interests in maintaining the relationship, which African leaders could use to their advantage.

The interests of the former metropole might well diverge at particular points from those of the new government, and the areas of collaboration and potential conflict had to be carefully explored by both sides. In economic terms, the African government relied on the colonial economic structure to raise its own revenues, and needed to maintain that structure and the relationship with the former metropole that went with it; but at the same time, it had an interest in extracting as much revenue as possible from the economy, bringing it into competition with the metropolitan companies which – especially for mineral-exporting states – were often the major sources of foreign exchange. In political terms, the advantages to be gained from the tacit protection of the ex-colonial power had to be balanced both against forgone opportunities for other relationships, and against the costs of continued colonial involvement (or interference) in matters which an African government might well regard as falling into the sphere of its own domestic sovereignty. A relationship close enough to arouse accusations of neocolonialism could remove the opportunity for the leader to seek a glamorous role on the continental scene or in the Non-Aligned Movement, let alone to establish connections with the Soviet bloc. The attempt to broaden relationships could arouse retaliation, not only from the former metropole itself, but from groups within domestic politics who were associated with it.

As already noted, the structure and ideology of the nationalist movement was the most important factor in determining the initial nature of a relationship which essentially amounted to a continuation of that combination of conflict, bargaining and co-operation in which decolonisation had consisted, through into the independence era. The personality of the new ruler, and his own sense of security, also had a significant influence. Over time, the relative size and economic strength of the African state became an increasingly important factor: the close connections at independence between Nigeria and Britain, for example, could not survive the fall of the First Republic in 1966 and the civil war of 1967–70, and became increasingly strained once the oil boom enabled the Nigerian government to exercise the influence to which it felt itself entitled. The resentments inherent in a post-colonial relationship were never very far from the surface, and became especially evident when the formerly colonised state sought to challenge the assumption of inequality which such a relationship embodied. Nigerian suspicions of British involvement in the attempted *coup d'état* of 1976 which resulted in the death of Murtala Muhammed, and the Umaru Dikko affair which erupted when the Nigerian government sought to kidnap an exiled politician in Britain to face corruption charges in Nigeria, illustrated the tensions in the relationship.[2] Zaïre's relations with Belgium were even more sensitive.

Though the closeness of the post-colonial relationship varied markedly, according to the identity of the colonial power and the choices of the African leadership, its content was constant: where a working relationship could be maintained, what African leaders needed from it was security; where it could not, they still more evidently needed to find security from some equivalent relationship elsewhere. 'Security', as already discussed in the opening chapter, is of course a contested concept, and can scarcely be mentioned without raising the questions of *whose* security is involved, and on what terms.[3] The security which the major colonial powers helped bring to Africa was very clearly predicated on the territories which they had themselves established, on the interests which they had acquired within them, on the institutional structure which they had bequeathed to them, and – very often – on the maintenance in power of the individuals and groups who were best disposed towards them. It was security of a particular kind, and both its costs and its benefits were unevenly distributed.

At the level of *territorial security*, former colonial powers almost invariably had a commitment to the preservation of the state's integrity against secession or dismemberment. The sole exception was the

Belgian flirtation with Tshombe's secessionist regime in Katanga in the immediate aftermath of independence and collapse in Congo/Zaïre. When territorial integrity was threatened, those groups who controlled the central government of the African state concerned, and whose power thus depended on maintaining the formal principles of juridical sovereignty, could almost always call on the former coloniser for help. The Nigerian civil war of 1967–70 was particularly instructive, since pressures from economic interest groups in favour of British support for the federal government (which within a very short time of the outbreak of war secured by far the most important areas in which British economic interests were concentrated) were to some extent offset by an active lobby on behalf of the secessionist Biafran regime which had some support within the governing Labour Party. British military aid to the federal government was as a result both limited in quality by excluding heavy weapons, and to a large extent concealed from the public. Though this exasperated the Nigerian government, and deprived the United Kingdom of the diplomatic advantages to be gained by backing what proved to be the winning side, British weapons were in practice instrumental in winning the war.[4] The principal reason given by the British Prime Minister, Harold Wilson, for supporting the federal side was redolent with a sense of post-imperial responsibility: refusal would have been 'a hostile act against a fellow Commonwealth country ... whose integrity we supported'.[5] The former French colony most explicitly threatened was Chad, where Libyan intervention was at least tacitly predicated on claims to the Aouzou strip, an area in northern Chad, the transfer of which to then-Italian Libya had been raised but never implemented during the appeasement era of the 1930s.[6]

This commitment to the territorial security of their own former colonies did not, however, necessarily apply to anyone else's. In the Nigerian case, the major (though secretive) external support for the secessionist Biafran regime came from France, guided at that time by de Gaulle's geopolitical ambition to secure France's hegemony in the West African region by helping to dismember its largest anglophone state. French military aid to Biafra, provided at second hand through Côte d'Ivoire and Gabon, was instrumental in prolonging the war for about eighteen months after it would otherwise have ended.[7] Nor did former colonial powers have the same commitment to maintaining the integrity of unions which subordinated one of their ex-colonies to a larger African territory with which they did not maintain such close ties. The Italians retained an ambivalent attitude towards the incorporation of Eritrea into Ethiopia, as between a policy which sought to extend Italian influence over Ethiopia as a whole (and thus strengthen the central government), and one which sought to separate Eritrea from Ethiopia (and thus enhance the Italian role in their former colony); this ambivalence reflected alternative approaches to Italian policy in the region which stretched back over more than a century.[8] Analogously, once the former British Somaliland had declared its secession from the Somali Republic in May 1991, the British government was, without formally recognising the new 'Republic of Somaliland', much readier than other outside powers to treat it tacitly as an independent state.[9]

At a second level, the former colonial powers were also concerned with *state security*, or with aiding African regimes to maintain an effective central government. This likewise corresponded to the demands of juridical sovereignty, and amounted in practice to supporting the project of monopoly statehood and the hegemony of those who sought to impose it. Some of this support took an essentially institutional form: it sought to strengthen the structures of the state, in ways that would be helpful to whoever controlled that state. The great majority of African states continued, at least for some years after independence and in many cases indefinitely, to depend on the former colonial powers for training the military and police, and for the provision of weapons. The combination of administrative and educational linkages, coupled with the fact that institutions in most African states were constructed according to metropolitan models, was reflected in technical assistance programmes which continued to send trainee administrators to the metropole even after independence, while training establishments within the country were often manned by colonial expatriates. In this respect, Commonwealth states had options which were not open to members of the smaller and much more centralised francophone community, since they could look for training on the British pattern at one remove, in states other than the United Kingdom, such as Australia or India. Much of the post-colonial aid programme was in practice directed towards state maintenance, whether it took the form of technical assistance, or of development projects which enhanced the distributive capacities and hence the patronage networks of the recipient government. In some cases, notably with the British in Malawi and the French in Benin and elsewhere, direct budgetary support was provided after independence to recipient states which would otherwise have been unable to pay their own bureaucracies.

The third level of support, *regime security*, was much more problematic, and its connection with the principle of juridical statehood was ambivalent. Whereas on the one hand, the sovereignty principle permitted incumbent rulers to seek external military aid, on the other hand the maintenance of a regime in power by external military forces could plausibly be regarded as a negation of national sovereignty. The Soviet role in Afghanistan after December 1979, which could be treated either as Soviet imperialism maintained behind the front of a puppet regime, or else as an expression of the Afghan government's sovereign right to call on aid from its allies, provides the classic case. In practice, external support was much easier to invoke when a regime was threatened by an insurgent movement operating from the countryside or even from across its borders, than when it was threatened from within. Even though the Shaba invasions of Zaïre in 1977 and 1978 were directed against the Mobutu regime, rather than against the territorial integrity of Zaïre, the Belgians and French intervened in order to defeat the insurgents and keep Mobutu in power – and, in the process, to protect their mining interests in the Shaba region. Most of the numerous French interventions in Chad were likewise concerned to protect the regime in power; the French attempt to protect the Habyarimana regime in Rwanda against the RPF invasion in 1993/94 was less successful.[10]

It was generally much more difficult for African heads of state to secure the assistance of the former colonial power against *coups d'état* launched by their own armed forces. For one thing, these were generally launched with little warning, ousting the incumbent regime before any external assistance could be organised. For another, external intervention against coups offended the norms of juridical statehood much more directly than equivalent intervention against invasions. Equally, however, coups usually involved only the replacement of one leader by another, without threatening the state itself, or the interests of the former colonial power in it; given the close relations between many African militaries and the metropolitan states in which their leaders had often been trained, they could even be welcome. There were none the less a number of cases in which the former colonial power intervened in order to reinstate an ousted or threatened African leader. Most commonly, these occurred in the years immediately after independence, as with the British interventions to protect the leaders of

Kenya, Uganda and Tanzania against army mutinies in 1964, or the French intervention to keep President Mba of Gabon in power in the same year. British special forces none the less played a significant if unpublicised role in restoring President Jawara of The Gambia after an attempted putsch in July 1981; the fact that President Jawara was in London at the time, attending the wedding of the Prince of Wales, may help to account for the readiness of the British government to support him.[11] The presence of metropolitan forces in an African state, such as the small French detatchments permanently stationed in Senegal and Côte d'Ivoire, could also be taken as indicating tacit support for the government in power, since even if they were nominally there for other purposes, they constituted a deterrent to intervention by the army of the state concerned.

Direct military involvement was the most spectacular means used by the ex-colonial powers to maintain their former colonies, but for routine purposes economic instruments were more significant. All former colonial powers directed their aid programmes disproportionately towards their former colonies. Prior to 1975, for example, some 82 per cent of British aid to Africa went to Commonwealth states, a proportion slightly but not greatly diminished by British accession to the European Community.[12] French aid, discussed in the next section, was probably even more exclusively reserved to the countries of the francophone community. Italian aid was correspondingly concentrated on those states in the Horn of Africa, including Ethiopia, in which Italy historically had an interest, while even Germany paid particular attention to such former German colonies as Tanzania and Namibia, though the formal link had been severed by the First World War, and few Africans in either country were German-speaking.[13]

More generally, the European metropoles retained a residual sense of responsibility for their former colonies on the broader international stage, and provided them with access points which they would not otherwise have possessed. When the European Community was formed, for example, the maintenance of special trading privileges for the African colonies of its founding states had to be built into the Treaty of Rome, through provisions for association with the Community which were later extended into the Yaoundé Conventions; France was the major instigator of these arrangements, even though the Belgian colonies and Italian-administered Somalia also benefited from them.[14] British accession brought with it a further set of obligations, and ultimately resulted in the negotiation of the Lomé Convention, discussed in a later section. The former Portuguese colonies gained the right to accede to the Lomé Convention, even before Portugal itself became a member of the Community.

The parameters of the post-colonial relationship also depended to an appreciable degree on the European state by which the African one had been colonised. Some former colonisers had the capacity to maintain an effective post-colonial relationship, whereas others did not. Put simply, this distinguished the British and French on the one hand, from the Belgians, Italians, Portuguese and Spaniards on the other. Britain and France both possessed considerable colonial empires and developed industrial economies, and were able to develop complex linkages with their colonies which in turn (though in rather different ways) provided the basis for a generally peaceful transfer of power and for reasonably viable post-colonial states. The others had few colonies (though Belgium and Portugal had important ones), and lacked the capacity either to build up the same range of links, or to manage a successful transition to independence. The argument was often made during the struggle for independence from Portuguese rule that Portugal could not decolonise because it could not neocolonise; and though the conclusion did not follow (since the consequences for Portugal of disengagement from empire were almost entirely beneficial), the premise was certainly correct.

The advantages for African states of colonisation by one of the two major powers were clearly illustrated by the dramatically greater level of insecurity in those which were *not* colonised by Britain or France. Following the collapse of Congo/Zaïre, and the ethnic bloodletting in Rwanda and Burundi, the former Belgian colonies effectively attached themselves to France, with which they built up quasi-post-colonial links, which were to lead in two of the three states concerned to direct military intervention on behalf of the incumbent government. Though Belgium retained important links, especially with Zaïre, it lost most of the peculiar status which ex-colonial powers generally retained elsewhere.[15] The major Portuguese colonies, Angola and Mozambique, came to independence after long wars which shattered the possibility of any normal post-independence relationship with Portugal, and subsequently suffered crippling civil wars which elevated the need for protection into the overwhelming priority of their foreign policies; the re-establishment of relations with Portugal was a long and difficult process.[16] The Italian colonies of Somalia and Eritrea, and the Spanish ones of Equatorial Guinea and Western Sahara, experienced either internal breakdown or external takeover. The breakdown of both Chad and Uganda demonstrated that French or British rule carried no guarantee of subsequent stability, but the two major powers generally bequeathed to their former colonies both a level of internal statehood and a supportive external environment which at any rate placed them at a considerable advantage by comparison with those African states with different colonial origins.

For both Commonwealth and francophone states, the connection with the former colonial power enabled them to benefit at second hand from that power's place in the international order, and the linkages that this brought with it. Through membership of the Commonwealth or the Franco-African community, it opened the door to association with a larger group of broadly like-minded states, with at least some sense of common identity and mutual obligation. To a certain degree, British and French permanent membership of the United Nations Security Council provided a channel of access, at least for those of their former colonies which retained good relations with them. The same went for relations with UN specialised agencies, and international financial institutions such as the World Bank.

The differences between the two groups of states were none the less startling. The Commonwealth or anglophone connection provided nothing resembling the level of protection on the one hand, or dependence on the other, created by the complex of francophone relationships. The French role in Africa requires a section of its own, but the relative weakness of the British role also calls for examination. In essence, this derived both from what the Commonwealth African states wanted from Britain, and from what Britain was willing to provide.

The second of these has generally attracted more attention. Whereas Africa formed by far the greater part of the French empire, especially after the loss of Indochina, it was no more than a generally insignificant part of a British empire which had historically been dominated by the 'white dominions' and India; and while France sought to retain a global role through the Franco-African association, the post-1945 generation of British foreign policy makers was obsessed by the idea of a 'special relationship' with the United States. Way back into its national past, moreover, France had sought to assimilate outlying territories into its national political life, whereas Britain (or perhaps more precisely England) had tended to exclude them; in more than nine centuries of government under a common crown, for example, successive English and British governments had never even tried to incorporate the Channel Islands into the structures of national government. From this point of view, British politicians were simply uninterested in mobilising (or paying for) a clientele of African states, and the support that African leaders might have sought from them was diminished accordingly. British interests were largely concerned with southern Africa, and much of the British aid budget for the continent was essentially a matter of compensating successor African elites for the consequences of white settlement – such as buying out white farmers in Kenya and Zimbabwe, meeting some of the costs to Zambia of Rhodesian UDI, and technical aid programmes to states such as Malawi and Lesotho.[17] Few if any senior British politicians had any serious interest in Africa, and such personal relationships as they developed with their African counterparts – like Mrs Thatcher's friendship with President Machel of Mozambique – were largely a matter of chance. By 1987, British aid to sub-Saharan Africa, at $325m, had shrunk to a level equivalent to that of Canada and Sweden, less than 35 per cent of Italian aid, and a mere 16 per cent of the $2,046m provided by France.[18] British economic interests in Africa were by this time negligible; in 1987, the continent received no more than 3.2 per cent of Britain's exports, and provided only 1.9 per cent of its imports.[19] Only one British company, Lonrho, was sufficiently closely involved in a number of African states to become a significant element in their politics; but whereas a number of French companies were closely involved in the complex of relationships through which the French government pursued its interests in Africa, Lonrho was kept at arm's length from British policy-making, and its activities treated – at least within the Foreign and Commonwealth Office – with considerable suspicion.[20]

But the African viewpoint also mattered. For a start, the former British colonies in Africa were much larger than their French equivalents: of the ten sub-Saharan states which in 1980 had populations of over ten million, seven (including South Africa and Sudan) were former British colonies, whereas none had been French.[21] Though Commonwealth Africa included such microstates as The Gambia and Swaziland, the larger states set the tone of the relationship, led by Nigeria with a population which was greater than Britain's, and well over twice that of any other sub-Saharan state. A less supplicatory relationship was inevitable. It was enhanced by the use by African states of the Commonwealth, not as a forum within which they could seek aid from a British patron, but rather as one in which they could combine to make demands on the former colonial power. This pattern went back to the 1961 Commonwealth meeting, at which South Africa was forced to withdraw from the grouping, and was greatly reinforced by the Rhodesian Unilateral Declaration of Independence in 1965, which once more put the British government on the defensive in dealing with Africa. In essence, the Commonwealth became a setting in which the ambivalent legacies of British colonialism could be exposed; and though the Lusaka summit of 1979 provided essential diplomatic support for the British-managed mechanism through which the Rhodesian issue was eventually resolved, no sooner had this been achieved than the issue of sanctions against *apartheid* South Africa displaced it. Commonwealth African leaders generally welcomed their freedom of action, and some like Nkrumah scorned what they saw as the grovelling neocolonialism of their francophone neighbours; but their independence, and the perception of Africa by British policy-makers as a source of trouble rather than of opportunity, was in some degree paid for in the loss of British interest in maintaining a relationship from which the Africans might have been able to extract greater benefits.

The international politics of francophonie

The French role was strikingly different. The complex of relationships between the francophone African states and France formed by far the most comprehensive set of mechanisms for maintaining African states and their rulers, and had no equivalent either among the other colonial powers, or in the clientele networks established by the United States and the Soviet Union. These relationships, moreover, extended over a substantial part of the continent, including a continuous block of states from Mauritania to Zaïre; taken together, the francophones (including the three former Belgian colonies) accounted for eighteen of continental sub-Saharan Africa's forty-two states, and for just over a quarter of its estimated half a billion people.[22] They provided the clearest example of the external ramifications of African state security, and their implications not only for foreign policy but for the domestic structure of power.

Like any complex set of relationships, francophonie can be analysed in terms of three interlocking elements: people, money and force. In personal terms, it may be viewed as an association for mutual benefit between two groups of people: on the one hand, not so much the French State – that mythical monolith which falls apart on close inspection – as a limited number of French people who, whether or not they held official positions, had some kind of access to state power; on the other, an equally limited number of leading figures in the eighteen francophone states. Those within this association emphasised, over and again, its personal aspects: the long-established friendships, the networks of personal trust and obligation, the connections formed by freemasonry and occasionally marriage, which linked its members across the divide between France and Africa.[23] Politics everywhere comes down to a set of personal interactions between individual human beings, and what distinguished relations between African leaders and France – in sharp contrast to those with Britain, the United States, or the former Soviet Union – was the way in which they were incorporated into a network which was intimate in character but international in scope. It provided a means of conducting diplomacy which sometimes more closely resembled the world of domestic politics than that of formal inter-state relations.

The importance of these personal links was immeasurably aided by the fact that they reached to the highest level of the French political system. All but one of the four presidents of the Fifth Republic between de Gaulle's accession in 1958 and Mitterrand's departure in 1995 had close contacts with Africa, indicating a priority which African affairs never came close to attaining in the foreign relations of any other major state. De Gaulle's links with Africa went back to June 1940, when the obscure Saharan colony of Chad was the sole territory to declare immediate allegiance to the Free French; he retained a mystique in francophone Africa which carried over beyond independence. His successor, Georges Pompidou, appears to have accepted the African role only as part of the obligations of office, but the election of Valéry Giscard d'Estaing in 1974 revived but also altered the relationship. On the one hand, Giscard championed the role of France as the defender both of Western interests in Africa during the 'Second Cold War' of the later 1970s, and of those African leaders who were most closely associated with the West; this led to a level of military intervention that was most strikingly illustrated by the protection of the Mobutu regime against the invasions of Shaba province by dissidents based in Angola in 1977 and 1978. On the other, he became involved with a number of leaders with unsavoury personal reputations, notably Mobutu in Zaïre and Bokassa in Central Africa, who offered commercial opportunities to himself or members of his family; the revelation that he had received a gift of diamonds from Bokassa, regardless of their actual value which was hotly disputed, came to symbolise the dubious features of these relationships, and contributed to his defeat in the elections of 1981.[24]

The fourteen-year reign of François Mitterrand reinforced the personal and indeed dynastic aspects of Franco-African relations. Mitterrand's own connections with Africa went back to his role as Minister for Overseas France in 1950, when he played a critical part in persuading the future President Houphouet-Boigny of Côte d'Ivoire to abandon his links with the communists; and despite his election on a Socialist Party platform of reducing French support for African regimes with extremely poor human rights records, the old connections were rapidly resuscitated.[25] They were moreover patrimonialised by the appointment of Mitterrand's son, Jean-Christophe, first as a presidential adviser on African affairs and subsequently, from October 1986, as head of the secretariat for Afro-Malagasy affairs attached to the presidency. This secretariat, established under de Gaulle by the legendary Jacques Foccart, expressed both the official status of Franco-African relations at the highest levels of the French state, and equally the personalisation of these relationships through channels which largely circumvented the government hierarchy. While foreign affairs as a whole, under the constitutional conventions of the Fifth Republic, remained within the 'reserved domain' of the president, African affairs became an enclave even within this domain, often conducted without reference to the Ministry of Foreign Affairs. During the Nigerian civil war, when the Quai d'Orsay remained openly hostile to the Biafran secessionists, these were able to procure French arms through an arrangement with Foccart.[26] A similar disregard for formal government channels, and a preference for conducting business through his personal contacts with African leaders on the one hand, and his father on the other, prevailed in the time of Jean-Christophe Mitterrand, who thus acquired in Africa the nickname of Papamadit or 'Daddy says'. The annual Franco-African summits, whose very title conveyed the bilateralism of the relationship, by contrast with the multilateralism of the Commonwealth, conducted little formal business, but provided a congenial milieu within which to reinforce the sense of familial solidarity.[27]

This personalism was not, however, confined to the level of the head of state, but spread throughout the world of French business and diplomacy through the 'Messieurs Afrique' whose web of contacts have been brilliantly described by Smith and Glaser.[28] Similar networks were maintained by the public works contractor, Martin Bouyges, the agro-industrialist Vincent Bolloré, or the commodity broker Serge Varsano; here too the patrimonial principle applied, both Bouyges and Varsano having inherited the businesses established by their fathers, along with their portfolios of contacts. The world of journalism was represented by Philippe Decraene, longstanding Africa correspondent of *Le Monde*, whose wife Paulette was private secretary to François Mitterrand. Most powerful and secretive of all were the oil companies, and especially Elf, whose president Loik le Floch-Prigent was an intimate associate of Mitterrand; the Elf network, concentrated in the oil-producing African states and especially Gabon, was dominated by Corsicans, who constituted within the closed world of French–African relations a distinctive tribe of their own.

From the viewpoint of the African leaders who dealt with them, these networks provided a powerful source of support combined with an equally powerful pressure for conformity. The major coastal former colonies which were at the centre of Franco-African relations – the intellectual capital of Senegal, the primary produce centre of Côte d'Ivoire, and the oil-producing states of Cameroon and Gabon – all had stable domestic political systems, at least in the sense that the same leaders remained in power, though French intervention was needed to rescue President Mba of Gabon from a *coup d'état* in 1964.[29] In each of the above four states there were only two presidents between 1960 and 1995, with the second peacefully succeeding the first, and the French connection thus served the correspondingly stable function of supporting the regime in power. In less stable systems such as Dahomey/Benin and Chad, no single leader could maintain the undivided support of France, and the French role was more ambivalent. President Tombalbaye of Chad was overthrown and killed in April 1975, after the commander of the French force in the country had made an apparently innocuous statement to the effect that the French army's role was to protect Chad's territorial integrity, not to intervene in domestic politics – a statement interpreted as withdrawing French support from the regime.[30] In Niger in April 1974, a *coup d'état* took place over a weekend when French security personnel all happened to be off duty.[31] The clearest case of direct French intervention to remove an African leader occurred in the Central African Republic (or Empire, as it had briefly become) in 1979, when Bokassa had become an embarrassment whose immediate overthrow was required. French involvement was also a factor in the *coups d'état* in the Comoros in August 1975 and May 1978.[32] Leaders who had lost the support of the French government could not rely on its protection.

To some extent, the network of relationships extended beyond the francophone states, into neighbouring territories where French businesses had interests. The role of the French–Ivoirian connection in supporting Charles Taylor's NPFL insurgency in Liberia will be examined in a later chapter. The most significant non-francophone state was, however, Angola, which mattered especially as the largest single source of supply for the French state oil company Elf, and where different French interests, and indeed different individuals within Elf itself, were able to maintain contacts simultaneously both with the MPLA government in Luanda and with Jonas Savimbi's Unita.[33] With the decline of tropical Africa's economies, the French looked increasingly towards South Africa.

Like any patron–client relationship, however, the Franco-African one could in some degree be manipulated by the clients as well as by the patron. At times, the French found themselves obliged to support leaders for whom they can have had little sympathy. The ability of Hissene Habre in Chad to gain French support by invoking the Libyan threat and mobilising the concern of other francophone leaders has already been noted. The most difficult relationship of all, however, was that between France and President Mobutu of Zaïre. Though French-speaking, Zaïre as a former Belgian colony lacked the intimate links with France of other francophone states; with a population three times the size of any other francophone state, lucrative mineral resources, and a vast and strategically located territory, its government also had a bargaining power denied to the other francophones. Its full incorporation into the francophone community dated only from the later 1970s, when the expansionist presidency of Giscard d'Estaing coincided with a reduction in United States support for Mobutu, who desperately needed foreign help in the Shaba invasions of 1977 and 1978. Though Mobutu was one of the principal targets for Socialist Party criticism of Giscard's African adventures, the relationship was (after a fairly short interval) restored by Mitterrand, only to be threatened once again when Zaïre became an obvious target for the democracy and human rights agenda of the early 1990s. Mobutu's capacity not merely to survive these pressures, in the course of which the French ambassador to Zaïre was assassinated by his troops, but to emerge as co-chair of

Mitterrand's farewell Franco-African summit at Biarritz in November 1994, provided the clearest example of the way in which a skilful African leader could manipulate the francophone relationship to his own advantage.[34]

Both Hissene Habre and Mobutu were able to secure French support at least partly through a tacit threat to look instead to the Americans. Nothing aroused French protective instincts so sharply as the danger that one of their clients might defect to the Anglo-Saxons. French aid to Biafra had, as already noted, been designed to neutralise an anglophone Nigeria. Any regime threatened by the Americans' *bête noire*, Colonel Qadhafi, could expect to be helped by Washington. Mobutu was as much an American client as a French one. The emergence of an anglophone candidate as a leading contender in the Cameroonian presidential elections of 1992 cemented French support for President Biya.[35] The extreme case was, however, that of Rwanda, where the invasion by English-speaking Rwanda Patriotic Front exiles based in Uganda led not only to military support for the Habyarimana regime, but to a high level of French complicity in the 1994 massacres in which between half a million and a million Rwandans died, and to subsequent support – once the RPF had gained power – for the authors of the genocide who had taken refuge in Zaïre.[36] The usefulness of Zaïre as a base from which to destabilise the new regime in Rwanda was indeed one of the levers through which Mobutu was able to restore his relations with the Mitterrand government.

These mutually beneficial relations between groups of French and African politicians were lubricated by financial arrangements from which each could gain. In some respects, the most significant was the common currency zone denoted by the CFA Franc, which encompassed almost all of the former French colonies but not the former Belgian ones. The CFA Franc was maintained, from 1948 until its 50 per cent devaluation in January 1994, at a fixed rate against the French Franc, with which it was fully convertible, of FF1.00 = CFA50. In maintaining monetary stability at the price of a privileged role for France, and external support at the price of dependence, the Franc Zone aptly encapsulated the Franco-African relationship as a whole.

A convertible currency pegged to the French Franc assured ready access to Western goods, and this sustained the lifestyles of those urban elites, heavily dependent on the public sector, who had the highest propensity to consume imports.[37] In this sense, the CFA Franc maintained the entire political class on which the French relationship depended, at the expense – especially as the rising exchange value of the French Franc from the mid-1980s dragged the CFA Franc with it – of the export-producing rural areas. Although this bias towards the interests of politically influential urban groups was by no means restricted to francophone Africa, the Franc Zone none the less helped to protect member elites from the imposition of IMF structural adjustment schemes, with their crippling effect on bureaucratic standards of living, for more than a decade after these had been imposed on other African economies. In addition, heads of state could lay their hands on substantial sums in convertible currency which they could transfer abroad: President Houphouet-Boigny regularly diverted as much as one-sixth of Ivoirian cocoa revenues to foreign banks, while President Ahidjo did the same with up to 70 per cent of Cameroonian oil revenues.[38]

While some critics regarded the Franc Zone as a neocolonial mechanism which enabled France to make large profits out of its former colonies, in practice the subsidy operated in the opposite direction: since African elites continued to consume imports, while primary produce export revenues declined, the French treasury had to stabilise the operating accounts of the CFA central banks at a cost in the late 1980s of some $1bn a year.[39] Though French exporters to some extent benefited from a relatively protected market, and some of the subsidy was thus recycled back into the French economy, the idea that the French economy as a whole benefited from the zone does not bear even cursory inspection. The system survived because it had discriminatory effects, not only in Africa but also in France. A number of French companies with close African connections were able to mount extremely effective lobbying operations within the closed world of the French elite, at the expense ultimately of the French taxpayer. A very significant part of this lobbying operation consisted in the provision, both by these companies and by African leaders themselves, of secretive and doubtless illegal financial support for French political parties and their leaders.[40] Although all of the mainstream French political parties, except for the Communists, received their regular 'watering', the lion's share was obviously reserved for the party in power. This in turn helps to account for the close personal and even family relationships between the Elysée and the individuals responsible for French relations with Africa.

A similar logic applied to the French aid programme, which at

$2,046m in 1987 amounted to nearly 50 per cent more than the World Bank's allocations to sub-Saharan Africa, and over twice as much as any other bilateral aid donor.[41] Disbursed through the *Fonds d'Aide et de Coopération* (FAC) and the much larger *Caisse Centrale de Coopération Economique* (CCCE), this money went not only to support normal development projects, and a large number of French *coopérants*, but also to fund speculative ventures and patronage payments. In December 1988, for example, the CCCE was urgently convened on the initiative of Jean-Christophe Mitterrand to approve a payment of FF4,000m to meet the storage costs of a 200,000 tonne stockpile of cocoa which President Houphouet-Boigny hoped to use to force up the world market price; not only did this venture fail, but nearly half of the sum involved remained in the hands of the French produce-broking company responsible for managing the stockpile.[42] Some construction companies depended to a significant extent on aid-funded public works in Africa. Cases such as this amounted not to aid in the normal sense at all, but to the recycling of French taxpayers' money to well-connected French companies, through the medium of the aid budget.

The French readiness to intervene militarily in Africa has attracted greater attention than the currency or the aid programme, because it is less easily concealed. Whereas aid counts as part of a 'normal' relationship, moreover, military intervention is readily regarded as deviant and illegitimate. In proportion to the totality of the Franco-African relationship, the military element was not great; but it provided the ultimate guarantee of the French presence in Africa, and its overall impact may have been more significant than the individual cases suggest. In any event, France intervened militarily in Africa far more often than any other external power, and that in itself made its role of particular importance.

The means available in 1993 included some 13,000 troops deployed in and around Africa, and a *force d'action rapide* of some 20,000 men based in France;[43] though small in relation to any major military commitment against an opponent armed with modern weapons, this was a significant force in many African conflicts, where the numbers, armament and organisation of potential opposing forces were generally at a relatively low level. After an early period between 1960 and 1964, when the French were involved in a number of policing operations which culminated in the reversal of the Gabon *coup d'état* of 1964, direct intervention until 1976 was limited to operations in the

Central African Republic and Chad. A rapid escalation under the Giscard presidency included operations in Zaïre, Chad and Western Sahara (where the French assisted Mauritania against Polisario), and the ousting of Bokassa in the CAR. During the first eight years of Mitterrand's tenure, from 1981, direct intervention was limited to Chad, and briefly Togo in 1986, but the scale of operations increased with the wave of demands for democratisation in the early 1990s. In some cases, notably Rwanda, these turned into direct military support for the regime in power; in others, including Djibouti, Gabon and Zaïre, the French role shaded between the protection of French and other European expatriates, the bringing of pressure on incumbent rulers to democratise their regimes, and the protection of those same regimes against internal opposition or insurgent movements launched from across the frontier.

Though a number of African states had formal military agreements with France, these had little effect on actual cases of intervention, which depended on relations between the French and African governments concerned. By the late 1980s, only Cameroon, the Central African Republic, Djibouti, Gabon, Côte d'Ivoire, Senegal and Togo retained defence agreements with France, whereas other states in which French forces had intervened to a significant extent, such as Chad, Rwanda and Zaïre, did not.[44] Alongside the formal military relationship were less formalised security operations, including notably the provision – often through former French intelligence officers who had established their own private security services – of personal protection for heads of state. 'Beside almost every president from the *pré carré* is to be found a colonel from the DGSE.'[45] The activities of these individuals were not always easily distinguished from those of 'mercenaries' engaged in covert operations directed at the destabilisation as much as the protection of African regimes.[46] Though the security aspect of French policy in Africa could in general terms be regarded as a mechanism for protecting the access of favoured individuals, both French and African, to funds generated both in France and in Africa, there were also more direct connections between military and economic interests. On the one hand, funds were on occasion diverted from the development budget to serve military purposes, such as the payment of mercenaries provided to help Hissene Habre fight against the Libyan-supported regime in Chad in 1983.[47] On the other, much of the military assistance budget went to pay for armaments supplied by French companies which were thus given access to a captive market. French military aid to Africa remained essentially static between 1960 and 1977, but then rose rapidly from FF414m in 1977 to FF644m in 1978, and to a peak of FF954m in 1986.[48] Much of this was in turn recycled back to France in the form of arms sales.

Despite its tenacity, the Franco-African relationship was threatened, not so much by generational change in France and Africa as by the decline of African economies, and accordingly their interest to France. The personal elements in the relationship proved remarkably resistant to the march of time: each major change in the personnel of French (and to some extent African) politics, such as the departure in turn of de Gaulle, Foccart, Giscard d'Estaing and most recently Mitterrand, was hailed as indicating the end of an era. On each occasion, at least until 1995, another and remarkably similar era replaced it. Both French and African elites showed a capacity for renewal which was best symbolised by the friendships struck by Jean-Christophe Mitterrand and the sons of several francophone African presidents, such as Ali-Ben Bongo in Gabon or Jean-Pierre Habyarimana in Rwanda.[49] Each new generation of French politicians brought with it its African networks. In the Balladur government which came to power following the 1992 legislative elections, the African connection was represented by Charles Pasqua, who inherited both the contacts associated with his membership of the *Service d'Action Civique*, a Gaullist organisation with close African connections, and his Corsican origins which enabled him to tap into the Corsican mafia which was associated especially with Gabon. Though minister of the interior under Balladur, Pasqua had a presence in Africa which overshadowed those of the ministers of co-operation or foreign affairs. The astonishing level of French commitment to the Habyarimana regime in Rwanda against its anglophone opponents was ascribed in the French press to the 'spirit of Fashoda', which (nearly a century after that celebrated confrontation) remained a living force at least within the Elysée and the French defence establishment, but could equally be attributed to the partnership between the sons of the two presidents.

The declining level of French economic interests in Africa represented a more serious threat to the relationship. As the number of branches of French businesses on the continent rapidly declined, and many of those that remained were kept open largely for sentimental reasons, so the clout of the Franco-African lobby fell with them. The rapid escalation of the deficits which the French Treasury had to meet in maintaining the Franc Zone imposed a direct financial burden which could not be indefinitely maintained: the devaluation of the CFA Franc in January 1994 represented at least a partial victory for the technocrats in the Treasury over the political and economic interests of the Elysée and the Franco-African business establishment. With the end of the Cold War, the unification of Germany, and the opening up of Eastern Europe, the pretence that the maintenance of a special relationship between France and the francophone states of Africa served any valuable function became increasingly difficult to sustain. It had become not so much a policy as a habit for sections of the French political elite.[50]

Multilateral post-colonialism

Post-colonialism was the most exclusive of relationships, between a single former metropole on the one hand, and its former dependencies on the other. Even multilateral organisations such as the francophone community and the Commonwealth were in essence clusters of bilateral relationships, in which the connections of each of the individual members with France or Britain were on a different plane from those which they had with one another. The incorporation of all of Africa's former colonisers into the European Community,[51] and their creation of a multilateral relationship among themselves, none the less brought with it a multilateralisation of their relations with Africa, and in turn broadened the linkages which African states could seek in Europe.

Academic analysis of this relationship has almost exclusively been concerned with the Lomé Conventions, which from 1975 linked the two groups of states within a common trading structure, and within that with the impact of the Conventions on African economic development. This discussion will take a different emphasis. The effects of the Lome Conventions on African development were in any event negligible,[52] and their provisions are of interest largely as indicating the balance of relative advantage which existed at the time when each of them was negotiated. The aid provisions of the Conventions, however, provided African states with a significant source of income, while at the same time subjecting them to the peculiar pressures and tensions which any aid relationship creates. More generally, the Lomé regime – without displacing bilateral relationships – gave African states alternative points of access to Western Europe, while also providing

European Community states with a mechanism through which to pursue their individual or collective interests in Africa.

In its origins, the initiative for establishing special links between the Community and its former African colonies came very largely from France. At its most cynical, indeed, it could be regarded as a mechanism through which other states in the Community (and especially Germany) could be induced to contribute to the French aid budget, and through which the special trading relationship between France and the former colonies could be extended to the rest of the Community, while remaining essentially under French control. Among the founding members of the Community, France had overwhelmingly the most important interests in Africa, and though the arrangements made for former French colonies had also to be extended to those of other member states, the French none the less stood to be by far the greatest gainers. This largely French connection led first to the provision for the 'association' of the African colonies of Community members under the Treaty of Rome, and subsequently to the negotiation of the Yaounde Conventions between the Community and eighteen of their former African colonies.[53] The first Yaoundé Convention came into effect in 1963, and the second in 1969; but though they put the relationship between the six EC states and their African former colonies formally on the basis of an agreement between independent states, and maintained the European Development Fund for EC aid, they were too restricted in scope, and too uneven in the bargaining power of the two sides, to constitute more than a partial multilateralisation of previously bilateral post-colonial economic relationships.[54]

The negotiation of the first Lomé Convention of 1975, on the other hand, presented one of the very few occasions on which African states were able to bargain with external powers on something approaching a position of equality. For this, two developments were responsible. First, the accession of the United Kingdom to EC membership made it necessary to extend the EC–African relationship to Commonwealth African states, and in the event led to the inclusion of all independent sub-Saharan states which wished to take part, except for South Africa. Rather than dealing with a group of small states, most of which had a high dependence on France, the EC found itself confronted by the virtual totality of sub-Saharan states, led by the larger and more self-confident anglophones. Second, the negotiation of the Convention fell immediately after the oil price increase of 1973, and the short-lived commodity boom which accompanied it, when for the only time in the post-independence era the exporters of tropical primary products enjoyed substantial bargaining power in global economic relations. These two factors were combined in the chairing of the African (and Caribbean and Pacific, or ACP) negotiating group by Nigeria, which, as by far the most populous ACP state and a major oil exporter, had the capacity both to impose its leadership on the ACP group, and to present a relatively powerful negotiating front to the European Community.

These advantages enabled the ACP states to gain a number of concessions, going well beyond what the EC had been intending to concede at the start of the negotiations, which amounted in the political and ideological circumstances of the time to a highly favourable package. This included aid under the European Development Fund of 3,052.4m EUA (about $2,800m, at the 1975 exchange rate), funds (known as Stabex) designed to help cushion the impact of sudden falls in primary produce prices on exporters, and 'non-reciprocity' clauses which enabled ACP states to impose protective tariffs on imports from the EC without jeopardising the access of their own exports to EC markets. That these measures failed to lead to the predicted upsurge in ACP development (or even to reverse the decline in living standards that took place over the period when the Lomé I Convention was in effect) was, in a sense, neither here nor there. Politically, they demonstrated the capacity of united African states, favoured by the current condition of the international economy, to reach an agreement with a major group of northern industrial states which met at least some of their more important objectives.[55]

By the time that subsequent Lomé Conventions were negotiated, the boot was on the other foot. The commodity boom had collapsed, and EC states had proved more able than had seemed likely in 1974/75 to cope even with the increase in global oil prices. The 'Second Cold War' from 1975 onwards had increased the level of external military intervention in Africa, and weakened the unity of African states. From the negotiation of Lomé II in 1978/79 onwards, the ACP were the subordinate partners in a supplicant relationship, which ultimately depended on what the EC was willing to concede, and on the conditions which the EC sought to impose. The clearest indication of declining ACP bargaining power was the fall in the value of EC aid: though the nominal total increased to 5,530m EUA ($7,960m at June 1980 exchange rates) in Lomé II, when account is taken of new states joining the ACP group, increased population, and inflation, it represented a fall of some 20 per cent in real per capita terms. The 8,500m ECU ($11,220m, at February 1985 exchange rates) allocated for Lomé III in 1985 amounted to roughly the same as the Lomé II real per capita total.[56]

As the relative position of the ACP states weakened, so the Lomé Conventions shifted in emphasis from trading provisions which were at least in principle designed to enhance the prospects for ACP development, to aid provisions which exposed the inherent inequalities between the two sides. Rhetoric aside, the renegotiations of the Convention from Lomé II onwards essentially consisted in the EC telling the ACP states how much aid they were going to get, and the ACP complaining that it was not enough. The amendments introduced on each occasion reflected EC rather than ACP priorities. At the time of the Lomé II negotiations, when access to strategic minerals was relatively high on the agenda of industrial states, the Stabex system was supplemented by a scheme called Sysmin, which covered ACP mineral exports. The Lomé III negotiations, coinciding with the 1984 Ethiopian famine, gave special emphasis to food self-sufficiency and emergency relief.[57] By the Lomé IV negotiations five years later, the emphasis had shifted to the environment. By the 1980s, moreover, the bargaining framework had shifted in other ways, as the EC states sought to introduce into the conventions elements of the economic and political conditionalities which were by then increasingly prominent in relations with other donors. The issue of human rights, first raised in 1979 over the EC's obligation to provide aid for the Idi Amin regime in Uganda, achieved a nominal place in the Lomé III Convention and was more explicitly built into the aid programme in 1991.[58] Over time, the capacity of African leaders to shape the Lomé relationship to their own priorities diminished, and the level of control by the EC states increased.

The Lomé relationship, however, went well beyond the negotiation of the terms of the successive conventions. Their implementation was equally important, and allowed ample scope for manipulation. EC aid accounted for only a relatively small proportion of total aid to Africa,[59] but came on favourable terms. A large and increasing proportion of it was allocated as grants rather than loans, culminating in the Lomé IV Convention in which all but 10 per cent of the total of 12,000m ECU ($14,000m at December 1989 exchange rates) came as grants. Despite some tightening in the 1980s, moreover, the political and economic conditionalities attached to the aid were less stringent than those applied either by most bilateral donors, or by the major international financial institutions. Bilateral aid was often strongly related to the foreign (and indeed domestic) policy objectives of the donor, and imposed corresponding constraints on the recipient. Within the Lomé framework, however, such constraints were greatly eased, with the result that the Mengistu regime in Ethiopia was able to maintain the closest military and diplomatic relations with the Soviet Union, at the same time as becoming the largest single recipient of EC development aid;[60] EC aid was even used to repair the runway at Addis Ababa airport which had been badly damaged during the 1977/78 Ogaden war by heavy Soviet tank-transporting aircraft. Nor was EC aid restricted to goods and services supplied by any single state, while economic policy conditionalities were less exacting than those imposed by the World Bank.[61] Levels of donor control over the projects funded by EC aid were also relatively lax, enabling the governments of recipient states to allocate it in the form best suited to their own domestic political priorities: the resulting proliferation of economically worthless prestige projects led the EC Development Commissioner in the early 1980s, Edgard Pisani, to refer in scathing terms to the use of EC aid for financing 'cathedrals in the desert', and led to greater EC control over project aid from the Lomé III Convention onwards.[62]

The value of the EC relationship to African states was also, however, affected by the peculiar domestic politics of the Community itself, and the intricate management of the interests of the member states which this involved. As has already been noted, the whole EC–African relationship originated in large part from the French determination to integrate their African relationships into the European Community under their own control, and something of this emphasis remained. The Directorate-General within the European Commission which dealt with the associated territories, DG VIII, was from the start regarded, within the peculiar conventions of the Community, as a French preserve, and all of its commissioners from its foundation in 1958 until 1985 were French.[63] The suggestion in 1980 that the portfolio might be allocated to a national of another EC state aroused intense reactions from Paris. Though this predominance had to be balanced by the appointment of a Director-General from another member state, usually Germany, many of the other key staff were French as well.[64] This in turn was reflected in a disproportionate allocation of EC aid to francophone African states.[65]

From the mid-1980s, however, the EC development portfolio was monopolised by southern Europeans, in turn from Italy, Spain and Portugal. As a group, these states had a particular interest in impeding the access to EC markets of ACP agricultural goods which competed with their own produce, and in classic EC fashion, the allocation to them of responsibility for relations with the African states served to reassure them that their own interests would take precedence. Each of their states also had particular interests to pursue in relations with Africa: Italy's African concerns were heavily concentrated in the Horn, and helped to favour EC relationships with Ethiopia and Somalia during the later 1980s.[66] Spain's Manuel Marin, who represented the Galician region which provided the base for the massive Spanish deep-sea fishing fleet, was especially interested in the access of this fleet to African waters, and was accused by African diplomats of applying pressure to allow such access as a covert condition for the release of EC funds; Spanish trawlers also engaged in illegal fishing, for example in Namibian waters.[67] The appointment in 1995 of a Portuguese Commissioner gave EC backing – diplomatic and potentially financial – for the restoration of Portugal's relationship with its former African territories.

Conclusion

The independence which African nationalist leaders sought and achieved from the late 1950s onwards did not, and could never be expected to, cut their links with their former colonisers. Nor could it alter the fundamental inequality that was built into the relationship between colonised and coloniser, and which was reinforced by cultural dominance, political and military weight, and economic penetration. What it did, rather, was to convert a relationship which had hitherto been expressed largely through dominance and subjection within the colonial territory, into one which took the form of diplomatic interaction between the representatives of states on different continents. In this interaction, African leaders did at least possess a bargaining position substantially superior to that which they had had under colonialism. The formal norms of sovereign statehood protected them to a large extent against expressions of post-colonial power which would excite the condemnation of an international community in which such power was widely regarded as illegitimate. Those same norms allowed African rulers access to an international system in which they could seek alternative alliances. Their takeover of the instruments of domestic government gave them considerable leverage over former colonial powers which retained substantial interests within African states, but which were restricted in the actions which they could take to protect such interests directly.

The post-colonial connection was, as a result, generally supportive to African states and those who ruled them. The rhetoric of anti-colonialism, and the eagerness of analysts and observers to emphasise their nationalist credentials and their sympathy for the African cause, has often led to a stress on the conflictual elements in the relationship at the expense of the co-operative ones. Even the most radical of African leaders, however, generally retained some sense of identity with the former colonial power, some personal links with it, and an appreciation for its culture if not necessarily for its politics.[68] At a diplomatic level, the former metropole provided a European state, normally a relatively wealthy and secure one, on which an African leader had some claim. It was usually the most important source of aid, military as well as economic, and it could almost invariably be relied on to come down on the side of its former colony in case of serious trouble. In a potentially threatening world, it provided even the smallest and weakest African state with some assurance that it was not alone. And while in the post-Second World War decolonisation period, the Western European colonial states were eclipsed by the superpowers, as time went by their economies and self-confidence recovered, and their incorporation into the European Community opened the way for a broader and less exclusive relationship for their former African colonies, and for additional sources of aid.

The problem was that the greater the level of support which the former colonial power was prepared to provide, the greater the concern for its own interests that was likely to accompany it. Conversely, the more an African leader sought to pursue an independent course of action, the less reliable the post-colonial connection became. This is, of course, part of the logic of any power relationship, and especially of any unequal one, in which each party seeks to pursue its interests and assesses the value of its alliances accordingly. What made the post-colonial relationship particularly sensitive in this respect was the depth and range of the former metropole's linkages with the African state, and the legacy of subordination on the one hand, and superiority on the other. The differences in French and British relations with independent Africa indicated widely separated points on a spectrum between protection and control on the one hand, and tolerance but relative indifference on the other.

Insofar as the relationship faded, after more than thirty years in most cases since independence, it did so quite as much because of the growing indifference of the European states, as because of the growing autonomy of the African ones. The decay of African economies, and the increasingly evident fragility of African political structures, reinforced their need for protection at precisely the time when the rapid decline of Western European economic interests in Africa, and the opening up of new economic and political opportunities and dangers with the end of the Cold War, were leading the former colonial powers to look elsewhere. Whereas in the early 1960s, the call was for the colonial powers to get out of Africa, the end of the Cold War was greeted by pleas not to abandon it. In the 1970s, control of the Co-operation portfolio was one of the key French goals in the allocation of Commissioners to posts in the European Community; when EC posts were redistributed in October 1994, the main battle was for control of relations with Eastern Europe, and the new French Commissioner, Madame Edith Cresson, was reported as saying 'Please, not the Africans'.[69]

A further critical feature of the post-colonial role in Africa was the concern of the former metropoles with the maintenance of the state, at any rate in those territories for which they had been responsible. Though they had no special commitment to the principles of juridical statehood, and were sometimes cavalier about intervention in African states, they were overwhelmingly concerned to uphold the structure of statehood itself, and were normally inclined to act on the side of the person or group in government. Despite the transfer of power at independence, in most cases, to the winner of a reasonably democratic election, they rarely showed any serious commitment to the maintenance of democracy and human rights, at least until these became fashionable in the late 1980s, and at times they connived in abuses of power of the most appalling kind. Their actions almost invariably favoured those who had power against those who did not. The weakening of post-colonial concern for Africa could thus only intensify the pressure on the maintenance of the African state, and the interests of those who depended on it.

5 The politics of solidarity

African states: allies or rivals?

Those African rulers who sought to supplement or displace their dependence on the former colonial power had an obvious alternative source of diplomatic support in their relations with one another. Some of them, such as Kwame Nkrumah of Ghana, had already been closely involved in the Pan-African movement, and associated their own achievement of independence with broader aspirations to continental liberation and union. Others, like the francophone leaders or those of former British east and central Africa, had established links with their counterparts in neighbouring states within an essentially colonial setting. A proliferation of meetings, starting with the Accra conference of independent African states called by Nkrumah in April 1958, established a continental diplomatic network which rapidly expanded as it was joined by newly independent states. The value of these inter-African relationships depended, however, on two basic questions. First, to what extent did African states share common interests, which would enable them to act internationally as allies rather than rivals? Second, even if they did act as allies, what effective support could such weak states give to one another?

The relations between African states were suffused with a rhetoric of solidarity which constantly emphasised their 'unity', characteristically in opposition to external domination and especially colonialism. Like any political rhetoric, that of Pan-Africanism served in large part to conceal unpalatable truths. The rhetoric of anti-colonialism papered over the close relations which most African states maintained, and needed to maintain, with their former rulers. The rhetoric of unity papered over the extreme reluctance of any but a very small minority of African rulers to sacrifice any of their power in the interests of any continental grouping. There were none the less significant sources of common interest. First, there were those identities which Ali Mazrui summed up as 'the concept of "We are all Africans"'.[1] Regardless of the inability of African rulers even seriously to consider any programme of continental union, the sense of being African had an impact which went beyond the merely rhetorical level. Derived from commonalities of race and historical experience, this imposed on African rulers a sense that, at any rate, they *ought* to act in harmony, and that Africans in one part of the continent had some kind of claim or obligation on those in another – a sentiment which was most sharply aroused by opposition to colonialism or white minority rule. It meant that over issues where a broad continental consensus had been established, there was some pressure on the rulers of individual states not to step out of line. Such a maverick as Dr Hastings Kamuzu Banda of Malawi might delight in going against the grain, without suffering any evident ill effects, but a small state whose leaders had no strong foreign policy commitments, such as Sierra Leone, generally found it easiest just to discover what most other African states were doing, and then do the same.[2]

Second and more basically, African rulers overwhelmingly shared a common 'idea of the state', which removed many potential sources of conflict between them, and made it possible for them to devise generally agreed principles by which to regulate their relations with one another. One important expression of this was, as already noted, that the artificiality of their boundaries normally created a shared interest in boundary maintenance, rather than a mass of boundary conflicts. This in turn was, however, only one element in a common commitment to the idea of juridical statehood, from which almost all of them had much more to gain than to lose. It was their interest in their own individual sovereignty, and their determination to maintain it both against their own neighbours and against the outside world, that led them both to reject continental union on the one hand, and to seek the protection of fellow African states on the other.

Since one critical element in the idea of the state was that it should be governed by indigenous Africans, conflict automatically arose between African states and territories that remained under colonial or white minority rule. That apart, states which were deviant in terms of their domestic political structures, but which conducted their foreign policies within the conventions of juridical statehood, could as already noted be accepted as members of the African international community with very few questions asked. Neither Haile-Selassie's imperial Ethiopian government, nor its revolutionary Marxist successor, had any difficulty in fitting into the continental framework, and in the process denying legitimacy to their separatist opponents in Eritrea. The governments of Somalia over most of the period until 1991, and of Libya under Colonel Qadhafi, were far less deviant in terms of their domestic political systems than either the Haile-Selassie or the Mengistu regimes in Ethiopia; but each of them challenged the assumptions of African juridical statehood, and was regarded with suspicion by most other African regimes.

Where conflicts arose between African regimes, these largely resulted from the contrasting and implicitly competing 'packages' through which the rulers of different states sought to maintain their security. Such packages were a composite of personal preference, domestic political ideology and need, and external alliance. During the early years after independence, the differences between them turned largely on the relationship with the former colonial regime, and divided African states into 'anti-colonial' and 'neocolonial' camps. When an intensified level of superpower involvement divided Africa in the mid-1970s, this in turn became the major source of differentiation. Even though it made little difference to the principles of juridical statehood whether African regimes were kept in place with the aid of France, the United States, or the Soviet Union, competing external backers or domestic ideologies aroused at least a suspicion that one state would seek to undermine the sovereignty of another.

Some latent conflicts between African states did arise as a result of structural features of the African state system, of the sort that have been familiar from the history of Europe, but these were relatively muted. The Ethio-Somali conflict could be seen at its most basic as reflecting divisions between highland and lowland, Christianity and Islam, agriculturalists and pastoralists, which derived from the physical and social endowment of the Horn. The differences between Ethiopia and Sudan were likewise a perennial source of tension. The presence of Nigeria in West Africa, as a massive state with a large number of much smaller neighbours, aroused a sense of 'manifest destiny' on the part of many Nigerians, and a corresponding fear of hegemony on the part of their neighbours. The regional domination of South Africa, long subsumed under the much more directly threatening shadow of white minority rule, remained a potentially difficult issue after the transition to majority government.[3] For the most part, none the less, the principles of juridical statehood, coupled with the ability of threatened states to seek countervailing protection from outside the continent (from France by francophone West African states, from the Soviet Union by Angola), kept these tensions under control.

By far the greatest threat to collaborative relations between African states therefore resulted from the breakdown of the conventions of juridical statehood which helped to insulate them from one another. To quite a large extent, of course, internal breakdown was fomented from outside, most evidently in the Horn and Angola. Its most important sources were none the less overwhelmingly domestic. It was the failure of African states to maintain their own statehood that pushed them into conflict with one another. The resulting upheavals will be examined especially in the chapter on the foreign relations of insurgency.

This in turn leads back to the second question raised at the start of this chapter: how much support could African states provide for (or, conversely, how much damage could they do to) one another? In terms of hard resources, whether military or economic, the answer was usually, not a lot. Nkrumah's Ghana provided vital economic aid to help meet the crisis of independence in Guinea. There were also quite a number of mostly small-scale African military interventions in neighbouring states, almost always at the invitation of their governments, which will be examined in a later section. But these resources were generally dwarfed by those available from outside. In terms of the maintenance of the conventions of juridical statehood, none the less, the influence of African solidarity was critical. So long as African states were able to maintain a broad consensus among themselves, they could help set the conditions for acceptable intervention by non-African states in the affairs of the continent. Intervening states, and especially the superpowers, were concerned not only with the immediate consequences of intervention, but with maintaining a coalition of friendly client states, and this placed pressure on them to act in accordance with the conventions of the regional system. The conventions governing the international relations of the continent were in turn most explicitly formalised in the Organisation of African Unity (or OAU), and the successes and failures of this organisation most clearly illustrate the possibilities and limitations of continental diplomacy.

The continental coalition

The division of African states after independence into blocs named after the cities where they were created – Casablanca, Monrovia, Brazzaville – and the subsequent absorption of these blocs into the Organisation of African Unity at the Addis Ababa conference of May 1963, are among the most familiar events of African diplomacy. The OAU, much criticised though it has been, did establish a common forum for the conduct of continental diplomacy, and in the process helped to define the assumptions and conventions that would guide it. By examining the OAU, one can therefore gain an overview of the principles that were at least formally expected to govern the relations between African states, and an indication of the extent to which these principles could actually be implemented, and the reasons why they frequently could not.

The success of the Addis Ababa summit, and the establishment of a single continental organisation encompassing all African states (save only colonial territories and those under white minority rule), was at the time by no means the foregone conclusion that it subsequently appeared to be.[4] It was certainly a diplomatic triumph, and one which helped to ensure that, at least in the early years of independence, those interests which African states broadly shared with one another would be emphasised, rather than those issues over which they differed. The price to be paid for this was that the organisation created at Addis Ababa had to be one which all independent African states would agree to belong to, and that in turn meant one which would protect, and not threaten, the sovereignty of its individual member states. Though often described as a compromise between 'radical' and 'moderate' states, the Charter of the OAU actually represented the most clear cut possible victory for the principle of juridical sovereignty, over any pretensions to supranational continental union.

That this was indeed the only basis for agreement was clear from the support that it received, not only from conservative states like Ethiopia, Nigeria and most of the francophone states – all of which were concerned about the undermining of their territorial integrity or domestic structures of government, either by secessionist movements like that in Eritrea, or by the potentially subversive doctrines of Nkrumaist Pan-Africanism – but equally from most of the 'radical' states as well, including notably Sekou Touré's Guinea. Only Nkrumah, with some support from his Ugandan ally Milton Obote, clung to a belief in continental 'union government' which belonged to the realm of fantasy. The Charter of the OAU was in consequence one of the purest statements of the elements of juridical statehood to be embodied in any international organisation, stopping a very long way short even of the concessions to supranationality made in the Charter of the United Nations.[5]

The only body capable of taking decisions on behalf of the organisation was the annual meeting of its heads of state and government, which itself had no power to impose decisions on any dissenting member. There was no body equivalent to the Security Council of the United Nations, which could meet at short notice and take decisions on behalf of African states as a whole, since this would have involved a level of delegation which member states were not prepared to accept. Though a permanent secretariat was set up, it likewise had no authority to take decisions on behalf of the organisation as a whole, and its head was accorded the deliberately insignificant title of Administrative Secretary General. The formal statement of its aims committed all of its members to defend the sovereignty, territorial integrity and independence of African states, and obliged them to adhere to the principles of non-interference in the internal affairs of member states, and the condemnation of political subversion. Though the Charter also committed member states to the emancipation of dependent African territories, and to international non-alignment, the first of these in any event expressed the aspirations of all African states, while the second did not in practice impose any constraint on their foreign policies. The 'unity' referred to in the organisation's title was entirely rhetorical.

It may seem surprising that an organisation founded on such anodyne principles could have any impact on the international relations of the continent. A case could, however, be made that its influence during the first twelve years after its foundation was quite significant. In particular, by reinforcing the emphasis on juridical statehood, it helped to ensure that most African states during the critical early years after independence enjoyed a generally supportive international environment, both within the continent and outside. This was the most peaceful of the three and a half decades of independent Africa. External military intervention in the continent was at its lowest,[6] and the few incipient conflicts between African states, notably between Algeria and Morocco and between Ethiopia and Somalia, were defused. The major trauma of the period, the Nigerian civil war of 1967–70, was not entirely isolated from either African or external involvement: four African states recognised the government of Biafra, two of which were actively involved in providing it with arms;[7] while among non-African states, the Soviet Union and United Kingdom supplied arms to the federal government, and France and Portugal aided Biafra. The contrast with the level of external involvement in Angola, Ethiopia and Zaïre from 1975 onwards was none the less dramatic. While the specific influence of the OAU is difficult to isolate, that organisation did embody the principles of non-intervention and respect for the territorial integrity of African states which were maintained by the great majority of its members. Though the provision in the Charter for the establishment of a Commission of Mediation, Conciliation and Arbitration to deal with disputes between member states was never formally activated, the idea that such disputes should be peacefully mediated within an African framework was generally accepted. The normal format for such mediation was through a small group of carefully chosen senior heads of state.

Another way in which the OAU helped to insulate the African diplomatic system from conflicts arising within its member states was through the recognition of whoever held power in the national capital as the government of the state concerned, which was then entitled to call on the support of the system as a whole. Though contested, for example, by Nkrumah after his overthrow in the Ghanaian *coup d'état* of February 1966, this provided a practicable means of averting involvement in disputes which could otherwise have divided African states between the supporters of rival domestic regimes. The resolution at the OAU's first ordinary summit, at Cairo in 1964, committing member states to respect the frontiers inherited on their accession to national independence, likewise defused what could otherwise have been a mass of intractable disputes.

Even in its early years, however, the OAU was unable to displace the much more important links between African states and their external protectors, notably the former colonial powers. This was demonstrated in 1965, when the organisation called on its members (though at a meeting of foreign ministers, not of heads of state) to break diplomatic relations with the United Kingdom in protest at its failure to prevent the unilateral declaration of independence by the settler regime in Rhodesia. Among the few states that did so, the only one for which it had significant consequences was Tanzania, which under the presidency of Julius Nyerere was virtually alone in seeking to base its foreign policy on principle rather than the pragmatic pursuit of state interest.[8] The francophone states did not interpret the formal commitment to non-alignment in the OAU Charter as affecting their own close relations with France, and even in several cases had French troops permanently stationed on their soil. Insofar as the principle of sovereignty conflicted with that of non-alignment, it was sovereignty – and hence the right of any national government to invite military assistance from any external ally – that prevailed.

On only one occasion did the OAU play a significant role in inducing its members to conduct their foreign policies in a way which many of them could not otherwise have been expected to do, and that was over the breach of diplomatic relations with Israel in 1973. The formal basis for this was that Israel was occupying the territory of an OAU member state, Egypt, in defiance of the OAU's commitment to the territorial integrity of its members. Following the Israeli occupation of Sinai during the 1967 Arab–Israeli war, the organisation had set up an investigatory committee which – because its terms of reference necessarily had to respect Egyptian territorial integrity – was bound to come down on the side of its member state. Once Egypt had accepted the resulting report, and Israel had rejected it, the way was open for a resolution recommending member states to break relations with Israel to be passed at the 1973 summit. That this recommendation was subsequently implemented by all but a handful of African states owed much to the 1973 Arab–Israeli war, and to the rise in oil prices which vastly increased the economic and diplomatic weight of the Arab states. It was none the less greatly helped by a sense of African solidarity, which induced even reluctant states, such as Haile-Selassie's Ethiopia and Tolbert's Liberia, to break relations with Israel in order to retain their credibility within the African setting.[9]

The OAU was, however, ineffectual in liberating the remaining African territories from colonial or settler rule. It established a liberation committee based in Dar-es-Salaam, which maintained relations with the leaders of recognised liberation movements, but its achievements were at best slight, and largely limited to attempts to get competing movements within a given territory to present a united front. African states were in no position to provide effective military aid, except through the use of neighbouring territories as bases and refuges for movements operating across the border, and the provision of training facilities in states further removed from the 'front line'. At the critical moments in contested decolonisation, such as the Angolan war of 1975 and the negotiation of settlements in both Zimbabwe and Namibia, the organisation was not involved.[10]

So long as the OAU was involved in policing the boundaries of juridical statehood, it generally had a useful job to do. At every point at which the formulae dictated by this approach were inadequate, the inadequacy of the OAU was likewise revealed. These formulae, in essence, had to assume that the problems of the continent could be resolved by dividing it into its constituent states, and then supporting the right of whoever held power in the capital of each of those states to exercise unfettered control over the whole of the territory allocated to it. They made the organisation into a governments' trade union.

The first test that the organisation clearly and publicly failed, after the Rhodesian UDI of 1965, was that posed by the independence of Angola in November 1975, and the civil war between contending nationalist movements which started before independence and continued after it. Prior to independence, the OAU had followed the conventional path of seeking to induce all three rival movements to unite, in order to present a single nationalist front. There was no pre-independence election to determine which movement had most popular support, and the Portuguese left without designating a successor. This left African states with a choice between recognising the MPLA regime which controlled the capital, or giving equal status to all three movements – a choice which, since the MPLA was strongly supported by the Soviet Union, while the rival FNLA and Unita were backed by the United States, instantly turned into a Cold War conflict with profoundly divisive consequences. Though the specific question of Angola was eventually resolved in favour of the MPLA, both in practical terms through its victory (with Soviet and Cuban help) in the civil war, and in terms of legitimacy through the support given to Unita by South Africa, the divisions remained.

Two further issues which likewise raised the question of which *was* the government entitled to OAU support arose in Western Sahara and Chad. In Western Sahara, the departing Spanish colonial regime had in 1976 partitioned the territory between its two main neighbours, Morocco and Mauritania, while ignoring the claims of the Polisario nationalist movement to separate independence. Though Mauritania soon withdrew, African states still had to choose between the claims of the Polisario and one of the OAU's own members. The issue was in some degree pre-empted for the OAU by the decision of a majority of its member states to recognise Polisario as the government of what became the Sahrawi Arab Democratic Republic, even though it did not control the capital or much of the rest of the territory. This led to Polisario being invited to join the OAU, and in turn to Morocco leaving it.[11] In Chad, which from the late 1970s was fractured between a bewildering number of armed factions, neighbouring states became concerned in 1981 over the right of the leader of a transitional government, Goukhouni Waddeye, to declare a union with Libya, which at the same time had territorial claims on part of northern Chad; Libyan troops then entered Chad to help keep Goukhouni in power. Goukhouni was persuaded to accept an OAU peacekeeping force in place of the Libyans, in the belief that this would protect him against his domestic rivals; on its arrival, however, it stood aside while Goukhouni, shorn of Libyan aid, was overthrown. The divisions this aroused were such that the 1982 summit, which fortuitously was due to be held in Tripoli, had to be abandoned for lack of a quorum.[12]

While disputes over who had the right to represent a state in the OAU were ultimately capable of resolution, any issue which raised the question of what a government had a right to *do*, within its own territory, challenged the principle of juridical sovereignty directly. During the 1970s, three regimes in particular – those of Jean-Bedel Bokassa in the Central African Republic, Fernando Macias Nguema in Equatorial Guinea, and Idi Amin in Uganda – aroused a level of external criticism for their abuse of human rights which was damaging to Africa as a whole, and in particular to African criticism of human rights violations in South Africa and other settler governed territories. As discussed in a later chapter, they significantly weakened external acceptance of juridical sovereignty in Africa, and were to open the way to the imposition of political conditionalities.

The management of Africa's international relations through the defence of juridical statehood was undermined, finally, by the failure of the state itself. States such as Angola, Chad, Sudan and Ethiopia were locked into apparently endless civil wars, in which the central government's opponents received the barely disguised assistance of neighbouring African states. With the independence of Eritrea in 1993, and its admission to the OAU, the first recognised secession took place from an existing African state. In Liberia and Somalia, the state collapsed altogether when the government was overthrown by insurgent movements which were incapable of putting any alternative regime in their place. Though there was some response to these disasters both at the sub-continental level, through the West African peacekeeping force in Liberia, and at the extra-African level, notably through the United States and United Nations operation in Somalia, the OAU lacked any capacity even to help set the rules within which attempts at resolution could be made. Nor was it qualified to do much to help meet many of the challenges which faced African states from the mid-1980s onwards, and which went beyond the capabilities of individual states, such as economic failure, famine, environmental degradation, and refugees. It did help to promote a convention on refugee problems in Africa, and passed a number of resolutions on the dumping of toxic waste, but these operated at a declamatory level which could make little practical difference to the problems themselves.[13] The OAU's forays into plans for continental economic union, in the 1980 Lagos Plan of Action and the subsequent programme for the creation of an African Common Market by the year 2025, were entirely unrealistic.

Much of the criticism heaped on the OAU derived essentially from the gap between the aspirations for liberation, peace and development aroused by an organisation with so ambitious a name, and the extremely limited capabilities of the organisation itself. As the failure of juridical statehood as a formula for resolving domestic conflicts became increasingly evident, moreover, so the OAU was tagged with a measure of responsibility for the actions of governments which most blatantly used this formula to deflect any criticism of their own abuse of power. African leaders such as Yoweri Museveni of Uganda and Isaias Afewerki of Eritrea, who came to power after years of fighting regimes which were backed by the OAU's commitment to territorial integrity and unfettered domestic sovereignty, were eloquent in their scorn. In the first summit which he attended as president of an independent Eritrea, for example, Isaias branded the OAU as 'an utter failure'.[14]

Some effort at reform was therefore needed in order to enable the OAU to regain a measure of moral authority, not only outside the continent but even among some of its own members. One of these efforts, the African Charter of Human and Peoples' Rights, was proposed by President Jawara of The Gambia in an attempt both to rebut external criticisms of Africa's human rights record, and to lay down at least some minimum standards which African states might be expected to meet. Ineffectual even in its wording, let alone in its implementation, it is examined in a later chapter. Another was the attempt made by Salim Ahmed Salim, the Tanzanian foreign minister who became Secretary General of the OAU in 1989, to improve the organisation's decision-making capacity by creating a smaller body, to be called the Bureau of the Summit, which would carry out some of the functions (without enjoying the powers) of a security council analogous to that of the United Nations. Presented to the 1992 summit in Dakar, this proposal was referred to the subsequent Cairo summit in 1993, at which it was approved in a modified form as a Mechanism for Conflict Prevention, Management and Resolution. The key difference was that the original Bureau had the appearance of a Security Council or politburo, standing above the rest of the organisation, whereas the Mechanism was no more than a subordinate commission. It would, however, have the right to concern itself, with the agreement of the state concerned, with conflicts inside member states, and the Central Organ of the Mechanism, as it was cumbersomely entitled, met for the first time early in 1995.[15] Though the principle of OAU concern for conflicts within member states was thus established, the capacity of the OAU to regulate Africa's international relations once juridical statehood ceased to provide any adequate guide none the less remained at a minimal level.

The politics of regionalism

One evident problem of the OAU was that an organisation with over fifty members was too large and diverse to be able to meet many of the needs of its individual states. In practice, much African diplomacy was therefore conducted within the more manageable framework of groups of neighbouring states which had some affinity with one another. Much of the continent could be divided without difficulty into large regions whose member states had at least an element of common identity. The states of Arabic-speaking North Africa had such strong links with those of the Arab Middle East that they could for most purposes be separated from sub-Saharan Africa altogether. The fifteen or so states of West Africa, from Senegal and the Cape Verde islands east to Nigeria, encompassed numerous languages, both indigenous and post-colonial, as well as both Moslem and Christian populations, and a wide range of ecological zones; but they none the less formed a fairly compact regional grouping, with a good deal of population movement between its members. The ten states of southern Africa, north to a line from Angola through Zambia and Malawi to

Mozambique, had the identity imposed by the regional presence of South Africa, and a set of transport links which integrated the region into a common infrastructure to a greater extent than any other similarly sized part of the continent.

There was no equivalent central or east African region, in the area from Chad south to Zaïre, but rather a series of much smaller groupings: francophone north-central Africa, the Horn, former British East Africa, the former Belgian territories. Similar clusters could be identified within the larger regional groupings, such as a number of francophone ones within West Africa which coexisted awkwardly with the regional organisation.[16] Some states were pulled in different directions – most obviously Sudan, with the largest territory of any state in Africa, which looked north to Arab North Africa, east to the Horn, south to Uganda and the Zaïre basin, and west to the Sahel. Despite the inevitable existence of boundary zones, however, African states generally fell into self-defining clusters, relationships within which were considerably more significant than those with other parts of the continent.

When one asks what these relationships actually consisted in, one can come up with two very different kinds of answer. First, Africa spawned a proliferation of regional 'communities' or 'unions', all of which were ostensibly dedicated to the promotion of economic integration between their members. Each of the two large sub-Saharan regions, southern Africa and West Africa, was defined by its regional grouping: the Southern African Development Community (SADC, formerly SADCC), and the Economic Community of West African States (ECOWAS). The absence of any equivalent east and central African region was indicated by the lack of a similar regional organisation, save for the Intergovernmental Authority on Drought and Development (IGADD), which had negligible functions beyond serving as an occasional meeting point for regional heads of state, and the amorphous and virtually meaningless Preferential Trade Area (PTA) which also included most of the states of the SADC. Smaller groupings were established both within the large ones, like the Mano River Union of Liberia, Sierra Leone and Guinea within ECOWAS, or outside them, like the Central African Customs Union (UDEAC) which linked the francophone central African states and Equatorial Guinea.

None of these schemes had any discernible positive impact on the economic welfare of the people incorporated into it. Virtually every commentary on them, indeed, consists in little more than a recital of the failure of the institution concerned to work in the way that was ostensibly intended.[17] There were good economic reasons for this, notably in the tiny internal markets even of the groupings created by a number of African states, the high dependence of all of them on trade outside the region, and the non-complementarity of the economies within it. There were also important political reasons, the most basic of which was that African states depended on extracting resources from external trade, to an extent that made their leaders extremely reluctant to release control over this trade to any supranational body. Any challenge to the statist policies followed by rulers within their own territories was consequently interpreted as infringing their national sovereignty. Similar challenges imposed by international financial institutions eventually proved to be irresistible, but these had the effect of integrating African states with global markets, rather than just with the economies of their continental neighbours.

A further problem of regional integration schemes was that such schemes almost inevitably had a differential impact on their members, which worked to the advantage of the largest, most developed and most centrally placed among them. The Central African Federation established under British colonialism favoured Southern Rhodesia (now Zimbabwe) over the present Zambia and Malawi.[18] The East African Community favoured Kenya over Uganda and Tanzania. In ECOWAS, the lead position was taken by Nigeria. The exclusion from the SADC of the region's dominant economy, South Africa, effectively removed any economic rationale from the organisation, except as a platform from which to appeal for outside aid. Even when a measure of economic integration did occur, necessarily involving the transfer of resources from one state within the community to another, this in turn created political resentments on both sides. These were most clearly expressed by the political consequences of population movement. The poorer and more peripheral states saw many of the most qualified members of their workforce going to take jobs elsewhere; the richer and more centrally placed ones, through precisely the same process, saw jobs within their own countries being taken by foreigners. The expulsion of West African aliens from Nigeria in 1983, as part of an electoral strategy through which the ruling National Party of Nigeria sought to create jobs for Nigerian voters, perfectly illustrated these tensions.[19]

This unrelieved catalogue of failure raises the question of why African leaders sought to establish such regional communities in the first place. Part of the answer lay in the rhetoric of internationalism, for which the creation of a regional organisation neatly combined two functions. First, it could be fitted into the ideology of Pan-Africanism, as a mechanism ostensibly designed to promote collaboration between African states which, even though it was limited both regionally and functionally, could be regarded as a 'building block' or 'stepping stone' in the wider process of achieving continental union. Second, it could draw on examples of economic integration among industrial states, and notably the European Community, to present a scenario that combined political integration with mutual economic benefit, but which was entirely irrelevant on both economic and political grounds to the states of sub-Saharan Africa.[20]

The second and more important basis for regional co-operation resulted from the second element in African regional relationships: that the region was one of the critical arenas within which the security of the state and its rulers was threatened, and within which it could equally be protected. In those cases where regional organisations amounted to anything more than rhetorical creations, this was because the region constituted a 'security complex' in Buzan's terms,[21] within which the organisation could serve as a security community, rather than as a development one. In southern Africa, the security role was effectively performed within the framework of the Front Line States, which provided an informal forum which enabled heads of state to meet under the chairmanship of the senior regional president (initially Nyerere of Tanzania, then Kaunda of Zambia, and subsequently Mugabe of Zimbabwe), whenever the occasion required it. With the achievement of majority rule in South Africa, Mandela was invited to participate, and discussions were held in March 1995 over its re-creation as a regional security forum. The creation of ECOWAS reflected an attempt by Nigeria, born of the confidence engendered by its size, its oil wealth, and the successful (for the central government) conclusion of its own civil war, to achieve the role within the West African region to which its rulers felt that it was entitled. It had no viable pretensions to cut across the north–south economic linkages which were reinforced, in the very year that ECOWAS was founded, by the first Lomé Convention; it did however have pretensions to cut across north–south security linkages, and especially those between the francophone states and France. Regions such as the Horn, which were too riven by conflict to have much prospect of developing any plausible regional security structure, were correspondingly unable to develop any regional economic community.

The security element was equally evident within smaller regional groupings. The most explicit of these, the Senegambian Confederation, was the expression in political terms of the Gambian government's dependence on the Senegalese army to reverse the attempted *coup d'état* of July 1981. The formation of the Mano River Union between Liberia and Sierra Leone was correspondingly related to the insecurity of Presidents Tolbert and Stevens, and its extension to Guinea reflected the willingness of President Sekou Touré to use Guinean troops to maintain order and protect the regime in both Freetown and Monrovia.[22] Where regionalism amounted to anything more than a formality, it did so because it helped to serve the cause of state and regime preservation.

Regional security none the less raised critical issues of power, and was ultimately inextricable from the problem of hegemony. No regional security structure – certainly not NATO or the Warsaw Pact, to take the most obvious examples – can be considered in isolation from the distribution of power among its members. Any such structure can only protect the weaker alliance members against external threats, at the price of subordinating them to some extent to the alliance leader. In the case of African states, the common calculus of alliance systems raised particularly sensitive issues, which made it extremely difficult for would-be regional powers to establish their claims to leadership.

First of all, the very idea of regional leadership ran up against the commitment to equality between states which was strongly entrenched in the culture of African international relations, and which was inherent in the ideology of juridical sovereignty. Though asserted most strongly against the pretensions of external powers, the claim to sovereignty – ideals of African unity notwithstanding – was never likely to be abandoned in favour of regionally dominant states. Would-be regional hegemons consequently had to step extremely carefully, for fear of raising an alliance of smaller states against them. Nigeria, easily the largest of African states and one whose elites were especially prone to express aspirations to regional or continental leadership, had great difficulty in turning its size and wealth into effective diplomatic influence.[23] South Africa, the other potential hegemonic state within its own region, is likely to face similar difficulties.

Secondly, small African states were able to counteract the influence of would-be regional powers by looking instead to patrons outside the continent. For a small state, protection by a distant power was often less threatening than dependence on a large and potentially predatory neighbour. Nigeria's aspirations to leadership in West Africa were constantly frustrated by France. Angola and Mozambique, during the period of South African destabilisation, sought to protect themselves through an alliance with Cuba and the Soviet Union in the first case, and by trying to use Western influence to fend off South African pressure in the second. The end of the Cold War, with its resulting diminution in superpower interest and (for the ex-Soviet Union) ability to intervene in African conflicts, together with the declining role of the former colonial powers, may open the way for a greater assertiveness on the part of African states; indeed, the Nigerian leadership of the ECOMOG force in Liberia has been seen as just such a development. A regional power structure has none the less yet to be established.

A third major impediment to the emergence of regional leadership was the internal division of would-be hegemonic states themselves. It was an almost inevitable consequence of the generally small size of indigenous African political communities, and the externally dominated process of state formation, that any state with a large territory and population should have serious problems of internal coherence. Every large state in sub-Saharan Africa – Nigeria, Ethiopia, South Africa, Zaïre, Sudan – was deeply riven by internal conflict, and most suffered civil wars. Given that effective external leadership by any state, even one as large as the former Soviet Union, requires a government that is firmly established within its own territory, it was not surprising that few African states were able to provide it. Nor, finally, did most African states possess the political, social and economic instruments required to exercise influence over their neighbours without the overt use of force. Only South Africa stood at the centre of a network of connections through which pressure could be exerted on other regional states, and even these were largely displaced during the period of minority rule by military destabilisation.

Though African states fairly readily intervened in the domestic politics of their neighbours, the influence that this brought them was therefore generally short-lived. By far the greater number of overt interventions were on the side of the existing authorities, and thus upheld the norms of juridical statehood.[24] Even where the authorities in the target state evidently retained power as a result of external intervention, as was for example the case in The Gambia after the Senegalese intervention of 1981, this was not translated into long-term influence. Indeed, the greater the level of external dependence, the more anxious the domestic authorities were to regain their freedom of action. The Senegambian Confederation, formed after the Senegalese intervention, had become a dead letter within a few years, and was eventually wound up in 1989.[25] Guinean intervention in Liberia and Sierra Leone likewise led to no long-term association.

In only one case did the direct invasion of one African state by another lead to the overthrow of the regime in power and its replacement by a government acceptable to the invading state. This was the Tanzanian invasion of Uganda in 1978/79, which ousted Idi Amin and resulted in a number of unstable governments, until eventually Yoweri Museveni seized power in January 1986. Though the Tanzanian government had a high level of influence over the initial establishment of a post-Amin regime, this was steadily reduced as each succeeding government took over.[26] Nor did support for insurgent movements seeking to displace the government of a neighbouring state carry any greater potential for influence, since even if the insurgents gained power, they needed to consolidate their rule by building internal alliances, in the process distancing themselves from their sources of external support. Both the EPRDF in Ethiopia and the allied EPLF in Eritrea benefited considerably from a succession of generally supportive governments in Sudan during their long struggles against the Mengistu Haile-Mariam regime in Addis Ababa. Once Mengistu had been overthrown in May 1991, however, their differences from any Sudanese government – and especially one with the Islamist tendencies of the al-Bashir regime – rapidly reasserted themselves. A counter-example was the support given by the Frelimo regime in Mozambique to Robert Mugabe's ZANLA forces during the Zimbabwean independence war, and the corresponding help given by Mugabe to Frelimo against Renamo, after he had taken power in Harare. Mugabe even exercised some influence over the selection of the new president, Joachim Chissano, after Samora Machel's death in October 1986. This can, however, be explained by Mozambique's exceptional degree of continuing dependence, in the face of the Renamo insurgency and South African destabilisation.[27]

The most intense demands on regional security arose when the threatened state as a whole, and not merely the regime in power, was in danger of collapse. The first such case occurred in Congo/Zaïre immediately after independence in 1960, and led to the deployment of a United Nations force with some African participation. There was likewise a limited level of African participation in the UN force in Somalia in 1993/94. In two other cases, Chad and Liberia, the attempts at state maintenance were essentially African. Chad, like neighbouring Sudan, was a 'border' state in regional terms, stretched between North Africa, West Africa, and francophone central Africa, with the result that it was difficult to construct any generally accepted regional framework for intervention. The major intervening states were Libya, Nigeria, and a number of francophone west and central African states, each of which had connections with particular factions within Chad. At the same time, each implicitly sought to incorporate Chad into rival security communities – whether Arab North African, ECOWAS West African, or francophone. Any stabilising impact of intervention was consequently short-lived.[28]

Liberia, on the other hand, fell squarely into the West African region, and its institutional expression, ECOWAS. The intervention of the ECOMOG force in August 1990 provided the most explicit example of the use of an ostensibly economic grouping as a structure for regional security, and illustrated many of the difficulties in establishing a regional security structure.[29] The first of these concerned the standing of the intervening force itself: though ECOMOG was despatched at the invitation of the then incumbent Liberian leader, Samuel Doe, and could draw on the provisions of an ECOWAS Defence Pact which had been designed largely to protect the region against external attack, its status became less clear once Doe had been killed, and the force became involved in the choice of a successor. A respected Liberian academic, Amos Sawyer, was selected as interim president by a meeting of Liberian groups held under ECOWAS auspices, but this excluded Charles Taylor, leader of the major insurgent group, the National Patriotic Front of Liberia (NPFL). In the process, ECOMOG became inextricably involved in Liberian domestic politics, and the country was divided between the capital city and its immediate environs, which were controlled by ECOMOG under the nominal authority of Sawyer, and most of the rest of the country, which was (initially at least) controlled by Taylor and NPFL. The intervention also raised the issue of regional leadership, and thus at least tacitly the division between the region's anglophone and francophone states. ECOMOG was led by Nigeria, which provided by far the greatest number of troops and finance for the operation. The Nigerian military leader, General Babangida, had an association with Doe which from the start raised issues about the internal political neutrality of the force.

Nigeria was supported by the other anglophone states of the region, with contingents from Ghana, Sierra Leone and The Gambia. Though a clear division was prevented by the involvement in ECOMOG of Guinea and Mali, and for a period Senegal, Charles Taylor's NPFL operated from Ivoirian territory and was also supported by Burkina Faso. French companies took the major role in exporting produce from the areas of the country controlled by the NPFL.[30]

Though ECOMOG helped to maintain order in Monrovia, at a time when it might otherwise have collapsed into the level of bloodshed seen the following year in Mogadishu, it is doubtful whether it eventually contributed much to the stability of Liberia, the intervening states, or the region as a whole. The division of Liberia into ECOMOG-controlled and NPFL-controlled zones, with the opportunities which this provided for the proliferation of further armed factions, impeded the negotiation (or even imposition) of any political settlement. The war spread into Sierra Leone, largely as the result of Taylor's attempt to gain access to Sierra Leonean diamonds by fostering an insurgent movement across the border. Troops which had been engaged in ECOMOG were responsible for *coups d'état* in both Sierra Leone and The Gambia, and also presented a security threat in Nigeria. In the event, the outcome of the ECOMOG intervention in Liberia was little different from (and certainly no worse than) that of the United States and United Nations in Somalia; but whereas the Somali operation was carried out by troops from distant countries which could pull out relatively easily, the Liberian one had longer-term destabilising effects for the region as a whole.

In the period following the end of the Cold War, the creation of effective regional security structures emerged as one of the major challenges facing the management of any new world order. In the face of the evident failure to create such structures in much of the rest of the world, and notably the former Yugoslavia and the Caucasus, the failure to do so in Africa was scarcely surprising. In each case, once the structure of statehood had proved inadequate, the possibilities for rescuing states and their peoples through international action were extremely limited.

The Afro-Arab relationship

Despite the rhetoric of non-alignment and Third World solidarity, the relationships between African states and most other regions of the

'Third World' were generally slight. Such linkages as existed, moreover, arose largely in the context of north–south institutions such as the Commonwealth or the ACP group of states associated with the European Community. The triennial summits of the Non-Aligned Movement scarcely challenged this conclusion, since they provided little beyond solidaristic rhetoric, and largely ineffectual attempts to construct a Third World bargaining bloc against the capitalist industrial states. With the end of the Cold War, the imposition of economic and political conditionalities, and the increasing differentiation in levels of development between the various regions of the Third World, its already marginal influence completely disappeared.

The most important exception to the general insignificance of 'south–south relations' to African diplomacy was provided by the relations between the states of sub-Saharan Africa and those of the Arab and Moslem Middle East, including those North African states which formed part of both groupings. These were the only Third World states in immediate proximity to Africa, and their relations with the continent had been formed, not just by modern diplomacy, but by linkages which stretched back long before the colonial period. Islam in particular had profoundly influenced the entire Sahelian zone of sub-Saharan Africa, and the east African coastal region as far south as northern Mozambique. To see whether international relations with states beyond their own number on the one hand, and the major industrial powers on the other, had any significant impact on the states of sub-Saharan Africa, it is therefore necessary to look to the Middle East.[31]

At its broadest, the Afro-Arab relationship was characterised by two inherently clashing features: a structure of equality on the one hand, and one of inequality on the other. The structure of equality, which understandably provided most of the rhetorical flavour of the relationship, emphasised the common subjection of both Arab and African peoples to the domination of Europe, and provoked common demands for both development and liberation. Although in a sense Arab states were generally less intensively colonised than African ones, as a result of the conquest of almost the entire Arab world by the Ottoman empire which shared their religion and much of their culture, Arab societies often had a much more intense hostility to the 'West' than was commonly found south of the Sahara. Whereas for African states, anti-colonialism most prominently took the form of a demand for political independence, Arab ones were more concerned with the cultural threat which imperialism presented to their language and religion. A process of westernisation through European languages, formal education and conversion to Christianity which presented opportunities to Africans was more likely to be seen as a threat by Arabs. There was none the less a substantial shared set of interests and identities which could be mobilised by an alliance of the two groups.

Each group of states, too, had a specific focus for regional solidarity through the equivalence of the Arab concern for the liberation of Palestine from Israeli occupation on the one hand, and the African concern for majority rule and the affront presented by *apartheid* in South Africa on the other. Though the cases were not identical, each had a symbolic significance in reinforcing the internal solidarity of each group of states, and provided a touchstone for external sympathy with their aspirations. Despite the friendly relations which Israel had established with a number of African states soon after their independence, there was an obvious basis for combining the two causes within a framework of Afro-Arab solidarity.

On the other hand, in every significant respect by which the two groups of states could be compared, the Arab states were in a markedly stronger position than the Africans. Any aspect of Afro-Arab relations which raised these differences thus created a sense of Arab power and African subordination, and was inherently subject to the resentments that any unequal relationship gives rise to. Even though Islam was a religion shared by almost all Arabs and a great many Africans, it was in essence an Arab religion which had spread into Africa; its language was Arabic, its holy places were in the Arab lands, and Islamisation was no less an arabising influence than Christianity was a europeanising one. Moslem 'fundamentalism', with its emphasis on a return to the original purity of Islam, threatened those indigenous elements of popular Islam which had softened its impact in much of sub-Saharan Africa. For some Africans, too, especially in southern Sudan and east Africa, the most prominent historical legacy of Arab involvement was not the relatively benign one represented by conversion to Islam, but the hostile one represented by the slave trade. It is often hard to be sure to what extent Arab slaving was a continuing indigenous folk memory, or to what extent it was fostered by colonial rulers, Christian missionaries and indigenous elites as a means of warding off a threat to their own power. For a number of Christian African leaders, none the less, a revived and militant Islam was a source of intense concern. The massive Roman Catholic basilica constructed by President Houphouet-Boigny at Yamoussoukro in Côte d'Ivoire could indeed be regarded, at one level at least, as a symbolic bulwark against Islam.

Arab states were likewise more strongly placed than African ones in terms of almost all the indicators that are commonly used to measure 'development': urbanisation, literacy, industry, and GNP per capita.[32] Oil wealth, coupled with their location in a highly conflictual region, also enabled and encouraged many Arab states to acquire exceptionally high levels of sophisticated weaponry. All this meant that for Arab states, Africa was a hinterland into which they could seek to extend their own power and influence, while for African ones, the Arab world was a potential source of wealth, military protection and diplomatic support – and, at the same time, a potential threat. The terms on which African states could gain these resources in turn inevitably reflected Arab interests and priorities, and were correspondingly liable to provoke African resentment. An early example was the Arab demand that African states should break off diplomatic relations with Israel, offending the African sense that their sovereignty entitled them to establish relations with whoever they wished; it was not until the Arab–Israeli dispute could be brought within the African principles of juridical statehood, as a result of Israeli occupation of Egyptian territory after the 1967 war, that the demand to break relations was agreed to.[33]

The shift from an equal to an unequal relationship between the two groups of states was perfectly expressed by the issue of Arab aid to Africa.[34] The great majority of African states had severed relations with Israel, following the recommendation of a special committee of OAU heads of state appointed to investigate the Egypt–Israel dispute in 1971, which in turn reported shortly before the October 1973 Arab–Israeli war. For most of them, the breach coincided with the 1973 oil price rise, which greatly enriched the Arab oil-producing states, while doing immense economic damage to the African oil-consuming ones. The least that African states could expect was, in their own view, a substantial flow of aid which would both compensate them for their economic losses and reward them for their political solidarity. The Arab Bank for Economic Development in Africa (generally known by its French acronym, BADEA) was accordingly established in November 1973 as a conduit for Arab aid, and started operations early in 1975. Over the following decade, it approved loans and grants of close to $1bn to African states.[35] In the process, however, it aroused all the resentments inherent in any aid relationship. The Africans complained that control over its allocations remained exclusively in Arab hands, arousing suspicions that Moslem African states would receive the lion's share of the money, and that continued subservience to Arab goals would be expected from recipients; Malawi, which had never broken relations with Israel, received nothing. The total amount on offer was moreover substantially less than the sum lost to African states through increased oil prices. From the Arab viewpoint, the diplomatic benefits from their perceived generosity were slight, and after the early 1980s allocations tailed off rapidly. By the mid-1980s, a number of Western-leaning and largely Christian African states, notably Côte d'Ivoire, Liberia and Zaïre, had restored relations with Israel.

Further difficulties arose from the differences between the Arab and African 'idea of the state'. The inevitable association of Arab nationalism and statehood with Islam was a unifying factor in the Arab world, but a divisive one in sub-Saharan Africa.[36] Internationally, the Islamic factor discriminated in favour of Moslem African states, a few of which like Djibouti and Somalia became members of the League of Arab States, even though their own indigenous populations were not Arabs in any sense of the word. More significantly, it discriminated within states in favour of Moslems against Christians, and even within Moslem states in favour of particular groups who were able to establish priority claims on Islamic status or clientelist links with particular Arab patrons. Across the line to the south of the Sahel, which had historically marked the southern limit of Islam, from Sierra Leone through Nigeria and Chad to its extreme expression in Sudan, the Arab link was an inherently divisive one.

This divisiveness was in turn enhanced by the relatively low priority which Arab leaders, in sharp contrast to African ones, gave to the principles of juridical statehood. In part, this doubtless reflected the ambivalent status of secular political authorities in Islam, and the disregard for territorial boundaries characteristic of pastoralist peoples. It was likewise strikingly illustrated within the Arab world by the readiness of Arab leaders such as Nasser or Qadhafi to appeal beyond the frontiers of their own states to the people of other Arab countries. Arab nationalism in this sense implied the existence of a political community extending across state frontiers, in a way that was not true of African nationalism. At all events, Arab leaders seeking to extend their influence into sub-Saharan Africa were often unconcerned with issues of juridical statehood, and their intervention in continental affairs was correspondingly liable to undermine the bases of African statehood. Not only the Arabs, but also Iran as the most self-consciously Islamic state of all, were correspondingly ready to support insurgent movements against sub-Saharan governments.

Qadhafi in Libya, the Arab leader most often accused of undermining sub-Saharan regimes through military or financial support for opposition groups, combined the financial and military resources available to a 'hydrocarbon prince' with an intense anti-imperialism and a public hostility to the very idea of the state which led to the formal abolition of the Libyan state and its replacement by a 'People's Arab Jamahiriya'.[37] Though some of the accusations brought against him may well have reflected the usefulness of the Libyan bogy in extracting Western aid, especially from the United States, there were plausible indications of Libyan involvement in attempted *coups d'état* in Benin, Niger and Sudan, as well as the amply documented intervention in Chad. Despite Libyan support for regimes regarded as anti-imperialist, including those of Idi Amin in Uganda and Mengistu Haile-Mariam in Ethiopia, the overall impact of Libyan intervention did more to weaken than to uphold the principles of African statehood.

On the other side of the ideological divide, Morocco likewise followed a policy of active intervention in sub-Saharan Africa, to which norms of juridical statehood were only incidental. Whereas Qadhafi's disregard for states sprang from hostility to the state itself, Hassan II's derived from a determination to restore a postulated pre-colonial empire whose territories had in his view been truncated by colonial incursions. This led first to Morocco's role in the Casablanca group, an alliance of otherwise radical states with which Morocco shared only a desire to challenge inherited colonial frontiers, and later to support both for regimes in power (as in Zaïre) and for insurgent movements (as with Unita in Angola). Morocco's refusal to accept the admission of Western Sahara to the OAU – and thus to accept the principle of independence within existing colonial boundaries which underlay the whole idea of African statehood – led to its becoming the only state to withdraw from the organisation altogether.

The other major North African states, Egypt and Algeria, generally played a 'correct' role in continental politics, save for Egypt's support for the Somalis in the Ogaden war of 1977/78. Arab states outside the continent were not constrained by the same need to maintain diplomatic alliances in the OAU, but had little interest in African affairs beyond a general desire to seek African support over the Palestine/Israel conflict, and a particular concern for the Horn. Iraq and Syria were among the first states to aid the Eritrean Liberation Front in the mid-1960s, though the rubric of an 'Arab' and 'Moslem' Eritrea within which they did so was inherently divisive inside Eritrea itself, and led to the eventual defeat of the ELF and its displacement by the Marxist and non-sectarian EPLF. The radicalisation of religion throughout the Moslem world which derived from the Islamic revolution in Iran spread into Africa largely through the Islamist *coup d'état* in Sudan in 1989, and the new government's search for armaments through which to pursue the civil war in southern Sudan. In this sense, the aid provided first by Iraq and subsequently by Iran might be regarded as state-supporting, even though the ideology which underlay it was profoundly anti-statist. The extension of support for Islamist groups into Eritrea, Ethiopia, Somalia and Kenya, together with aid (especially from Saudi Arabia) for established Moslem authorities, formed part of broader processes undermining juridical statehood which are examined in a later chapter.

Conclusion

Relations with their immediate neighbours, and beyond that with other states in the continent and even in the Middle East, thus had a significant impact on the security of African states and regimes. Much of this can be appreciated by contrasting parts of the continent in which regional relationships were broadly consensual and supportive, with ones in which they were largely conflictual. West Africa, at least until the stability not just of Liberia but also of its neighbours was threatened by the increasing brutality of the Doe regime, provided the clearest example of a supportive regional environment, in which external intervention in the affairs of other states was generally slight; even on those occasions when it did occur, moreover, as with Guinean intervention in Liberia and Sierra Leone, and Senegalese intervention in The Gambia, it characteristically took the form of support for incumbent regimes. Even after insurgencies designed to overthrow the Doe regime had been launched both (unsuccessfully) from Sierra Leonean territory and (successfully) from Ivoirian, a sufficient element of consensuality remained both to make possible the ECOMOG intervention (which, regardless of its eventual effect, was at least intended to restore regional stability), and to debate regional action within the forum provided by ECOWAS and the numerous meetings in President Houphouet-Boigny's home town of Yamoussoukro. Elsewhere in the continent, and notably along the two 'front lines' represented by the limits of Arab and Islamic influence in Chad, Sudan and the Horn, and the frontiers of white rule in southern Africa, no such regional consensus was possible, and a greatly intensified level of conflict resulted. Such conflicts almost indiscriminately involved rivalries between states on the one hand, and internal wars on the other. In Chad, Sudan and Ethiopia, as in Angola, Rhodesia/Zimbabwe and Mozambique, the rivalries between neighbouring states with alternative and conflicting concepts of statehood were closely associated with conflicts within the state and the support given to each side by other regional powers.

As these cases indicate, regional relations carried a high potential both for destabilisation and for mutual support. Despite the rhetorical association of the African arena with 'unity', and the north–south one with imperialist intervention, destabilisation in practice operated far more effectively across borders within a regional setting, than it did when the would-be destabilising power was a long way away. Even in cases such as Angola, where the role of the United States in undermining the MPLA regime after independence in 1975 was undeniable, this was only practicable because of the opportunities provided by hostile states (and notably Zaïre and South Africa) on Angola's borders. Equally, regional support for incumbent regimes often required only a modest level of intervention, well within the capabilities of neighbouring states such as Guinea and Senegal in the cases referred to above. With time, however, and notably with the explosion in the availability of armaments explored in the next chapter, and the growing role of insurgent warfare, the possibilities for effective small-scale regional intervention diminished. Cases of extended insurgent warfare, as in Angola and Mozambique, or of state collapse, as in Chad and Liberia, were beyond the stabilising capabilities of regional actors. At best it was possible only to launch operations designed to hold the fort, in the hope that a settlement could be negotiated in the meantime, as with the ECOMOG intervention in Liberia, and the attempts by Zimbabwean and other forces to protect the lines of communication through Mozambique against Renamo attack.

At a continental level, the OAU did at least have some initial effect, in promoting peaceful relationships between African states on the only basis – that of respect for juridical statehood – on which these could plausibly have been achieved. In the process, the OAU also helped to restrict the scope for external intervention in African affairs, at least until the upheavals of the later 1970s which will be discussed in the next chapter. The problem, for which the OAU could scarcely be blamed, was that the unfettered exercise of juridical sovereignty induced levels both of internal conflict and of external involvement which consigned the OAU itself to virtual impotence. Ultimately, regional relationships were subordinate both to the internal dynamics of African states – since it was essential for national governments to maintain reasonably peaceful conditions within their own states if the principles of juridical statehood were to survive – and to the relations between Africa and the major industrial powers, whether superpowers or former colonial metropoles, which had vastly greater economic and military resources at their disposal than were available within the continent. The relationships between internal instability, regional conflict and superpower rivalries, and their disastrous effects especially on southern Africa and the Horn, are therefore examined in the next chapter.

6 The resort to the superpowers

Africa in the superpower world

For the first thirty years or so of their independent existence, until the collapse of the Soviet Union in the early 1990s, African states were incorporated into the bipolar global structure defined by superpower confrontation. While every state in the world, apart from the two superpowers themselves, was consigned by this structure to a position of subordination, the gap in terms of every indicator of international power between the two giants and the new, artificial and impoverished states of sub-Saharan Africa was peculiarly acute: to travel from Moscow to Mogadishu, or from Washington to Ouagadougou, was to be confronted with a level of inequality that verged on the surreal.

Analysis of the Afro-superpower relationship has therefore focused on the superpower rather than the African side of the connection. For one thing, it mattered more: to claim that so large a dog as the United States or the Soviet Union could be wagged by so small a tail as their African 'partners' appeared to stretch plausibility beyond any acceptable limit. In addition, while the two superpowers were intensely concerned with their own policies and those of their global rival, they were not to any comparable degree concerned with the policies of African states which barely figured in the international calculus. American analysts in particular, encouraged but also in some degree seduced by the openness of their own policy-making apparatus to external and even academic influence, tended to concentrate their attention on issues of interest to their foreign policy establishment, and this in turn imposed an emphasis firstly on what the United States should be doing in Africa, and secondly on what the Soviet Union was doing.[1]

One result of this emphasis was that the contours of the Afro-superpower relationship from an African perspective were often neglected, or reduced to the sterile formula of African independence versus superpower imperialism. At the very least, however, bipolarity had a significant impact on the struggle for state maintenance and regime survival in Africa, which would be worth exploring even if the initiative which it left open to African states and leaders were slight. In addition, African leaders were not always as powerless in the face of the superpowers as a crude comparison of relative capabilities would suggest: they often had at least a certain freedom of action, which the bipolar system itself and the support which it tended to give to the principles of juridical sovereignty actually enhanced. Finally, the peculiar interaction of superpower involvement and domestic regime priorities affected not only individual states but also the whole structure of African statehood in ways which were sharply revealed by the collapse of bipolarity, and the stumbling attempts to create some new form of global and continental order.

For all that, any attempt to set out the parameters of the Afro-superpower relationship must start from an appreciation of the *unimportance* of Africa to either the United States or the Soviet Union. The distinguishing feature of the superpowers' view of the world – in contrast notably to the largely economic priorities of the middle level powers – was their emphasis on their strategic contest with one another. This in turn led to a demarcation of the world in essentially spatial terms, in which different regions and territories were characterised firstly according to their overall strategic importance, and secondly according to their actual or potential allegiance to one side or the other in the great game of global domination. In this contest, sub-Saharan Africa barely figured. Africa, as already noted, did not form part of the security perimeter with which each superpower sought to protect itself, while only the Horn fell into the contested zones, most evidently represented by the Middle East and south-east Asia, which formed the 'front line' of superpower confrontation and attracted by far the greater part of their military commitments beyond the central alliances represented by NATO and the Warsaw Pact. Apart from a number of 'strategic' minerals, its economic resources were negligible.

In the second half of the 1970s, superpower interest in Africa rapidly increased, as a result partly of a Soviet challenge to the Western alliance throughout the Third World, following the American collapse in Vietnam, partly of developments in Africa, and notably the Ethiopian revolution and the Portuguese withdrawal. The cover of a book published at that time showed the Soviet Union and United States in eyeball-to-eyeball confrontation across an inert African continent.[2] The level of superpower engagement, especially on the part of the Soviet Union, was indeed appreciably greater at this period than it had been earlier; but the disparity in power between the superpowers on the one hand and African states on the other still meant that a disproportionate effect in Africa could be produced by a fairly modest level of superpower engagement. On no occasion, for example, were either the United States or the Soviet Union prepared to commit their own armed forces to Africa, in the way that they had done in Vietnam and Afghanistan.

Policy towards Africa was generally handled, by both superpowers, at a level several times removed within the governing hierarchy from the top political leadership. In the United States, from the presidency of John F. Kennedy, an Assistant Secretary of State was assigned special responsibility for Africa, a device which on the one hand gave US–African relations a certain profile, but on the other insulated them from the mainstream of US foreign policy. Only on exceptional occasions, such as the Angolan civil war of 1975 or the Ogaden war of 1977, were African affairs brought to the attention of the President, or even the Secretary of State. Concern for Africa outside the executive branch was generally restricted to a small congressional caucus, a few pressure groups involved with race relations and humanitarian issues, and a very few companies with interests in the continent.[3] In the Soviet Union, policy towards Africa generally remained within the control of the foreign ministry, in collaboration with the Africa Institute of the Soviet Academy of Sciences, but with relatively little input from the secretariat of the Communist Party of the Soviet Union which was closely involved in more important areas. Not until the mid-1970s, when the international profile of Africa was suddenly (if temporarily) raised, did either superpower's head of state so much as visit the African continent. Even then, the visits of President Podgorny to Somalia in 1974 and of President Carter to Nigeria in 1978 were largely symbolic, and Podgorny found himself on the losing side within the Soviet policy-making apparatus when the USSR had to choose between Somalia and Ethiopia during the Ogaden crisis of 1977.[4] That crisis, encapsulated in the comment by Carter's National Security adviser Zbigniew Brzezinski that 'SALT lies buried in the sands of the

Ogaden', furnished the sole occasion on which Africa impinged in any significant way on superpower relations.[5]

Much of the relative freedom of action which African states enjoyed within the bipolar order therefore sprang from the fact that they did not matter enough to the superpowers to make it worth their while to expend significant resources on seeking to control them. From the viewpoint of the United States, most African states were closely enough connected to the Western alliance through their association with the former colonial powers to obviate the need for an active American policy – an attitude classically if tactlessly defined at the time of the Nigerian civil war when the Secretary of State, Dean Rusk, was quoted as regarding the crisis as 'primarily a British responsibility'.[6] From that of the Soviet Union, Africa was both distant from its areas of primary concern, and so poorly developed as to make it an unlikely setting for the establishment of genuinely socialist states. Though each superpower sought global allies in its contest with the other, this search was, at least until the mid-1970s, more a matter of collecting support on generalised issues within the context of institutions such as the United Nations, than of looking for specific advantages to be gained from alliance with (or control over) particular states.

This in turn helps to account for the broad support of the superpowers for the principles of juridical statehood upheld by the African states themselves. The superpowers, unlike the Africans, had no inherent commitment to an idea of statehood which served to protect weak states against strong ones. The Soviet Union in particular espoused an ideology which treated states as no more that the expression of the class interests of the groups who ruled them, and which through the idea of 'proletarian internationalism' explicitly legitimated support for socialist opposition movements against the governments of their own states. The self-image of the United States as the protector of the 'free world' against international communism lent itself to a similar readiness to disregard the domestic sovereignty of Third World states. In zones of superpower confrontation, both of them engaged with little compunction in activities designed to destabilise regimes associated with their opponents. In Africa on the other hand, for so long as the OAU consensus on juridical sovereignty held, such activities risked alienating the support of African states as a whole, without offering any appreciable advantages in return. The fragility of African regimes likewise meant that any investment of resources in relations with a particular state was always liable to be wasted if the government of that state was overthrown by a domestic *coup d'état*; the new government would then, as in Ghana after the coup that ousted Nkrumah in 1966, or Ethiopia after Haile-Selassie's overthrow in 1974, be likely to oppose the international allies of the previous regime. Both superpowers tacitly accepted, at least until the mid-1970s, that their interests were best served by doing business with incumbent governments. The means through which they tried to maintain their position in Africa were correspondingly state-supporting, much more than state-subverting, and notably included both economic and – especially from the mid-1970s – military aid, which was channelled through governments.

Attempts to raise the strategic profile of Africa generally came from interests within Africa itself which sought to attract superpower attention and support in pursuit of their local objectives, or else from relatively insignificant interested parties in the superpower. In particular, the *apartheid* establishment in white-ruled South Africa tried to emphasise its importance to the defence of 'Western civilisation' as a means of gaining the support, or at any rate deflecting the opposition, of the United States and its allies. This notably involved an ideological invocation of white South Africa as a bastion against communism, and an attempt to present both access to southern African minerals and the 'Cape route' for oil supplies as central Western strategic interests.[7] Some black African rulers, notably President Mobutu in Zaïre, raised the anti-communist and minerals issues in a rather similar vein. On the other side of the ideological divide within the Western community, academic and other sympathisers with black African nationalism sought to encourage US support as a form of enlightened self-interest, and tried to prevent concern for African welfare from slipping over the threshold of American indifference. The connections between white minority rule and the struggle for racial equality within the United States were helpful in this respect.[8] African commentators likewise tended to exaggerate the importance of the continent to the superpowers.

The relative insignificance of Africa to the superpowers meant that their activities in the continent were in practice fuelled by the agendas of African actors, every bit as much as by their own. This is clearly indicated by patterns of superpower involvement which are distinguished more by the internal characteristics of the African states in which it occurred, than by criteria such as strategic location or economic resources that might have been expected to make those states of any special interest to outside powers. Superpowers did not impose themselves on Africa, nearly as much as they were sucked into it through the search by competing forces within the continent for external resources through which they could pursue their internal rivalries. The Afro-superpower relationship provides a classic example of the politics of extraversion.

The most important criterion in accounting for levels of superpower intervention was consequently the failure of the post-colonial relationship, either because the African state concerned did not have access to a colonial power capable of providing the normal level of protection, or else because it wished to escape from the post-colonial embrace by seeking alternative sources of support. In some cases, and notably the Horn, domestic and superpower interests coincided. On the one hand, Ethiopia, Somalia and Sudan all for one reason or another lacked a normal post-colonial relationship, while on the other hand the Soviet Union and United States both sought allies in the region because of its proximity to the Middle East. Even there, however, external involvement was fuelled largely by a search for support (and especially armaments) on the part of regional combatants, rather than by any superpower search for hegemony.[9] Elsewhere, the most evident cases of post-colonial failure, already explored in a previous chapter, were in the Portuguese colonies and Zaïre, while the French rejection of Guinea led both the Americans and the Russians to try their luck with Sekou Touré.[10] The failure of post-colonialism was also, as already noted, closely associated with political breakdown and conflict, and this in turn increased the demand for armaments, which the superpowers were especially well equipped to provide – with results that are explored later in this chapter.

For African rulers, the superpowers could therefore be regarded very largely as a resource. The threat which the United States and Soviet Union posed to their own security was relatively manageable, even though the USSR in particular presented problems in this respect, whereas the benefits that they had to offer were potentially considerable. The problem that African states faced was how best to manage the relationship in order to maximise their own pay-offs from it. Many of the factors involved, and their connections with domestic politics, have been considered in chapter 3. Central to the analysis presented there was what David has termed the 'omnibalancing' of domestic and external threats and resources.[11] This in turn encompassed the nature of the regime's domestic base and the sources of internal opposition; the pattern of regional relationships and its association with external powers; and the nature and level of the resources which the superpowers were prepared to dedicate to the protection of their clients.

In this context, the option of non-alignment was open only to those rulers with a relatively high level of control over their domestic political systems, and a relatively unthreatening regional environment. Superpowers were jealous partners, and though a strategy of playing off one against the other might help African states to win low value resources such as development projects from either side, they made major commitments only to rulers who were similarly committed to them. Rulers in zones of high insecurity, such as the Horn, did indeed have some choice over which superpower to align with, but not over the possibility of aligning with neither. In calculating their policies, they therefore had to consider the advantages and costs of commitment to one side or the other within their own specific situation.

An example of how such calculations could produce different answers even for similar regimes was provided by the reponses of Angola and Mozambique to the threat posed by South African destabilisation.[12] Both the MPLA regime in Angola and Frelimo in Mozambique shared the Marxist ideology derived from the liberation struggle against Portuguese rule, and from the external alliances which they had formed in order to wage it; Mozambique was the more orthodox Marxist state of the two, and unlike Angola, had even sought to join the CMEA.[13] Both faced South African-backed insurgencies – Unita in Angola, Renamo in Mozambique – which posed a major threat to political stability and even regime survival. The MPLA responded to this threat by calling on Soviet and Cuban military aid, with which to present a direct riposte to South Africa and indeed the United States, which also backed Unita. Mozambique pursued the much weaker or more conciliatory policy of seeking association with Western states, which in turn it used in an attempt to bring pressure on South Africa to end support for Renamo. Part of the reason for this difference lay in strategic location. Angola was separated from South Africa by Namibia which, even though Namibia was at that time under South African control, gave it a defensible space; its capital, Luanda, was towards the north of its territory, and its principal foreign exchange earner, the Cabinda oilfield, was further north still. Mozambique, by contrast, directly adjoined South Africa, and its capital Maputo, at the extreme south of the territory, was just across the South African frontier and open to attack. Another major difference was economic strength. Angola was well supplied with natural resources, notably oil and diamonds, which it could use to maintain its economic independence and pay for Soviet and Cuban military support. Mozambique, desperately poor, relied for a very high proportion of its gross national income on aid which could come only from the West, and could not afford to alienate its donors by too close an association with the Soviet bloc. The calculations which induced governments in the Horn of Africa, notably Ethiopia and Sudan, to seek alignment with either the Soviet Union or the United States have been considered in chapter 3.[14]

There were none the less significant differences in the roles of the two superpowers in Africa, and in the resources which African states could seek from them. As a result both of its dominant position in the global power structure, and of its close relations with the former colonial powers, the interests of the United States lay broadly in support of the status quo. This brought with it both advantages and disadvantages. On the one hand, though American incursions into the *pré carré* were a source of French suspicion, the United States enjoyed relatively unfettered access to most of the continent, and could pursue its generally low profile interests with little opposition either from African regimes or from the former colonial powers. Only where it was pushed into a salient position by the absence of a post-colonial framework, notably in Ethiopia in the later years of the Haile-Selassie regime, did it find itself incurring local hostility through its support for unpopular governments, in the way that frequently affected its role in the Middle East, south-east Asia, and Latin America. Few major American companies had extensive interests in Africa, and these did not attain the political prominence of US corporations in Latin America; in Angola, Gulf Oil was widely recognised for its tacit support for the MPLA government, despite US government aid to the Unita opposition. Even in South Africa, the United States did not attract the same level of international opprobrium as the United Kingdom for the role of Western companies in upholding *apartheid*; US companies were generally quicker than British ones to take protective action, initially through adherence to principles such as the Sullivan Code for treatment of African employees, and subsequently through disinvestment. The Comprehensive Anti-Apartheid Act of 1986, passed over President Reagan's veto, went substantially further than comparable British measures.[15]

Enjoying the advantages of the status quo, the United States was, however, correspondingly unable to challenge it, or consequently to provide an effective alternative to incumbent ex-colonial powers. This was most strikingly illustrated by American ineffectiveness in the face of the determination of a minor ally, Portugal, to cling to its African possessions by force. Despite an undoubted American preference for decolonisation, the United States was rendered virtually impotent by its fears for its vital base on Portuguese territory in the Azores should Portugal withdraw from NATO; and even though the NATO operational area did not extend into tropical Africa, the United States was unable to prevent Portugal from using weapons supplied for NATO purposes in its African wars. In Angola, it pursued the twin-track strategy of maintaining relations with Portugal on the one hand, while covertly supporting the FNLA (as the most pro-Western and anti-communist liberation movement) on the other; both tracks ran into the buffers when Portugal was obliged to withdraw, and the FNLA was decisively defeated in the subsequent civil war.

The Soviet role

The Soviet Union possessed neither the advantages nor the disadvantages of the United States in Africa. It had no commitment to the global status quo, and had consistently opposed colonialism in Africa and elsewhere. It had no economic interests in the continent to defend, and could attack Western capitalism with impunity. At the same time, it was regarded with deep suspicion, not only by the United States and the former colonial powers, but by many African regimes which viewed it as a potential source of subversion. The lack of any contact with the continent during the pre-independence period (save for an embassy in Ethiopia which dated from czarist times) gave it a certain freedom of action on the one hand, but denied it potential sources of leverage on the other. The Afro-Soviet relationship thus constituted an attempt on the part both of the Soviet Union and of its African allies to reorient the continent's international relations away from the linkages established under colonialism, which illuminates not only a particular episode in a global epoch that ended in 1990, but also more deep-seated features of Africa's position in the international system.[16]

For a start, the Soviet role in Africa depended almost entirely on African initiatives. Facing a continent sealed off from it by colonialism, the USSR could gain a foothold in Africa only through the willingness of its African partners to provide one. This in itself imposed on the Soviet Union a respect for the norms of juridical statehood upheld by

African states, except insofar as these were prepared to collaborate with it in the covert destabilisation of their neighbours. It also meant that the Soviet presence, superpower though it was, was always inherently precarious: a change of regime, or even a reversal of policy by the existing regime, could lead to its immediate expulsion even from states – such as Ghana in 1966 or Somalia in 1977 – in which it had established a considerable presence over several years. The need to stabilise its position was thus a perennial Soviet preoccupation.

The Soviet Union none the less had appreciable resources with which to attract the interest of African partners. The first was simple anti-Westernism: it provided a counterweight which African states could use in order to reduce their dependence on historically dominant powers. One of the clearest examples of this was the signing of a military aid and training agreement between the USSR and the newly independent Somali Republic in 1963, which established a Soviet military presence in the Horn. Since the Somali government was committed to bringing all ethnic Somalis within the boundaries of an enlarged Somali state, its 'idea of the state' threatened not only all of its immediate neighbours – Ethiopia, Kenya and the then French colony of Djibouti – but also the Western powers which protected them, respectively the United States, the United Kingdom and France. None of these was willing to provide any military assistance that might endanger their own clients, and the Soviet Union made a useful ally simply because it had no clients of its own. In much the same way, the Federal Government in Nigeria could look to the Russians for weapons in its war against the Biafran secession which the British and other Western states were unwilling to provide.

Second and more positively, the Soviet Union could serve as an active partner in the struggle for 'liberation', which always effectively amounted to liberation from established Western interests. This was clearest, as already noted, in the unalloyed support which the Russians could give to movements fighting against colonialism or white minority rule. In South Africa, it was closely associated with the banned South African Communist Party, which in turn was intimately linked with the ANC; this connection helped to guide Soviet relations with other regional liberation movements.[17] It was also helpful for radical regimes in already independent states, which wanted to reduce their dependence on the West. Even as simple a step as the establishment of a Soviet embassy could be used as a warning to Western states not to trespass on the sovereignty of the African state concerned. Though the

Sino-Soviet dispute impinged on Africa in the later 1960s and 1970s, and to some extent gave radical African states and liberation movements an alternative to the Soviet alliance, the Soviet Union maintained a more active presence on the continent, and was much more reliable especially as a source of arms. China was sometimes a useful source of aid, especially for large public works projects such as roads and stadiums, and after the Rhodesian unilateral declaration of independence in 1965 it took on the high profile project of building the TanZam railway from Dar-es-Salaam to free Zambia from dependence on rail networks through white-ruled territory. On the whole, though, African states and liberation movements turned to a Chinese alliance only when the Soviet option was closed because of existing ties between the USSR and a local rival; and after the death of Mao Zedong in 1976, Chinese interest in Africa declined.[18]

Third, the USSR was the global standard-bearer of an ideology which was particularly attractive to African leaders, not merely because it provided an alternative to the dominant mode represented by the capitalist Western states, but because it appealed to the state-centred interests of these leaders themselves. Few African states adopted either the centrally planned economic system or the Leninist vanguard party structure that characterised Soviet Marxism–Leninism.[19] Even an approximation to a Soviet-style economy required a level of control over resources (including notably the labour force and external trade) which were well beyond the capabilities of all African states, and a level of administrative capacity which was beyond the great majority of them. The selectivity, training and hierarchical structure expected of a Leninist party were likewise far removed from the inclusive and ill-organised single parties characteristic of sub-Saharan Africa. Soviet diplomats and academics had few illusions about the efforts even of ostensibly Marxist–Leninist regimes in Africa to aspire to Soviet-style socialism.[20] In a popularised form, none the less, 'socialism' appeared to offer a formula by which state control of the economy could achieve rapid economic growth, while actually providing the means through which leaders could increase their access to the resources required for patronage and state maintenance. The single party, which from a Western liberal perspective appeared to be merely a device for concentrating power and suppressing opposition, could be treated within the framework of Leninist rhetoric as a means for expressing popular aspirations and building national unity; at a rather more sophisticated level, of which few

African leaders availed themselves, the Stalinist doctrine of nationalities could be adopted as a means for reconciling strong and centralised government with the ethnic diversity bequeathed to African states by their colonial origins.[21]

Fourth, the Soviet Union was useful as a supplier of those resources which its own domestic political economy caused it to overproduce. By far the most important of these, armaments, is considered in the next section. Soviet aid as a whole was strongly oriented towards the maintenance of the centralised state, and thus generally coincided with the interests of African rulers. It included security services, a field in which the East Germans developed a particular expertise.[22] Although the Soviet Union did not itself provide troops to fight in Africa, it provided the logistical back-up that enabled its Cuban allies to do so. The role of the Cubans in Africa, at one time a topic arousing considerable controversy, can be briefly summarised. The Castro regime was prepared to commit a remarkably high level of military resources to aiding what it regarded as revolutionary governments in Africa, notably in Angola and Ethiopia. These resources went well beyond what it could have been expected to provide as a mere agent or surrogate of the Soviet Union, and gave Cuba a certain autonomy in dealing with African governments which enabled it, for instance, to exercise its own initiative over the Alves attempted coup in Angola noted below. At the same time, Cuba was logistically incapable of deploying troops in Africa without Soviet support, and its first allegiance was to the USSR; when, for example, Ethiopia aligned itself with the Soviet Union, Cuba abandoned its previous support for the EPLF in Eritrea.[23] North Korea, which also acted to some degree in association with the Soviet Union, was rather more independent. Its most significant single involvement in Africa was in training the Fifth Brigade of the Zimbabwe army, which was used by President Mugabe in the mid-1980s for the brutal suppression of dissent in Matabeleland, the base area of ZAPU which, during the liberation war, had been backed by the USSR.[24]

In all these respects, the Soviet Union and its associates made potentially attractive allies for those African states which sought an alternative to the Western connection. Its support, once achieved, was moreover relatively consistent; rather than trying to extend its influence over the whole continent, and burdening itself with the conflicts of loyalty that this would involve, it tended to concentrate its efforts on a small number of countries, and on particular groups and leaders within them. In supporting liberation in territories under minority rule, for example, the Soviet Union normally selected a single movement with which it sought to establish a close alliance, such as MPLA in Angola and ZAPU in Zimbabwe, rather than seeking the kind of artificial unity between competing movements which both the OAU and Western states normally tried to achieve. Only in Somalia in 1977, in the special circumstances created by the Ethiopian revolution (which provided it with a much more attractive potential partner) and its failure to reconcile the diametrically opposed interests of the Ethiopians and Somalis, did the Soviet Union unilaterally abandon a longstanding alliance.

In other ways, however, it suffered from crippling defects. One of these simply reflected the mutual lack of familiarity between Russians on the one hand, and Africans on the other, and the difficulty which each side had in adapting itself to structures and attitudes which had little in common with one another. Sheer ignorance was an initial obstacle, classically illustrated by the case of the Soviet snow ploughs delivered in the course of re-equipping the airport at Conakry in Guinea.[25] The education which the Soviet Union provided for large numbers of African students was invariably regarded in Africa as inferior to Western education – sometimes justifiably, but also very often for reasons of pure snobbery, or because Soviet qualifications (in medicine or engineering, for example) were designed to fit into a structure very different from the Western colonial systems prevailing in the African state. Many African students, too, found the racism of Soviet society even worse than that prevailing in the West. Language and custom, and the extraordinary formalism and rigidity of the Soviet system, created further difficulties. In a host of ways, the Soviet Union was unable to displace the linkages established with African states by the colonial powers which had, after all, formed those states themselves.

Further problems arose from the ineradicable tendency of the Soviet Union to interfere in the domestic affairs of African states, in ways which African rulers regarded as infringing on their own sovereignty. Most basically, this was a tension inherent in any clientelist relationship: African rulers, occupying a middleman role between the Soviet giant on the one hand and their own societies on the other, needed to maintain their bargaining strength by monopolising the interactions between the two levels; the Soviet patron, on the other hand, could improve its own bargaining position by undermining the middleman and dealing directly with different elements within the client state. It was, however, exacerbated both by the carryover into the African setting of attitudes inherited from the experience of the USSR and Eastern Europe, and by the understandable anxiety of the Soviet government to build some insurance against the precariousness of its position.

Soviet officials coming to Africa had been trained within a system in which the idea of a boundary between legitimate diplomatic activity and unwarranted interference in the internal affairs of another state carried very little meaning. Officials drawn from the secretariat of the Communist Party of the Soviet Union, which controlled Soviet relations with the closest African clients, had frequently no diplomatic experience at all, but had been engaged in managing relations between Moscow and the Union Republics within the USSR;[26] Russian apparatchiks used to dealing with Tadjiks or Azerbaijanis within the monolithic Soviet state could well have trouble adapting to the sensibilities of Angolans or Ethiopians. Even those with experience of Eastern Europe were used to a system which was in the last resort held in place by Soviet military power. The special status of the Soviet Union as the world's senior socialist state was deeply entrenched in the attitudes of many Russians serving in Africa, and was reflected in unselfconsciously Orwellian references to the USSR as the 'elder brother' of African socialist states.

Coupled with this was a need for the Soviet Union to protect its investments in African alliances by seeking to put them on the basis, not of personal deals with individual leaders which could be revoked at will – either by the overthrow of the leader concerned, or by a change of policy – but rather of long-term relationships which could be expected to survive changes in personnel. The problem here was that the mechanisms pursued by the Soviet Union in order to increase its own security were simultaneously threatening to the security of the African leaders with whom they had to deal, and thus generally self-defeating. From the mid-1970s onwards, when the Ethiopian revolution and the independence of the former Portuguese colonies led to the emergence of a small number of African regimes with a strongly expressed commitment to Marxism–Leninism, the USSR sought to build up multifaceted alliances with these states, which were cumbersomely designated in Soviet jargon as 'states of socialist orientation'.[27] The formal expression of this alliance was a treaty of friendship and co-operation with the Soviet Union which, although formally phrased in very general terms, none the less marked a sharp change in the way in which the state concerned was treated within the Soviet system; notably, responsibility for relations was transferred from the foreign ministry to the CPSU central committee secretariat. Such states, if they did not have one already, were expected to establish a Leninist vanguard party, and to organise their structures of political and economic management in conformity with the Soviet model. This would permit party-to-party relations, which in turn would open the African state to penetration by the USSR and its Eastern European allies.

The Soviet Union's capacity to build such multifaceted linkages with its African allies was, however, sharply restricted, in part by the determination of African leaders to maintain control over their own domestic politics, in part by the alienness of the whole Soviet system and the frequent arrogance of its local representatives. In practice, then, the USSR found itself limited to clientelist relations with particular individuals who – whether from genuine ideological commitment or from political calculation – sought to associate themselves with the Soviet alliance. Soviet diplomats then found themselves involved in counter-productive attempts to promote the fortunes of their local clients, which sometimes – as in Sudan in 1971 and Angola in 1977 – extended to apparent complicity in attempted *coups d'état*.[28] The Cubans, who in other respects played an important part in maintaining Soviet alliances in Africa, had their own experience of Soviet penetration, and tended to side with the African national leadership.

Finally, the Soviet Union was entirely incapable of displacing the economic linkages between African states and their Western markets and suppliers. The economies of the USSR and its CMEA associates rarely produced the goods which their African partners required, and when they did so the products concerned – such as tractors or trucks – were generally of poor quality and ill-suited to African conditions. Nor did they have markets for the cash crops which most African states exported; and even though there was some speculation in the later 1970s that the Eastern European economies in particular might benefit from shifting their sources of mineral imports from the USSR to Africa, and a considerable number of exploratory ventures were undertaken, these did not in the end result in any major CMEA investments or trade flows.[29] On top of that, trade relations with CMEA states had to be negotiated through an extraordinarily cumbersome system of bilateral negotiations, which were generally characterised by hard bargaining on the CMEA side, and a resulting sense on the part of the African negotiators that – far from benefiting from trade with their socialist allies – they were actually being exploited because of their dependence on Soviet support.[30]

One African state, Samora Machel's Mozambique, formally applied in the summer of 1980 for membership of the CMEA, but was refused admission. Full membership would have required the existing CMEA members, and notably the Eastern Europeans, to accord to Mozambique the level of aid required to help it attain the level of development reached by the existing members; and with its resources already badly stretched by the need to aid Cuba and Vietnam, whose membership had been forced on the CMEA by their strategic importance to the Soviet Union, there was no prospect of accepting a state which commonly figured as the poorest in the world. Mozambique's subsequent reluctant adherence to the Lomé Conventions with the European Community graphically demonstrated that Western Europe could help Africa while Eastern Europe could not.[31] Rather than full membership, African states of socialist orientation were accorded only 'observer status' with the CMEA, which in practice amounted to nothing. Their economic relations with the Soviet bloc were restricted to barter deals in which each side sought to dispose of prospective exports for which it could find no hard currency market; the exchange of Ethiopian skins for Bulgarian jam was never going to provide the basis for a viable economic relationship.[32]

So far from seeking to incorporate its African allies into a Soviet-dominated economic bloc, the USSR became increasingly concerned to use them as a source of hard currency, with which it could in turn buy food and technology from the Western industrial states. It therefore sought to encourage client states to engage in export-oriented cash-crop agriculture and mineral production, destined for hard currency markets in North America, Western Europe and the Middle East, with which they could generate the revenue required to pay the Soviet Union for the weapons which supplied by far the greatest quantity of Soviet exports to Africa.[33]

In practice, therefore, Soviet relations with Africa became increasingly dependent on the single commodity – armaments – which African leaders often desperately needed, and as a supplier of which the USSR was not merely the equal but greatly the superior of its Western rivals. The resulting militarisation of Africa's external relations, by other suppliers as well as by the USSR, marked a critical phase in the decay of African states which is discussed in the next section. It effectively left the Soviet Union, however, with an open-ended commitment to leftist African regimes with an urgent need for weapons. These in turn were necessarily engaged in intractable civil wars, and their potential for economic development and thus for any long-term stability from which the USSR might eventually benefit was correspondingly slight. Instead, the Russians were left propping up the political superstructures of regimes whose economic base was rapidly decaying – an irony which the Marxists among them must have appreciated.

More broadly, the failure of the Afro-Soviet relationship, which was evident long before the final collapse of the USSR itself, indicated the extreme difficulty faced by African leaders in seeking to break out of the pattern of external dependence established by colonialism, and the integration of African economies into the Western capitalist structure of international trade. Specific regimes or movements might for specific reasons – a determination to escape from Western control, a commitment to Marxism–Leninism, or a search for arms – establish relations with the Soviet bloc which for a period gave the impression that they were definitively aligned with the socialist camp in the bipolar global contest. This impression was misleading. As soon as the reason for the Soviet commitment faded or disappeared, these states would revert, often virtually overnight, to the relationship with the West that had been created by history, language, culture and economic need.

The militarisation of Africa's external relations

The rapid if short-lived expansion of Soviet involvement in Africa from the mid-1970s certainly reflected, on the Soviet side, the boost in confidence, and the greatly increased willingness to engage in 'adventurist' policies in the Third World, which followed from the collapse of American-supported regimes in South Vietnam and Cambodia, and which was reflected across other areas of the globe from Nicaragua to Afghanistan. This was a period, in the Soviet terminology of the time, when 'the world constellation of forces' was favourable to the advance of socialism. On the African side, however, it also reflected a breakdown in a significant number of African states of the incumbent regime's capacity to control its territory and maintain itself in power with a minimal actual use of force. The wars in southern Sudan and

Eritrea apart, the only major armed conflict to afflict independent African states in the decade and a half after 1960 had been the Nigerian civil war which, however, had been decisively resolved with the victory of the federal forces in January 1970. Even the Sudanese civil war had ended, temporarily as it transpired, with the Addis Ababa peace agreement of 1972; while the war in Eritrea, though still rumbling on, did not by 1974 appear to present any major threat to the maintenance of Ethiopia's national unity or the survival of its government.

From about 1975 onwards, however, state security in much of Africa rapidly deteriorated. For this change, both internal and external factors were responsible. Probably the most important single precipitant was the refusal of one minor European colonial power, Portugal, to disengage from empire in Africa, and the consequent resort of nationalist movements to insurgent warfare in the three continental Portuguese colonies of Angola, Mozambique and Guinea-Bissau; insurgency was impracticable in the island colonies of Cape Verde and São Tomé and Principe. The need to resort to arms in order to achieve independence pushed the nationalist movements into external alliances which, given the reluctance of Western powers to support insurgencies against one of their NATO allies, necessarily involved an appeal to one or other of the socialist states. In the small and isolated West African colony of Guinea-Bissau, the effects of militarised nationalism could be contained, despite a retaliatory Portuguese attack on Guinea in November 1968. In the much larger southern African colonies, such containment was rendered impossible by the greater scale of insurgent operations, the involvement of neighbouring white-ruled states which regarded continued Portuguese rule as a buffer against African nationalist activities in their own territories, and crucially in Angola the division of the nationalist opposition into three different movements which fought against one another and appealed to rival sources of external support. The Portuguese withdrawal in 1975, following a military coup in Portugal in 1974 which was induced by the African wars, did not therefore lead to a return to peace, but instead prompted further violence, induced partly by the civil war in Angola, partly by the intensified assault on the remaining redoubts of white control and consequent retaliatory measures by the white regimes, and in part simply by the proliferation of weapons and of people whose main resource was the ability to use them.

A second precipitant, the Ethiopian revolution of 1974, was only marginally the result of external factors, and followed almost entirely from the domestic decay of the imperial regime, and its eventual overthrow by a radical military government bent on a revolutionary transformation of Ethiopian society. Ethiopia had a long indigenous tradition of insurgent warfare which was reflected in the readiness of some conservative leaders to contest the revolution from the hills. More important, the accession to power in early 1977 of a military Jacobin regime, bent on achieving national unity through ruthless centralisation, prevented any peaceful resolution of the conflict in Eritrea, and helped to lead to the eventual displacement of the relatively ineffectual and Moslem-dominated Eritrean Liberation Front (ELF) by the Marxist and vastly better organised Eritrean People's Liberation Front (EPLF). At the same time, the regime's ruthless campaign of terror against its rivals within the urban revolutionary elite led the survivors to resort to guerrilla warfare and start the insurgencies which, in alliance with the EPLF, were to overthrow it in 1991.

The Ethiopian conflict was in turn internationalised, initially through the greatly increased supply of arms in the mid-1970s by the Soviet Union to its regional client, the Somali Republic, which in mid-1977 used them to invade Ethiopia, in the hope of realising its claims on the Somali-inhabited areas of south-east Ethiopia at a time when the Ethiopian government was incapacitated by domestic upheavals. When the Ethiopian regime was then able to persuade the USSR to change sides – on the strength of its greater size, more strategic location, and superior claims to Marxist–Leninist commitment – this in turn led to an influx of Soviet armaments that dwarfed any previous supplies to the region.[34] After the Ethiopian victory over the Somalis in March 1978, the Mengistu government was still unable to crush the EPLF and TPLF insurgencies in the north of the country, and this created a continued dependence on fresh supplies of Soviet arms. Both the EPLF and other insurgent movements were able to take advantage of Ethiopia's long western frontier with Sudan for refuge and logistical support; and once the Sudanese peace agreement had broken down in 1983, the Addis Ababa regime was able to retaliate by supporting the Sudan People's Liberation Army (SPLA), which then emerged as the main source of resistance to the Khartoum government in southern Sudan.

A further source of conflict was what can only be described as sheer bad government in a number of African states, and the resistance which this eventually prompted. The return to war in Sudan resulted from the central government's encroachment on the autonomy promised to the south under the Addis Ababa agreement of 1972, exacerbated by the conversion of the military ruler, General Nimairi, to militant Islam.[35] Sudan's western neighbour, Chad, had since the 1960s suffered from insurgencies which were initially induced by the repression of the north of the country by a government based in the south, and which subsequently fragmented into a mass of different factions, some of which were then armed and supported by Libya. Its southern neighbour, Uganda, came in the 1970s under the brutal regime of Idi Amin, one of a trio of African dictators – the others being Jean-Bedel Bokassa of the Central African Republic and Macias Nguema of Equatorial Guinea – who were overthrown in 1979. On Uganda's western frontier, the corrupt regime of President Mobutu in Zaïre was in 1977 and 1978 the target of invasions by Zaïrean dissidents based in Angola, thus completing a continuous chain of states with serious problems of internal order, stretching from the Red Sea and the Gulf of Aden to the South Atlantic Ocean. Though the collapse of Liberia as a result of the depredations of the Doe regime was not to occur until the early 1990s, in both Liberia and Sierra Leone in the late 1970s the incumbent governments of Presidents William Tolbert and Siaka Stevens were obliged to call on Guinean military intervention in order to keep themselves in power.[36]

This rapid escalation in political disorder in the later 1970s, coupled with the decline in African economies which became evident at much the same time, challenged the assumption that monopoly statehood could be maintained largely with the domestic resources available to African rulers. Their almost automatic reaction was to call on aid from the international system, in order to make good the deficiencies in their domestic political power. This was, in a sense, the ultimate recourse of juridical statehood, and it was reflected in a dramatic increase in external arms flows to Africa from the mid-1970s onwards. From some $150m (at constant 1985 US$ prices) in the late 1960s, the annual average value of major weapons imports into sub-Saharan Africa rose to $370m in 1970–3 and $820m in 1974–6, before peaking at nearly $2,500m in 1977–8, the years of the rearming of Ethiopia by the USSR during the Ogaden war. For the period 1980–7, annual weapons imports remained fairly constant at some $1,575m at 1985 prices, but then collapsed with the end of the Cold War to $350m in 1989–93; the 1993 figure was the lowest since the mid-1960s.[37] The majority of the weapons during the arms boom of the later 1970s and 1980s came from the Soviet Union, which as an arms supplier was in every respect – quantity, quality, delivery and price – enormously superior to any of its Western rivals.[38] Quantitatively, Soviet arms were mass produced for supply to the labour intensive armies of the Warsaw Pact and its allies, whereas Western ones were generally produced to order; the Soviet disinclination to scrap outdated weapons when these were replaced by new products meant that large stocks of previous generations of weaponry were available for supply to African and other Third World armies at negligible opportunity cost. Though Western weapons were generally much more sophisticated than Soviet ones, this in turn tended to restrict their use to the highly trained armies of industrial states, and called for expert and time-consuming maintenance and a large stock of spare parts; Soviet weapons, in contrast, were designed for use by poorly educated armies, generally required less maintenance, and were more robust in use. They were also, for the most part, better suited to the kinds of warfare in which African armies were engaged. In delivery terms, any but the most basic Western weapons had to be produced to order, and this often imposed long delays: the F5–E fighter aircraft ordered from the United States by the imperial government in Ethiopia in 1973 were not actually delivered until July 1976, by which time the emperor had been overthrown by the revolutionary military regime which was then on the point of concluding an alliance with the Soviet Union. No sooner had this change of alliance taken place, at the height of the 1977 Somali invasion of the Ogaden, than the USSR was able to supply Mengistu Haile-Mariam's government, within a few months, with all the material – from assault rifles to tanks and aircraft – required to re-equip an army of 300,000 men.[39] And while Western arms supplies required payment at market prices to the mostly private companies which produced them, Soviet arms exports, though valuable to the USSR as a source of foreign exchange, were provided by the state on terms which reflected the balance in any particular case between its strategic and financial interests. Though Angola as a major oil exporter could be required to pay for its massive imports of Soviet weaponry at something approaching market prices, there was no conceivable way in which either Somalia or Ethiopia, two of the poorest countries in the world, could have been expected to pay for the Soviet arms which flowed into them, before and after mid-1977 respectively.

The Western powers none the less responded in kind, thus providing anti-communist African leaders (or more precisely, those who could claim that they were threatened by communist states or insurgents) with an ideal opportunity to profit from their patronage. The Mobutu regime was probably the major beneficiary, since Zaïre's vast and strategically located territory and its mineral wealth, coupled with Mobutu's extremely bad relations with the neighbouring and Soviet-supported MPLA regime in Angola, made it the most sensitively placed 'domino' in any scenario which envisaged the progressive takeover of central Africa by the USSR and its Cuban allies. The geostrategic concern for mineral resources which dominated Western security policies in the immediate aftermath of the OPEC oil price increases of the mid-1970s encouraged leaders such as President Giscard d'Estaing of France to view Africa as the natural security hinterland of Western Europe, and to devote considerable resources to its protection.[40] The sheer ineptitude of the Zaïrean armed forces meant that direct military intervention was required both in 1977 and 1978 to rescue the Mobutu regime from collapse. The takeover of Chad (a state virtually worthless in itself, but with an impressively large surface area and frontiers with more important states such as Sudan and Cameroon) by a local warlord allied with Colonel Qadhafi prompted support for a rival warlord from both the United States and France, while the United States also sought to prevent the Soviet Union from expanding from its Ethiopian base by providing military assistance not only to Sudan, which in the late 1970s and early 1980s was still aligned with the West, but also to Somalia which until 1977 had been one of the USSR's closest clients in the continent.[41] Even in Liberia, the increasingly autocratic regime of Master Sergeant Samuel Doe received a level of US military and financial aid which had never been made available to his predecessor, President Tolbert.[42]

This flood of weaponry meant that from the mid-1970s those African states which faced any serious threat to their security were vastly better armed than they had previously been. Even though the insurgent movements which threatened them were also better armed, and though some of the weapons which flowed into the continent were destined for these, by far the greater part of the imports from the world's major arms producers went to strengthen the militaries of the governments of juridically constituted states. Paradoxically, however, the ultimate effect of this massive import of armaments was not to strengthen the states which received them, but to weaken and, in some cases, eventually to destroy them. A rollcall of Africa's major arms recipients – Angola, Chad, Ethiopia, Liberia, Mozambique, Somalia, Sudan, Zaïre – also provides a list of its failed and collapsed states.

This paradox cannot be explained simply on the ground that these recipients were in any event those states with the most intractable problems of national integration, though with some of them – Angola, Ethiopia and Sudan, for example – that could well be the case. Somalia, by contrast, enjoyed a level of cultural homogeneity shared by few if any other African states, and before Siyad Barre's seizure of power in 1969 had operated a democratic system of government which, however chaotic, authentically mirrored the society in which it was set.[43] The True Whig Party of Liberia had before Doe's *coup d'état* in 1980 been the longest continuously governing political party in the history of the world, and without being able to make any plausible claim to democracy, it had none the less developed political mechanisms which were capable of handling the affairs of a society with a small population and a relatively high level of resources.[44] Political failure derived from bad political management, not merely from the inherent difficulty of the problems that the government had to face.

Part of the explanation was that an apparently inexhaustible supply of arms and aid from an all-powerful external patron encouraged rulers to suppose that their own hegemonic ambitions were ultimately unstoppable, and that they could therefore proceed with the establishment of a monopoly state which need take no account of internal opposition or the indigenous characteristics of the societies which they governed. Such an attitude was all too evident in the rule of Mengistu Haile-Mariam in Ethiopia, where every set-back in the struggle to create a disciplined and centralised socialist state prompted a still more determined effort to impose central control. In fact, the control capacity of virtually all African states was weak – Ethiopia under Mengistu's government was indeed one of the strongest of them – and the attempt to impose by force a level of autocratic control which they were ultimately incapable of sustaining merely led to the eventual emergence in all the states noted above of insurgent opposition movements.

A second and related problem was then that armaments did not in themselves endow a government with power. The actual level of control which they conferred depended firstly on the ability of the military to make effective use of them, but secondly and more importantly on the mechanisms of *social* control available to the government to secure the loyalty of the people who handled them. This problem was particularly evident in the collapse of the Somali regime of Siyad Barre. Siyad sought to manage dissent by manipulating the hostilities between different Somali clans, and arming 'loyal' clans in order to control the clans which were opposed to him. As the resources available to the central government declined, and its authority weakened, previously 'loyal' clans gained an incentive to cross over to the opposition, and the whole exercise had to be repeated, but from a weaker starting point than before. In the process, numerous clan armies were established which only hastened the collapse of the country into the fiefdoms of competing warlords.[45] In Liberia, Doe's attempt to retain power by packing the army with members of his own Krahn group worked only for as long as no organised military force could be mustered in opposition to it. The moment such a force appeared, even in the relatively feeble form represented by Charles Taylor's National Patriotic Front of Liberia (NPFL), much of the rural population rallied to it, and the Krahn represented too small an ethnic base to enable Doe to retain power. In Ethiopia, an initially disciplined and effective army was ground down over fifteen years of ceaseless warfare, until eventually it depended on reluctant conscripts who could see no further point in fighting. Ultimately, it was not the imported armaments which conferred power on the government, but the indigenous people who had to use them. When they failed, it failed.

In the event, then, the attempt to shore up African states by seeking the aid of the superpowers proved to be entirely counter-productive. The lesson apparently conveyed by the Nigerian civil war of 1967–70, that the existing structure of statehood could be sustained by ensuring that the central government received preferential access to external arms supplies, no longer applied once opposition movements resorted to guerrilla warfare and were able to gain the acquiescence and often the active support of the rural population. African states were generally incapable of surmounting the organisational challenges which the defeat of such guerrilla movements required, and the attempt to compensate for their weakness by importing armaments which they then often could not control only compounded the problem. Ultimately, in those parts of the continent which were most affected by insurgent warfare, and notably the Horn and parts of southern Africa, the supply of weapons became too complex to control. They passed from one group to another – by purchase, capture or exchange – and the distinction between organised forces committed to some political goal and simple robber bands became impossibly blurred.

Africa in the post-Cold War world

Even before Gorbachev came to power in 1985, Soviet policy-makers were aware that the costs of engagement in Africa were too high, not only in financial terms but equally because the Soviet Union's commitments in Africa stood in the way of the improvement of relations with the West in areas that were of vastly greater consequence.[46] Since American interest in supporting client regimes in Africa was also receding, it was already evident before the end of the Cold War that the superpowers were not prepared to devote the level of resources to the continent that the maintenance of African monopoly states required. The end of the Cold War in 1989, and the subsequent disappearance of the Soviet Union, then definitively removed the global conditions which had encouraged the massive oversupply of armaments to Africa, and – since African states rarely had the financial resources to buy weapons in the market-led arms trade that followed – the import of arms to Africa instantly dropped. Only a few states, notably Sudan, were able to continue importing weapons which they could not afford by turning instead to Middle Eastern patrons, and substituting the ideology of political Islam for that of Marxism–Leninism or anti-communism.[47] At the same time, the previous emphasis of the major actors in the international system on the maintenance of existing states and boundaries likewise disappeared, with the fragmentation of the Soviet Union into fifteen different states. If such a fate could befall a superpower, then African states could have little hope of getting much external assistance to maintain their own integrity. The EPLF in Eritrea, having finally captured the capital city of Asmara at the same time that their allies to the south swept the Mengistu regime from power in Addis Ababa, found no opposition outside the continent (despite considerable misgivings within it) to their accession to independent statehood.[48] The declaration of independence by the former British Somaliland, seceding from the defunct Somali Republic, went virtually unnoticed.

Both in the Horn and in southern Africa, the end of the Cold War either helped to resolve conflicts, or at any rate provided a political environment within which domestic actors could resolve them without needing to fear that disappointed combatants would be able to appeal for superpower support. The most explicit superpower contribution to conflict resolution was the Angola/Namibia accords of December 1988, brokered by the United States with the active support of the Soviet Union.[49] These opened the way to Namibian independence in March 1990, and laid the basis for the Angolan settlement which was subsequently aborted by Unita's refusal to accept the results of the 1992 elections.[50] In South Africa as in Ethiopia, the end of the Cold War may have helped to end conflicts which were basically both caused and resolved at the domestic level.

Despite these favourable outcomes, and equally despite the level of suffering induced by Africa's incorporation into the 'Second Cold War' from 1975 onwards, the end of bipolarity was overwhelmingly greeted by African rulers with regret.[51] The opportunities which it had given them to impose the project of monopoly statehood were abruptly removed, and African states were exposed instead to the monopoly diplomacy of a triumphant Western alliance. United States troops, unseen in Africa throughout the Cold War, arrived in Somalia as part of a postulated new world order. Pressures for democratisation, considered in a later chapter, became at least temporarily impossible to withstand. In retrospect, the principles of juridical statehood as these were applied in Africa may be regarded, in part at least, as a product of the Cold War, and the end of that epoch in international history exposed African states to external pressures from which they had hitherto been largely protected. More basically, however, the inadequacies of juridical statehood had already been revealed by the impact of the Cold War on Africa itself, which had led to an oversupply of armaments that eventually exacerbated the very weaknesses of African states which it had been intended to correct. The end of the Cold War did not so much cause the crises of African statehood which in some cases became increasingly obvious after 1989, as coincide with the failure of a conception of the state in Africa which had already become unsustainable.

Part III
Struggling with decay

7 The international politics of economic failure

The failure of African economies

By far the most important factor underlying the international weakness of African states, and their vulnerability to internal fragmentation and external penetration, was their record of economic failure.[1] The trajectories of different groups of Third World states since 1960, and notably the contrast between the capitalist states of east and south-east Asia on the one hand, and the states of sub-Saharan Africa on the other, provided the clearest indicator of the roles of economic success in ensuring political autonomy and diplomatic respect, and of stagnation and decay in leading to dependence on the uncertain and conditional charity of Western donor states and international institutions. There was, of course, no one-way causal relationship between economic failure and political weakness. The structure of African statehood certainly contributed to the dismal record of African economies, just as the structure of African involvement in global production and trade helped to induce political alienation and institutional decay. The economic and political crises of African statehood could most plausibly be regarded as different facets of a common complex of problems. From the early 1980s onwards, however, these problems were most clearly reflected in the economic needs of African states, and their subjection to the conditions imposed by external donors as the price for meeting those needs, which in turn became the overriding preoccupation of Africa's external relations.

Any attempt to quantify the economic failure of African states over the third of a century or so after most of them became independent is subject to the reliability of statistics which were affected by the same processes of institutional decay as the economies which they purported to describe. The World Bank, which made the most systematic effort to collect and publish figures relating to the global economy, abandoned the attempt for such important African states as Angola, Sudan, Zaïre and Zambia, not to mention the collapsed states of Liberia and Somalia.[2] These were, of course, the states for which economic decline was likely to be most marked; figures for other states were often subject to a wide margin of uncertainty. Across the states of sub-Saharan Africa as a whole for which data were available, average per capita gross national product was recorded as declining at a rate of 0.8 per cent a year between 1980 and 1992.[3] The great majority of individual sub-Saharan states also showed declines in per capita GNP over the same period, with only Botswana recording sustained economic growth. In twenty-five of the thirty-six states for which data were available, moreover, per capita food production declined during the same period, helping to account for an increase from 1.6m to 4.2m tons in the provision of food aid in cereals.[4] This translated into a figure of some fifty million Africans (or 9 per cent of sub-Saharan Africa's total population) who would be liable to death or severe malnutrition were it not for donations of food which came overwhelmingly from the wealthy industrial states of North America, Western Europe and Australasia; this figure in turn had some claim to be regarded as the single most important indicator of Africa's economic relations with the rest of the world.[5]

Figures for the flow of exports out of Africa, and of private investment capital into it, suggested that the continent had virtually dropped out of sight as a participant in the world economy. Africa's world market share of non-oil primary produce exports fell from 7 per cent to 4 per cent between 1970 and 1985, while returns on investment in the continent dropped from 30.7 per cent in the 1960s to a mere 2.5 per cent in the 1980s.[6] Given these returns, it could be no surprise that external private commercial investment in the continent totalled only $504m in 1992, or 1.6 per cent of the total private investment in Africa, Asia and Central and South America as a whole.[7] The end of the Cold War, which reduced the demand for some of Africa's strategic minerals, while making alternative sources of supply and investment available in the former Warsaw Pact states, can only have intensified the economic marginalisation of the continent. The recorded gross domestic product of the whole of sub-Saharan Africa in 1992, at $270bn, amounted to appreciably less than that of the Netherlands.[8]

There were, it is true, additional sources of income which did not show up in the figures, notably in the 'informal sector', where appreciable quantities of goods undoubtedly evaded detection; one such source of unrecorded income was certainly Africa's increasing role in international drug trafficking.[9] Any possibility that this significantly affected the overall picture of economic decay was, however, belied both by those indicators (such as foreign investment and industrial production) for which fairly reliable statistics were available, and by the all too evident economic misery of very large numbers of Africans. Even though official figures often did not accurately measure overall levels of economic activity, moreover, they were much more accurate as an indicator of the amount of income which the state was able to monitor and hence to tax. The growth of the informal sector both reflected and exacerbated the declining capacity of the state.

This economic decline directly affected Africa's external relations, because of the critical importance of foreign exchange in maintaining the state itself, and the lifestyles of those who were most closely associated with it. African economies, most of which were individually minuscule, depended on imports for a high proportion of their consumption, and this dependence was particularly high for products consumed by wealthy and urban groups, including the state itself.[10] The search for foreign exchange, or 'forex', was as a result a constant preoccupation not just of individuals but of governments, and vast ingenuity was dedicated to devising means of squeezing the last possible drop of it from any potential source. The insistence of the Ethiopian government in 1984/85 on demanding $12.60 in port dues and other fees on every ton of the famine relief needed to keep several million Ethiopians alive was no more than a particularly striking example of a universal phenomenon.[11]

For many African states, the onset of a crisis in foreign exchange availability was abrupt and unexpected. Most were caught by the oil price rises of the later 1970s, which had an especially severe impact on economies which depended very largely on motor transport, while markets for their exports in the industrial states were simultaneously hit by the recession caused by precisely the same price rises. The price of copper, for example, on which Zaïre and Zambia's export earnings were largely dependent, collapsed in 1975, and by 1984 was 57 per cent lower in real terms than in 1970–4.[12] The few and fortunate African oil exporters, notably Nigeria, revelled in their sudden wealth and expanded their consumption to meet it, only to be caught when the price of oil proved to be subject to the same fluctuations as any other commodity. Foreign exchange, which had previously been fairly easily available, was suddenly turned off like a tap, leaving those who had previously enjoyed it with a desperate need to find some alternative source; the transition from wealth to penury in previously oil-rich Nigeria was particularly traumatic, and helped to explain the number of Nigerians who sought to maintain themselves by acting as couriers for illegal drugs.[13] Since foreign exchange was essential to sustain the whole range of modern sector activities, the impact of its sudden disappearance was dramatic, affecting the availability not just of raw materials and spare parts for industry or fertilisers for agriculture, but even of prophylactics against malaria. In many African university libraries, the onset of the forex crisis may be precisely dated by the disappearance of foreign publications and the cancellation of subscriptions to journals. But in political systems heavily dependent on patronage networks to keep themselves going, the disappearance of foreign exchange also signalled a crisis of the state. The bases of political support were rapidly narrowed, and access to forex was restricted to the highest levels of the political order, and to those vested interests, most obviously the military, which could not prudently be denied it. In states which maintained their domestic currencies at artificially overvalued exchange rates, and which thus required stringent import licensing, the allocation of licences became a means of rewarding favoured cronies and political supporters. Not everyone could be accommodated, and although causal connections are difficult to pin down, the foreign exchange crisis probably does much to account for the increase in autocracy, militarisation and armed resistance which took place at about the same time.

Fortunately, as it appeared, the initial foreign exchange crisis of the later 1970s coincided with the fairly ready availability of loan finance. It was, indeed, no coincidence at all: the surplus cash extracted from oil consumers by the price rise was invested by the producers in Western banks, which in turn needed to lend it to someone else. Most African states were in addition able to borrow on favourable terms from Western governments and international institutions. The easiest short-term expedient, for African (and other) states, was therefore to borrow the money which they were no longer able to earn. The result was a rapid increase in levels of African indebtedness, which until the late 1970s had been kept within what appeared by later standards to be very modest limits. The rate of increase in African debt was startling. From $5,244m in 1970, the total African outstanding public debt rose to $48,793m in 1980, and $151,176m in 1991.[14] For a number of the smaller individual African states, the debt rose to levels at which any prospective ability to repay could only have been greeted with derision; by 1992, to take the extreme case, Guinea-Bissau's outstanding debt amounted to double its annual gross domestic product, while the annual outstanding interest and capital payments came to 92.7 per cent of export earnings. Even for many of the more substantial African economies, such as Côte d'Ivoire, Kenya or Nigeria, annual debt payments amounted to 27–32 per cent of export earnings.[15]

Indebtedness is, of course, a perfectly normal way of financing the acquisition of productive resources, the income from which can then be used to repay the debt, leaving the borrower with a more productive economy and enhanced opportunities for raising additional capital with which to finance further development. There was, however, little to suggest that anything more than a minimal proportion of African debt was raised, or was even seriously intended, for this purpose. Much of it accumulated automatically from the failure to meet outstanding obligations, or went to meet shortfalls in government revenues, which in turn were the result, partly of declining primary produce export prices and levels of production, partly of the failure to restrain public expenditure, especially on the bureaucracy. Much of it likewise went to fuel 'crony statism', in which politicians, bureaucrats, traders, industrialists and public works contractors formed a powerful alliance designed to augment their own wealth at the public expense.[16] When, as very soon happened, the inability to repay the borrowed money became all too evident, the African debt crisis was at hand.

At this point, it becomes necessary to ask *why* Africa's economies should have been so unsuccessful, particularly at a time when the astonishingly rapid growth of some of the Asian economies was destroying any plausible basis for those 'dependency' theories which had argued that the economic development of the Third World was rendered impossible by the domination of the global economy by the already industrialised capitalist powers. In simple political terms, the answer to that question essentially came down to two alternative sets of arguments, each of which was understandably adopted by those whom it exonerated from the major share of the blame. Those responsible for running African states, and their sympathisers, argued that most of the problem lay with the structure and management of the international economy. Conversely, those responsible for running the international economy, and their colleagues in the industrial countries, argued that most of the problem lay with the structure and management of African states.

Each side could put up a plausible case. The African states could point to the extreme dependence of their tiny economies on international economic conditions over which they had not the slightest control: the traumatic effects of the oil price rises; the wildly fluctuating world market prices of their primary produce exports; the underlying tendency, irrespective of these year-to-year fluctuations, of primary produce prices to decline relative to the cost of the industrial goods which they had to import; and the increase in global interest rates, and hence in the amount of interest that they had to pay on their debt, which was due largely to the deficit run by the United States.[17] Even the level of debt, and the inappropriate development models which they had followed, were in some measure the result of policies advocated by the World Bank and other donors in the 1960s and 1970s. The major capitalist states and international financial institutions could correspondingly point to numerous ways in which the efficient operation of African economies was obstructed by the policies pursued by African states, and indeed and more basically by the structure of the African state itself: the maintenance of artificial exchange rates, which benefited urban consumers at the expense of rural producers; state control of produce marketing, which was driving many potential producers out of the market altogether; the massive debts run up by badly managed state corporations and nationalised industries; the inflation of the government payroll, caused in part by militarisation, in part by the state's attempt to carry out functions for which it was inherently unsuited; and, least excusably of all, the ample evidence of gross corruption and abuse of power.[18]

The question of which of these alternative explanations was broadly right, or more plausibly, the share of the responsibility for Africa's economic plight which should be apportioned to each of them, scarcely however mattered. What mattered was that one side (or in other words, those who had the money) was in a position to enforce its explanation for the problem, and the policy measures which followed from it. The other side (or in other words, those who needed the money) was not. This was the origin of the structural adjustment programme.

The externalisation of economic management

The phrase 'structural adjustment', used to denote a set of policies designed to reform the economies of indebted Third World states, was coined by the then president of the World Bank, Robert Macnamara, at a meeting of the Bank's board of governors in Belgrade in October 1979.[19] Though the precise content of structural adjustment packages varied, both over time and as between the different states to which they were applied, they generally constituted a set of measures with a strong 'family resemblance' to one another.[20] These measures were designed to address the problems in African economic management identified by Bates and other authors, and were articulated in a number of reports commissioned by the World Bank, starting with *Accelerated Development in Sub-Saharan Africa* (commonly known as the Berg Report), published in 1981.[21] In March 1989, the Bank issued a report, *Africa's Adjustment and Growth in the 1980s*, which claimed (over the virulently expressed opposition of its opponents) that those states which had adopted economic reform programmes had managed better than those which had not.[22] This was followed in November 1989 by *Sub-Saharan Africa: From Crisis to Sustainable Growth*, which moved away from the anti-statist approach contained in earlier reports, and recognised the need for a more balanced relationship between the state and the market, while raising the need for improvements in state capabilities.[23] These were further spelled out in another report, *Governance and Development*, in 1992.[24] In 1994, the Bank attempted to produce a balance sheet, which argued that in at least some cases its policies had been successful, while emphasising the extent to which they had often not been implemented.[25] Despite the evolution of the Bank's policies, to take account of the recognition that the rehabilitation of African economies would have to be a much longer-term operation than it had at first supposed, and to incorporate governmental factors as well as straightforward economic measures, it consistently took a 'liberal' or market-oriented approach to economic management, which rested on the assumption that economic 'rationality' was a constant across all societies, which applied regardless of the level of development reached by any particular economy. This approach, which denied the relevance of any specific 'development economics' geared to the special needs of developing states, has been described as 'monoeconomics'.[26] Accordingly, the central requirement of macroeconomic management was to control budget deficits and money supply, and to liberalise the foreign exchange regime; this in turn would ensure that the market was given free rein to allocate resources within the economy, and rectify the distortions created by undue and inefficient state intervention in economic management.

In essence, then, structural adjustment programmes constituted exchanges, in which on the one hand, international financial institutions and other donors provided loans to indebted African states, and on the other hand, the states concerned agreed to pursue the economic policies stipulated by those institutions as a condition for receiving the loans. These exchanges were, however, negotiated under conditions of very unequal power on the two sides. One African negotiator compared the process to a Wild West shoot-out, in which his revolver emitted no more than a series of ineffectual clicks, while his opponent's was fully loaded.[27] The African state, unable to meet its debts or even pay for its essential imports, and denied any access to further credit until it had reached some arrangement with its existing creditors, was in no position to do more than plead for lenient treatment, while drawing attention to any special needs or mitigating circumstances. Ranged against it were the Bretton Woods institutions, the International Monetary Fund and World Bank, whose bargaining power was greatly enhanced by the fact that, as lenders of last resort, their approval was also the key to securing loans from other international lenders and individual states, which were generally happy to leave the Fund and Bank with the unpopular task of imposing conditions which they could then endorse. It escaped no one's notice that the meetings of the 'Paris Club', in which arrangements for rescheduling public debt were negotiated, took place in the building which, during the Nazi occupation of France, had housed the Gestapo.

Though the IMF had been involved in dealing with financial crises in several African states since the 1960s, the first structural adjustment loans were introduced in 1980/81, in Kenya, Malawi, Mauritius and Senegal; they subsequently spread to the great majority of African states. Some donors, notably the Scandinavian states, were willing to provide aid to states which defied the demands of structural adjustment, and Tanzania in particular, despite 'socialist' economic policies of often awe-inspiring stupidity,[28] was able to benefit from the sympathy attracted by its founding president, Julius Nyerere, to avoid succumbing until 1986.[29] By 1993, none the less, virtually all of sub-Saharan Africa and its adjacent islands had been obliged to implement adjustment programmes of one sort or another, with the sole significant exceptions of Angola and the states of the Southern African Customs Union.[30] Most of them had by then negotiated several successive programmes, and Ghana was on its ninth.

The policies which African states were normally obliged to accept in exchange for these loans fell into four broad groups.[31] First, states with heavily overvalued domestic currencies were obliged to devalue them, preferably to the level dictated by the foreign exchange market. This devaluation could be drastic. In Ghana from May 1983 onwards, the cedi (C) was devalued from an initial $1=C3 to $1=C30 by October 1983, and by September 1991 it had dropped to $1=C400, a loss of over 99 per cent of its previous exchange value.[32] In Nigeria, the value of the naira (N) fell from N1=$1.54 in the early 1980s to N1=$0.08 in 1991.[33] This in principle multiplied both the price that had to be paid in local currency for imported goods, and the amount that was earned, in local currency, from the sale of exports for foreign exchange, leading to a massive transfer of local currency resources from those who consumed imports to those who sold exports. In practice, given the limited ability of states to police their economies, many people were already subject to market-driven prices; but employees on fixed incomes who had previously been able to buy imported goods at official prices were very badly affected. In the states of the Franc Zone, where the value of the currency was maintained at a fixed parity against the French franc, devaluation was resisted by France until January 1994, by which time the overvaluation of the CFA franc had done considerable damage to the export earnings of the CFA states, and was imposing an increasing burden on the French budget; the eventual 50 per cent devaluation was none the less far smaller than that imposed on most states with floating currencies.[34]

Second, economic activities which had previously been controlled by the state had to be opened up to private enterprise. Two of these were particularly important. The first was the dismantling of the government buying monopolies for locally grown primary produce which, as noted in chapter 3, had initially been established by the colonial administrations as a means of extracting foreign exchange from peasant producers. Instead, private commodity traders would be obliged to compete with one another, and would in the process have to offer favourable prices to producers. The second was the privatisation of the state corporations, commonly known as 'parastatals', which had been formed either by the nationalisation of formerly private businesses (which had almost always been foreign-owned), or else to run newly established industries such as steel mills and oil refineries on the government's behalf. It was rare to find any such corporation which did not run up massive losses, while many were run as little more than patronage operations on behalf of their employees.[35]

Third, governments were obliged to change state-imposed pricing structures which had the effect of distorting markets, and in the process redistributing wealth towards some social groups and away from others. These characteristically included protective tariffs designed to shield otherwise uneconomic local industries, and controls on the prices of foodstuffs designed to meet the demands of urban food consumers at the expense of food producers; such controls, by rendering local food production unprofitable, were also regarded by the international financial institutions as the source of much of the decline in food production, which in turn made African societies increasingly dependent on food aid. Amongst other measures, consumers were often required to pay at least part of the cost of services such as health and education which had previously been supplied free of charge.

Finally, governments were expected to maintain macroeconomic stability, especially by balancing their own budgets, and in the process to cut government spending and reduce the size of the bureaucracy. Many if not all African governments had run massive budget deficits, which they had financed either by borrowing or by printing money and thus inflating the currency. In the process, they had diverted economic resources, including skilled labour, away from productive enterprises and into unproductive government employment. In keeping with the underlying ideological assumption that the state was at the root of most of the problems of African economies, its reduction in scale was seen as a benefit in itself, over and above the desirability of balancing the budget.

By far the greater part of the massive literature devoted to analysing the effects of structural adjustment programmes has been concerned, understandably enough, with assessing whether they actually produce the benefits which their proponents have expected of them.[36] There is also a considerable amount of research on the impact of adjustment on specific (and especially disadvantaged) population groups, such as women.[37] My concern here, however , is with the impact of adjustment on the politics, and in particular the international relations, of African states, a subject which has certainly not been overlooked, but which has generally attracted rather less attention.[38] From this viewpoint, the critical point about structural adjustment was the challenge that international instititutions posed to control by African states and rulers over their own domestic economies, and thus more broadly to the whole project of state consolidation in Africa. Structural adjustment challenged the political as well as the economic basis of monopoly statehood, by which governing elites had sought, first to extract resources from the economy in order to sustain state power, and second to direct economic benefits towards those who either ran the state, or were in a position to threaten it. Control of the currency was central to this enterprise, either through the ability of states with 'independent' currencies to manipulate access to imported goods, or else through the rather different mechanism represented by the Franc Zone, which achieved very similar results.[39] Most of the other common elements in structural adjustment programmes, and especially those relating to parastatals and government employment, threatened the patronage basis of regimes which, in the absence of any underlying sense of legitimacy, depended heavily on the allocation of benefits to maintain themselves in power. Structural adjustment riots, prompted especially by increases in urban food prices, clearly demonstrated the link between economic benefits and political stability.[40]

But although structural adjustment propelled many African regimes into confrontation with seemingly omnipotent international financial institutions, and severely threatened their control over domestic political resources, the contest was not as one-sided as it may have seemed. First and foremost, African regimes were the powers in possession. The IMF and its partners had neither the capacity nor the desire to take over direct management of African economies themselves, but depended on the government to implement the very policies that were intended to undermine its power. And if there was one area in which many African regimes had of necessity developed political skills of the highest order, it was in the complex manoeuvres required in order to ensure their own survival. In practice, though some conditions (notably currency devaluation) were straightforward in implementation, and could therefore be readily monitored and enforced, others (such as budgetary arrangements and institutional innovations) were much more open to obfuscation or delay. Frequently, governments could plausibly claim that implementation had been prevented by factors beyond their control. It was therefore possible for them to gamble that they could get away with relatively high levels of what was termed 'policy slippage', which essentially amounted to taking the money without delivering the promised policies.[41]

On a number of occasions, external aid donors attempted to impose their own financial management on African states in an attempt to ensure a basic level of honesty and efficiency. These attempts invariably ended in abysmal failure. In 1978, the World Bank recruited a team of experts to assume direction of the Bank of Zaïre, but its leader, a German, left in disgust after a year; his Mauritanian successor was more diplomatic, but lasted only for two years.[42] In the mid-1980s the United States government recruited a team of 'operational experts', swiftly dubbed 'opex', to supervise the financial operations of the Doe regime in Liberia, in an attempt to prevent the massive diversion of US aid to unauthorised uses which had been revealed by the US General Accounting Office. As an external imposition of direct financial control over a nominally sovereign state, it recalled the British management of Egyptian state finances in the 1880s, and it was only made possible by the Doe regime's desperate need for aid, the Reagan administration's determination to keep supplying that aid despite ample evidence of corruption, and the US Congress's ability to specify the conditions under which it would be made available. When, after long delays, the opex were eventually recruited and despatched to Monrovia, the impossibility of their task soon became apparent, and after a short time they were withdrawn.[43]

The international financial institutions, moreover, soon had to recognise that a well-run state was an essential participant in any effective structure of economic management. The initial and rather simplistic characterisation of the state as the major obstacle to the development of economies which would do much better without it, had to give way to the realisation that development actually required not only a state but even a strong state. The contrast between the *laissez-faire* approach initially recommended for Africa, and the powerful role played by states in the economic success of eastern Asia, could not go unnoticed for long. In addition to maintaining basic public order, which was a problem in an increasing number of African states, they also had to enforce property rights, maintain the physical and social infrastructure, and create market institutions such as stockmarkets.[44] Equally, the economic and social upheavals that would necessarily accompany any successful process of structural adjustment could scarcely be contained in an anarchical political void, but would require a regime that enjoyed a substantial level of popular legitimacy and support – a point that was forcibly made by the successes and failures of structural adjustment in Central and Eastern Europe. By the time that the World Bank published *Sub-Saharan Africa: From Crisis to Sustainable Growth* in November 1989, it had come to recognise the need for a balance between the roles of state and market.[45] The corollary of this was that the state itself would have to change; but despite their anxiety to bring about major changes in the economic role of African states, the World Bank and its allies had to make sure that they did not destroy the basis of statehood itself, and this likewise placed bargaining counters in the hands of African regimes.

And if African governments were under pressure to demonstrate the effectiveness of structural adjustment, so also were the international financial institutions themselves. By 1994, concessional loans to Africa accounted for some 44 per cent of the World Bank's total disbursements,[46] and if the Bank was to justify its existence, it would need to show that this was a worthwhile activity. Given the level of political opposition and academic scepticism that the programmes attracted, the Bank's own reputation was at stake; and even if the intellectual argument for structural adjustment seemed unshakeable, it soon became clear that its implementation would take much longer to produce demonstrable benefits than optimistic early assessments had assumed. In part, the damage done to African economies by over two decades of statist management had created interests, and set in train processes, which it would take a long time to reverse; although (or indeed because) peasants might be rational economic producers, they would not rapidly recover enough from an all-too-often justified scepticism of government to risk investment in what might well prove to be transient market opportunities. In part, too, there were genuine structural problems in African economies and societies that made it difficult for them to respond to market incentives in the way that the adjustment model took for granted; the weakness of indigenous entrepreneurial classes, the lack of capital, and the difficulty of creating and maintaining effective economic organisations beyond the level of the small family enterprise all made the 'supply side' much slower to respond than the experience of already functioning capitalist economies suggested. Nor could the continued impact of changes in the international economy be ignored. As a result, structural adjustment programmes had to be adapted in ways that generally increased the bargaining power of African governments: the timescale had to be greatly lengthened; the 'sequencing' of the different elements in the programme had to be carefully worked out; and, in particular, it became clear that programmes had a vastly better prospect of implementation if the government had a sense that it 'owned' them, and thus if it had a role in their articulation and an interest in their success.[47]

Responses to adjustment

African states were thus not merely the passive victims of programmes imposed on them, but were able to devise alternative responses to the demands made on them. These depended on a variety of factors, including the economic interests and political strength of governing elites, their international bargaining power, and in some degree the personal ideologies and decisions of individual rulers. In principle, three broad responses were possible: resistance, acceptance, or, lying between the two, the formal acceptance of adjustment programmes coupled with attempts to subvert them by failing to implement their least desirable provisions.

It soon became clear that outright resistance was not a viable option. Though a few states, such as Tanzania as already noted, were able to mobilise international sympathy in order to put off the evil moment, the virtual totality of continental African states north of the Southern African Customs Union were eventually obliged to succumb. Attempts to articulate any viable alternative to adjustment, moreover, failed intellectually as well as politically. Particularly embarrassing was the attempt by the United Nations Economic Commission for Africa to devise an *African Alternative Framework to Structural Adjustment Programmes for Socio-Economic Recovery and Transformation*, issued in July 1989, which sought to revive the OAU's economically illiterate Lagos Plan of Action for an African Common Market, initially put forward in 1980, and linked it to vague and contradictory policy proposals which called for increased external aid on the one hand, and indicated a deep suspicion of the role of the world economy on the other.[48] Though convincing arguments could be made that the transformation of African economies would require changes in addition to structural adjustment, notably at the international level, the claim that no changes were required in the management of African states themselves was unsustainable.

The second option, that of accepting but subverting adjustment programmes, offered in contrast ample scope for flexibility and manoeuvre. Underlying it was the assumption that the African state and its external economic mentors were in a competitive bargaining position, in which 'winning', from the African state's point of view, consisted in getting as much adjustment aid as possible from international financial institutions and other donors, while delivering as little policy reform as possible in exchange. This was a viewpoint diametrically opposed to the ideology underlying adjustment, which regarded it as an essential set of reforms from which African states themselves would ultimately be the main gainers, and treated the accompanying aid package as the sugar coating required to get the patient to swallow the pill which would eventually make him better. It was, however, a perfectly understandable attitude for African rulers, who were anxious to get their hands on the money, but whose long-established practices and possibly political survival were threatened by the conditions which accompanied it; African governments, indeed, rapidly became as adept at evading the demands of international financial institutions as their people were at evading those of their own governments.

For some regimes, subversion was not so much an option as a necessity. Kenneth Kaunda's Zambia, with a massive and inefficient parastatal sector, and a level of urban bias in government policy which had resulted from the need to appease the powerful mining sector, was – from the World Bank's viewpoint – crying out for reform. The calamitous collapse of copper prices had left the government in desperate need of aid. But the government, having presided over two decades of often rapid economic decline, had exhausted whatever political credit it had once possessed, and any attempt to impose unpopular policies aroused an instant reaction, especially in the form of urban protest. The politics of reform in Zambia therefore followed a cycle, in which the government was driven by financial crisis to accept a structural adjustment programme, which led to a popular reaction that threatened the government and forced it to backtrack on its promised implementation measures, which in turn resulted in a cutback in aid, and in a further financial crisis that eventually pushed the government back into acceptance of another adjustment programme.[49] This cycle was eventually broken by the government's acceptance of multiparty elections which it then lost, though the subsequent Chiluba government faced similar problems in its turn.

Other regimes, whose predicament was not quite so desperate, were able to drag their feet on implementing at least parts of the programme. In Kenya, the number of conditionalities attached to World

Bank loans had by 1991 reached 150, many of which were not precisely quantified and virtually impossible to monitor.[50] And since some policies, such as the privatisation of parastatal corporations, could only be implemented over a long period, governments had a fair chance of getting away with it. It was not easy for international financial institutions to specify precise criteria for cutting off aid, where programmes had been partly but not entirely implemented, or to determine whether such criteria had in fact been met. Regimes which enjoyed the political support of major Western powers were able to use this to exert leverage on donor institutions, or to play off different donors against one another. The Mobutu regime in Zaïre, in particular, was able to get exceptionally favourable terms from international financial institutions, as a result of pressures behind the scenes from the United States and France.[51] The Biya regime in Cameroon could play off the IMF against France over the reform of parastatal corporations; and at a critical moment in the presidential election campaign of 1992, when Biya faced a strong challenge from an anglophone Cameroonian opposition candidate who might well have threatened French interests in the country, the extension of new aid facilities by both France and the IMF gave him a considerable boost.[52]

There were also some respects in which parts at least of structural adjustment programmes could be manipulated to serve the economic and political interests of governing elites. At its simplest, rulers could lay their hands on the loan money, while ensuring that the costs of adjustment were passed on to people with no access to political influence. In Côte d'Ivoire, the programme helped the political leadership to reimpose control over its own bureaucracy.[53] In states such as Kenya or Zimbabwe, where political elites had substantial economic interests in agriculture, the external demand to liberalise agricultural marketing and remove restrictions on food prices enabled them to implement policies which served these interests, while blaming external agencies for their repercussions on the living standards of the urban poor.[54] Some policies, notably in the area of privatisation, offered scope for downright fraud; many African politicians and bureaucrats had, after all, been adept at 'privatising' state assets for years. The sale of state assets in Cameroon enabled political elites to acquire government vehicles at knock-down prices.[55] In other parts of francophone Africa, French businessmen were able to take over privatised state utilities, in collaboration with local politicians who gained shares or other favours as a result.[56] In Sierra Leone, President

Siaka Stevens formed his own company, in collaboration with a Lebanese businessman, and sold the most profitable state corporations to himself.[57] Nigerian privatisation likewise became a mechanism through which politically influential businessmen could gain additional assets.[58] In all these cases, external pressures for privatisation took for granted a distinction between the 'public' and 'private' spheres that was by no means always evident even in developed industrial states, and which certainly did not apply in much of Africa.

Finally, however, some African leaders – notably Jerry Rawlings, the populist military ruler of Ghana, and Yoweri Museveni of Uganda – accepted structural adjustment, and set about trying to implement it in their own countries. In part, this acceptance derived, especially in the case of Ghana, from the intellectual conversion of the leader and his immediate entourage, at a time when the credentials of socialist and dependency-oriented development strategies had collapsed.[59] A plausible case could indeed be made that 'socialism' in an African context was an ideology that appealed largely to the class interests of the state bureaucracy, whereas the market approach favoured under structural adjustment would empower and enrich the hard-working rural masses. In addition, however, a wholehearted acceptance of structural adjustment was a rational strategy at least for a limited number of African leaders. For a start, it ensured solid Western support, and correspondingly favoured access to external finance, by contrast with those states whose adherence to World Bank policies was only partial and grudging. This support, moreover, could carry over from the economic into the more explicitly political field: neither Rawlings nor Museveni, one of whom had come to power by military coup, the other by guerrilla insurgency, was subjected to as much pressure for multiparty democratisation as were other leaders whose economic policies were not so closely in tune with current Western thinking. In addition, were structural adjustment actually to yield the economic benefits that it promised, the government that introduced it would (if it could last that long) be the ultimate gainer.

Acceptance of structural adjustment none the less implied a domestic political strategy that was open only to some leaders and not to others. Since it immediately attacked the interests of state elites, including the military, it required a leadership that both controlled the instruments of force, and was at the same time autonomous from them and from the ordinary state bureaucracy. Rawlings and Museveni met these criteria. Both were 'outsiders', with little commitment to the interests of established elites; Rawlings was able to maintain himself in power with the help of his appeal to the rank-and-file of the Ghanaian armed forces, while Museveni had formed his own independent National Resistance Army which had defeated the armed forces of the previous regime. Each of them eventually adopted the reform programme despite an initial commitment to broadly 'leftist' ideas, and after a year or so of confused economic policy-making that was evidently getting nowhere. Two other leaders, Meles Zenawi in Ethiopia and Isaias Afewerki in Eritrea, came to power with a level of autonomy that would have permitted them to follow similar reform policies, but – despite a formal conversion to market economics – retained too strong a commitment to their Marxist–Leninist past to be able to accept them. Both Ghana and Uganda (and also Ethiopia and Eritrea) had likewise suffered a level of economic damage that had undermined the position of established economic interests which might otherwise have been able to mount effective opposition to reform.

Beyond this, however, economic reform programmes carried profound implications for the structure of political life, since they sought to undercut the basis for the neopatrimonial techniques through which African leaders had characteristically tried to keep themselves in power.[60] They removed from the government much of its capacity to buy support and reward followers, through such mechanisms as the allocation of import licences or posts in parastatal organisations, and weakened its ability to manipulate the politics of ethnicity by discriminating in favour of (or against) particular groups or regions. Ultimately, the effect of a successful adjustment programme would be to create a state which depended on the sources of wealth generation within the economy, rather than an economy which was manipulated by the patronage available from the state. Since politicians, civilian as well as military, generally rose to power within an established set of social institutions and interests, on which they usually continued to depend for their survival, few of them were in a position to embark on such a strategy.

But even if some African leaders had at least an element of choice and bargaining power in responding to the demands for economic reform pressed on them by international financial institutions, these demands still represented a dramatic reduction in their freedom of action. Whereas previously, the domestic economic policies which they chose to follow had been regarded as falling unambiguously within the sphere of national sovereignty, they were now obliged to bargain or dissemble in an attempt to retain some influence over those aspects of economic management which were most critical to their hold on political power. Frequently, and especially over the drastic devaluation of their national currencies, they were not able to achieve even that. Even in those cases, such as Ghana and Uganda, where leaders pursued adjustment policies with a relatively high level of commitment, it was extremely unlikely that they would have adopted them in the first place, had it not been for the bankruptcy of the economies which they inherited when they came to power. And even though the World Bank and its allies eventually came to recognise the importance of the state in African economic management, and to treat it as a partner to be bargained with, rather than a mere obstruction which should be removed as far as possible from the economic realm, this changed appreciation also carried with it assumptions about the desirable character of the state itself which were markedly at variance with important features of most African states as they currently existed. The World Bank's discovery of a relationship between 'governance' and development carried with it the danger of still more threatening conditionalities relating to the structure of domestic government itself.

The politics of aid dependence

At the time of independence, the more radical African nationalist leaders had understandably been concerned that their formal achievement of national sovereignty might be undermined by the continued dependence of their economies on the structures of production and exchange which during the colonial era had been closely associated with the colonial power. The idea of 'neocolonialism', for which ample theoretical foundation could be derived from the work of Lenin and other Marxist writers, was articulated in order to account for any of the numerous ways in which the economic power of the world's major capitalist states continued to penetrate the domestic economies and class structures, and restrict the governments, of nominally independent African states.[61] In many respects, indeed, the concerns expressed under the heading of neocolonialism were eminently justified. The ruthless French reaction to the Guinean vote for independence in the 1958 referendum demonstrated the power of an outgoing colonial regime to damage the economy of any African state which challenged or even offended it. Nor did one have to be a Marxist to recognise the connections between the subservience of many African rulers to the capitalist states and especially the former colonial power, and the dependence of their economies on trade flows and corporations which linked them to the former metropoles, and very often on a level of aid which provided the African states concerned with a powerful inducement not to offend the countries which supplied it.

The policies required to avert the dangers of dependence seemed so obvious as to be simply logical. In order to prevent the penetration of one's own domestic economy and politics by the agents of international capitalism, it was essential to bring that economy so far as possible under domestic control; and in societies where the indigenous capitalist class was extremely weak, that necessarily meant bringing it under the control of the state. Beyond that, moreover, the damaging effects of incorporation on a subordinate basis into the global economy could only be contained by reducing one's exposure to international trade and capital, and attempting so far as possible to rely on one's own internal human and material resources. No African state was remotely in a position to cut itself off from the world economy, as Burma and Khmer Rouge Cambodia had attempted to do, but if that economy was inherently exploitative and destabilising, it was clearly incumbent on socialist African regimes to protect themselves from it as far as they could. In Nyerere's famous phrase, 'socialism and self-reliance' were two sides of the same coin.

This apparent logic proved to be fundamentally misconceived. Given that the economic development of small and poor economies (and even, indeed, of large and rich ones) actually depended on production for an international market, and given likewise the counter-productive effects of trying to introduce statist systems of economic management in countries which lacked the capacity to implement them effectively, the result was merely to induce a level of impoverishment which could ultimately only intensify dependence. 'If Ghana and other poor African countries are unusually vulnerable to the international economy, such vulnerability is in good part a result of government policies that kept them poor.'[62] Thirty years after most of them became independent, those African countries which had attempted to pursue socialist development policies proved to be the most dependent not only on structural adjustment funds, but more directly on the charity of Western capitalist states expressed as aid. By 1991, official development assistance (ODA) receipts amounted to 9.3 per cent of the gross national product of sub-Saharan states, in contrast to 2.2 per cent for the Middle East and 2.1 per cent for South Asia, and less than 1 per cent for East Asia and Latin America.[63] In Mozambique, ODA came to no less than 69.2 per cent of GNP, followed by figures of 43.4 per cent for Guinea-Bissau and 33.8 for Tanzania. The total for Tanzania, the only one of the exceptionally aid-dependent states not to have suffered from liberation war or periods of profound political instability, provides the clearest commentary on the policies of 'self-reliance' that helped to account for it.[64]

This discussion is not concerned with the effectiveness or otherwise of aid as a mechanism for achieving economic development, or with controversies over the moral justification for aid, or the purposes to which it is put, from the viewpoint of donor states, international agencies and non-governmental organisations.[65] It is concerned, rather, with the advantages and disadvantages of aid from the viewpoint of recipient African states, and notably with the extent to which it supported or undermined the attempts of recipient governments to maintain their states and their own control over them, and to further their other aspirations. For a start, of course, even though a high dependence on aid indicated weakness, states which accepted aid could be assumed to get something out of it. For deeply impoverished states, with often desperate problems in raising domestic revenue, aid provided the essential means for the functions of government to be carried on. For most African states, it characteristically furnished a high proportion of the disposable resources which could be used to maintain political support. 'Development projects' of one sort or another provided the currency in which the demands of political constituencies were commonly expressed, and through which they could be gratified. So long as the government could exercise some influence over the form which they took and the locations in which they were implemented, they could help to strengthen the domestic acceptability and bargaining capacity of the state. Recognition by the donors that their aid was being used in this way led to the imposition of conditions designed to ensure that it also met their own political priorities, and to a contest between donor and recipient in which the donor normally had the upper hand; but so long as aid was provided through the state, and could be associated with it, it was broadly state-strengthening. Much aid, indeed, was specifically targeted at enhancing state capacity, not only through aid to the military and other instruments of control like the police,[66] but through programmes designed to enhance economic policy-making and implementation.[67]

In addition, aid projects commonly enabled state officials to achieve personal goals of maintaining their own political networks or of self-enrichment.

It was by no means always evident that such aid had to be 'bought' by the recipient state at the price of its own freedom of action. Some recipients, such as Tanzania, were able to present their independence from external pressures as a positive inducement to would-be donors; indeed, regardless of the ineffectiveness of the Tanzanian policy of self-reliance as a strategy for achieving economic development, it was remarkably effective as a mechanism for attracting foreign aid. Other aid could not be used to impose political conditionalities without arousing opposition from public opinion in the donor states themselves: at the time of the Ethiopian famine of 1984/85, for example, it was not politically feasible for Western states to use famine relief as a means of inducing the Ethiopian government to reduce its close military and ideological association with the Soviet Union. Under other circumstances, however, aid could play at least some role in international alignment. As noted in the previous chapter, one factor which may explain the difference between Angola's and Mozambique's response to South African destabilisation was Mozambique's much greater dependence on Western aid.

Frequently, none the less, aid dependence had to be paid for in terms of the external penetration of domestic policy-making, rather than in terms of international alignment. Even though the provision of famine relief aid for starving Ethiopians could not directly be used by donors for diplomatic leverage, the close relationship between famine and warfare turned famine relief into a critical instrument in the struggle for control by both the government and its opponents over contested populations; the use of this instrument not only by governments but by NGOs with varying political agendas is considered in a later chapter. When the Ethiopian government sought aid funds for agricultural development programmes designed to ensure that such famines did not recur, moreover, this came into a sphere in which policy-conditionality was politically acceptable, and instantly created a conflict between the collectivisation policies sought by the Marxist–Leninist regime then in power in Addis Ababa, and the peasant-oriented approaches that were by this time favoured by the virtual totality of the Western development community. Only the Italians, whose aid was frankly intended to curry favour with the Mengistu regime, could for example be persuaded to finance the government's resettlement programme.[68] The major agricultural development programme funded by other Western donors was blocked until the Ethiopian government eventually agreed to the conditions on which donors insisted.[69]

In this case, it could plausibly be argued, firstly that the market-oriented approach favoured by the donor states was demonstrably more effective at increasing agricultural production than the statist policies of the government, and secondly that these policies were themselves in large part designed to impose the power of a particularly brutal regime on a recalcitrant subject population. Had Western donors agreed to subsidise the Mengistu regime's collectivisation schemes, they would have laid themselves open to a charge of abetting the gross abuse of the human rights of Ethiopians. As this indicated, however, the provision of aid could not be separated, for the donor, from judgements not just about the efficacy of particular policies, but equally about the moral or political standing of the government concerned. This in turn meant, for the recipient, that in accepting aid, it was also offering its domestic political credentials for the approval of its creditors.

This dilemma excited most controversy in the case of Mozambique, a state which was both the poorest in the world among those whose per capita GNP was assessed by the World Bank, and the most dependent in terms of development aid as a percentage of gross domestic product.[70] Although Mozambique, like Ethiopia, had a government of broadly socialist orientation, this generally attracted far greater sympathy than the Mengistu regime from Western commentators, a sympathy enhanced by its evident victimisation by the *apartheid* regime in South Africa. When, however, by far the major source of wealth and welfare in the country was discretionary spending controlled by foreigners, the capacity of the government to govern became very questionable indeed.[71] Mozambique, like other aid recipients, was also affected by the changes in donor attitudes towards African governments which were likewise reflected in structural adjustment programmes. These resulted firstly in a much greater readiness to impose policy prescriptions on recipient governments, and secondly in a preference for non-governmental organisations (NGOs), rather than the government of the recipient state itself, as the agency of implementation.

Whereas macroeconomic policies of the kind imposed under structural adjustment could only be implemented by government, project aid could often be implemented by NGOs, even in areas such as health or education which had previously been regarded as the province of the state. In a climate of opinion in which African governments were widely regarded as corrupt, inefficient and autocratic, NGOs provided a means of by-passing them, and delivering the aid directly to those who were intended to benefit from it – a development which is discussed in chapter 10. Given the high standing of many NGOs in Western public opinion, their employment by donor governments as implementing agencies could likewise be presented as 'depoliticising' aid, and ensuring that the money was both properly and efficiently used. That NGOs could afford to pay salaries in convertible currencies, both to their expatriate staff and to indigenous employees, at a level greatly exceeding those of senior government officials, compounded the problem and enhanced the consequent resentment; it also led to many of the best-qualified indigenous officials being drained out of government service and into employment with NGOs. It was equally understandable that local populations should transfer their attention and even their loyalty to those agencies that could provide most for them.[72]

Much of the controversy surrounding the issue was concerned, on the one hand with the role of donor governments and implementing agencies in subverting the proper role of government, on the other with the efficiency and accountability of governments (and indeed of NGOs) themselves. The underlying problem was, however, that the economic and political failures of African states removed from them both the resources required to govern their own territories, and their legitimacy in the international and often also in the domestic spheres. The capacity of African governments to manage the connections between their own societies and the outside world was consequently reduced or even extinguished, and instead such connections were taken over, to the extent that they were sustained at all, by external agencies operating on their own account. The use of the term 'recolonisation' to describe the consequent takeover of governmental functions by the agencies of external donors was polemical but not entirely unjustified.[73]

8 The externalisation of political accountability

The decline of sovereignty

Over a period of close to thirty years after independence, African rulers were remarkably successful in protecting their control over their domestic political systems against external pressures for change. Whereas the domestic economies of African states were heavily penetrated by external forces which limited the power of the state, African governments were to a very large extent left free to manage domestic politics as they wished. Although control over the economy was often a matter of aspiration, political control was for the most part a matter of fact. Domestically, while the withdrawal of rural producers from markets controlled by national governments had an important impact on state revenues, an equivalent withdrawal from political participation merely left the government with the freedom to operate as it wished. In terms of regional relationships, though few African states could control their frontiers against smuggling, they were generally far less threatened – save in parts of southern Africa and the Horn – by cross-border political movements. African rulers understandably supported the principle of unrestricted domestic sovereignty, and at least for the first two decades after independence, even the most muted criticism of the internal autocracy of other African states was virtually non-existent.[1] Most evidently of all, the major external (and especially capitalist) powers which continued to exercise influence over African economies were for the most part unconcerned about any equivalent influence on domestic political structures. Regardless of their commitment (in most cases) to liberal democracy within their own territories, there was no attempt by Western states to protect the multiparty political systems which they had established in colonial territories as a prelude to decolonisation. They readily assumed that such systems were unsuited to Africa, or that they had no right to intervene in issues of domestic jurisdiction; and in any event they could normally establish adequate working relations with the government in power, and had no interest in seeing it subjected to the potentially destabilising influence of democratic accountability.

Eventually, however, the principle of unfettered domestic sovereignty proved to be unsustainable. Over a period, it lost the moral legitimacy which it had enjoyed at independence, while the economic and political weaknesses of African states, together with changes in the international system, exposed them to an increasing level of external control. This loss of legitimacy could most evidently be ascribed to a gross and public abuse of power in a relatively small number of African states which excited the interest and condemnation of Western electorates. Such abuses were, of course, far more evident to the African populations which chiefly suffered from them, but since these had few if any means of bringing their opinions to international attention, they generally suffered in silence.[2] Three rulers in particular came during the 1970s to symbolise the degradation of political power in Africa, and since these came from three different colonial traditions, they helped to spread an awareness of African personal rule more widely than if they had all been associated with a single former coloniser. In anglophone Africa, most attention centred on Idi Amin in Uganda, whose overthrow of the previous regime of President Milton Obote in January 1971 had initially been greeted by the British government with a measure of relief, but whose rule rapidly descended to a level of indiscriminate brutality that was symbolised by the murder of the Anglican archbishop as well as of a large number of less eminent Ugandans.[3] Among the francophones, an equivalent role was taken by Jean-Bedel Bokassa of the Central African Republic, who like Amin had come to power by a military coup, in December 1965, and who rendered himself conspicuous not just by the brutality of his government, great though this was, but by a personalised exercise of power that was extraordinary even by the standards of African dictators. This culminated in his coronation as emperor in December 1977, in a ceremony brazenly adopted from the coronation of Napoleon Bonaparte in 1804, which reputedly cost over a quarter of the annual foreign earnings of the country which he ruled. His excesses also implicated the French governments which had helped to sustain him in power, and notably the regime of President Giscard d'Estaing, whose domestic political credit was seriously damaged by his acceptance of a gift of diamonds from Bokassa.[4] The third and least widely known of the trio, though possibly the most barbaric of them, was Fernando Macias Nguema of Equatorial Guinea, who was credited with the deaths of at least 20,000 people during his tenure of power.[5]

African states also rendered themselves more vulnerable to international pressures on human rights grounds through their readiness to use such pressures in their attack on the *apartheid* regime in South Africa. In terms of their own 'idea of the state', opposition to the South African regime was based on the conception of a collective right to self-determination for African peoples as a whole, which was independent of any criteria governing the behaviour of African governments. The South African regime was condemned for what it was, not for what it did. In bringing their outrage to the attention of an external and especially Western audience, however, African governments and other anti-*apartheid* campaigners both explicitly breached the frontiers of juridical sovereignty, and raised issues relating to the treatment of individuals which could equally be raised with reference to their own states. Once the human rights records of African-ruled states started to attract external attention, it was correspondingly harder to claim the protection of sovereign statehood.

Despite the bad publicity and consequent embarrassment which rulers such as Amin and Bokassa caused to the external reputation of the continent, there was none the less no concerted attempt to bring pressure on them to amend their behaviour, from either inside or outside Africa. The United Kingdom turned a blind eye to human rights violations in Uganda, under both Amin and his successors (including notably the second Obote government),[6] while Bokassa as already noted enjoyed very close relations with France. Macias Nguema not only played off the French against the Spaniards, but was also supported by the USSR, Cuba and North Korea; Libyan troops were sent to guard both Amin and Macias Nguema. Amin served for a year as chairman of the Organisation of African Unity, and though the Nigerian press took an important role in exposing conditions in Equatorial Guinea, which affected Nigerian migrant workers on Fernando Po, the OAU was conspicuous by its silence.[7] When all three were violently overthrown in 1979, however, the sense of continental relief was such that external involvement was tacitly ignored. Amin had exacerbated his already bad relations with Tanzania by attempting to annexe a small area of Tanzanian territory, thus providing President

Nyerere with the pretext for an invasion by Tanzanian forces and Ugandan exiles, in the face of which Amin's army collapsed. Bokassa had become such an embarrassment to his protector, President Giscard d'Estaing, that he was ousted by a French military force, whose intervention was thinly disguised as an internal military coup. Macias Nguema was eventually deposed by his own family and executed after a sketchy trial, though such was the awe in which he was held within Equatorial Guinea that Moroccan troops had to be brought in to shoot him.[8]

These three cases did enough harm to the external reputation of African states to induce heads of state to pay at least some attention to the need for damage limitation. In April 1980, the then Chairman of the OAU, President Tolbert of Liberia, was assassinated in the course of a *coup d'état* led by Master-Sergeant Samuel Doe, and the new regime then proceeded to execute several of Tolbert's leading officials by firing squad amid scenes of gruesome celebration on a Monrovia beach. A delegation of neighbouring heads of state was immediately despatched to see Doe, in a temporarily successful attempt to persuade him to abide by internationally acceptable norms of public behaviour; the inclusion in the group of President Eyadema of Togo, who was widely credited with personal responsibility for the murder of one of his own predecessors, President Olympio, might have been taken as a tactful indication that such actions did not exclude Doe from eventual acceptance into the fraternity of African rulers.[9]

A more systematic attempt to convey a sense of continental concern for the internal government of individual African states was undertaken with the drafting of an African Charter on Human and Peoples' Rights, under the chairmanship of President Jawara of The Gambia, one of the few African leaders whose own country's generally fair multiparty elections and respect for the rights of its people gave him the credentials for the task. The Charter was approved in 1981 by the Assembly of Heads of State and Government of the OAU, and came into effect in October 1986 after being ratified by a majority of OAU member states.[10] It thus formally established the principle that the domestic conduct of African leaders was subject to generally accepted criteria of international morality. That was about as far as it went. The Charter was not legally binding, and provisions in the original draft placing states under an obligation to 'guarantee' rights and 'ensure' respect for them were taken out in order to gain acceptance from member states. Many important rights were made subject to domestic law, and therefore placed no restraint on it, such as the provision (art. 9) that 'every individual shall have the right to express and disseminate his opinions within the law'. The inclusion of 'peoples' rights' allowed for supposedly collective rights, which were implicitly subject to interpretation by the government of the state concerned as the custodian of the rights of its people, to take precedence over the rights of individuals. Nor was the Charter in any way legally enforceable, and although an African Commission on Human and Peoples' Rights was established under the Charter, this had no independent fact-finding ability, or even any right to make its recommendations public without approval by the OAU Heads of State. All in all, the African Charter constituted a formal admission on the part of the OAU and its member states that human rights within their own territories were a matter of legitimate external concern, while stopping short of any means by which they could be held responsible for any abuse of such rights.[11]

Not until after the end of the Cold War, however, was any effective pressure brought by the outside world on African states to maintain any commitment to human rights, let alone any form of domestic political accountability. Though President Carter attempted to incorporate human rights criteria into the conduct of United States foreign policy after his inauguration in 1977, the main application of this doctrine to Africa was to justify the withdrawal of United States support from the Mengistu government in Ethiopia, which had in any event by that time declared its commitment to Marxism–Leninism, and started to build close connections with the Soviet Union; as a result, US support was transferred to the almost equally unsavoury regime of Siyad Barre in the Somali Republic.[12] President Mobutu of Zaïre was likewise able to use his value as a Cold War ally to deflect American attention from his human rights record.[13] In 1979, the British and Netherlands governments attempted to have human rights criteria built into the renegotiated Lomé II Convention between the European Community and the associated African, Caribbean and Pacific states; but the ACP states refused to contemplate even a passing reference to the issue.[14] The same two EC states returned to the subject with the negotiations for the Lomé III Convention five years later, but succeeded only in having an anodyne declaration of principles which had no operational significance annexed to the Convention.[15] Occasionally, some particular incident aroused a response: after the Liberian executions of April 1980, for example, EC aid was briefly suspended.[16] For so long as they were subject to the constraints imposed by the Cold

War, however, Western states did not risk the imposition on Africa of principles of human rights or democracy which would be applicable to their allies as well as to their adversaries, and which would tend to push African leaders into the less demanding arms of the Soviet Union.

In the absence of action by Western governments, the major role in bringing external pressure on African governments over human rights related issues was taken by non-governmental organisations or NGOs.[17] Over a long period, going back to the campaigns against slavery and the activities of Christian missions, Africa had been viewed in Western societies as an appropriate arena for non-governmental organisations seeking to extend the application of moral principles which were regarded as being of universal validity. The new generation of NGOs concerned with human rights, led by Amnesty International which was founded in 1961, may be regarded as continuing this tradition into the post-colonial era, even though Amnesty was equally concerned over human rights issues in other parts of the world. Other NGOs with a specifically African focus included the United States-based Human Rights Watch/Africa (formerly Africa-Watch), and African Rights which split from it over the US intervention in Somalia in 1992. The increasingly important role of NGOs in the international relations of Africa will be considered more generally in chapter 10. In the area of human rights, though their impact on African governments was – to judge from the levels of human rights abuse that actually took place – fairly slight, they kept human rights issues before the attention of Western governments, and helped to ensure that they would be taken up at governmental level once changes in global political conditions made them a source of potential power rather than weakness.

The imposition of political conditionalities

The end of the Cold War brought an almost instant transformation. Prompted by its newly appointed Secretary-General, Salim Salim, the OAU approved a declaration in July 1990 which recognised the need to promote popular participation in government and to guarantee human rights.[18] By 1991, the great majority of African regimes had declared their commitment to the principle of multiparty electoral democracy, while several had experienced a political phenomenon never seen in any continental African state since independence: the peaceful transfer of power from a governing party to the former opposition after its victory in a multiparty election. This metamorphosis was the culmination of a series of pressures, both external and domestic, which made it extremely difficult for them to cling to their previous insistence on unfettered sovereignty in the international arena combined with monopoly statehood in the internal one. In some degree, these political changes followed on from the economic conditionalities discussed in the last chapter. Whereas it had been plausible to argue in the early 1980s that the implementation of structural adjustment policies would require 'a courageous, ruthless and perhaps undemocratic government',[19] by the end of the decade the World Bank and other donors were becoming convinced that such policies could only be carried out by regimes which enjoyed broad popular support. This was partly a matter of straightforward political effectiveness: given that reform policies had an inevitable initially unfavourable impact on a number of important domestic political interests, notably those of urban dwellers and state employees, governments had to be popular and self-confident enough to withstand the resulting protests. Beyond that, however, it could be argued that political structures which empowered rural producers, who were the main expected beneficiaries of adjustment programmes, would build a constituency in favour of economic reform which could outweigh the numerically usually smaller urban vested interests that were against it. In short, and in contrast to the argument that had seen autocratic regimes as essential to impose necessary but unpopular measures on a recalcitrant population, economically efficient and democratic government could be seen as going together.

Secondly, however, the end of the Cold War gave an enormous boost both to the power and to the self-confidence of the Western capitalist states. By virtually destroying the ideologies of single-party statehood and statist economic management which had served to uphold African as well as communist regimes, it left Western liberal capitalism in sole possession of the field, and provided a precise political equivalent to the 'monoeconomics' (the belief that the same economic principles applied equally to developing as to industrial economies) which had sustained structural adjustment. The application to Africa and elsewhere of Western liberal political models could be regarded, not as the imposition of values derived from one culture or stage of development on other cultures or developmental trajectories to which they were fundamentally unsuited, but rather as the transfer of political technologies of universal validity. The Soviet model had moreover been terminally discredited, not only as an ideology of development, but equally and perhaps more seriously as an ideology of 'nation-building'. In the wake of the collapse of both the Soviet Union and Yugoslavia into squabbling ethnic fragments, the idea that a single party and even a measure of autocracy were needed to create a sense of common purpose and identity among ethnically diverse populations within a single state could scarcely be sustained. On top of that, since the Soviet Union itself had disappeared, the inducement to Western states to maintain their own clientelist alliance systems in Africa in competition with those of the USSR had gone with it, removing one of the main bargaining counters which African regimes had been able to use to protect their domestic political hegemony from external attack.

Surprisingly, given its record of close association with the personalist autocracies of francophone Africa, one of the first Western governments to declare its support for multiparty democracy in Africa was the Mitterrand regime in France. At the Franco-African summit held at La Baule in June 1990, Mitterrand announced that those African governments which sought to defy the demands for popular political participation arising throughout the continent could not expect to receive French support.[20] For Mitterrand as for his audience of African heads of state, this sudden conversion evidently included a substantial element of calculation: it was indeed the association between France and personal rule in the past that made such nimble footwork necessary to preserve French interests in the continent under changed international circumstances. At the same time, the commitment to democracy also opened a door through which it would be possible to withdraw from parts of the continent where French interests no longer justified a continuing presence on the same scale as in the past.

For the United States, whose defence of the 'free world' against international communism had previously involved it in uncomfortable alliances with states which could not by any plausible criterion be described as free, the new dispensation promised a return to ideals which had consistently figured in American perceptions of their foreign policy, and also associated these ideals with the spread of Western capitalism. US aid programmes in particular were geared towards sustaining the bases for democracy by supporting the development of 'civil society' in African states.[21] The United Kingdom, normally sceptical about the introduction of grand moral principles into the conduct of diplomacy, announced that 'governments which persist with repressive policies, with corrupt management, and with wasteful and discredited economic systems should not expect us to support their folly with scarce aid resources'.[22] The European Community, reversing its earlier indifference, linked its aid to respect for human rights, democratisation, a free press and honest government in a resolution adopted in November 1991.[23] Even the Japanese, normally reticent in such matters, joined the bandwagon.

This response could in turn be linked both to the domestic constituencies represented by human rights NGOs, and to an awareness in the West of the concern about human rights and democracy being expressed by Africans themselves. In any assessment of the process of democratisation within Africa, the demand by a very large number of Africans for an improvement in the way in which they were governed would have to take pride of place. In assessing the decline of juridical sovereignty and the imposition of political conditionalities, however, it was the external recognition of these demands that mattered. The existence of a popular African voice, protesting against bad government, had hitherto been largely ignored within an international system that operated on the basis of relations between states. In the new international order, where the primacy previously accorded to states was being challenged – most generally by the spread of information and other elements of the process of 'globalisation', but more specifically by the growth of citizens' organisations concerned with international affairs – the emergence (from suppression rather than non-existence) of an African public opinion helped to convince Western publics and governments that, rather than merely imposing their own values on Africans, they were instead helping to empower Africans to bring about the changes which they themselves desired.

In short, 'political conditionalities' (as they soon came to be called, mirroring the economic conditionalities imposed under structural adjustment) could be regarded as the programme of an alliance, comprising international financial institutions, seeking to bring about the capitalist transformation of African economies; Western governments, flexing their diplomatic muscles in the aftermath of the Cold War; Western public opinions, outraged at the brutality and corruption of at least a significant number of African regimes; and finally, at least vicariously, the African publics who were vociferously demonstrating their own discontent with the existing order, and on whose behalf the Western aid donors could claim (often misleadingly) to speak. Directed against African governing elites, and the failing projects of monopoly statehood that they had sought to implement, this made a powerful combination.

Like the economic conditionalities which they resembled, these political conditionalities could be broken down into a number of common elements. The most basic and widely shared was a concern for 'human rights', which were in practice difficult to specify and monitor (the United Nations' famous Universal Declaration of Human Rights providing, in this respect, remarkably little guidance), but which could without much controversy be regarded as encompassing freedom from the politically motivated killing, torture, imprisonment without trial and similar abuses to which many Africans had been subjected. The United States government was from 1977 onwards obliged by Congress to publish an annual report on the extent to which other governments met a large number of specified human rights criteria, and which could then be used as a basis for US aid and other policies.[24] Voluntary organisations, and notably Amnesty International, published their own annual reports.[25]

Second was a concern for 'democracy', characteristically conceived in Western liberal terms and notably including the installation of governments freely chosen in multiparty elections. Up to a point, this requirement could be regarded in essentially technical terms, encompassing the promulgation of a constitution in which certain rights were guaranteed and essential procedures laid down; the lifting of any previous restrictions on activities such as the formation of political parties, publication of newspapers, and holding of public meetings; the holding of parliamentary and presidential elections, which in turn were subject to monitoring by international agencies; and the continued observance of democratic procedures by the regimes which were thus elected. In practice, however, it was recognised that democracies could not simply be legislated into existence, but that their maintenance required a range of supportive conditions which could to some extent be encouraged with external aid. Much of this aid concentrated on sustaining the institutions of 'civil society', or in other words organisations outside government which might be expected to act as a constraint on the abuse of power by governments of the sort that had occurred in the past, while also helping to shape the attitudes and values of the government itself. This evidently required aid programmes which not only evaded the state, by directing resources to non-governmental organisations within African societies, but which also explicitly sought to undermine it. The search for 'civil society' brought aid donors into a direct engagement in social reconstruction which would previously have lain outside their accepted role.[26]

Third, there was a more general concern for what was often described as 'governance'. At its most technical, this could be regarded as encompassing a set of procedures for ensuring that the business of government was carried out as honestly and efficiently as possible, together with training measures designed to create a body of civil servants capable of understanding and implementing these procedures – an enterprise which showed pronounced similarities to the programmes of 'africanisation' carried out by the departing colonial powers, which continued in most cases for several years after independence. At its broadest, it could be extended to include any measures that were intended or expected to produce a 'better' government, including all those that might be covered under the headings of democracy and human rights. 'Good governance' programmes were characteristically most concerned with measures designed to enhance the honesty, efficiency and accountability of bureaucratic departments.[27]

Taken together, then, political conditionalities constituted an ambitious project for reforming and reordering African states, in accordance with external models and subject to external controls. Some of the elements involved, notably the more technical requirements of 'good governance', were incorporated into structural adjustment programmes negotiated with the World Bank, and were subject to the same bargaining processes as economic conditionalities.[28] The Bank and other international institutions none the less had only a very limited competence to intervene in the domestic political management of individual states, and many of the criteria covered under political conditionality lay beyond their scope. These therefore usually came directly under the initiative of individual states. By far the most activist state in this respect, as a result both of its power and of its readiness to inject its political values into its conduct of diplomacy, was the United States. In some countries, and notably in Kenya, US ambassadors publicly criticised African regimes and called for their reform in terms which would previously have been regarded as well beyond the bounds of acceptable diplomacy.[29] The Scandinavian states, which likewise combined a high profile as aid donors with a concern for moral values in international relations, were often not far behind. In November 1994, Norway and Sweden cut off aid to

Tanzania, previously one of their most favoured recipients, in protest at corruption;[30] the money was used to pay off the arrears of debt owed to the World Bank by Uganda and Ethiopia – a shift which neatly encapsulated the changing priorities of aid donors.

Unlike the economic conditionalities imposed by the World Bank, political conditionalities were often not directly linked to aid, but formed part of the normal business of diplomatic relations. United States aid to Kenya, for example, was negligible by the mid-1990s, and all of it was directly allocated to non-governmental groups. In some cases, when the attitudes of the major Western states broadly coincided and their interests were not strongly engaged, they set up a formalised system of consultation, normally chaired by a senior ambassador to the state concerned, in order to compare notes and co-ordinate policies; at the time of the Kenyan elections in 1992, for example, the Canadian ambassador chaired a group set up by the consortium of Western donors to monitor the elections.[31] The point at which a normal process of diplomatic co-operation gave way to a consortium of Western states seeking to exercise tutelary guidance over African regimes was potentially hard to discern. Regular meetings between diplomatic missions of the European Union, held under the political co-operation provisions of the Maastricht Treaty,[32] potentially served a similar function, though the fact that one EU state, normally the United Kingdom or France, almost invariably had the peculiar position conferred by post-imperial status, and the set of special interests that went with it, impeded the formulation of any single EU policy.

Underlying the whole issue of political conditionality, as this was pursued by Western states, there was indeed a considerable element of sleight of hand. The language of human rights, democracy and governance provided them with a discourse through which they could greatly enhance their bargaining power against African governments, and in particular gain a freedom of action which they could use either to intervene in what would previously have been regarded as the sphere of domestic politics, or else to withdraw from previous obligations. Whereas structural adjustment was for the most part pursued – regardless of how successful it proved to be – by international financial institutions which had a genuine commitment to the policies which it entailed, political conditionality was the instrument of other goals.

At one level, Western states faced a genuine dilemma. Having abandoned the principle of juridical sovereignty, and acknowledged that the attempt to maintain African states by giving military or financial aid to the incumbent government was often merely counter-productive, they still had to decide what to do instead. At the broadest conceptual level, it was easy enough to assert that African states could only be preserved and strengthened by making them more accountable to the societies which they ruled. In practice, as the experience of Gorbachev in the Soviet Union made all too clear, it was difficult to reform the political structure of authoritarian states while preserving their governmental effectiveness; and in arbitrating between the demands of greater participation on the one hand, and the maintenance of authority on the other, the instincts of Western governments generally favoured authority, especially if democracy appeared to be leading to the recrudescence of ethnic conflict and the possibility of state collapse. President Moi in Kenya constantly emphasised the dangers of tribal violence should Western states persist with their demands for multiparty democracy – and then took covert steps to ensure that such violence would indeed occur.[33] The principles of democracy and good government did not avert the need for difficult judgements which had to take into account the specific problems of often very different African states: what was appropriate for Kenya was not necessarily appropriate for Uganda, even though the language in which action had to be justified was the same. However widely the Western liberal multiparty model might be touted as the solution to Africa's political problems, the prospects for successfully implementing such a model varied enormously; and whereas a single economic package might be imposed almost indiscriminately on nearly all African states, there was no way that donors could realistically expect the same degree of uniformity in political systems.

At another level, Western states also retained interests in the continent, and sought to ensure that these would be served and not undermined by political conditionalities. The 'spirit of La Baule' proclaimed by the Mitterrand government proved to be of very short duration, except in places where – as in Rwanda, where it translated into support for Hutu demands for power against the Tutsi minority – it could be made to serve the government's own agenda.[34] Both the American and the British governments likewise differed in their approach to African regimes which they regarded with greater or lesser degrees of sympathy. There were thus significant cracks in the alliance of Western powers that sought to further the new democratic agenda. In the absence of a single external body such as the World Bank, which could be used to help present a united front of the major capitalist powers, and in the process protect each of them from having to take much of the blame, the imposing states were much more directly confronted with the potential consequences of their own policies. While in some African states, moreover, their interests were negligible, there were others in which these were significant – and inevitably, those who had the most important interests in any particular state, and were therefore in the strongest position to impose their preferred outcome, were also those who had most to lose and were therefore most prone to temporise. Former colonial powers in particular tended to take a gentler and more nuanced approach to demands for political reform than states which did not have the same range of local connections. They had often built up good working relations with the regime currently in power, and could not always be sure about their reception by the opposition. Especially in francophone states such as Gabon or Cameroon, there was a real question about whether a new government would look as favourably on the French connection as the old one. When it came to the crunch, external patrons might prefer to stick with the government that they knew.

The ambivalence of the democratising ethos was nowhere more clearly demonstrated than by the role of external election monitoring. On the one hand, the validation of elections by groups drawn variously from international institutions, bilateral aid donors, and associated non-governmental groups strikingly symbolised the loss of sovereignty. Aid donors were able to insist that elections be policed to their satisfaction as a condition for the continued supply of aid. On the other hand, election monitors were then extremely reluctant to dismiss any election as fraudulent; and even in cases where there were considerable doubts about their validity, monitoring organisations generally phrased their reports in a manner acceptable to the government, softening evidence of fraud into references to 'difficulties' or 'irregularities' in the electoral process. Commonwealth electoral observers viewed their mission, indeed, largely as one of assisting the government in holding the election, an attitude which was difficult to reconcile with acting as an independent referee.[35] Rather than serving as a guarantee against the manipulation of the electoral process by the government, they could instead indicate international acquiescence in the means used by governments to maintain themselves in power.[36]

The African state response

These differences and ambiguities in Western approaches to political conditionality allowed African rulers a measure of flexibility. In principle, they faced the same range of possible responses to this additional challenge to their jurisdiction over their domestic political systems as they had to structural adjustment: compliance, subversion, or defiance. In practice, however, the situations were rather different, and the range of options was rather more complex. For one thing, even though their continued tenure of power was now explicitly threatened, in a way that it had not been by the external imposition of unwelcome economic policies, they still had the chance of winning outright by holding acceptable multiparty elections in which they might defeat whatever opposition forces were mustered against them. For another, although contestants for power mushroomed in most African states, as soon as it became clear that there was to be a free-for-all in which hitherto suppressed opposition movements or ambitious defectors from the governing party might have their chance of glory, the capacity of the opposition to launch a viable challenge varied greatly from state to state. Incumbent governments therefore needed to position themselves carefully as between external pressures and domestic political groupings, and if possible prevent these from combining against them.

On the whole, the new opposition parties were only too ready to seek the support of Western embassies, since it was through Western pressure on their own governments that they hoped to win power. They accordingly took care not to put forward programmes which might seem threatening to the lords of the new international order: nowhere in the continent did the upsurge in political participation lead to the formation of socialist or even radical parties, while even existing parties with a long history of socialist commitment, such as the ANC in South Africa, recognised the need to adapt to the new global realities. Having taken it upon themselves to impose democratic systems of government on African states, Western diplomats soon found themselves the targets of a new form of the politics of extraversion, in which opposition politicians were constantly knocking on the embassy door to complain about the undemocratic practices of the government. For opposition parties, as previously for governments, the way to power led as much through external support as through the mobilisation of their domestic constituencies.

There were several cases, including some quite surprising ones, in which established African rulers acceded to the demand for multiparty elections presented (with more or less overt external support) by their domestic oppositions, conducted them fairly, and then peacefully handed over power once they had lost. Mathieu Kerekou in Benin and Kenneth Kaunda in Zambia led the way respectively in francophone and anglophone Africa. In each of these cases, the demand for democracy was largely a domestic one, and external pressures were relatively muted, though the changes in the global system evidently influenced the willingness of the incumbent ruler to depart.[37] In Benin, a state with a long if chaotic tradition of popular political participation, the domestic pressures for change were especially vibrant. In Malawi, the nonagenarian president-for-life Dr Hastings Kamuzu Banda was eventually induced by external pressure, first to hold a referendum on whether there should be a multiparty system, second (when this had been overwhelmingly approved) to hold the resulting elections, and finally to depart when these were won by one of the opposition candidates.[38] In the island microstates of Cape Verde and São Tomé and Principe, the ready acceptance of multiparty elections could most simply be ascribed to an urgent need for aid.

A variety of strategies was available to those who were determined to cling on. The most effective was that followed by President Houphouet-Boigny in Côte d'Ivoire, who agreed to the opposition demand for immediate elections, and then held them before his outsmarted rivals could organise any effective challenge.[39] President Moi in Kenya, as the ruler of another relatively wealthy state with a strong pro-Western orientation and appreciable Western economic interests, might well have been expected to enjoy an equally easy ride. That he did not was due partly to the relative strength of organised opposition, which was capable of mobilising a threatening ethnic coalition; partly to a particularly outspoken United States ambassador, Smith Hempstone, who was prepared to criticise the government far more openly than any other senior diplomatic representative in Africa; but partly also to his failure or refusal to go through the motions of reform, until this had been forced on him by the refusal of his principal creditors to reschedule Kenya's debts until an acceptable system of multiparty democracy had been put in place.[40] Kenya was indeed the most explicit case of the imposition of multiparty elections as a result of external pressure. Given the presence of an active opposition which appeared to have every prospect of ousting the incumbent regime were it given the chance to do so, the United States could press ahead with pressures for democratisation in reasonable confidence that it would then be able to work with a friendly regime which its own efforts (and, of course, the support of the electorate) had helped to put in power. In the event, however, the opposition split into three competing fragments, and Moi was able to win re-election on a minority vote.[41]

Other rulers were able to survive through a combination of fraud, force and external acquiescence. In the case of Cameroon, this meant falsifying the election results, in connivance with a French government which was concerned that the election of an anglophone Cameroonian president might endanger its position in a significant oil-producing state.[42] In Togo, where parliamentary elections produced a government hostile to the incumbent President Eyadema, he was able to retain a formally titular presidency, and use his continued control over the army to frustrate the government and reassert his power.[43] In Nigeria, the outgoing military regime of General Babangida organised elections under a carefully contrived two-party system, in which the presidential candidates of both parties were Moslem businessmen who had been closely associated with Babangida himself. When, however, the less favoured of Babangida's two candidates won the election, demonstrating in the process a less deferential attitude than he had expected and drawing support from well beyond the ethnic constituencies which had traditionally shaped electoral politics in Nigeria, Babangida took fright and cancelled the election. After an initial and unsuccessful attempt to quieten the resulting popular protests by installing an unelected civilian regime, this led to the imposition of another military government under General Sani Abacha.[44]

The most determined and resourceful attempt to cling to power was, however, that maintained by President Mobutu in Zaïre, who as the leading example in Africa of a corrupt but Western-backed dictator was under particularly strong pressure to give way to a more accountable regime. He was eventually able to avoid having to hold any elections at all, and survived through a combination of the manipulation of opposition politicians, whom he appointed to government positions and then undermined, and a judicious use of force – in the course of which the French ambassador to Zaïre was killed, whether accidentally or not, by Mobutu-supporting soldiers engaged in violent demonstrations against a regime which had been installed in power as a result of external pressure. Eventually, Mobutu was able to use the Rwandan crisis of mid-1994 to restore himself to French favour, by allowing Zaïrean territory to be used as a base by the French intervention force, and subsequently by Hutu militias ousted by the new RPF regime. His prominent role as doyen and co-chair of Mitterrand's farewell Franco-African summit at Biarritz late in 1994 symbolised his triumph.[45]

While some African leaders were desperately struggling to sustain themselves in the face of domestic opposition backed by external pressure others, however, appeared to face no such challenge. In Zimbabwe, for example, President Mugabe had made no secret of his preference for a single-party regime, and had used the most brutal methods to force the major opposition movement, the Ndebele-based ZAPU of Joshua Nkomo, into his ruling ZANU party in the mid-1980s.[46] Though a formal single-party system had been avoided, largely as the result of pressure from within ZANU itself, ZANU was so dominant as to form a single party in all but name. Its pre-eminence was fortified, despite growing public indifference indicated by low turn-out at elections, by its access to generous government financial support denied to other parties, by its control of the electoral machinery, and by the right of the President to nullify even a strong electoral showing by opposition parties by appointing thirty members of parliament himself.[47] Though levels of official corruption probably did not approach those found in Kenya, there was none the less ample evidence of self-enrichment by leading politicians, exemplified by a scandal in which ministers were found to have confiscated valuable farms run by white commercial farmers in order to redistribute them among themselves.[48] The press was appreciably more subservient than in Kenya to government control.[49] Yet Western pressure on the Mugabe government to institute a more open and accountable political system was virtually non-existent. This was doubtless partly because, unlike Kenya, the weakness of the opposition was such that Mugabe was likely to stay in power anyhow, and little was to be achieved by offending him; but equally, unlike Moi, Mugabe was prepared to accept the formalities of a multiparty electoral system before these were forced on him.

Another group of states to escape the full rigours of external pressure for democratisation might be described as 'reconstructing autocracies'. These were states which had been in an advanced condition of collapse, and where power had been seized – usually by guerrilla warfare, sometimes by military *coup d'état* – by an efficiently organised though militaristic regime with a commitment to reconstruction, even at the cost of continuing autocracy. Among Commonwealth African states, the clearest examples were Ghana under Jerry Rawlings and Uganda under Yoweri Museveni, but equivalents could be found in Meles Zenawi's Ethiopia and Isaias Afewerki's Eritrea, as well as in the attempts of the RPF regime to restore some semblance of government in the aftermath of the Rwandan genocide of mid-1994. Here, a plausible case could be made for putting the requirements of order before those of participation, and external demands for political reform were correspondingly softened or delayed, despite the vociferous complaints of civilian political parties which sometimes, as in Uganda, bore a high degree of responsibility for the original collapse. Thus Uganda was permitted to continue for the best part of a decade with a no-party system in which representatives of the former parties were allowed to participate on a personal basis, while little pressure was placed on either the EPLF in Eritrea or the EPRDF in Ethiopia to go much beyond the formalities of a democratic system.[50] When elections eventually took place, as in Ghana in 1992, the incumbent regime was able to contest them, and its victory (if not an entirely foregone conclusion) occasioned neither surprise nor regret among the foreign diplomatic community.[51]

In other cases, a programme of externally monitored democratisation was promoted – with a greater or lesser degree of success – as a basis for a political settlement between warring movements, and, in the process, as a means of restoring some degree of legitimacy to the government of fragmented states. The management of fair elections in states which had been subject to decades of civil war, and in which only a precarious ceasefire had been put in place, was inevitably an uncertain business, in which the losers would have little difficulty in contesting the fairness of the poll. On the first occasion on which it was tried, in the Angolan elections of 1992, the electoral process broke down as soon as the results were announced, when Savimbi's Unita resumed the war rather than accept that it had lost. It is a matter of dispute whether a more effective UN peacekeeping operation might have induced or compelled Savimbi to abide by the political settlement.[52] In Mozambique in 1994, where the opposition movement Renamo likewise lost the elections to the incumbent regime, the settlement at least initially held, aided by the fact that Renamo was appreciably more dependent than Unita on external assistance, and was consequently more open to external pressure.[53] In Liberia and Somalia, on the other hand, attempts to negotiate a political settlement based on an eventual appeal to the electorate broke down long before the elections could take place.

Straightforward defiance of the Western attempt to impose multiparty electoral systems required a state to devise both an alternative source of legitimacy with which it could appeal to at least a core of domestic support, and an alternative source of external aid which it could use to suppress internal dissent. The one African state to opt openly and unapologetically for a policy of defiance, Sudan under the al-Beshir regime which seized power in 1989, found both of these in Islam. As a source of legitimacy, the appeal to Islam enabled the regime to reject Western multipartyism as an alien and indeed immoral system of government, while gaining the support of an appreciable constituency in northern Sudan, where a commitment to Islam formed an important defining element in local political culture. As a source of external support, it enabled the regime to appeal for military assistance first to Iraq, and then after the Kuwaiti crisis of 1990–1 (in which Sudan was one of the very few states to side openly with Saddam Hussein) to Iran.[54] The set of circumstances which enabled Sudan to take this deviant course was, however, replicated in few if any other African states.

The other regimes which sought to evade Western demands for multiparty electoral systems, and notably the three anglophone West African military regimes of Nigeria, Sierra Leone and The Gambia, appeared to lack either the domestic or the diplomatic support necessary to sustain this stance for long. The Sierra Leonean regime of Captain Valentine Strasser, which seized power in April 1992 from a single-party government of notable corruption, which had presided over a long period of economic decline and was making only token efforts at political reform, evidently aspired to emulate Flight Lieutenant Jerry Rawlings in Ghana; but despite gaining support in Freetown, it could establish itself neither with donors nor in the countryside, and as disorder spread from the civil war in neighbouring Liberia, aided by indiscipline in the Sierra Leonean army itself, its control shrunk progressively to the area surrounding the capital.[55] The Gambian military regime which ousted President Jawara in 1994 was in an even more precarious position, since the minuscule Gambian economy depended heavily on package tours organised by British holiday companies, most of which cancelled their bookings in November 1994;[56] the perils of economic dependence were never more graphically illustrated. The Nigerian military regime of General Sani Abacha was scarcely comparable with that of a microstate such as The Gambia, and Nigeria's exceptionally low dependence on foreign aid insulated it from one potential source of external pressure; but the combination of domestic opposition with high international indebtedness left it, too, facing an impasse from which it could be rescued only by political reform.[57]

Such cases of failed democratic transition indicated that the ability of African regimes to resist external economic and diplomatic pressure gained them only partial and temporary relief. African states were not weak because of their level of external dependence; rather, they were dependent because they were weak. If those weaknesses could not be addressed through reform programmes which brought governments at least a measure of external (and indeed internal) support, then they were likely to manifest themselves in other ways. In an increasing number of African states, these took the form of guerrilla insurgencies.

9 The international politics of insurgency

Insurgency and the African international order

One of the clearest symptoms – and also causes – of state decay in Africa was the growth of armed opposition movements against the state, originating usually in the least accessible areas of the countryside, which came to pose a serious challenge not just to individual states, but to the African international order as a whole. Variously described as guerrilla movements, liberation struggles, or indeed as private armies, terrorists or secessionist bandits, these movements may – without overlooking the important differences between them – be examined together under the reasonably neutral term, insurgencies. Two regions of the continent, the Horn and southern Africa, were particularly affected by insurgent warfare, and in each case fostered a mass of competing movements which interacted with the states of the region to exercise a powerful effect on its international relations. Insurgent warfare also affected other states, including Chad, Uganda, Rwanda and Zaïre in central and eastern Africa, and Liberia and Sierra Leone in West Africa, which, however, was generally the least insurgent-affected part of the continent. A small but significant number of African governments came to power as a result of insurgency; and two states, Liberia and Somalia, were destroyed by insurgent movements which, fragmenting into numerous different factions, were unable to establish any effective regime. Occasionally, however, and notably in Uganda, insurgency provided the means for reconstructing states which appeared to have almost collapsed.

The origins of insurgency lay almost entirely in the domestic politics of the states concerned, and notably in the actions of governments which not only excluded substantial sections of their national populations from any form of effective political participation, but governed them in a manner so brutal and exploitative as to induce eventual resistance. Insurgency was the ultimate proof of the failure of monopoly statehood. In several cases – as for instance in Chad, Somalia, post-Amin Uganda, Angola and Mozambique – the weakness of incumbent governments made it easier to launch insurgencies which a more effective regime might have been able to suppress. Only in Mozambique, where Renamo was clearly the product of deliberate destabilisation measures taken first by the Rhodesian and subsequently by the South African intelligence services, was any African insurgency evidently external in origin.[1] Virtually all of them none the less drew to a significant extent, and some of them indeed to an overwhelming extent, on the international system, and their impact on African international relations was profound.

Despite some excellent studies of individual movements,[2] the international implications of insurgency in the continent as a whole have, however, been neglected. In part, this is doubtless because the patterns of international politics revealed by insurgency often ran sharply counter to the ideologies or mythologies of African statehood and unity. Insurgencies, too, were violent, often secretive, and subject to often intensely held mythologies of their own, and they were consequently difficult to study. They none the less formed an integral part of the international relations of Africa, and their incorporation into an understanding of the subject is overdue.

Many of the earliest insurgencies to occur in modern Africa did indeed fit clearly into the conventions of African statehood, and consequently acquired a legitimate and even honoured place in the international relations of the continent. Normally characterised as 'liberation movements', these were directed against those colonial and white minority regimes which refused to permit any peaceful transition to African majority rule. The ideology of decolonisation imposed on African states an obligation to aid these movements which was accepted even by the most conservative regimes, and which was formalised through the establishment of the Liberation Committee of the OAU with its headquarters in Dar-es-Salaam. Acceptance of the legitimacy of the decolonisation struggle, not only within Africa but also through the celebrated Resolution 1514 of the United Nations General Assembly,[3] opened the way to support from other states in the international system, and notably from the Soviet Union and its allies, which could use their unequivocal commitment to African decolonisation as a means to make common cause with African states, against Western powers which were reluctant to go beyond merely formal support for the principle of majority rule. Even though the United States provided some aid to the FNLA in Angola before Portuguese withdrawal, this was due simply to the need to find a counterweight to the Soviet-supported MPLA, rather than to any commitment to liberation in itself.

Apart from Guinea-Bissau in West Africa, these liberation insurgencies were heavily concentrated in the southern cone of the continent, where they were internationalised through the support provided by the 'front line states' on one side, and through collaboration between the white minority regimes on the other. Patterns of alliance between movements in different territories, and between insurgent movements and states, therefore long predated the achievement of independence. These patterns were complicated, not only by the encouragement of divisions within liberation movements by the threatened minority regimes, and by retaliatory insurgencies directed against states which aided them, but also by the existence of competing movements with access to alternative sources of external support. The Sino-Soviet split, in particular, led to the formation of rival client networks and helped to create rivalries and alliances between movements in different southern African states which owed little to their domestic strategies or ideologies.[4] For African states, these rivalries were an embarrassment, since they offended the principle of African unity against minority rule. Wherever possible, the OAU Liberation Committee sought either to unify competing movements within a single common front – a strategy which rarely worked, but which achieved at least a partial success with the formation of the Patriotic Front of ZANU and ZAPU in Zimbabwe – or to designate one movement as 'authentic' for purposes of African support.

A second group, which may be termed 'separatist insurgencies', directly offended against the most basic principles of the African international order, by seeking independent statehood, or sometimes a special and separate status within an existing state, for one particular people or region. This threatened the inherited structure of state boundaries which OAU members were pledged to uphold. The early attempted secessions of Katanga from Congo/Zaïre, and of Biafra from Nigeria, do not qualify as insurgencies in the sense defined above, since they were proclaimed by the constituted regional authorities of the territories concerned, and did not take the form of guerrilla warfare, though the patterns of international opposition and support which they elicited were comparable to those found in other cases. The separatist insurgencies in southern Sudan and Eritrea gave rise to two of Africa's (and the world's) longest wars. The southern Sudanese movements did not for the most part seek the formal secession of the South as a sovereign state from the rest of Sudan, whereas sovereign independence was always the goal of all the different movements in Eritrea, and was eventually achieved in 1993. The movements for Somali self-determination in Ethiopia and (in a much more muted form) Kenya, and for eventual union with the Somali Republic, belonged in the same category, along with the movement for Ewe unification in Ghana.[5] In all these cases, the insurgents could win the tacit support of the governments of neighbouring states, but since their cause explicitly offended against continental norms, only the Somali government with its commitment to Somali unification openly supported separatism. The Ethiopian government in particular had the strongest reasons to uphold the territorial sovereignty of existing states, and could not publicly support secession in neighbouring Sudan. This in turn helped to explain why the southern Sudanese movements generally expressed their goals in terms of regional autonomy rather than outright independence.

A third group, of 'reform insurgencies', sought to transform the governing structures of their own states, but did not make explicit demands on the international system. These only emerged relatively late in the day, once the inadequacies and worse of existing African governments had become all too evident, and they were most clearly exemplified by the NRA in Uganda, the TPLF and later EPRDF in Ethiopia, and the RPF in Rwanda. All of these movements owed much of their support to specific ethnic or regional constituencies within their own states, but expressed their demands in national rather than ethnic or regional terms. Whereas the EPLF in Eritrea could justify a demand for independence within the boundaries of the former Italian colony of Eritrea, and challenge the legality of Eritrea's incorporation into Ethiopia, the TPLF in neighbouring Tigray could not similarly justify the secession of a region which had continuously formed part of Ethiopia since the earliest times. The Tutsi in Rwanda, who dominated the RPF, were not geographically separated from the Hutu who controlled the government in power until 1994, and in any event recognised the futility of seeking to establish a state based on only some 15 per cent of the Rwandan population. Museveni in Uganda sought national goals, even though he had largely regional support. But even though these insurgencies did not explicitly challenge the African state system, they none the less almost inevitably affected regional relations.

A fourth group, finally, had poorly defined aims, and could largely be associated with the personal ambitions of their leaders. Though they formed a diverse category, they can broadly be grouped together as 'warlord insurgencies', and were found throughout the continent, from Liberia and Sierra Leone through Chad to Somalia, and down to Angola and Mozambique.[6] They were distinguished by personal leadership, generally weak organisational structures, and still weaker ideological motivation. In those cases where they managed to overthrow incumbent regimes, they generally proved unable to establish effective governments in their place. They affected Africa's international relations in two major ways. First, they sought external patronage on an almost entirely opportunistic basis, even if this was at times disguised by a rhetorical commitment to the principles espoused by their current patron – to multiparty democracy and a capitalist economy on the part of Renamo in Mozambique, for example, or to unification with Libya by factions in Chad. Secondly, their inability to establish or manage viable states was a major factor in almost every case of African state breakdown, and ultimately posed a far more serious threat to the African state system than that presented by separatist or secessionist movements.

These insurgencies often differed markedly, both in their internal structure and effectiveness, and in their relations with the international order. Liberation insurgencies, in particular, constituted a distinctive form of nationalist movement against colonial rule, and one which was invariably adopted only after any constitutional means of expressing African aspirations had been blocked by the incumbent regime, rather than as part of the international relations of independent Africa. There are none the less compelling reasons for considering them together. For one thing, very different kinds of insurgency were often closely associated with one another in their actual operations. It is, for example, difficult to understand external support for Unita in Angola without also considering SWAPO in Namibia, or to separate Rhodesian support for Renamo from Mozambican support for ZANU. In the Horn, the separatist insurgencies of the SPLA and EPLF formed part of a common 'security complex' with the reform insurgency of the TPLF, and these in turn affected the warlord insurgencies of Somalia. For another, almost all insurgent movements had common needs, deriving from the tactical requirements of their struggle against incumbent regimes, which included access to an open frontier, across which they could attack or maintain communications with the outside, a measure of external patronage, and means of acquiring essential resources such as arms and money. These created important points of comparison, even between movements which differed markedly from one another in other ways. Finally, insurgencies of all kinds were deeply affected, both in the thinking of many of those who led them and in the ways in which they were analysed by outsiders, by common theories of insurgent warfare deriving largely from Mao Zedong; the experience of African insurgency could in turn be used to appraise and reassess these theories.

One of the most significant ways in which African insurgencies could be distinguished from one another, and one which then shaped the nature of their external relations, was in the relative balance in each case between their external and diplomatic relationships on the one hand, and their internal military effectiveness on the other. Virtually all insurgencies required some combination of the two. Among the African cases of which I am aware, only the NRA in Uganda was able to achieve ultimate success, or even a reasonable level of effectiveness, without continuing access to external resources, and in this it was greatly helped by the virtual collapse of the Ugandan state as a result of the Amin era and the subsequent instability. The NRA appears to have obtained some initial aid from Libya, but operated throughout the war from 1981 to 1986 without significant cross-border support. At the other extreme, no externally based opposition movement which operated without any attempt to contest military control of the territory of the regime which it opposed could properly be described as an insurgency at all.

The most significant difference in this respect lay between what may be termed 'internal' and 'external' insurgencies. *Internal* insurgencies were those which were able to establish a substantial presence inside the territory of the 'target state' (the state against which the insurgency was directed), and could normally maintain themselves without needing to retreat across the frontier into the territory of a neighbouring 'host state' (a state which was prepared to give support to an insurgent movement). Their leadership was accordingly established in the area of military operations, and many of them were able to administer extensive 'liberated areas', which government troops were able to penetrate, if at all, only by temporary and unsustainable concentrations of force. Such insurgencies normally needed to engage in external relations, both with neighbouring states and with more distant powers, in order to maintain their communications and logistical support, as well as to pursue their goals in the diplomatic arena; they needed to retreat across the frontier, however, only in cases of emergency. They could be quite sharply disinguished from *external* insurgencies, which were unable to maintain a permanent presence inside the territory of the target state, and which were consequently obliged to conduct their operations from the territory of a host state across the frontier. The leadership was in that case based abroad, and the movement's effectiveness and even survival were deeply affected by its relations with the governments of the states in which it had taken refuge. Its diplomatic activities, which could scarcely be described as 'external' relations in that there was no 'internal' sphere of operations with which they could be contrasted, then acquired an extreme importance. Military operations even sometimes became an offshoot of diplomacy, in that they were undertaken in order to establish the movement's credentials with its external backers, rather than with any plausible expectation of achieving military objectives.

Because of their legitimate international status, liberation insurgencies could maintain an autonomous external existence which was virtually independent of any effective military presence within the target territory; and though some liberation insurgencies, especially in the Portuguese colonies, were directed against relatively weak regimes, others sought to challenge some of the most formidably organised states in Africa. The South African army in particular, both in its own territory and in Namibia, was in military terms virtually invincible, without a commitment of troops by other states which would have taken the war beyond the sphere of insurgency altogether. ZANU (and to a much lesser extent ZAPU) were eventually able, at considerable cost, to establish a permanent presence inside Rhodesia/Zimbabwe, but their leadership remained outside. Even though liberation insurgencies generally enjoyed a high level of support amongst the people of the target territory, the balance of diplomatic and military factors in this case therefore generally tilted in the external direction.[7] In Namibia especially, the combination of military weakness with an exceptionally powerful diplomatic position, deriving from Namibia's special status as a United Nations trust territory and the recognition of

SWAPO by the UN General Assembly as 'sole and authentic representative of the Namibian people', meant that SWAPO pursued an essentially external strategy, which in turn had lasting effects not just on its diplomatic relations but also on its internal structure, ethos and ideology.[8]

At the other extreme, those movements which could not obtain ready access to international diplomatic support had to establish an effective presence within the territory of their target state, or else perish. Though a measure of sympathy was sometimes available from neighbouring states, these could not be expected to jeopardise their relations with the target state, in support of a movement which had only negligible prospects of success. It was thus essential for the movement to be able to maintain itself inside the country, if it was to attract the attention of the international community. The EPLF's ability to demonstrate that it controlled a large part of the population of Eritrea, for example, enabled it to bid for external food supplies during the famine of 1984–85, and for the valuable outside contacts that these brought with them. The EPLF indeed provided the classic example of a movement which was largely shunned by the international community, because of the unacceptability of its secessionist goals to the idea of African statehood that was upheld not only by the OAU but by both superpowers and by the former colonial metropoles. Though it engaged in a vigorous campaign for diplomatic recognition, this depended much more on its strength on the ground than vice versa. Other movements combined their military and diplomatic resources in the manner best suited to their individual circumstances.

The politics of the border

Paradoxically, given the subversive impact of insurgency on the formal norms of African statehood, insurgent movements depended much more directly on their relations with states in the immediate vicinity of their target than on those with the developed industrial world. This was indeed the one area in which regional relations between African states were of primary importance. Although the superpowers in particular had a significant impact on African insurgencies, they were able to operate only through the medium of neighbouring African states through which their aid to insurgents could be channelled. In any military conflict, physical access is vital; and since public access to the target state was almost always controlled by the incumbent government, insurgents had to import their external resources by covert means. Despite occasional cases where insurgents were supplied by sea from international waters, or by airborne routes overflying neighbouring states, they almost always had to be supplied across land frontiers, and this in turn required the acquiescence of a neighbouring host state which was prepared to give them at least tacit support.

The point of entry to any analysis of the international politics of insurgency is thus to explain why African states should have been willing to support insurgent activity against their neighbours. This willingness in turn normally depended on the host state having an idea of the state which differed from that of the target state. This was most obviously the case with liberation insurgencies, where the whole basis of insurgency rested on the unacceptability of the domestic political structure of the target state, both to the insurgents and to the 'front line' states across the border which shared the insurgents' conception of legitimate statehood. In these cases, the willingness of neighbouring states to offer access to insurgents was normally determined largely by their vulnerability to retaliation by the target state. Accordingly, much of the counter-insurgency strategy of the Rhodesian and South African regimes in particular was concerned with raising the costs of support to neighbouring front line states to a level at which they would be obliged to deny access to the liberation movements. Angola's ability to maintain support for SWAPO, at a time when Mozambique had been obliged to abandon support for the ANC, derived from its lower level of geographical vulnerability to South African attack, and from its access to countervailing military support from Cuba and the Soviet Union.

Differing ideas of the state likewise accounted for the willingness of the Somali Republic, with its emphasis on ethnicity as the basis for statehood, to support insurgencies against the Ethiopian and Kenyan states which rested on a basis of territoriality. More generally, the limited role of territoriality as a basis for political legitimacy in Islam helped to explain why Arab North African states were often readier to support insurgencies than their sub-Saharan neighbours. Colonel Qadhafi's Libya, with its peculiar conception of statehood based on the idea of a people's *jamhariya*, provided the clearest example, but Morocco (which had pursued territorial claims against all its neighbours) was also relatively uninhibited in its support for insurgents elsewhere in the continent. In most of West Africa, where ideas of statehood were relatively uniform, external support for insurgency was correspondingly slight, and insurgencies themselves were rarer than elsewhere.

The introduction into Africa of a greatly intensified level of Cold War competition in the mid-1970s helped to prompt support for insurgencies which reflected global alliances. Whether or not the invasions of the Shaba region of Zaïre from Angolan territory in 1977 and 1978 were tacitly supported by Cuba and the Soviet Union, they certainly helped to encourage United States support for Unita through Zaïre.[9] American support for Renamo in Mozambique, which was much harder to associate with Cold War rivalries, was limited to the activities of private organisations such as the Heritage Foundation.[10] In the other part of the continent affected both by insurgency and by superpower rivalry, the Horn, local rivalries often appeared to guide superpower involvement, rather than vice versa. The close alliance between Ethiopia and the Soviet Union led to the association of Somalia and in some degree Sudan with the United States, and imported an implicit (though never explicit) element of superpower rivalry into the support given by each state to insurgencies against its neighbours. Simple retaliation was the major element in Ethiopian support for the SPLA, a movement with which the Mengistu government had little in common, and whose aspirations for regional autonomy (if not secession) were implicitly threatening to Ethiopia. Finally, it is possible to detect an element of sheer exasperation in the willingness of both Sierra Leonean and Ivoirian governments to permit attacks from their territories on Samuel Doe's Liberia, though Côte d'Ivoire may also have been influenced by the prospect of diverting Liberian exports through its own territory.

For externally based insurgencies, the role of the border was clearly critical. The independence of Angola and Mozambique, for example, opened up frontiers through which SWAPO and ZANU could launch vastly more effective attacks on the regimes in Namibia and Rhodesia/Zimbabwe. The availability of friendly frontiers also affected the relative fortunes of rival movements operating in the same country. The preference of Kenneth Kaunda's Zambian government for ZAPU over ZANU in the struggle for Zimbabwe made it very difficult for ZANU to operate effectively from Zambian territory; it also impeded ZANU's attempts to gain wider international backing, since an insurgent movement's access to the diplomatic community was characteristically mediated in some degree through the host state from which it had to operate. The Soviet Union's strong preference for ZAPU provided another obstacle. It was therefore only with the independence of Mozambique, which provided ZANU not just with a long frontier across which to conduct its military campaign, but with an alternative source of diplomatic backing, that ZANU was able to mount an effective diplomatic challenge to its rival liberation movement, as well as an effective military challenge to the white regime in Rhodesia. ZANU's African alliances were also associated with the support of the PRC against the USSR in the context of the Sino-Soviet split.[11] In Angola on the other hand, the potentially crippling effects for the MPLA of its failure to secure the support of any of its neighbours were offset by the strong backing which it received from Cuba and the Soviet Union.

The role of the border as a resource for insurgent movements was often associated with its importance as a haven for refugees.[12] Africa's unenviable status as the source of by far the largest number of refugees in relation to population of any continent in the world was certainly in part the result of its large number of states with permeable boundaries, and in consequence the relative ease of the 'exit' option as a response to political oppression or disturbance.[13] Getting out of a massive state such as China was nothing like so simple. Exit was also a much more straightforward option for pastoralists or shifting cultivators than for those whose livelihood bound them to permanent settlements. The major concentrations of African refugees were none the less in practice closely associated with insurgency. On the one hand, the two phenomena were often simply alternative responses to political alienation and the failure of the monopoly state: while some people sought to contest government control through armed conflict, others (and especially the most vulnerable sectors of the population) just wanted to escape. On the other hand, insurgency almost invariably caused mass population movement, as people tried to get away from the government forces, the insurgents, or simply the destruction and insecurity that any insurgent conflict inevitably brought with it.

In many cases, the flight of refugees led to the formation, just over the border, of refugee camps comprising people from the same population as the insurgents. The camps then became a refuge, a recruiting ground, and a source of supplies (notably of food, provided as relief for refugees by international agencies) for the insurgents. In some cases, it was even difficult to distinguish refugee camps from insurgent bases. The very high proportion of young men in the southern Sudanese refugee camps in south-west Ethiopia in the late 1980s may have been – as was claimed – the result merely of the fact that this section of the population was best equipped to reach safety; or it may have been that these were in effect SPLA training camps. The clearest case of the control of camps by insurgents arose, however, in Rwanda after the 1994 genocide, when the Hutu militias largely responsible for the killings, driven out of Rwanda by the Rwanda Patriotic Front, took with them other members of the Hutu community and used the resulting camps in Zaïre (and to a lesser extent Tanzania) as bases from which to organise their return.[14]

It could by no means be taken for granted, however, that local populations necessarily sympathised with the insurgents who were fighting in their territory, and that refugees therefore provided support for insurgency. The enormous influence on the study of insurgency of the work of Mao Zedong, with its image of guerrillas swimming around in the supportive environment provided by the local population like fishes in the sea, has fostered an impression of insurgency as 'liberation war', which it was impossible to pursue unless the insurgents were virtually indistinguishable from the people. Often, indeed, this was the case, especially in liberation and separatist insurgencies in which the insurgents explicitly claimed to represent the political identities of local populations. Even then, the insurgents often killed people who were identified, rightly or wrongly, as the representatives or supporters of the regime in power, or exploited local populations through forced recruitment, looting, rape or murder.[15] In the case of warlord insurgencies, however, even this basic association of the insurgents with the population could not be assumed. Renamo in Mozambique was particularly notorious for its forced recruitment and atrocities against the people of the areas which it controlled, a record which cannot be discounted even in the light of the support which it obtained from many of these areas in the 1994 elections.[16] In states such as Mozambique, where both insurgents and government forces were rapacious and ill-trained, the common assumption that insurgent warfare consists in a struggle between insurgents and conventional forces simply did not hold, and neither group differed much from the other in its relations with the population.[17] The people fleeing to the towns from violence in Sierra Leone early in 1995 often did not know whether they had been attacked by the government forces or the RUF insurgents; the word 'sobels' was coined for attackers who may have been soldiers, rebels, or indeed both.[18]

The support that insurgent movements were able to gain from their host states was inevitably balanced by the dependence on them that this support brought with it. One danger was simply that insurgents were vulnerable to changes in government or policy, or to pressures imposed from outside, which induced the host state to withdraw its support from insurgents and expel them from its territory. The ANC was expelled from Mozambique and other front line states because these were unable to bear the consequences of South African destabilisation measures, with the result that by the time it was permitted to assume an open and legal role in South African politics in February 1990, it had been forced to withdraw further from the frontiers of South Africa than at any time since it had embarked on its strategy of armed struggle.[19] The SPLA had been permitted to operate openly from Ethiopian territory under the Mengistu Haile-Mariam regime, in retaliation for Sudanese support for the EPLF and EPRDF; but when Mengistu was ousted by these very movements in May 1991, one of the EPRDF's first actions was to repay its Sudanese hosts by expelling the SPLA from Ethiopia, an action which in turn had knock-on effects in weakening John Garang's control over the movement, and leading to its division into two and later three competing factions.[20]

In at least one case, such an expulsion brought paradoxical success. Following the defeat of the Ethiopian army by the EPLF at Afabet in Eritrea in 1988, the Mengistu government needed to concentrate its military resources in an attempt to rescue the situation there, and this in turn led to an agreement with the Siyad Barre regime in Somalia that would enable it to withdraw troops from the Ogaden. The price for this was that Ethiopia had to expel the Somali National Movement (SNM) and other Somali insurgent groups which had been operating across its frontier. Forced into the territory of its target state, the SNM took over most of its ethnic homeland in northern Somalia, and – at an appalling cost in suffering over the next three years, including the bombing by government forces of the northern capital of Hargeisa – set in train the course of events which led to the overthrow of the Siyad regime in January 1991, and the establishment under SNM control of the breakaway Republic of Somaliland.

Even when insurgent movements were permitted to operate within their host states, their presence normally carried with it an obligation to support their host in their own external diplomatic contacts, and to agree with it in other respects. The inability of the SPLA to promote a secessionist agenda for so long as it operated from Ethiopian territory has already been noted. In southern Africa, ZANU's search for regional patrons to counteract Zambian support for ZAPU forced it into dependence on Tanzania and Mozambique, and consequently into acceptance of their international alliances and domestic political agendas.[21] The most dependent of all the liberation insurgencies was, however, probably SWAPO, a pragmatic movement with negligible ideological commitment, which took on a chameleon-like protective ideological coloration from the state in whose territory it was based at any given time, and at the same time became adept at using the different 'languages' of the prospective outside patrons – Western European, Soviet bloc, non-aligned – from which it was seeking support. Its political programme adopted in 1976, which gave it the appearance of a Marxist–Leninist movement, was drafted in the context of its move from Zambia to Angola, and the consequent need to establish an appropriate ideological relationship with its new host. This history of adaptation in turn affected its approach when it eventually came to power.[22]

Movements which were solidly based within the territory of their target states were evidently much less vulnerable to such pressures, even though they usually still needed access across the frontier for logistical support and external communications. The EPLF in Eritrea was able to run its lines of communication fairly freely through Sudan under the Nimairi, al-Dahab, Sadiq al-Mahdi and al-Beshir regimes, with no more than token interruptions on occasions when the Sudanese government of the day felt the need to improve its relations with Ethiopia. Such periods of *détente* placed the EPLF under intensified military pressure from the Ethiopian forces, but they always proved to be short-lived, and the EPLF generally had advance warning of them and was able to stockpile resources accordingly.[23] Indeed, given the effectiveness of the EPLF forces, and their strength in parts of eastern Sudan, it would have taken a courageous Sudanese government to challenge them.

The existence of a frontier as a real line of demarcation between states, rather than as a merely formal dividing line which acquired physical expression only on maps, depended minimally on the ability of at least one of the states involved to control the territory up to its border, and in its full sense on the ability of both of them to do so. Where insurgent movements were able to operate freely across frontiers, this second and more stringent requirement was evidently not met, and the territory across the border of the target state which was effectively occupied by insurgents associated with the host state became an informal extension of the host state's own domain. The host state's currency, for example, often circulated freely in the area controlled by insurgents, and the direction of international trade was re-oriented back across the frontier into networks controlled from the host state, and away from the routes which previously linked the area to its national capital. In relatively exceptional cases, the military forces of the host state operated with impunity beyond their own frontiers; and in the extreme case, the South African army remained in effective occupation of substantial areas of southern Angola over a period of several years.[24]

In some cases, as for example on the Sierra Leone–Liberia frontier after the launching of the Revolutionary United Front (RUF) attack on Sierra Leone in 1991, or much of the long frontier between Angola and Zaïre, the border zone was controlled by neither of the two states which ostensibly shared it. It then became a no-man's-land, possibly subject to the rule of a local warlord, providing a haven for drug dealers and diamond smugglers, or anyone else who wanted to escape from the impositions of statehood.[25] As the administrative reach of African states declined, with the shrinking of their revenue base and the spread of armed challenges to their power, so the number and size of such zones increased, in a sense withdrawing parts of Africa from the formal scope of international politics, but in the process creating a new international relations of statelessness.

Insurgent diplomacy

Although formal participation in international diplomacy is restricted to properly constituted states, which are recognised as such by other states and permitted to belong to international institutions such as the United Nations, insurgent movements may for many purposes be regarded as quasi-states themselves, and they exercise many of the functions of statehood, including the conduct of external relations. They also possess armed forces and administrative structures, control varying amounts of territory, extract resources from the populations under their control, and enjoy a level of legitimacy among those populations which certainly varies but which frequently exceeds that of formally constituted governments. The diplomacy of 'non-juridical states', to adapt Jackson's terminology, thus provides an intriguing counterpoint to that of juridical statehood, as well as being of considerable interest and importance in its own right.

The functions of international relations for African insurgents were, in many respects, little different from those for recognised states. Insurgent leaders, like heads of state, used international contacts in order to strengthen their own control over their domestic political structure, gain access to external resources, and so far as possible ensure their own survival. Like heads of state, insurgent leaders presided over domestic systems of variable stability, and insurgencies embodied their own idea of the state – or idea of the movement – which might be more or less widely shared. The leader of a powerful structure with widely shared goals, such as Isaias Afewerki in the EPLF, had little need of international backing for his own personal position, and could use diplomacy in pursuit of the common goals of the movement itself. Leaders of weak organisations with poorly defined goals, such as Charles Taylor's NPFL or Mohamed Farah Aidid's SNA, had to devote much of their diplomatic effort to securing their own position. Sam Nujoma in SWAPO, as the leader of an insurgency with widely shared goals but a weak internal structure, had to seek external support for his own leadership, while associating himself as closely as possible with the international legitimacy accorded to the movement.

There were, however, additional tasks required of insurgent diplomacy. One of the most sensitive was maintaining the close relations with the host state that were imposed by a position of dependence, while at the same time retaining as much autonomy as possible. Access to external resources was essential in order to pursue the conflict, but since these could not usually be obtained through the normal public channels, insurgent representatives had to undertake discreet and precarious negotiations with any plausible supplier. In the public arena, since insurgencies lacked the international legitimacy conveyed by official statehood, they needed to establish their legitimacy in other ways, and notably by publicising the justice of the struggle. The international diplomatic activities of insurgent movements were therefore often much more intensive than those of ordinary states.

In the more institutionalised insurgencies, the insurgent 'foreign ministry' was normally established in the capital of the main host state, where informal access could be gained to the diplomats stationed there. Before May 1991, foreign countries wanting to conduct business with the EPLF or EPRDF did so through their embassies in

Khartoum, while those seeking links with the SPLA did so usually through their embassies in Addis Ababa. In warlord insurgencies such as Charles Taylor's NPFL or Jonas Savimbi's Unita, the need for the leader to retain control over external relations was often too great to allow him to delegate it to any subordinate beyond his immediate reach, and external relations could only be effectively conducted by seeking out the leader himself; in this respect, insurgents did not differ significantly from formally established states, whose leaders likewise often conducted their external relations in person. Insurgent diplomacy also operated at second remove through 'godfather states', which helped them to establish external contacts and bring their activities under the cover of legitimate diplomatic missions. Sometimes, these godfather states were geographically far removed from the scene of the insurgency; King Hassan of Morocco for example provided such services for Unita in Angola, in the process both reinforcing his own connections with his Western patrons, and laundering relations with states which did not want to maintain direct contact with Unita.[26] President Moi of Kenya did the same for Renamo, which because of its peculiarly close connection with the South African security services had an urgent need for an alternative channel of access to the African diplomatic system.[27]

The role of external diplomatic missions was also affected by the international legitimacy and internal structure of the movement. Movements such as SWAPO or the ANC enjoyed quasi-official status, whereas less internationally legitimate organisations had to open offices which were in principle dedicated only to publicity and had no acknowledged diplomatic role, but were in effect embassies under other names; these were, however, liable to be closed, permanently or temporarily, when the government of the state in which they were located felt the need to improve its relations with the target state. Some Western countries took a tolerant view of such shadow embassies; the United States government indeed lacked the power to close the offices in Washington even of movements of which it disapproved, while virtually every insurgency enjoyed the support of an exile community of its own nationals in the United States, many of whom were US citizens. Elsewhere, the presence of an insurgent office generally provided a clearer indicator of the sympathies of the government of the state concerned. Insurgent diplomats, though sometimes able to travel on refugee papers or even the passports of the state against which they were fighting,[28] were also in some cases able to travel on papers provided by friendly states; EPLF and TPLF representatives travelled on Somali diplomatic passports.[29]

The ultimate objective of insurgent diplomacy was to secure parity with the representatives of the target state itself in the capitals of the major powers, a goal which was normally pursued through escalating levels of access. Initial contacts with junior members of foreign ministry staff, often conducted away from the ministry building itself, would be followed by attempts to see increasingly important officials in an increasingly public setting. The ultimate recognition of status was a public meeting between the leader of the insurgent movement and the head of the state concerned, a triumph achieved by Jonas Savimbi in his meeting with President Reagan in January 1986.[30] The willingness of the major powers to become publicly involved in diplomatic contacts with insurgent movements reflected not only the increasing military effectiveness of many of the movements themselves, but also the decline in the conventions of juridical statehood, since any public meeting between the official representatives of a major state and the representative of a movement engaged in violent conflict against the government of another state constituted a challenge to the sovereignty of the state concerned.

As in so many other respects, this challenge to juridical statehood was greatly enhanced by the end of the Cold War, and the resulting imposition of political conditionalities. In the most general sense, this brought with it a major change in the assumptions governing diplomatic behaviour towards conflicts in other states. Before 1989, insurgency could broadly be characterised as constituting a challenge to the government of a sovereign state, and in the event of this threatening one of its own clients, the patron state concerned would be expected to respond by support for the incumbent regime – even if this regime, like that of Mobutu in Zaïre, was in other respects undeserving of assistance. Afterwards, it could be taken as indicating a level of political conflict which called for resolution through negotiations between the parties involved, preferably in the context of an agreed constitutional structure leading to multiparty elections. The result of this change in the external perception of domestic conflict was to elevate insurgent movements to the status of legitimate participants in the political process, in which their standing scarcely differed from that of incumbent regimes. Post-1989 internationally sponsored attempts to reach a settlement in Liberia, Ethiopia, Sudan, Rwanda, Angola and Mozambique all conformed to this basic pattern, even though it was only in

Mozambique that the process resulted in an at least initially successful resolution of the conflict. In Ethiopia and Rwanda, the insurgents eventually seized power by force, while in Sudan and Angola the breakdown of the peace process was followed by a government military offensive, and in Liberia numerous attempts to constitute a coalition government collapsed.

The substantial diplomatic advantages provided by juridical statehood to formally constituted governments thus declined, while at the same time some of the *disadvantages* of statehood also became apparent. States were subject to international obligations which did not trouble their insurgent rivals. As a legal entity, the Interim Government of National Unity in Liberia, powerless and bankrupt though it was, was liable to be sued by foreign companies for damage incurred in the Liberian civil war, whereas the insurgents who had caused most of the damage were legally untouchable. Obligations in the field of human rights could in some degree be imposed on governments, especially when these were signatories to international conventions, but could scarcely be enforced against insurgents. Reports by human rights monitoring groups were characteristically more severe in dealing with abuses by governments than with those by insurgent movements.[31] No one attempted to subject an insurgency to a structural adjustment programme, or to impose a democratic constitution on its internal power structure. Though statehood conveyed a level of symbolic gratification that no insurgency could match, and on the whole still constituted an advantage in the exercise of political power, there were occasions when a warlord could find it advantageous to remain in the non-juridical sphere.

The NGO connection

The external relations of insurgent movements were not confined to their relations with governments. In their constant search for resources with which to maintain themselves, they needed to seek contacts with any potentially useful partner. In at least some parts of the continent, they established relationships with non-governmental organisations or NGOs which were both significant in themselves, and provided an illuminating picture of international relations in the non-official sphere. Though the role of NGOs in African international relations as a whole is discussed in the next chapter, their sometimes intimate connections with insurgent movements call for examination here.

NGOs entered the world of African civil conflict largely as the suppliers of resources. Most of them, including prominent organisations such as Oxfam and Save the Children Fund, World Vision and *Médécins sans Frontières*, saw their mission as the relief of human suffering; and since human suffering was in plentiful supply in any insurgent war, there was ample scope for their activities. They were most often involved in famine relief, especially in the Horn where an already food deficient region was pushed into disaster by constant warfare, in looking after refugees, and in providing other social services such as medical welfare; the inevitable abuse of human rights in conflict situations also aroused their concern. Given their number and variety, and the fact that they existed basically in order to distribute resources, they provided a host of potentially useful points of contact for insurgent movements.

Until the mid-1980s, none the less, the overwhelming majority of NGOs worked closely with African governments. Operating within the constraints of juridical statehood, they took it for granted that the permission of the state concerned was an essential precondition for carrying out relief work in its territory, and the possibility of working through insurgent movements did not arise. Even when access to parts of a country was prevented by insurgent warfare, government forces almost invariably controlled the ports, roads and other infrastructural facilities through which famine relief food and other resources had to be distributed. Famine relief supplied through government-controlled channels necessarily favoured the government side in civil wars, by forcing hungry people into government-held areas. Western relief agencies in Ethiopia thus found themselves, willy nilly, supporting the war effort of one of the Soviet Union's most important African clients.

Although the involvement of Western NGOs with opposition forces in African civil wars dated back to the role of Christian aid agencies, notably Caritas and Joint Church Aid, in providing relief on the Biafran side during the Nigerian civil war of 1967–70,[32] the breakthrough in their relations with insurgent movements came as a result of the Eritrean conflict, which in this as in many other respects set precedents which would be followed elsewhere. Contacts between relief agencies and the Eritrean insurgents dated back as far as the mid-1970s, and thus long predated the end of the Cold War and the resulting challenge to the principle of state sovereignty. On the NGO side, War on Want came out in full public support for the Eritrean secessionist movement from the later 1970s, and subsequently for the

TPLF in Tigray.[33] Scandinavian church groups were also involved from an early stage. The relationship was assisted by two critical organisational innovations. On the insurgent side, the EPLF in 1975 set up a nominally independent humanitarian organisation, the Eritrean Relief Association (ERA), which provided a mechanism through which agencies could provide relief aid in EPLF-held territories without appearing to fund an armed insurgency; the TPLF established an equivalent, the Relief Society of Tigray (REST), in 1978. On the NGO side, two Scandinavian Lutheran agencies in 1981 formed an innocuously named umbrella organisation in Khartoum, the Emergency Relief Desk (ERD), through which to manage aid to insurgent-occupied areas. This enabled large and 'official' agencies such as Oxfam, which also operated in Ethiopian government-controlled territory, to channel aid into these areas without jeopardising their work elsewhere.

The level of external engagement greatly increased with the Ethiopian famine of 1984. In some respects, this was a triumph for the Ethiopian government, since through its Relief and Rehabilitation Commission it was able to control by far the largest share of relief aid. It none the less drew sharp attention to the political issues involved in famine relief amidst civil war, and raised the international profile of ERA and REST. For American agencies in particular, channelling aid through the insurgents enabled them to help relieve the famine without assisting a Soviet client regime. From then onwards, interaction between agencies and insurgents continued at an increasing level up to the eventual EPLF and TPLF/EPRDF victories in 1991. In the final stages of the war, the weakened Mengistu regime in Addis Ababa was forced to allow the passage of relief food from government-controlled territory into insurgent areas, while the EPLF capture of the port of Massawa early in 1990 made the remaining government-held areas of Eritrea dependent on food supplied through EPLF territory.

The relationship between insurgents and NGOs has aptly been described by DeMars as one of 'tactical interaction'.[34] Even though their aims were often very different, each side benefited from the services provided by the other, and a close partnership was often established. The NGO needed access to a beneficiary population: like a bank which can only survive by lending money, it could only justify its existence by finding someone to help. The insurgents controlled just such a population, which was rendered all the more attractive by its high level of need, and its inaccessibility to other means of delivering aid. The ability of the insurgents to collaborate with the NGO in delivering this aid both strengthened their control over the population, and also provided numerous spin-off benefits. It was, for example, virtually impossible to prevent food destined for civilian populations from being diverted to feed the 'fighters'; channels of communication established to deliver relief food could also be used for military supplies. NGO solidarity with the insurgents was enhanced by shared danger from government air strikes, and the sense of delivering aid to desperately needy people despite the efforts of the government to prevent it. The two parties readily became partners in a common enterprise.

This partnership in turn served other functions, one of the most important of which was external publicity. NGOs were in any event closely attuned to the needs of the media, as a result of their own fund-raising needs; operations in conflict zones were especially newsworthy. In addition, the NGO itself on some occasions became the source of publicity designed to enhance the external image of the insurgents; one of the first accounts of the TPLF insurgency in the Tigray region of northern Ethiopia was published by War on Want in 1982.[35] NGO personnel were even involved in 'black propaganda', designed to restrict the supply of famine relief to the government side: a claim that the Ethiopian government was diverting aid to the Soviet Union, published in the British press under the emotive headline 'Food for Starving Babies Sent to Russia for Arms', proved to emanate from the former General Secretary of War on Want;[36] exhaustive investigations by the United States government and the European Community failed to find any basis for the claim.[37] Beyond their own direct involvement, NGOs also provided channels of access for journalists and television crews reporting on the conflict from the insurgent side, which almost necessarily portrayed it in a form that favoured the insurgents. Coverage of conflicts from the insurgent side also often provided evidence of human rights abuses by government forces, whereas any equivalent abuses by insurgent forces could be concealed by the close control over visiting investigators maintained by the insurgents – a control which was in any event imposed by the exigencies of the war situation.[38] African governments were characteristically far less adept at managing external publicity; they were often reluctant to admit that any serious conflict was taking place, and did not allow foreign journalists into the war zone, for fear that they might be captured by the insurgents or reveal information discreditable to the regime. This was one area of external relations in which the insurgents normally had an advantage.

In addition to the financial benefits conferred by the NGO presence, which are discussed in the next section, NGOs also provided access to diplomatic contacts. In many African conflict zones, and especially in the Horn which possessed negligible economic resources of interest to the outside world, humanitarian aid and the publicity which it attracted were by far the most important element in Western policy – a priority clearly revealed by the Ethiopian famine of 1984 or the despatch of US troops to Somalia in 1992. Relief agencies were thus at the sharp end of Western policy, and did much to define the agenda to which governments had to react; their conceptions of the conflict, and their attitudes to the conflicting parties, helped to guide those of their national policy-makers. For insurgents, association with relief agencies thus provided an entrée to contacts with their governments, initially through their official aid bureaucracies, and subsequently with their diplomatic staff. For the NGOs, this quasi-political role was often an uncomfortable one. While a few of them revelled in political commitment, most retained a strong institutional ethos which distinguished their own humanitarian mission on the one hand from 'politics' on the other. The paradox that their engagement in humanitarian relief also provided resources with which both government and insurgent forces pursued devastating civil wars raised complex moral and political issues which they were often reluctant to face.[39] From the viewpoint of Africa's external relations, the often close association between insurgents and Western NGOs provided a further example of the mechanisms through which, for better or worse, the autonomy of African states was undermined.

The insurgent international economy

Fighting wars is an expensive business. Though insurgents normally fought them much more cheaply than governments, since they did not pay their troops and rarely had to buy their arms, they none the less needed all the foreign exchange they could lay their hands on – for essential supplies and all the other costs involved in running a large organisation, for external activities such as publicity and travel, and sometimes even for maintaining the lifestyles of their leaders. Insurgencies were characteristically accompanied by internal process of exploitation or 'asset transfer', through which those who held power (and at its simplest, those who had guns, whether on the government or the insurgent side) enriched themselves at the expense of those who did not.[40] The opportunities for taxing the local community were none the less limited by the fact that insurgencies generally took place in poor and isolated areas, and in addition had an extremely damaging effect on the local economy. Apart from direct destruction and looting, farmers were often prevented from tending their fields by landmines, fear of air attack and other forms of insecurity, while communications were badly disrupted and a large proportion of the population fled to places of relative safety. The Liberian gross national product was reported to have fallen from $US1.1bn in 1989 to $250,000 in 1993.[41] The international political economy of insurgency is therefore an important though often neglected subject.

The easiest means of obtaining funds was through direct external aid, but despite the readiness of governments to accuse 'foreign paymasters' of maintaining insurgencies, the amount of money available generally appears to have been very limited. The Soviet Union in its later years had little foreign exchange available, while United States support was largely limited to Unita in Angola. Scandinavian states were more willing than other Western donors to provide aid to liberation insurgencies, such as SWAPO and the ANC during their long period of exile, but the sums involved were relatively small.[42] The oil-producing states of North Africa and the Middle East provided an obvious source of funds, but their major commitment was to the Palestinians, and their aid to African insurgent movements often proved to be ineffectual. Saudi Arabia supported an Eritrean faction, the ELF-PLF, largely because as a Moslem and non-Marxist group it could be fostered as a counterweight to the EPLF, but its strength on the ground was negligible. The PAC in South Africa, having lost Chinese patronage with the death of Mao Zedong in 1976, turned to Libya and Iran.[43] Libya under Qadhafi was indeed constantly engaged in supporting movements deemed to be fighting against 'neo-imperialism' in Africa, and some of these movements, such as the NRA in Uganda, the NPFL in Liberia, and the RUF in Sierra Leone, achieved a high level of success; the extent to which Libyan support was responsible is, however, highly questionable.[44]

One liberation insurgency, SWAPO, was able to gain an exceptional level of external aid, because of its peculiar international status and standing with the United Nations. The UN channelled aid worth $US15m to SWAPO in 1979 alone, while Western aid to the movement over the five years to 1978 was reported to be over $US75m.[45] 'Rentier insurgency' was none the less generally ineffective and often indeed counter-productive, since gifts of cash directly to the movement's leadership often did not filter down to the fighting forces, helped to reduce the leadership's accountability to its members, and hence damaged the operational effectiveness of the movement as a whole. This was evidently the case with SWAPO.

Rather than seeking aid directly on their own behalf, movements could tap into aid flows designed for humanitarian purposes, through the linkages with NGOs already discussed. For a start, insurgents received 'payments in kind', through their ability to divert food, medical supplies, and essential services such as transport for the use of their own forces. Payments by NGOs for local purchases could be used to raise money directly. Famine relief organisations in the Ethiopia–Sudanese borderlands, for example, provided cash where possible for the purchase of food in local markets, an infinitely preferable course of action in developmental terms to importing it from outside, since it encouraged rather than depressed local production. By accounting for the food purchased at the official exchange rate, while actually converting foreign exchange into local currencies at far more favourable unofficial rates, the movements could make a substantial profit. The governments against which they were fighting could generally play the same game to even greater effect, since the sums of aid passing through their hands were usually much larger.[46]

On some occasions, this extraction of a 'rent' from NGO operations turned into straightforward extortion. Following the Rwandan genocide of mid-1994, and the ousting of the militias involved in the killing by the RPF, these established themselves in the refugee camps (especially in Zaïre) where they created a brutal control apparatus designed to extract relief supplies for sale or for their own benefit, while making preparations for a subsequent reinvasion of Rwanda.[47] The extreme case of extortion from aid agencies was, however, unquestionably that operated by the various 'warlords' in Somalia after 1991. Having first created the suffering which attracted the agencies to the country, they then charged them for house rents (reportedly at a rate equivalent to those in the West End of London), 'protection' by armed guards supplied by the warlord, and anything else that could be turned into dollars. When the United States and subsequently the United Nations sent large forces to Somalia in an attempt to protect the aid agencies, these in turn were drawn into the same process. The Italian forces were even alleged to have bribed the warlords not to attack them.[48] When they eventually withdrew in early 1995, the United Nations forces had to buy their way out at a cost of about $30 million.[49]

When insurgents were able to draw on the support of well-established exile communities, rather than recent refugees, they sometimes proved extremely efficient at raising money from supporters abroad. The EPLF, the leader in this field as in so many others, organised a regular system of taxation among Eritrean exiles in Europe, North America, the Gulf and elsewhere, which reportedly brought in about $US20m a month. Eritrean housemaids working in Italy were exceptionally dedicated, apparently devoting some 60–70 per cent of their earnings to the cause, and helped to organise the annual Bologna festival, which in addition to raising funds reinforced the cultural identity and political solidarity of Eritrean exiles worldwide.[50] The RPF, many of whose supporters had fled from Rwanda as early as 1959, was also able to raise money from the exile community, while the Somali factions had supporters working in the Gulf. In contrast to rentier insurgency, remittance insurgency fostered a high level of organisation and commitment, and helped to build links between the fighters in the field and the people whom they claimed to represent.

Since it was difficult for insurgents to develop regular structures of production, the export of goods from insurgent-held areas was liable to degenerate into a once-for-all sale of anything that could be carried away, with very damaging effects on long-term economic development. Given the problems of bulk transport under guerrilla war conditions, low bulk and high value items had an obvious attraction. This explained the lure of Angola's diamond mines to Unita, and the extension of the Liberian war over the frontier into the diamond-mining areas of Sierra Leone. Accounts of freelance traders with well-armed personal bodyguards, operating across the Zaïrean border to haggle for diamonds in Angola, recall the earliest and crudest days of the African trading economy.[51] Ivory and rhinoceros horn, stripped from animals in Angola and Mozambique and exported through contacts in the South African security services, helped to raise cash for Unita and Renamo.[52] Though relationships between insurgency and the international drugs trade are well-attested in Latin America and south-east Asia, there has been little available information on their role in Africa; the clearest example was the trade in *chat*, a mild and legal narcotic which was mostly grown in south-eastern Ethiopia and consumed in the Horn and the Arabian peninsula, which helped to supply supplementary income for warlords in Somalia. Some insurgents were in a position to export bulk items; Charles Taylor's NPFL, during the period when it controlled the whole of central Liberia, was able to export iron ore, rubber and timber, either through the port of Buchanan or through Côte d'Ivoire.[53] Straightforward booty exports included anything that could be carried away, including the corrugated iron sheeting that provides Africa's standard roofing material. One scholar even records an eye-witness account of a Peugeot car, being headloaded along forest trails from Sierra Leone into Liberia.[54]

Finally, insurgents could trade on the expectation that they might eventually come to power, and raise what were effectively insurance premiums from foreign firms which were anxious to protect themselves against that possibility. Given that the French state oil company, Elf-Aquitaine, depended heavily on Angola for its supplies, it was no more than commercial prudence for some of its senior managers to maintain close contacts with the MPLA government, while others did so with Savimbi and Unita.[55] Nor was it difficult to imagine that the smooth relations established between the SWAPO government and the major Namibian mining companies after independence may have been helped by informal contacts which had been built up beforehand.

Overall, the financing of African insurgent movements, with the partial exception of the remittance economy, illustrates the most destructive and dependent features of the African political economy. Its emphasis was almost inevitably on raising ready cash as fast as possible, and by any available means, often at the direct expense of those such as looted peasants and exploited refugees who were least able to bear the burden. This peculiar economy was none the less capable of yielding substantial benefits to at least a number of those who controlled it. Indeed, the creation of suffering could be a rational economic strategy, since it attracted resources which necessarily came under the control of the most powerful individuals in the society concerned, and could be used to promote their personal well-being or political control. At least in the Horn, Liberia and parts of southern Africa, a 'permanent emergency' was created, which in turn fostered individuals and groups with an interest in sustaining it.[56]

Controlling insurgency

The control of insurgency proved an exceptionally difficult business, not just for individual African states but for the African state system as a whole. This section is not concerned with the counter-insurgency warfare of African governments, or the processes of militarisation and alliance-formation associated with it, but rather with attempts to deal with insurgency at the diplomatic level.

The most basic problem was that the diplomatic assumptions of the African state system rendered it almost incapable of dealing with the challenge posed by insurgent movements. The principles of juridical statehood, including respect for existing frontiers and non-intervention in the internal affairs of other states, meant that in any insurgent conflict, the overwhelming weight of African official opinion came down on the side of the incumbent government. External involvement was possible only if this was acceptable to the government concerned, and this in turn enabled that government to lay down the conditions, favourable to itself, on which such involvement could take place. The insistence of the Nigerian federal government on specifying the terms of reference for the various attempts to resolve the Nigerian civil war of 1967–70 provided the clearest example.[57]

The two early cases of attempted secession in Biafra and Katanga, neither of which could be fully characterised as an insurgency, appeared to confirm the validity of this approach. In each case, the secessionist region was eventually reincorporated into the national territory. The southern Sudanese and Eritrean insurgencies, however, could not be dealt with in the same way, in large part because they involved not simply the defeat of ambitious regional rulers with aspirations to independence, but rather the suppression of deep-seated resentments which were only intensified by the attempted imposition of central government control. The diplomatic hegemony of the established government could not be converted into control on the ground.[58] As the number of insurgencies grew, and the inadequacies of monopoly statehood became increasingly evident, so both the practicability and the legitimacy of attempting to deal with insurgency through mere support of the established government declined. Stuck with the principles on which it was founded, the inability of the OAU to provide any diplomatic mechanism through which to resolve the problems created by insurgency likewise became obvious.

In one important group of cases, that of liberation insurgencies against white minority regimes, a permanent solution reached through international mediation eventually proved possible. This was not only because there was only one conceivable ultimate political outcome, that of African majority rule, but equally because an impasse was eventually reached in which both the minority regime then in power and the leaders of the insurgency had a strategic and not merely a tactical interest in a negotiated settlement. Once the minority government and its white constituency recognised that an indefinite tenure of power was unsustainable, they had an interest in reaching a settlement which would so far as possible maintain their established economic interests; majority rule was the price that they had to pay for it. The insurgent leaders not only stood to gain political power, but were also anxious to preserve both the state structure and the economic base which they would need to exercise that power once they had got it; continued white privilege, however disguised, was the price they had to pay for inheriting a working state and economy, rather than a shattered shell. The way was therefore open for a southern African equivalent of what has been described in the Latin American context as a 'pacted transition'.[59] Negotiating the precise terms of the pact allowed ample scope for wrangling and bargaining, which in two of the three cases, Zimbabwe and Namibia, was mediated by external actors.[60] The South African settlement of 1990–4 was by contrast almost entirely negotiated among the internal parties.

In the case of insurgencies within states already under African rule, no such basis for a settlement was available, even once the right of the insurgents to participate in negotiations was conceded. The parties were fighting either for control over the whole state, or sometimes for control over part of it, and what was gained by one was lost by another. Nor, since most of these conflicts were fought over the poorest and most devastated states in Africa, were there powerful interests in maintaining the state and the economy more or less intact. Attempts were made to mediate in many of these conflicts, notably in Sudan where the central government was often readier to allow some role for external involvement than in other African domestic conflicts.[61] With the end of the Cold War, as the international bargaining position of African governments was weakened, attempted mediation was extended to most of the continent's other outstanding conflicts. Its level of success was, however, generally slight. The parties involved were usually prepared to negotiate only when in a position of weakness (which in turn corresponded to their opponents' periods of strength), and negotiations were held either in order to secure a temporary respite while they sought to strengthen their position, or in order to give an impression of conciliation which would avoid alienating their external constituency. The number of supposed settlements – in

Angola, Liberia and Somalia, to take three of the most evident examples – that were triumphantly announced at the end of some international mediation, only to be disowned or ignored the moment the principals returned home, was past counting. On occasion, the attempted settlement itself had tragic consequences: in Rwanda, the RPF was induced by strong international pressure for a negotiated solution to agree to a ceasefire, under cover of which its opponents finalised their arrangements for the genocide of April–July 1994.[62]

Until the early 1990s, the only successfully negotiated settlement to an African insurgency was the Addis Ababa agreement of 1972 which ended the first Sudanese civil war. This came about because the incumbent Nimairi regime was threatened both by the divisions within its northern support base revealed by the nearly successful *coup d'état* of the previous year, and by the loss of its external patron, the USSR, which had supported the coup.[63] The shift to American patronage, combined with the need to build a new domestic coalition, dictated a settlement to the civil war, and the resulting peace lasted under increasing strain until 1983.[64] Subsequently, settlements were negotiated to the civil wars in Angola in 1991 and Mozambique in 1992, but these depended on elections to determine who would take control of the national government, and were thus in danger of being rejected by the side which lost the elections. In each case, the incumbent regime won the elections, at least averting the massive problems of transition that would have followed had they been won by the insurgents, but in Angola (though not in Mozambique) the losing party refused to accept the results and returned to civil war. The difference between the two cases is probably most convincingly explained by Unita's greater autonomy from its external patrons, as compared with Renamo, and the stockpiling of arms previously supplied by the United States which made renewed conflict a viable option.[65]

In a small number of cases, African or external states attempted to impose a ceasefire on both governments and insurgents, while using a multinational peacekeeping force in order to arbitrate a settlement. The first example, and the only occasion on which a multinational peacekeeping force was established under the auspices of the OAU, was in Chad in 1981–2.[66] Subsequently, ECOWAS sent the ECOMOG force to Liberia in 1990, while first the United States and then the United Nations attempted to keep the peace and resolve the civil war in Somalia between 1992 and 1995. In Chad, there was a basic misunderstanding between the incumbent regime of Goukhouni Waddeye and the other francophone states which constituted the OAU force as to what the functions of this force should be: Goukhouni believed that its role was to support his regime against the opposition forces, whereas the troop-providing states believed that their role was to impose a ceasefire by interposing themselves between the government forces and the opposition forces led by Hissene Habre. In the event, paradoxically, this misunderstanding resolved the war: Habre was able to regroup his forces under the protection provided by the OAU force, and launch a successful attack on Goukhouni which led to his flight and the installation of Habre in his place, at which point the OAU force withdrew. It is possible that this was indeed the outcome desired by the troop-contributing states in the first place, since several of these were suspicious of Goukhouni's close relations with Libya.[67]

The interventions in Liberia and Somalia, however, illustrated the classic problems of seeking to arbitrate in an on-going conflict, and both the ECOMOG and the US/UN forces found themselves sucked into the conflicts in a way which made it difficult for them either to settle them, or to withdraw with any credit. This was the result as much of the logic of the situation as of any particular ineptitude on the part of the peacekeeping forces, though that was certainly a contributory factor. Of necessity, external intervention aroused the hostility of the warlord – Charles Taylor in Liberia, Mohamed Farah Aidid in Somalia – who believed himself to be in a position to take over the government had intervention not occurred. The neutrality of the peacekeeping force was thus compromised from the start, regardless of whether it had arrived with any partisan intention – a possibility which cannot be discounted in Liberia, given the leading role of a Nigerian government which had close connections with the regime of the then incumbent dictator, Samuel Doe, but which was unlikely in the case of the United States in Somalia. The arbitration of a settlement was then obstructed by the unwillingness of the intervening force to broker a deal which would leave its local adversary in power, and its inability to enforce a deal which would, after its own withdrawal, leave power in the hands of its local allies. At the same time, the presence of the peacekeeping force encouraged the proliferation of further groups which were protected by its imposition of a ceasefire, and which wanted a share of the spoils from the political bargaining process. This in turn made a settlement even more difficult to negotiate. The resulting developments showed remarkable parallels between the two cases, including the outbreak of fighting between the peacekeeping force and the most powerful warlord, and an attempt to restore the neutrality of the force by broadening its composition. Eventually the UNOSOM force ignominiously withdrew from Somalia, leaving a situation as confused as that which had existed on its arrival, with the local insurgent factions both strengthened and enriched by its intervention; in Liberia, the ECOMOG force clung on with little prospect of averting a similar pull-out in its turn.[68]

In short, just as African insurgencies overwhelmingly resulted from internal factors, so they likewise had to be settled internally. In some cases, as in Uganda in 1986 or Ethiopia in 1991, they were resolved by the victory of the insurgents. In others, though very few of them, they were resolved by a negotiated settlement between the two sides. In Sudan under the Islamicist al-Beshir regime, as in Angola after Unita's rejection of the 1993 election results, the government persisted in the attempt to resolve them by military force. The role of the international community, whether African or external, was largely restricted to providing a face-saving cover or negotiating framework within which the local participants could resolve their own domestic conflicts.

The post-insurgent state

By 1994, all of the liberation insurgencies directed against colonial or white minority regimes had been resolved in favour of the insurgent movement – or at least one of them, in cases where there were two or more competing ones. Reform insurgencies had come to power first in Uganda, and subsequently in Ethiopia and – however precariously – in Rwanda. The sole separatist insurgency to have achieved unequivocal success was in Eritrea, where the EPLF victory was ratified by independence in 1993. Warlord insurgencies had come to power on several occasions in Chad, and had divided Somalia between them, while Charles Taylor's NPFL had been thwarted by the ECOMOG intervention from achieving victory in Liberia. Though the differences between these cases make it difficult to generalise about the impact of successful insurgency, the post-insurgent states made distinctive demands on the African international order.

Much of the initial impact depended on the circumstances of the insurgent victory. Some insurgents, including those in Ethiopia and in the former settler states of southern Africa, inherited state structures in working order, but run by bureaucrats from the old regime with different attitudes and loyalties from those of the new rulers. Others took over governments in a state of collapse, or even no government at all; in Rwanda, the surviving officials of the Habyarimana regime not only fled the victorious RPF in July 1994, but destroyed their files or took them with them. Though largely domestic in impact, the circumstances of the takeover also necessarily affected external relations.

The type of insurgency likewise made a difference. The liberation insurgent governments, in particular, were immediately welcomed into a supportive African state system; and even though legacies of the insurgent period often continued into the post-independence era, both in divisions within the nationalist movement and in the danger of destabilisation by the remaining white regimes, these were at least offset by the new regime's acquisition of the advantages of juridical statehood. Other types of insurgent regime, on the other hand, were by no means assured of such a welcome. For one thing, these regimes had come to power after an often long and bitter struggle against previous governments which had profited from the support automatically conveyed by the principles of juridical statehood embodied in the OAU Charter to whoever was currently in power. Both Museveni in Uganda and Isaias Afewerki in Eritrea took advantage of their first OAU meetings to launch scathing attacks on the ground rules of the organisation.[69] Though African states had to accept the independence of Eritrea, given especially that it was recognised by the state from which Eritrea had seceded, many of them regarded the breach of the hitherto sacrosanct principle of territorial integrity with misgiving. Reform insurgencies did not carry the same threat to the African international order, but they none the less constituted an implicit challenge to other states whose leaders could more readily be identified with the ousted former governments than with the ex-guerrillas who replaced them. The Museveni regime in Uganda aroused particular suspicion, especially from the Moi government in Kenya. These suspicions, not only in Kenya but in Zaïre, were intensified after 1990, when the RPF invasion of Rwanda was launched by Rwandans serving in the Ugandan army, who could plausibly be supposed to have acted with Museveni's encouragement.[70] On several occasions thereafter, the Moi government in Kenya publicly accused Museveni of fostering Kenyan insurgent movements in Uganda.[71] The RPF victory challenged not only the regional order, but implicitly also the structure of post-colonial relationships, since the RPF drew heavily on Uganda-based Rwandan exiles, and also on others who had taken refuge in the United States and elsewhere. Though Rwanda had never been a

French colony, it was viewed by the Mitterrand regime in France as falling within the French *chasse gardée*, and French hostility to the new regime – accompanied by bizarre mutterings of British complicity – induced Mitterrand to maintain much closer relationships with its genocidal predecessor than could otherwise have been plausibly expected.[72]

Another legacy of insurgency was the carryover into the post-insurgent period of alliances and hostilities formed during the struggle. Some leaders, such as Mugabe in Zimbabwe, remained intensely aware of who had, and had not, supported them. Within a very short time of Zimbabwean independence, troops were despatched to aid his old ally, Samora Machel in Mozambique, against Renamo insurgents who had been fostered by the former white Rhodesian security services. Relations with states such as Zambia and the USSR, which had backed Nkomo's ZAPU during the liberation struggle, remained cool.[73] Museveni in Uganda, despite the closeness of his relations with the United States and United Kingdom after taking power, remained on good terms with Libya, which had provided his one discernible source of external support during the NRA insurgency.

On the other hand, the transition from insurgency to government could also change both the interests and the attitudes of the new regime. The EPLF in Eritrea, though it had maintained essential lines of communication through Sudan throughout its long war for independence, prided itself on the strength of its organisation and support within Eritrea, and did not regard itself as in any way beholden to any outside state. Relations with Sudan might thus have been expected in any case to decline after independence, but this decline was greatly exacerbated by the presence of an Islamist government in Sudan whose idea of the state was highly threatening to the Eritrean regime, which with a population evenly divided between Christians and Moslems placed enormous emphasis on the importance of a non-confessional state. When Islamist insurgents backed by Khartoum started infiltrating Eritrea, albeit without success, this led to increasingly public differences between the two regimes, and in 1994 to Eritrea breaking diplomatic relations with the state which until three years earlier had been its major source of external support.[74] Sudanese relations with the EPRDF government in Ethiopia also deteriorated. At the other end of the spectrum of post-insurgent regimes, the eminently pragmatic SWAPO government in Namibia abandoned the socialist rhetoric which it had developed in order to strengthen relations with its Angolan hosts during the liberation struggle, and switched its attention to relationships with the capitalist states which would be of greater value to an independent Namibia.[75]

The most distinctive feature of post-insurgent statehood was, however, the idea of the state fostered in the minds of the new regime by the experience of warfare. This experience, reinforced by constant reference to the legitimating myth of 'the struggle', was expressed in a sense of *ownership* of the state much more marked than that found in other kinds of regime, and underlay the regime's approach to government and in turn its relations with other states. At its simplest, it was reflected in the view that only those who had participated in the struggle had the right to any major place in the new government – an attitude eminently understandable in the light of the sacrifices made by the 'fighters' in a case such as that of Eritrea. The tension between those who had gone into exile and pursued the struggle through guerrilla warfare, and those who had – subject to varying levels of resistance to or collaboration with the incumbent regime – stayed within the country, remained a sensitive issue in the politics of most post-insurgent states. More broadly, it affected issues of accountability and hence of democracy; even though post-insurgent states were obliged in the post-Cold War international climate to hold multiparty elections, in none did the government concede power to the opposition. Along with a sense of accountability to the movement and the fighters, rather than to the population as a whole, went a particularly intense resentment at external pressure, which helped to explain the relative success with which states such as Zimbabwe, Uganda, Eritrea and Ethiopia were able to fend off external demands for democratisation.

Post-insurgent states none the less had to face the problem of dealing with the decline and eventual collapse of the political formula – the Leninist single-party state – which most closely matched the idea of the state which they inherited from the struggle. Not only were the great majority of successful African insurgent leaders deeply imbued with Marxism–Leninism and especially with the ideas of Mao Zedong; the Leninist state also provided the perfect mechanism for carrying over into government the organisation and attitudes which had been developed for insurgent warfare. The insurgent movement could readily be transformed into the vanguard party, which expressed the movement's sense of representing the aspirations of the masses; any rival political movement which lacked this source of legitimation could properly be suppressed. The emphasis on discipline and command appropriate to the struggle for political power could likewise be carried into the struggle for reconstruction and development, and hence into ideologies of central planning and state control over the economy.

The declining sustainability of this formula in the light of changes in the international system can be traced through the experience of successive post-insurgent regimes. When Angola and Mozambique became independent in 1975, the prestige of Marxist–Leninist insurgency was at its apogee with the defeat in that year of the American-backed regimes in Vietnam and Cambodia, and the MPLA and Frelimo had little hesitation in establishing themselves as 'scientific socialist' states. Five years later, Mugabe in Zimbabwe retained an intellectual commitment to Marxism, and the ZANU-PF regime continued to employ a socialist political discourse, complete with references to 'comrades' and the 'politburo'; but the impracticability of trying to turn Zimbabwe into a socialist state on the lines of neighbouring Mozambique was already apparent. Museveni in Uganda likewise had a socialist past, derived from education in Tanzania and even, it was said, from experience fighting with Frelimo in Mozambique; for about a year after gaining power in 1986, the NRA struggled to implement an inchoate socialist economic policy, before recognising that alliance with the capitalist world represented the only possible way forward. The EPLF in Eritrea and EPRDF in Ethiopia had perhaps the most deeply rooted Marxist formation of any African insurgency, and as late as 1989, the EPRDF leader Meles Zenawi was looking to Albania as a model of autonomous socialist development. Much of this formation was ineradicable, and continued to affect the behaviour of both regimes after their victories in 1991; but as an official ideology for two deeply impoverished states in a world order dominated by the United States, it was simply unsustainable. Though post-insurgent governments continued to hold their own distinctive ideas of statehood, the external environment to which they had to adapt was the same as for more conventional African states.

10 The privatisation of diplomacy

African statehood and international relations

The increasing importance of insurgent movements in Africa, and especially their ability to gain access to the international system on terms approaching those available to formally recognised governments, constitutes a challenge, not only to the quest for survival of African states themselves, but also to the way in which the international relations of the continent has conventionally been analysed and understood. This challenge forms part of a wider questioning of the nature of international relations in the wake of the end of the Cold War, and the processes of globalisation which may be seen as underlying it.[1]

As was noted in the first chapter, international relations as a subject of academic study has conventionally been primarily concerned with the interaction between states. This has not, of course, excluded the recognition that states themselves are complex and variable structures, the behaviour of which in the international arena is often critically affected by their internal composition, and especially by the nature of their domestic power structure. Nor has it ignored the increasing importance of international institutions, and the development of an international system which exercises a very powerful influence over the behaviour of individual states. The recognition of the constraints on state policy imposed by incorporation into a single global economy, and the growth of the sub-discipline of international political economy to investigate these constraints, has played a very important part in this process. States none the less continue to provide the central focus of attention, linking the foreign or international sphere on the one hand, to the domestic or national one on the other.

States have, paradoxically, enjoyed an especially privileged position in the analysis of the international relations of Africa. It is paradoxical in that African states are not only among the weakest in the world, but are also among those most evidently formed by international action. If ever there was a case for regarding states as subordinate to the international system, then Africa – along with a number of other highly dependent states, such as the islands of the Caribbean – must provide it. Not only their boundaries, but their governmental structures and indeed their very names and identities were in most cases formed by international action, much of it in the shape of European colonialism. Their economies were so much part of global structures of production and exchange that it scarcely made sense to describe them as 'national' economies at all. Their independence, though it certainly followed in large part from the efforts of their own people, was also encouraged by changes in the structure of global power after 1945 and in international conventions regarding the minimal requirements for sovereign statehood. It was to a considerable degree maintained through international aid, including military aid, and the diplomatic support of the major powers.

The emphasis on statehood in the analysis of Africa's international relations rested in part, indeed, on the relative freedom of action which Africa's states (and thus, more precisely, its rulers) were accorded by international convention. The foreign policy behaviour of different states varied enough to indicate that these rulers could make real choices, for example as between 'capitalist' and 'socialist' strategies of economic development, and the international alignments that went with them. Most impressively of all, in the context of a Cold War global order, they could even change allegiance from one superpower to the other, or maintain a measure of non-alignment between them. These differences were evidently worth analysis. Until the failure of African economies brought about the imposition of structural adjustment programmes, and the end of the Cold War revealed the vulnerability of African states to direct external intervention in their domestic political management, it was easy to overlook the external setting that allowed them an apparent room for manoeuvre which was in retrospect misleading.

Beyond that, however, it was possible to discern a personal commitment on the part of many analysts of Africa's international relations to the project of African statehood. This again was only to be expected. All of the social sciences have in some degree been vulnerable to the danger of following, and in the process serving, the agendas set by actors with interests of their own.[2] International relations has been particularly at risk, because of its relatively weak theoretical structure, its strong concern with the events of the day, and the laudable desire of many of its practitioners to contribute to the improvement of the world in which they live and hence to influence policy-makers. The subordination of the sub-discipline of strategic studies to the demands of Cold War defence planning provides the clearest example of the association between 'thinkers' and 'doers' in the realm of international relations, but the entire analysis of the Cold War period can now be seen to have been guided to an astonishing degree by ahistorical assumptions peculiar to that particular epoch.[3] The tendency of American students of international relations in Africa to reflect the concerns of Washington has likewise been noted.

For both indigenous and expatriate scholars, the African state was the expression of an African identity and autonomy which were to be cherished and defended, against the attacks especially of the forces associated with Western imperialism. This too was eminently understandable, not least in the light of the position which Africans and people of African descent have, from the epoch of the slave trade to that of *apartheid*, come to occupy as the objects of European exploitation. It is difficult to read the mass of material by African and Africanist writers about structural adjustment programmes, for example, without being struck by the extent to which it was intended, not to provide any dispassionate analysis of an evidently important development, but rather to defend the continent (and in the process its states and its governments) against assault by institutions which could readily be associated with the old enemy of the capitalist West. Only with Jackson's work on quasi-statehood did scholars of Africa's international relations explicitly detatch the welfare of individual Africans from that of the states and even the liberation movements which claimed to act on their behalf.[4]

This conception of African international relations as the expression (and hence, at least implicitly, the defence) of African statehood obscured rather than illuminated the central issue in the study of African politics, international as well as domestic, which was the relationship between the people who ran African states and those whom they governed – or, at any rate, sought to govern. It was always clear, as students of African domestic politics consistently recognised, that the 'transfer of power' from colonial to indigenous rule altered but did not fundamentally resolve the problems of governing the political entities so haphazardly created by colonial partition. It still left unfinished the need to create some mechanism through which to reconcile the social habits, values and identities of Africans with the ways in which they were governed. Whatever form it took, the creation of such a mechanism necessarily affected the external as well as the domestic sphere of political action. Monopoly statehood, as the mechanism favoured by the great majority of independent African rulers, had as its external corollary the insistence on a juridical sovereignty which, while ostensibly protecting the state and nation against illegitimate external interference, actually provided privileged access for the rulers of the state to the external resources which they could then use to impose their power at home.

Outside the realm of international relations, the deficiencies of monopoly statehood became evident at a very early stage. Its inadequacy could indeed be traced to the failure of the initial single-party nation-building projects, epitomised by the military *coups d'état* which overthrew Kwame Nkrumah in Ghana in 1966, and Modibo Keita in Mali in 1967. Though other such efforts struggled on, in Sekou Touré's Guinea for example, the external recognition of juridical statehood continued long after the domestic nation-building ideologies which originally legitimised it had collapsed, and the hollowness of the pretensions of most African rulers to represent the people on whose behalf they claimed to exercise sovereignty had been exposed. The result was that sovereignty became a pretext for assuring external support for an increasingly disreputable and often brutal collection of domestic autocracies.

Much of the most interesting work in the sphere of domestic politics in Africa had in the meantime shifted to an examination of the ways in which governments sought to maintain control in the absence of any legitimating sense of nationhood, and of what happened when they could not do so. Into the first category came the concern for clientelism, neopatrimonialism and analoguous social relationships, the analysis of which was associated with the emphasis on 'politics from below' propounded by the group of scholars associated with the journal *Politique Africaine* – not least in reaction against an official French view, especially of francophone Africa, which was all too closely associated with government from the top down.[5] Into the second came Hyden's analysis of the implications for African development of an 'uncaptured peasantry'[6] – one which was not incorporated into structures of production and exchange controlled through the state – and Bayart's survey, under the heading of 'the revenge of African societies', of the numerous ways in which Africans resisted, subverted or simply ignored the attempts made by would-be monopoly states to incorporate them into the centralised structures of official nationhood.[7]

With the end of the Cold War, and the introduction of largely American-sponsored attempts to promote liberal democracy in Africa, the central concern for the relationship between African states and societies was introduced into the international sphere through the attempt to use foreign aid to promote African 'civil societies' which would in turn provide the foundations for democracy, an enterprise discussed in chapter 8. The major conceptual breakthrough in the analysis of state–society relations came, however, not from these rather contrived and official efforts but – surprisingly perhaps – from the realm of economics, through the discovery of informal markets. These were formed not only in order to evade state control of the economy, but equally to take advantage of the opportunities which ineffectual state control created. They impinged directly on the international sphere through the subversion of attempts to erect economic boundaries around states, through such devices as import controls, customs duties, and the maintenance of artificial exchange rates. Since all these things created artificial markets, and hence sources of profit for enterprising entrepreneurs, they fatally undermined monopoly statehood in the economic sphere; and given the centrality of economic allocations to political management in fragile African states, they rapidly came to have an equally subversive effect on the political process.

Informal markets therefore unsurprisingly gained their greatest political prominence where the state was weakest or most threatened, as for example in Ghana and Uganda during the periods immediately before the emergence of Rawlings and Museveni. In each case, indeed, 'black marketeering' became so significant that it acquired a local name – *kalabule* in Ghana, *magendo* in Uganda – which was widely known and used outside as well as inside the country.[8] In each case, too, the reformist regimes that came to power in 1982 and 1986 respectively were initially determined to stamp it out, but soon realised that the only way to do so was for the state to withdraw from attempting to regulate economic activities which it could not control. Rawlings' Ghana and Museveni's Uganda accordingly became two of the leading African exponents of economic liberalisation. The extreme case was, however, probably Zaïre, where the 'second economy' thrived on the rotting remains of Mobutu's state, and wealth – and indeed survival – were predicated on the ability to manipulate the opportunities that it provided.[9] While all informal economies were to a considerable extent concerned with international transactions, the Zaïrean one was particularly so, much of its wealth deriving from the long distance drugs trade to France, Belgium and other parts of Europe. A lifestyle and a vocabulary grew up around such activities: 'faire le sape' was to make one's fortune from them, and return in triumph to one's village in Zaïre.

But informal markets mattered not just empirically as a challenge to the power of the state, but also conceptually as an alternative way of understanding how state–society relations in Africa fitted together. As against the 'top-down' approach postulated by the nation-building scenario, in which people were brought together through participation in a common enterprise managed by the state, it put forward a 'bottom-up' approach in which people were brought together through the struggle for resources. In these terms, nation-building and the measures designed to impose control over both political and economic life that accompanied it, were merely attempts to fix the market by enforcing rules which would favour access to resources by those who controlled the state. Insurgent movements, with their attempts to maintain themselves through their own peculiar international economy, could correspondingly be regarded as rival entrepreneurs seeking to set themselves up in business by exploiting the failures – both political and economic – of their opponents. Rather than upholding official rules of international statehood on the one hand, or seeking to protect internationally accepted norms of human rights on the other, external international actors in Africa could likewise be treated as private traders, bent on establishing their own networks in collaboration with appropriate African partners. The next two sections will examine this 'privatisation' of Africa's international relations, from the perspective first of its African participants and then of its external ones.

The shadow state

The idea of the 'shadow state' – a concept devised by William Reno for analysing the peculiar relationship between politics and corruption in Sierra Leone – is in essence an attempt to extend the analysis of informal markets to understanding the operation of at least some African political systems.[10] The shadow state was, in Reno's terms, a system of personal rule, which was normally but not necessarily constructed behind the facade of formal statehood. It was founded, not on accepted concepts of legitimacy or even on governmental institutions, but on the control of markets, and on the ruler's ability to manipulate access to the resources created by those markets in such a manner as to enhance his own power. Control over a formally constituted state was, however, a matter of convenience rather than necessity: foreign aid, for example, was normally channelled through governments, and gave individuals in governmental positions the opportunity to benefit from the patronage that it provided; but it could equally, as discussed in the previous chapter, be captured and used as a resource by the leaders of insurgent movements. Structural adjustment programmes, designed by international financial institutions in an attempt to impose the discipline of the market on wayward African rulers, likewise often provided the rulers of states with increased resources through which to construct their patrimonial networks, which were not available to those who did not control states: the privatisation of state assets was especially useful in this respect. With the resources thus gained, rulers needed to buy the support of those who controlled independent resources of their own, and whose alliance was necessary for the effective exercise of power. Though these allies included those with access to important sources of wealth, the most critical among them were generally those who controlled the means of coercion, and who were needed both in order to maintain the obedience of everyone else, and because of their capacity to displace the ruler himself.

One critical insight provided by the idea of the shadow state was to show how it was often in the ruler's interest to undermine the formal institutions of the state itself. The state was needed, if at all, only as a kind of licence which facilitated access to certain kinds of resource; it was not needed, and could indeed be threatening, as a governing institution in its own right. Its officials could acquire interests, ideologies and powers which ran counter to those of the ruler. An army which was organised on an institutional basis, and whose officers were imbued with an ideology of military professionalism, could well present a greater danger to the leader's tenure of power than one whose commanders were bound to the president by personal or family ties, and mutual complicity in underhand business deals. The governor of the Bank of Sierra Leone, who reportedly objected to the means used by President Stevens to raise the funds needed to host the 1980 OAU conference, was summarily murdered.[11] While essential allies had to be assured of access to resources, moreover, states were also burdened with large numbers of people – such as health workers, schoolteachers, and many members of the administrative bureaucracy – who were of negligible value to the ruler's own objectives and whose salaries constituted a drain on the scarce resources that were needed for the tasks of political management. Up to a point, an effective and functioning state might provide a useful mechanism through which rulers could help to assure their long-term survival by meeting the needs of their people and building up a sense of their legitimacy. Once the state ceased to be able to perform such functions, much of it became an encumbrance. One of the numerous unintended consequences of structural adjustment programmes was that they helped to reduce African states – which were often, to be fair, already reduced – to a point at which personal networks rather than effective institutions provided the best road to survival.

This shadow state necessarily incorporated external as well as domestic elements, since the markets in which leaders operated extended beyond the frontiers of their territories. Most obviously, political control depended on access to foreign exchange, and as formal markets declined, so the ability to extract resources from the informal sector became critically important. Though conventional analyses of African economies distinguished between the formal economy which came under the control of state institutions, and the informal economy which evaded them, this distinction did nothing to prevent individuals who held high state office, from presidents downwards, from participating in the informal economy. Indeed, state power helped to create entrepreneurial opportunities, the profits from which could then be protected from taxation or the need to share them with other state employees. In Sierra Leone, to take another example from Reno's case study, control over the market in illegal diamond mining was critical to the maintenance of political power.

The management of the state as a private business evidently encompassed the whole range of activities which were commonly defined as corruption. Analysing these under the rubric of the 'shadow state' is certainly not intended to endow them with a spurious acceptability or even legitimacy. The use of power over other people for purposes essentially of private gain is corrupt, not merely because it fails to correspond to formal rules of essentially Western origin, or to meet the demands of 'good governance' laid down by external aid donors, but because of its impact on the lives of the people most harshly affected by it. This impact is in turn all too clear from an examination of those parts of Africa – Liberia, Nigeria, Sierra Leone, Zaïre, to take four of the most obvious examples – where it has been most evident. Corruption in turn goes a long way towards explaining both the governmental ineffectiveness of many African states, and their failure to generate political structures with any legitimacy or even public acceptability. It does not, however, do much to explain how such systems actually work.

One important way in which rulers used informal markets to bolster their control took the form of private deals with external companies, in exchange for which cash payments were made to the head of state. Since it was in the nature of such deals that neither side sought publicity from them, many if not most of them doubtless remained concealed, but enough cases have come to light to indicate their scope. One example was the agreement signed in March 1976 between President Mobutu of Zaïre and the West German Orbital Transport & Raketen AG (OTRAG), which gave OTRAG virtual sovereignty over a 150,000 square kilometre area of Zaïrean territory, including 'the right to possess and use the territory without restriction for the purpose of launching missiles into the atmosphere and into space ... and to take all measures which, in the opinion of OTRAG, are related directly, indirectly or otherwise.'[12] The dumping of the toxic waste generated in industrial countries where public opinion prevented it from being disposed of locally, in return for substantial payments to the president of the state concerned, provided another potentially lucrative opening for shadow state activities; an American company reportedly offered \$25m to President Stevens of Sierra Leone for this purpose in February 1980, when Stevens was desperately seeking foreign exchange with which to pay for hosting the OAU summit.[13] Enough other cases of attempted toxic waste dumping have come to light to indicate that this was by no means an isolated instance, and to suggest that dumping may well in other cases have been successfully concealed.[14] The involvement of Nigeria and some other African states in international drug trafficking has already been noted, and undoubtedly operated through informal networks which benefited from, and accordingly paid for, protection provided by rulers. By the first half of the 1990s, Nigeria had become a major transit point for Asian heroin and Latin

American cocaine, in additional to locally produced drugs, and was one of the world's major drug-trafficking centres.[15] The Habyarimana regime in Rwanda prior to 1994 reportedly protected, and may well have been directly involved in, drug production in the area of south-western Rwanda that was subsequently occupied by the French army in the course of 'Operation Turquoise' in mid-1994; persistent reports from Rwanda that this enterprise was in turn associated with a leading figure in the Mitterrand government have been impossible to confirm.[16] It cannot be assumed, however, that relations between African and external states were privatised only on the African side.

A number of companies specialised in exploiting the commercial opportunities to be gained through personal contacts with leading African politicians, either within or outside the bounds of formal statehood. French companies, including state corporations such as Elf-Aquitaine, characteristically did so within the complex of Franco-African relationships which operated on a highly personalised basis under the overall aegis of the Elysée.[17] Among British companies, by far the most prominent was LonRho under the chairmanship of Tiny Rowland, who was able to establish close personal ties which cut across divisions between African states, and extended to individuals who operated outside the state framework altogether. He was thus able to build links simultaneously both with the Renamo leader Alphonso Dhlakama, and with the ZANU-PF government in Zimbabwe which had sent troops to Mozambique in order to protect both the Mozambican government and its own vital export corridor to Beira from Renamo attack. When Rowland was ultimately ousted from control of LonRho in 1995, the Zimbabwean Minister of Mines, Edison Zvogbo, publicly regretted his departure.[18] Such contacts could be used not only for business dealings, but also for more direct involvement in international relations. LonRho provided an aircraft at a critical moment to help President Nimairi of Sudan defeat an attempted *coup d'état* in 1971,[19] while Rowland's mediation was suggested as the source of President Moi of Kenya's close association with Renamo in Mozambique.[20]

In the extreme case, it was even possible for African heads of state to hire private armies to maintain their personal security and fight their domestic opponents. The activities of the French soldier of fortune Colonel Denard attracted most attention in this respect, and encompassed operations undertaken both in support of incumbent regimes and against them. After the transition to majority rule in South Africa, the South African company Executive Outcomes supplied military services not only to Angola, where its operatives fought on the side of the MPLA regime which many of them had previously fought against in the course of South African support for Unita, but even as far away as Sierra Leone. Such private armies not only helped to control insurgents, but also provided some check on the political ambitions of the national armies which they were ostensibly employed to support.

The extent to which the external relations of African rulers were privatised in this way clearly varied from case to case. Zaïre under Mobutu was commonly taken as the classic example, and was subject to extensive investigation.[21] Reno based his analysis on the Stevens and Momoh regimes in Sierra Leone, where diamonds offered a vital resource for financing personal networks outside the supervision of formal state institutions. The close relations between French presidents and the leaders of francophone states discussed in a previous chapter incorporated them in a web of ties which offered not only access to aid funds but also a measure of personal security. Siyad Barre's increasingly desperate attempts to find external resources with which to maintain himself in power between 1978 and his eventual fall in 1991 had much in common with similar efforts by Stevens and Momoh in Sierra Leone. The less institutionalised the state, the more precarious its economy, and the more personalised the methods of rule employed by its leader, the closer it was likely to approach to the pattern of privatised diplomacy displayed by leaders such as Mobutu. At all events, the incidence of such deals was widespread enough to indicate that they constituted, not merely deviant cases, but a regular and important way of doing international business.

It should be emphasised that these were not simply examples of 'national' or 'state' policies pursued through informal means, in the way that United States presidents have for example sometimes conducted foreign policy through personal intermediaries. In such cases, even though the mechanisms of diplomacy were private ones, its substantive content was concerned with the realisation of national goals, for which the policy-makers were at some point accountable through normal institutional means to the public as a whole. In the case of African rulers such as Mobutu, Stevens or Siyad Barre, the substantive content of diplomacy was concerned with the wealth, welfare or personal survival of the ruler himself, even though the mechanisms through which it was conducted were sometimes official ones. If, for example, the ambassador in Switzerland was a relative or close personal associate of the president – and as President Houphouet-Boigny of Côte d'Ivoire is reported to have said, 'tout homme serieux place son argent en Suisse'[22] – it would be reasonable to assume that he was there in order to look after the presidential bank account. Diplomacy was then not merely unconcerned with the welfare of the state or its inhabitants, but often – as in the case of toxic waste dumping – ran directly contrary to it.

The private nature of such relationships, in the sense of their independence from the realm of formal statehood, was confirmed by the recurrence of identical patterns of behaviour in cases where no formally recognised state was involved at all. The clearest examples of this were provided by the shadow states created in different parts of Africa by the warlord insurgencies discussed in the previous chapter. One of these warlords, Charles Taylor, dignified the area under his control with the title of 'Greater Liberia', and though the regions controlled by such operators as Aidid and Savimbi remained anonymous, they too involved the creation of political authorities on the economic base provided by the control of informal markets, in ways that differed scarcely at all from the networks maintained by officially recognised rulers such as Stevens and Siyad Barre. In Taylor's case, the absence of a formal state structure did nothing to prevent him from reaching mutually beneficial deals with well-established multinational corporations operating from industrial states. An arrangement was reportedly reached with the Japanese rubber company Bridgestone, which by then had taken over the massive Firestone rubber plantation, for co-operation in rubber production and marketing.[23] French firms became so closely involved in the timber business that Greater Liberia became France's third largest source of imported tropical hardwoods by 1991. The former general manager of the Swedish-operating LAMCO iron ore mine returned under Taylor's aegis to supervise the resumption of iron ore production, an enterprise in which French and British companies were also involved.[24] Though Jonas Savimbi in Angola did not appear to have established such regular productive relationships with multinational companies, he was able to create his own export economy, especially through diamond sales.[25] Somalia provided less conducive territory for multinational operations or profitable primary product exports, but Aidid was able to gain an equivalent source of revenue from relief operations and eventually from the United Nations intervention force, as well as through the trade in *chat*. Though operating outside the sphere of formal statehood certainly carried costs, it also as already noted brought advantages. Whether a leader conducted his private foreign policy inside or outside the sphere created by the rules of juridical sovereignty depended on political opportunity or tactical calculation, but made little difference to the essence of the activity itself.

The 'de-stating' of external relations with Africa

Africa's relations with the outside world were privatised, not only through their subversion by the private interests of politicians both inside and outside the continent, but through the displacement of traditional state-to-state relations as a result of the processes of globalisation already discussed. The external world's relations with Africa were increasingly conducted, not by states, but by other kinds of organisation which acquired significant sources of power from the restructuring of social, economic and political life in the advanced industrial societies. This was facilitated by the reduction by outside states of their own level of engagement in Africa, and their partial abdication of policy-making to non-state organisations. In part, this resulted from the end of the Cold War, and with it the disappearance of such strategic significance to the great powers as Africa had previously possessed. This removed any incentive for these powers to become involved in Africa as part – however distant – of their own search for 'security'. The United States consequently switched to policies which emphasised the role of non-state activities such as those of private companies or civic associations, while the more state-centred and security conscious of the superpowers, the Soviet Union, disappeared altogether.

Other states, and notably the former colonial powers, became less directly concerned with Africa as a result of its declining economic significance. This in turn made it possible for them to hand over the conduct of their policy in some degree to other organisations, operating either at a multinational level like the European Union or the international financial institutions, or outside the formal state framework altogether. As demands on Western diplomatic services increased, with the proliferation of states in the former USSR and the intensification of relations within Europe both east and west, so the numerous, small and economically insignificant African states provided a convenient part of the world from which to withdraw redundant diplomatic representation. When Eritrea became independent in 1993, the United

States and Italy (as the former colonial power) were the only states from outside its immediate security zone to establish embassies in Asmara; as the possessor of a long coastal frontage to the Red Sea immediately opposite Saudi Arabia, if for no other reason, Eritrea could once have expected to attract a vastly greater level of external interest. It was difficult to imagine industrial states behaving with such indifference towards the rapidly developing countries of east and south-east Asia. With the decline in Western strategic and economic interests in the continent, it became for Western governments largely a source of problems rather than of opportunities. The eventual achievement in 1994 of majority rule in South Africa, which removed the last major issue from the colonial agenda, likewise made it possible for Western governments to reduce their profile on the continent.

Two rather different kinds of organisation arrived to fill the gap left by the reduction in the role of external states. The first of these, international institutions established by agreement between states, formed part of the official world of inter-state diplomacy, but none the less behaved in rather different ways from individual states. In particular, they placed a distance between the member states which formed or dominated the institution, and their African clients. The partial displacement of the bilateral relationship between European states and their former African colonies by the multilateral mechanisms of the Lomé Conventions, and the use of international financial institutions in order to impose Western conceptions of economic policy, provided the clearest examples. United Nations specialised agencies such as the UNDP, UNHCR, UNICEF, WFP and WHO also devoted a disproportionate share of their resources to Africa.[26] This was in large part because Africa suffered, to a vastly greater extent than any comparable area of the world, from the problems of refugees, disease, famine and underdevelopment with which these organisations were concerned. In some degree also, the interest of UN special agencies could also be accounted for by the number of votes which African states commanded in international organisations, and the consequent need for the directors of these organisations to retain the support of African governments.[27] Several million Africans in refugee camps were effectively governed by the UNHCR, rather than by any state administration.

The processes of globalisation, coupled with the partial withdrawal of external states from Africa, were, however, more directly signalled by the role of non-governmental organisations or NGOs. These have already figured prominently in the later chapters of this book: as the providers of famine relief, and the source of development aid and residual social services; as pressure groups seeking the implementation of basic human rights; and as a significant source of food, money, publicity and other resources for insurgent movements. They also reflected a change in the content of the external world's relations with Africa, in ways which reduced the role of outside states, and increased that of other organisations. For the populations of most Western states, Africa was largely synonymous with disasters which called for charitable aid. This aid was in turn most easily associated with private charitable organisations. The increasing concern for the environment in Western industrial states was most readily translated into an interest in the preservation of wild animals such as the elephant and the rhinoceros. The numerous television programmes which reinforced the popular Western image of Africa as an untamed wilderness where vast herds of game roamed wild and free, rarely ended without a reference to the threat which this wilderness was now under from some form of human encroachment. This too called for action which was rarely channelled through governments. The demand for human rights, which in all countries was largely directed against governments, necessarily gave prominence to non-governmental agencies.

Even though NGOs were usually based in single industrial states, and often received an appreciable amount of their funding from national governments, they broadly represented the privatisation of North–South relations, and nowhere more so than in Africa. In the most general sense, they expressed the involvement in Africa of Western 'civil society', and encompassed the full range of often contradictory attitudes and sentiments that the continent evoked. From the viewpoint of the African states and other social organisations that had to deal with them, they characteristically arrived as the bringers of gifts, and could also often (as in Somalia) provide welcome resources to fuel the patronage networks of indigenous operators. At the same time, they came equipped with the strongly held Western values which provided their own *raison d'être* (and explained their capacity to attract funding in their home countries), and were generally less respectful than diplomatic missions towards the niceties of juridical sovereignty. Some of them, and notably those concerned with issues such as human rights or nature conservation, had agendas which implicitly or explicitly involved the imposition of external controls on the behaviour of African governments.

The most dramatic incursions of external NGOs occured in the wake of famines or other highly publicised disasters, which provided photogenic opportunities for appeals for relief aid: the image of Africa as a disaster zone in the Western media indeed owes much to the funding needs of Western NGOs. The number of organisations which turned up on such occasions could be quite bewildering, and sometimes overwhelmed the resources of indigenous governments which – already overstretched by the initial disaster itself – were quite unable to cope with them. Western NGOs in turn sought counterparts in the recipient societies, creating parallel governments with often vastly greater resources at their disposal than the state itself – a situation all too visibly illustrated by the proliferation of four-wheel drive vehicles bearing aid agency logos, in countries where state officials disposed of no such resources and often had difficulty even in collecting their salaries.[28]

In Rwanda after the genocide of 1994, just over 150 NGOs arrived, many of them staffed by expatriates with few qualifications and little more to offer than a general desire to help.[29] The newly installed and RPF-dominated Rwandan government which had taken over in the wake of the genocide was severely understaffed and lacked even the most basic facilities: government ministers who had no means of transport observed with some bitterness the number of new four-wheel drive vehicles that were being driven round Kigali by the often young and unqualified employees of Western NGOs. In some cases, moreover, these NGOs had political agendas of their own which were at variance with those of the Rwandan government; French organisations were subject to particular scrutiny, because of the close relations between France and the previous regime, and one was discovered to have brought in a number of young men with inadequately defined functions who were expelled as suspected members of the French security services.[30]

Changes in the structure of international politics after the end of the Cold War helped to increase both the scope and the legitimacy of non-governmental relief operations.[31] The decline in respect for national sovereignty, coupled with the removal of the constraints imposed by superpower competition, helped to redefine such operations as a universal humanitarian obligation, rather than as an intervention in the domestic affairs of sovereign states. Relief agencies were thus not only entitled to intervene, but could also call, as in Somalia and Rwanda, on the military protection of the international community. The relationship between NGOs and insurgent movements has already been discussed, but this formed only part of a broader process through which the moral concerns of Western civil society came to shape the management of African external relations. This in turn affected the distribution of power, not only between indigenous African actors and the outside world, but also between different indigenous groups.

One way in which this happened was through the definition of emergencies in the essentially technical terms which corresponded to the self-perception of NGOs as organisations which existed to relieve human suffering: if people were hungry or sick, then the NGO's job was to provide the appropriate supplies of food or medicine. Both the initial political causes of the crisis, and the political impact of the relief operation, were easily overlooked or even suppressed, as a result of the reluctance of NGOs to concede that they were engaged in 'politics'; many of them indeed operated under legal provisions which explicitly prohibited political activities. Yet the resources which they distributed, and the mechanisms through which these were distributed, necessarily conferred power on some groups and in the process at least relatively disadvantaged others. The empowerment of the militias responsible for the Rwandan genocide of 1994, through the provision of international relief aid to refugee camps which they controlled, provided an extreme example.[32]

The involvement of external organisations in attempts to resolve political conflicts had rather similar effects. In broad terms, political disputes may be resolved either by a negotiated settlement, in which each contestant compromises on some of its demands while achieving others, or else by the outright victory of one contestant and the imposition of its power on the losers. Even though there was little in the historical experience of Western states to suggest that major conflicts could always be peacefully resolved by negotiation between the combatants, NGOs engaged in attempts at conflict resolution in Africa were characteristically reluctant to envisage force as a means to arrive at a solution, and sought instead to settle conflicts through reconciliatory mechanisms managed by external mediators. This in turn enhanced the position, both of the mediators and of the domestic groups who had most to gain from mediation. On some occasions, this approach did indeed succeed in resolving intractable conflicts in which neither side had any plausible prospect of winning an outright military victory; the 1992 settlement in Mozambique, in which a key mediating role was played by a Catholic lay community, provided the clearest example.[33] In other cases, such as the Sudanese civil war, endless external attempts at mediation proved fruitless.[34] Sometimes, as in Rwanda in 1993/94, the attempt to create the conditions for a negotiated solution actually exacerbated the level of suffering: NGOs called for a ceasefire in the war between the Habyarimana government and the RPF insurgents, in the course of which the government was able to pursue its preparations for the subsequent genocide, much of which might have been averted had the RPF been permitted by the international community to achieve an immediate military victory.[35] Even after the genocide, some NGOs continued to pursue programmes of 'reconciliation' which effectively amounted to demands for the reincorporation into Rwandan politics of those who had been responsible for killing close to a million people. What was common to all these cases was the insertion into African conflicts – sometimes with results that appeared to reduce the level of human suffering, sometimes with results that appeared to increase it – of concepts of legitimate and illegitimate means of resolving political disputes which were derived from the current values of Western civil society, and which were imposed through the influence exercised by this society, not only over African states but also over Western governments and Western-dominated international institutions.

The activities of NGOs engaged in economic development and human rights have already been touched on in the discussions of aid dependence and political conditionality. Human rights organisations, with their profound universalism and distrust of the powers exercised by governments, had an especially significant role as agents of Western civil society in Africa. As in the case of external attempts at conflict resolution, the attempt to enforce universal standards of human rights on African societies had results which in any particular instance could be regarded (according, inevitably, to the observer's point of view) as either beneficial or harmful: it could impose on African governments a badly needed element of accountability and reduce the incidence of human rights abuse, or else exacerbate conflict by encouraging political actors to make demands on local political institutions which were too fragile to cope with them. Its basic significance lay not in its impact on any particular situation, but in the extension to Africa of values derived from very different societies, which African states lacked the autonomy to resist.

A further example of globalisation was provided by NGOs engaged in environmental issues, which in the African context were very largely concerned with wildlife conservation and management. In part, this emphasis derived from the relative unimportance to Africa of many of the issues which attracted the attention of environmentalists in other parts of the world, and which resulted especially from industrial processes which affected African economies only to a minimal extent. In part also, however, it derived from a peculiar Western view of Africa as a wild and untamed continent, which was in turn reflected in wildlife tourism: indeed, popular Western images of Africa could be summarised in pictures of lions on the one hand, and starving children on the other. This conception of Africa went back to the origins of Western colonialism, and was initially encapsulated in big game hunting.[36] It was, however, adapted to the late twentieth-century Western concern with the global environment, and in the process led to the creation of a large number of conservation-oriented Western NGOs. Unlike many other areas of NGO activity, moreover, conservation was one in which NGOs had the field largely to themselves, and in which action by external governments was almost entirely subordinate to NGO initiative.

Conservation NGOs possessed sources of power which enabled them to exercise considerable influence both over African governments and over Western states and international institutions. In addition to the money directly at their disposal, they could benefit from the importance of wildlife tourism to the economies of states especially in eastern and southern Africa, where it constituted one of the most important sources of foreign exchange earnings. Tourism was also an extremely fragile source of earnings, since tourists could readily be put off visiting any particular country by adverse publicity, and NGOs were well placed to provide either favourable or unfavourable media attention. They were often very well connected to elite groups in industrial societies, where something of the traditional relationship between aristocracy and hunting was converted into a concern for nature conservation among the great and the good. Conservation, for example, provided a high profile but politically uncontentious arena for European royalty, and also one in which the wealthy and ambitious could exchange money for social credit. The list of patrons of the World Wide Fund for Nature, led by the Duke of Edinburgh and Prince Bernhard of the Netherlands, brought together royalty and aristocracy with industrialists and even African heads of state, among whom President Mobutu of Zaïre was particularly noteworthy.[37] In addition, conservationists were characteristically imbued with an ideology which was averse to compromise with opposing interests, and readily relegated all other considerations to insignificance. European conservationists could even support 'shoot to kill' policies against wildlife poachers in Africa, with little thought to the controversy aroused by the death penalty for convicted murderers in their own countries.

Though wildlife conservation thus became part of the currency of relationships between Africa and the industrial world, it also affected the balance of power within Africa. Hotly contested issues such as the ban on trade in ivory products aroused divisions both between rival interests in African states, and between states with relatively few elephants which supported the ban, such as Kenya, and states with excess elephants which were aggrieved at the loss of export earnings, such as Zimbabwe.[38] Within African states, the external wildlife lobby tended to favour the interests of the urban consumers of foreign exchange, who supported wildlife tourism for the earnings that it brought in, as against those of local peasant or pastoralist communities who resented their exclusion from areas designated for wildlife. In some cases, indigenous peoples were only permitted to remain within areas designated for wildlife tourism so long as they lived and dressed in a 'traditional' way, which effectively converted them into a form of wildlife themselves.[39] In states such as Kenya and Zimbabwe, not to mention South Africa, conservation was particularly associated with the settler community, and gave whites a source of international legitimacy and favoured relations with the outside world; several leading South African businessmen were among the patrons of the World Wide Fund for Nature.[40]

A final group of Western NGOs, the churches, were the oldest of them all. The major Christian denominations were indigenised, to a point at which it was even possible to speculate about the prospect of an African becoming pope,[41] but the churches continued to provide an external conduit both for financial resources and for moral influence. A visit by the Archbishop of Canterbury to southern Sudan, for example, helped to provide international legitimacy for the struggle against northern and Moslem rule,[42] while the Catholic hierarchy – reversing a history of close association with incumbent regimes – helped to promote democratisation.[43] These 'mainline' churches were, however, increasingly challenged and even displaced by Pentecostalist and other evangelical churches deriving from fundamentalist movements in the United States and the Protestant countries of northern Europe, which brought with them both material aid and a formidable missionary zeal. While most Western NGOs, including the longer established churches, generally acted as a constraint on African governments, these new denominations tended to support the authority at least of Christian rulers, regardless of their adherence or otherwise to Western democratic norms.[44]

It was evidently part of the 'mission' of a missionary church to indigenise and institutionalise itself by helping to establish African churches through which its converts could maintain and extend a religion which was initially of external origin. Other NGOs did the same. Creating a counterpart NGO could indeed be regarded as following in the footsteps not just of the missions, but equally of the colonial governments which created counterpart states to which they could transfer power. For NGOs concerned with democratisation and human rights, fostering counterpart local NGOs which would form part of an indigenous civil society was a central and explicit element in their agenda, since it was assumed to be the essential prerequisite for accountable government. For others, such as environmental groups, helping to establish local NGOs could be regarded simply as a practical mechanism for achieving their conservationist goals. In either case, the 'de-stating' of Western relations with Africa led to the establishment of institutions through which to reduce the role of the state both in the internal management of African societies, and in their relations with the outside world. To the extent to which they became effective and autonomous organisations, these 'southern NGOs' in turn became intermediaries which took African international relations beyond the sphere of the state.

Such African NGOs in turn acquired many of the characteristics, and faced many of the dilemmas, of African states in their dealings with the outside world. They depended on the outside world, even more directly than states, for the organisational models, the sources of funding, and the legitimating ideologies which they needed in order to maintain themselves and establish their influence. At the same time, their leaders had agendas of their own which differed from those of the 'parent' organisations in developed industrial states. On the one hand, the availability of external funds with which to establish human rights monitoring organisations or environmental action groups could encourage 'rent-seeking behaviour' by enterprising Africans: just as missionaries agonised over whether their African converts were genuine Christians, or whether they were simply pretending to be so in order to benefit from mission education and the access to elite employment which it offered, so human rights organisations could wonder whether their African counterparts had sprung up in order to take advantage of a new form of aid – bringing with it a measure of external protection and the chance of expenses-paid travel to conferences abroad – or whether they were committed to the concepts of human rights embodied in Western liberal thought. But equally, just as Christian churches – and indeed Moslem brotherhoods – needed to Africanise themselves in order to gain an indigenous base, so other organisations had to adapt in order to operate in an African environment. And just as external doctrines of sovereignty helped to provide African governments with a measure of autonomy in dealing with industrial states which were much more powerful than themselves, so the doctrines of rights and democracy (though not so much of environmentalism) protected their African protagonists against interference by the very external agencies which helped to establish them. Privatised international relations, like the foreign policies of states, had to strike a delicate balance between external dependence and domestic credibility.

This discussion of what I have termed the privatisation or de-stating of Africa's international relations is not intended to imply that either African or outside states were irrelevant to the international relations of the continent. It seeks, rather, to correct a view of international relations which has placed excessive or even exclusive emphasis on the role of states, and assumed that the actions of states should be explained in terms of the interests of the state itself (or even of the nation which the state claimed to represent), rather than those of the individuals who controlled it. In practice, even when the management of the state was almost entirely subverted by private interests, the mythology of statehood remained an important element in the exercise of political power, both because of its usefulness in gaining access to international resources and because it might retain at least some domestic legitimacy. African states varied very widely, moreover, in the extent to which they represented something more than the mere interests of their rulers; and even states which had been as thoroughly privatised as Ghana or Uganda proved capable of resuscitating themselves in some degree under regimes which articulated ideologies and programmes that sought to re-create a national political community. States could well be regarded as essential both to effective economic management – and the various forms of asset-stripping employed by shadow states evidently had nothing to offer in this respect – and to any attempt to combine the exercise of power with accountability to the governed. Only a small number of African states ceased to exist altogether, though an appreciably larger number were unable to exercise effective control over all of their formal territories; and the revival of states which appeared to have collapsed as thoroughly as Liberia or Somalia, or even the creation of new states in areas which the existing ones were no longer able to control, was not to be ruled out.

Africa's international relations were none the less in some degree independent of the states through which they were formally conducted. Both internal and external actors operated to a large extent through states, because states provided a convenient and internationally recognised mechanism through which to conduct relations; but when necessary they could none the less conduct their business outside the state framework, and increasingly did so. The state itself could correspondingly be used as a cover for activities which had nothing whatever to do with the functions for which it was formally deemed to exist. In areas of Africa where the state was no more than a fiction, the activities in which international relations essentially consisted still continued to take place: goods were imported and exported; external NGOs provided medical help or famine relief, and were sometimes even protected by outside powers; local rulers sought to control the exchanges between domestic and external resources, and in the process to maintain their own power and security. The connection between statehood and international relations was ultimately a contingent one.

11 Conclusion

The encounter between Africa and the Westphalian assumptions of sovereign statehood,[1] built into the practice of European powers and the international system that they created, underlies the entire modern history of the continent. It has been an awkward, ambiguous, unsatisfactory, and often indeed tragic combination. The international relations of African states since most of these became independent in the early 1960s provides no more than one aspect of that encounter. It is, however, one that reveals a great deal, not only about the nature of African statehood, but equally about the way in which the international system has operated in the late twentieth century, and one which has much to offer to students of international relations.

Decolonisation launched into independence close to fifty new states on the African continent and its adjacent islands, together with many more in other parts of the formerly colonised world. Many of these states were militarily and economically incapable of maintaining that independence against any sustained external challenge. Many of them were also riven by internal conflicts. Their independence consequently raised questions both about their own prospects for survival, and about the universal applicability of sovereign statehood as a mechanism for combining a measure of local autonomy with the maintenance of global security.

At first, it appeared that a satisfactory answer to these questions had been achieved. On the one hand, the enthusiastic acceptance of Westphalian principles by the governments of these states themselves, and the support which the majority of those governments apparently enjoyed among their own people, made it possible to incorporate them with minimal difficulty into the existing international system – an incorporation that was formalised in their admission to the United

Nations, and their adherence to its Charter. This system, which had been established in order to protect existing states and therefore also their governments, was indeed ideally suited to the needs of those states and governments which were in greatest need of protection. Regardless of the challenge which they had posed to the colonial powers, and the ambitious programmes for domestic transformation which some at least of them espoused, the new African and other Third World states were in international terms exceedingly conservative ones.

On the other hand, their claims to sovereignty were acknowledged by the major powers which would have to guarantee and if need be police them. The principal colonial powers – and notably in this context France, which had contested the nationalist claim to independence in both Indochina and Algeria – accepted that their interests could best be achieved by the 'transfer of power' to indigenous governments, and by their support for the territorial integrity of states which they had themselves created. The superpowers likewise accepted that competition between themselves was best regulated through the recognition of existing states and governments. In most of Africa, unlike other regions of the 'Third World', this recognition even extended to the Westphalian principle of 'cuius regio, eius religio' – that the ruler should be permitted to determine the religion of the state – converted into the Cold War equivalent of allowing African governments a choice between capitalist and socialist development strategies, and the international alliances that went with them. On occasions when this settlement was challenged by disorder or dissent within African states, as for example in the Congo crisis of 1960 or the Nigerian civil war of 1967–70, a broad consensus among both African and external states legitimated the use of international power to help restore the status quo.

This consensus was eventually undermined, not by any change at the international level, but by the decay of the domestic political settlements which had bound African rulers to the people whom they governed. As a result, the guarantee of external protection which had been conferred by international consensus on African states at independence was transferred from the state in a broad sense, as a corporate body representing the identities of the majority of people within it, to the state in the much narrower sense of the group of people who currently constituted its government. At times, the state became virtually coterminous with the single individual who ruled it. In the process, the international conventions which formally existed to maintain the rights of peoples to govern themselves, became converted instead into mechanisms for the maintenance of domestic control.

This change was by no means always unwelcome to the outside states which upheld the principles of sovereignty. For major powers, seeking African clients both for any local resources that they had to offer, and as part of their global diplomatic strategies, the level of domestic support enjoyed by any given African regime was vastly less important than its international allegiance. Neither the former colonial powers, nor the superpowers which took an increasing role in helping to maintain states in the continent from the mid-1970s onwards, showed many scruples about using their patronage and even direct military aid to uphold some of Africa's most brutal autocracies. African rulers, too, were generally able to benefit from the assistance or acquiescence of their fellows, occasionally in the form of direct intervention but more often through the maintenance of diplomatic conventions which helped to uphold their often precarious grasp of power. At the same time, given the inherent difficulties in governing territories in which the resources available for the purpose had since the earliest times been slight, and the arguments which could plausibly be made for maintaining public order even at the cost of autocratic rule, often no clear and obvious distinction could be made between regimes which were, and were not, deserving of external support. Patron states could consequently present their support for particular African regimes, regardless of their internal management, as essential to the stability of the African state system as a whole. Client regimes for their part became adept at manipulating the sympathies of their patrons, at least until the cost of external aid became prohibitive, or until the changing global structure of power altered the calculations involved.

The failure of the state in Africa long predated the transformation of the global system. It was first signalled by an experience of economic decay which was virtually continent-wide, and which – in addition to external shocks like the oil crisis, and the inherent weaknesses of such externally dependent economies – was greatly exacerbated by the demands of state maintenance and politically sanctioned consumption. It was marked, secondly, by the outbreak of armed opposition in a limited number of states, sometimes as a result of the militarisation of societies by liberation war against colonial and white minority regimes and by the deliberate destabilisation measures taken by these regimes themselves, but also as the result of levels of brutality by some African governments which their people were eventually unable to tolerate. In some regions, upheavals in adjoining states were rapidly enmeshed into clusters of related conflicts which were exacerbated both by regional states and by external patrons, and which readily spread to hitherto peaceful areas.

This failure was not in any direct or obvious way correlated with the process of colonial state formation, or with the endlessly reiterated artificiality of African states and of the boundaries between them. Those African countries which had an 'idea of the state' independent of colonial state formation were – as in Somalia, Ethiopia, Sudan, Rwanda or Liberia – more rather than less likely to succumb to widespread violence. Indeed, the very artificiality of African states induced their governments to agree on the conventions required for their preservation, and reduced rather than increased the dangers of conflict over their frontiers. The former colonies of the lesser European powers – Portugal, Belgium, Spain and Italy – were also far more likely to be engulfed by violence than those of France and the United Kingdom. While specific local factors, including the historic experience of different African peoples and the skills or otherwise of individual governments, bore an appreciable share of the credit or responsibility for state maintenance or collapse, across the continent as a whole the coexistence of artificial statehood with either French or British colonialism provided the best recipe for survival.

Faced by a level of economic and political decay which by the 1980s had become too obvious to be ignored, and by the withdrawal of the Soviet Union first from economic and later from strategic competition, Western states and their associated international institutions followed what appeared to be eminently rational strategies of reconstruction. In the economic sphere, these took the form of structural adjustment programmes designed to restore the role of the market, in place of the counter-productive distortion of the economy to meet short-term political goals. In the political sphere, they sought to restore the relationship between government and governed through an insistence on open multiparty elections. In each case, a plausible diagnosis was followed by the logical response. The success of that response was undermined to some degree by inherent difficulties in implementing the policies required under African conditions – notably by the weakness of the 'supply side' in the case of economic restructuring, and the absence or inadequacy of most of the normal structural requirements for successful democratisation in the case of political reform. To some extent too, regardless of the hope that they might be mutually reinforcing, the two reform projects undermined one another. In particular, in societies where the authority of governments depended to a large extent on their ability to manipulate patronage networks, it was difficult for new political institutions to attract lasting support when the government's power to distribute benefits was simultaneously being undermined by structural adjustment. Externally imposed reform strategies also failed to take account of the ingenuity with which African rulers, guided by 'governmentalities' long predating colonial rule, could manipulate the opportunities open to them in order to ensure survival. In this process the state, far from becoming the rational and accountable structure sought by the proponents of reform, was often still more radically privatised than during the pre-reform era. In some parts of the continent, certainly, the re-creation of competitive party systems and the imposition of a measure of accountability enhanced prospects for state survival. In others, the capacity of available political and economic resources to sustain even the minimal requirements of statehood was increasingly open to question. Given that these resources – again, in some but not other parts of Africa – had not been available in the pre-colonial era, a reversion to the historical condition of the continent, in which zones of reasonably settled government had been interspersed with broad tracts of territory in which political authority had been either extremely localised or entirely uncertain, was not to be excluded from the realms of possibility.

No academic study can escape the spirit and concerns of the period in which it is written – a point which is often particularly evident in reading accounts of the condition of Africa published in past decades. This one will prove no different. There are none the less a number of points, not only about African states but about statehood and the international system more generally, that it is possible to make from the vantage point that has now been reached. The first is that quasi-statehood – the recognition and support by the international system of states that are unable to sustain themselves internally – provides no bridge across which African or other states can pass in reasonable confidence from their post-colonial origins to the 'empirical statehood' that rests on national integration and a set of viable political and economic institutions. At best, it has provided only a temporary respite from external pressures, during which some steps towards viability could be made; at worst, it has badly damaged the prospects for any such viability, by sustaining rulers whose external support allowed them to escape accountability to their domestic populations, and to destroy such institutions as previously existed. African states, certainly, have continued in most cases to survive, and some of them have shown a remarkable capacity to reconstitute themselves from a condition of apparently terminal decay. If they are to sustain themselves, and to gain the capacity to carry out the functions for which no effective substitute for statehood has yet been devised, they will however, have to do so on the basis of their relations with their own citizens, rather than the support of international convention.

Second, the study of international relations needs to recognise, far more clearly than it has customarily been prepared to do, that it is concerned with political relationships within states, as well as between them. The importance of domestic politics in accounting for the external behaviour of states has indeed long been recognised, and has provided the staple fare of numerous works on foreign policy analysis. The role of the international system – and even of such apparently anodyne principles of international behaviour as those encompassed in the Charter of the United Nations – in moulding the structure of power within states has, however, been generally overlooked. The assumption that domestic power structures were in some sense beyond the scope of 'international relations' has led internationalists to ignore (and even, perhaps, enabled them to evade) the consequences of the fact that the relationships between domestic and international politics operate in both directions across the often artificial divide represented by the conventions of state sovereignty, and that the impact of the international on the domestic has often been every bit as important as its converse.

Third, a conception of international relations as consisting essentially in interactions *between* states, needs to be supplemented and in some degree displaced by a picture of the international system as a political arena driven by the struggle for control over the flow of resources across state boundaries. In this process, in which states collaborate every bit as much as they compete with one another, such control is needed for them to maintain themselves in both material and ideological terms. The epitome of sovereign statehood is not the diplomat but the customs officer. States need to extract revenue from the passage of goods across their frontiers, and devise mechanisms such as national currencies to assist them in the process. The evasion of control through smuggling undermines both the economic basis and the political structure of the state. But smuggling in a broader sense may encompass a wide range of intangible as well as material goods. In the case of food, 'smuggled' by relief agencies into territory controlled by insurgent movements, the inability of the state to regulate international resource flows strikes directly at its capacity for political control. The unauthorised flow of arms constitutes a still more evident challenge. But the passage of human beings across Africa's weakly regulated frontiers, whether as insurgents, refugees, or illegal immigrants; the provision of external financial aid through non-governmental organisations; the displacement of official currencies by alternative means of exchange – all these are the expression of an 'international relations' which consists, not in relations between one state and another, but in relations between states and those who seek to evade or sometimes displace them.

The most important international transactions which African states – and in some degree states in the global system as a whole – have proved decreasingly able to control have, however, been intangible ones. One such intangible, information, has indeed always lain beyond the control of African governments. Political information normally reaches Africans either from external sources, such as the BBC World Service, or from the often (but by no means always) astonishingly well-informed oral transmissions that are popularly known in francophone Africa as *radio trottoir* or pavement radio.[2] State control over the media in Africa has mattered more as a means of maintaining the mythology of monopoly statehood, an important objective in its own right, than as one of restricting access to politically relevant information. The information revolution has as yet challenged African states more through the transmission of information out of Africa than through the spread of new information technologies within it. Much more directly significant has been the impact of economic and political ideologies that have undermined the legitimacy of state action, and which – even though they have also affected Western governments – have had a particularly corrosive effect on states which have relied to an appreciable extent on external acceptance of their domestic regulatory power.

In some cases, finally, states have lost the struggle for control, either over significant areas of their formal territory, or occasionally through the collapse of the state itself. Some states, too, have been so thoroughly privatised as to differ little from the territories controlled by warlords, and retain their claim to the title only by international convention. These developments likewise pose a challenge to a conception of 'international relations' as the study of the interactions between states, which has consequently taken states as a given. During the long period of the Cold War, it was even possible to assume that, save for a few clearly exceptional instances, the particular states which constituted the current international order were a given too. The post-Cold War era has imposed a long-overdue recognition of the historicity of states, as organisations which have historically fought against and sometimes conquered one another, and in the process have amalgamated, split up, and sometimes disappeared. The idea that the world is divided into states, and that for any given territory or group of people there must necessarily be a corresponding state has, however, proved extremely tenacious. Yet as the African experience shows, states have to struggle for existence, not merely against the threat posed by other states, but against social forces that may dissolve them altogether. States are expensive organisations, in terms both of the material resources which they require for their maintenance, and of the demands which they make on the loyalty – or at the very least the acquiescence – of the people whom they seek to control. In most parts of the world, that expense is ultimately justified by the regulatory services which they are able to perform. In some parts, and notably in parts of sub-Saharan Africa, the demands made by states in relation to available resources have been high, the level of services offered in return has been slight (and even negative, where the state itself has constituted an important threat to the welfare of its people), and their capacity to call on the moral loyalty of those people has been lost. In such cases statehood itself, as a means of regulating not only domestic affairs but that range of transactions which are conventionally regarded as 'international', may cease to exist.

Historically, zones of statelessness in some parts of the world have coexisted with the maintenance of an international system that was confined to relations between states within the zone in which these had been effectively established. Expeditions beyond the frontier of what was then termed the 'civilised world' could be excluded from the realm of international relations, except insofar as these impinged on relationships within the zone of statehood. That frontier was closed by the imposition of European domination, and the forced incorporation of the rest of the world into the international structure defined by European conceptions of statehood. The creation of a global society, and especially the spread of global communications, means that it can no longer be reopened. The international relations of statelessness have imposed themselves as an issue, not only on the management of the international system, but on the analysis of international relations.

Notes

1 Fragile states and the international system

1 Robert H. Jackson and Carl G. Rosberg, *Personal Rule in Black Africa: Prince, Autocrat, Prophet, Tyrant* (Berkeley: California University Press, 1982), p. 18.
2 The idea of 'governmentalities' is taken from Jean-François Bayart, *The State in Africa: The Politics of the Belly* (London: Longman, 1993), who in turn derives it from Foucault.
3 For a discussion of developments in state theory and their application to international relations, see Fred Halliday, *Rethinking International Relations* (London: Macmillan, 1994), ch. 4.
4 Barry Buzan, *People States and Fear: The National Security Problem in International Relations* (Brighton: Wheatsheaf, 1983), pp. 44–53.
5 F. S. Northedge, *The International Political System*, cited in Halliday, *Rethinking International Relations*, p. 78.
6 Robert H. Jackson, *Quasi-states: Sovereignty, International Relations and the Third World* (Cambridge: Cambridge University Press, 1990).
7 Halliday, *Rethinking International Relations*, Introduction; for an examination of the creation of a 'British' identity, see Linda Colley, *Britons: Forging the Nation 1707–1837* (London: Pimlico, 1994).
8 United Nations General Assembly resolutions 1514(XV) and 1541(XV), 15 December 1960; from Dusan J. Djonovich, *United Nations Resolutions, Vol. VIII 1960–1962* (New York: Oceana, 1974), pp. 153 and 188–9.

2 The creation of an African international order

1 See John Iliffe, *Africans: The History of a Continent* (Cambridge: Cambridge University Press, 1995), for a study which relates the history of the continent to the hostility of its environmental base.
2 This theme is expressed in Jean-François Bayart, *The State in Africa: The Politics of the Belly* (London: Longman, 1993), pp. 20 ff.
3 See for example the classic study, John Middleton and David Tait (eds.), *Tribes without Rulers: Studies in African Segmentary Systems* (London:

Routledge, 1958); or Lucy Mair, *Primitive Government* (Harmondsworth: Penguin, 1962).

4 See Jeffrey Herbst, 'Migration, the Politics of Protest, and State Consolidation in Africa', *African Affairs*, 89 (355), 1990, pp. 183–203.

5 For a study which indicates the relevance of 'traditional' conceptions of authority to modern political conflict, see Stephen Ellis, 'Liberia 1989–1994: A Study of Ethnic and Spiritual Violence', *African Affairs*, 94 (375), 1995, pp. 165–97.

6 This can be demonstrated from the Oromo monarchies of what is now south-west Ethiopia, examined in Mohammed Hassen, *The Oromo of Ethiopia: A History 1570–1860* (Cambridge: Cambridge University Press, 1990), or from studies of the Moslem monarchies of the Sahel, as in Daryll Forde and P. M. Kaberry (eds.), *West African Kingdoms in the Nineteenth Century* (Oxford: Oxford University Press, 1967).

7 For Africa's boundaries in 1914, see Hermann Kinder and Werner Hilgemann, *The Penguin Atlas of World History*, Vol. 2 (London: Penguin, 1978) p. 108.

8 For the size of colonial administrations in Africa, see A. H. M. Kirk-Greene, 'The Thin White Line: The Size of the British Colonial Service in Africa', *African Affairs*, 79 (314), 1980, pp. 25–44.

9 For examples of how such deals worked in practice, see William Reno, *Corruption and State Politics in Sierra Leone* (Cambridge: Cambridge University Press, 1995), ch. 2; and Peter Woodward, *Sudan, 1898–1989: The Unstable State* (London: Lester Crook, 1990), ch. 2; for an example from francophone Africa, see D. B. Cruise O'Brien, *The Mourides of Senegal: The Political and Economic Organization of an Islamic Brotherhood* (Oxford: Oxford University Press, 1971).

10 The idea of 'extraversion' is taken from Bayart, *The State in Africa*, pp. 20–32.

11 A point made by Ali A. Mazrui, 'Africa and Other Civilizations: Conquest and Counterconquest', in John W. Harbeson and Donald Rothchild (eds.), *Africa in World Politics* (Boulder: Westview, 1991), ch. 4.

12 For an autobiography that conveys this message well, see Obafemi Awolowo, *AWO: The Autobiography of Chief Obafemi Awolowo* (Cambridge: Cambridge University Press, 1960).

13 These were Belgium, France, Germany (until 1919), Italy, Portugal, South Africa (displacing Germany in Namibia), Spain, and the United Kingdom.

14 Basil Davidson, *The Black Man's Burden: Africa and the Curse of the Nation-State* (London: Currey, 1992).

15 See James Mayall, *Nationalism and International Society* (Cambridge: Cambridge University Press, 1990), chs. 7 and 8, for a discussion of Third World nationalism and its relation to international society.

16 See R. W. Johnson, 'Guinea', in John Dunn, (ed.), *West African States: Failure and Promise* (Cambridge: Cambridge University Press, 1978), ch. 3.

17 See R. H. Jackson, *Quasi-states: Sovereignty, International Relations and the Third World* (Cambridge: Cambridge University Press, 1990), ch. 4.

3 Domestic statehood and foreign policy

1 Saadia Touval, *The Boundary Politics of Independent Africa* (New Haven: Harvard University Press, 1972), ch. 1.

2 Touval, *Boundary Politics*, ch. 2.

3 See David Brown, 'Borderline Politics in Ghana: The National Liberation Movement of Western Togoland', *Journal of Modern African Studies*, 18 (4), 1980, pp. 575–609.

4 For a study of French–Guinean relations in the period leading to independence, see Christine Ramsis, 'France and the Parti Democratique de Guinée', Ph.D. thesis, University of London, 1993.

5 But see Peter Skalnik, 'Why Ghana is not a Nation-State', *Africa Insight*, 22 (1), 1992, pp. 66–72, which argues that Ghana since independence has not been marked by any significant progress in nation-building.

6 For the classic exposition of this process, see Immanuel Wallerstein, 'The Decline of the Party in Single-Party African States', in Joseph LaPalombara and Myron Weiner (eds.), *Political Parties and Political Development* (Princeton: Princeton University Press, 1968).

7 See Robert H. Jackson and Carl G. Rosberg, *Personal Rule in Black Africa: Prince, Autocrat, Prophet, Tyrant* (Berkerley: California University Press, 1982).

8 On Doe, see Christopher Clapham, 'Liberia', in Donal B. Cruise O'Brien et al. (eds.), *Contemporary West African States* (Cambridge: Cambridge University Press, 1989), pp. 99–111; on Mengistu, see Christopher Clapham, *Transformation and Continuity in Revolutionary Ethiopia* (Cambridge: Cambridge University Press, 1988), esp. pp. 79–83.

9 See John A. Wiseman, 'Leadership and Personal Danger in African Politics', *Journal of Modern African Politics*, 31 (4), 1993, pp. 657–60.

10 See Olajide Aluko, 'Oil at Concessionary Prices for Africa: A Case Study in Nigerian Decision-making', *African Affairs*, 75 (301), 1987, pp. 425–43.

11 For a study of this process, see Nelson Kasfir, *The Shrinking Political Arena: Participation and Ethnicity in African Politics, with a Case Study of Uganda* (Berkeley: California University Press, 1976), esp. part III.

12 I have examined this problem in Christopher Clapham, 'The Politics of Failure: Clientelism, Political Instability and National Integration in Liberia and Sierra Leone', in Clapham (ed.), *Private Patronage and Public Power* (London: Pinter, 1982), pp. 76–92.

13 A classic example is the description of Sandhurst by the Ghanaian military leader, A. A. Afrifa, *The Ghana Coup* (London: Cass, 1966), pp. 49–52.

14 See Steven R. David, *Third World Coups d'Etat and International Security* (Baltimore: Johns Hopkins University Press, 1987), for an overview especially of United States and Soviet involvement.

15 See Thomas O'Toole, *The Central African Republic: The Continent's Hidden Heart* (Boulder: Westview, 1986), p. 55.
16 See Gary D. Payton, 'The Somali Coup of 1969: The Case for Soviet Complicity', *Journal of Modern African Studies*, 18 (3), 1980, pp. 493–508.
17 See Jeff Haynes, 'Ghana: From Personalities to Democratic Rule', in John A. Wiseman (ed.), *Democracy and Political Change in Sub-Saharan Africa* (London: Routledge, 1995), ch. 5.
18 See René Lemarchand, 'The State, the Parallel Economy, and the Changing Structure of Patronage Systems', in Donald Rothchild and Naomi Chazan (eds.), *The Precarious Balance: State and Society in Africa* (Boulder: Westview, 1988), ch. 6.
19 See Steven R. David, *Choosing Sides: Alignment and Realignment in the Third World* (Baltimore: Johns Hopkins University Press, 1991).
20 See Jeffrey A. Lefebvre, 'Donor Dependency and American Arms Transfers to the Horn of Africa: The F-5 Legacy', *Journal of Modern African Studies*, 25 (3), 1987, pp. 465–88; and for a more general overview, Lemmu Baissa, 'United States Military Assistance to Ethiopia, 1953–1974: A Reappraisal of a Difficult Patron–Client Relationship', *Northeast African Studies*, 11 (3), 1989, pp. 51–70.
21 See Michael P. Kelley, 'Weak States and Captured Patrons: French Desire to Disengage from Chad', *The Round Table*, No. 296, 1985, pp. 328–38. French hostility to Hissene Habre dated from the Claustre affair, when (as an insurgent leader in northern Chad) he kidnapped a French woman anthropologist as a hostage, and hanged the French army officer sent to negotiate her release.
22 See L. H. Gann and Peter Duignan, *Burden of Empire: An Appraisal of Western Colonialism in Africa South of the Sahara* (London: Pall Mall, 1968), ch. 15.
23 World Bank, *World Development Report 1993* (New York: Oxford University Press, 1993), table 16.
24 In Liberia and Sierra Leone in the late 1960s and early 1970s, between 61 per cent and 84 per cent of government revenues were directly attributable to foreign trade; see Christopher Clapham, *Liberia and Sierra Leone: An Essay in Comparative Politics* (Cambridge: Cambridge University Press, 1976), pp. 101–2; see also Douglas Rimmer, *The Economies of West Africa* (London: Weidenfeld and Nicolson, 1984), pp. 159–73 – though the figures on pp. 160–1 understate dependence on foreign trade, since some apparently domestic taxes, such as corporate income taxes, are effectively levied on foreign trade.
25 See World Bank, *Accelerated Development in Sub-Saharan Africa: An Agenda for Action* (Washington: World Bank, 1981), tables 4.1 and 4.2, p. 41, for figures on public sector employment and administrative costs for selected African states.
26 For an early and prescient analysis of this problem, see Immanuel Wallerstein, 'The Range of Choice: Constraints on the Policies of Govern-

ments of Contemporary African Independent States', in Michael F. Lofchie (ed.), *The State of the Nations* (Berkeley: California University Press, 1971), ch. 2.

27 However, the World Bank, *Adjustment in Africa: Reforms, Results, and the Road Ahead* (New York: Oxford University Press for World Bank, 1994), pp. 26–8, argues that (excluding Nigeria) these losses resembled those of other less developed countries.

28 Adebayo Adedeji, 'The Case for Remaking Africa', in Douglas Rimmer (ed.), *Action in Africa: The Experience of People Involved in Government, Business and Aid* (London: Currey, 1993), pp. 43–57.

29 This term was originally devised for analysing the oil-producing states of the Middle East, but has gained more general usage; see Hazem Beblawi and Giacomo Luciani (eds.), *The Rentier State* (London: Croom Helm, 1987).

30 Robert H. Bates, *Markets and States in Tropical Africa: the Political Basis of Agricultural Policies* (Berkeley: California University Press, 1981).

31 World Bank, *World Development Report 1993*, table 4; this notes declines in per capita food production in 26 of the 33 sub-Saharan states surveyed between 1979 and 1991. Like most African economic statistics, these should be treated with caution, but the picture of declining food production is broadly supported by figures for food imports, which are rather more reliable.

32 The classic case was that of Ghana; see Douglas Rimmer, *Staying Poor: Ghana's Political Economy, 1950–1990* (Oxford: Pergamon, 1992), pp. 93–9.

33 World Bank, *Accelerated Development in Sub-Saharan Africa.*

34 World Bank, *World Development Report 1993*, table 20; of the 33 African states noted in the table, official development assistance came to 10 per cent and over for 23, and under 10 per cent for 8, while for two (Sudan and Zambia) no figures were available. See further discussion in chapter 7.

35 A considerable literature has emerged on state–society relations in Africa: see, for example, Jean-François Bayart, 'Civil Society in Africa', in Patrick Chabal (ed.), *Political Domination in Africa: Reflections on the Limits of Power* (Cambridge: Cambridge University Press, 1986), ch. 6; Rothchild and Chazan, *The Precarious Balance*; and James S. Wunsch and Dele Oluwu (eds.), *The Failure of the Centralized State: Institutions and Self-governance in Africa* (Boulder: Westview, 1990).

4 The foreign policies of post-colonialism

1 See Daniel C. Bach, 'France's Involvement in sub-Saharan Africa: A Necessary Condition to Middle Power Status in the International System', in Amadu Sesay (ed.), *Africa and Europe: From Partition to Interdependence or Dependence?* (London: Croom Helm, 1986), ch. 5.

2 See Olajide Aluko, 'Nigeria and Britain since Gowon', *African Affairs*, 76 (304), 1977, pp. 303–20; and C. Galloway, 'The Dikko Affair and British–Nigerian Relations', *The Round Table*, 311, 1989, pp. 323–36.

3 See Barry Buzan, *People States and Fear: The National Security Problem in International Relations* (Brighton: Wheatsheaf, 1983), ch. 1.
4 For a detailed account, see J. J. Stremlau, *The International Politics of the Nigerian Civil War, 1967–1970* (Princeton: Princeton University Press, 1977).
5 Harold Wilson, *The Labour Government 1964–1970* (London: Weidenfeld and Nicolson, 1971), p. 556.
6 See Bernard Lanne, 'Histoire d'une frontière ou la "bande d'Aouzou"', *Afrique et Asie modernes*, 154, 1987, pp. 3–15.
7 John de St. Jorre, *The Nigerian Civil War* (London: Hodder and Stoughton, 1972), p. 218, compared France's Biafra policy to 'that of drugs on cancer: it kept the recipient alive but ensured – barring a miracle – a lingering death.'
8 On Italian policy in the Horn, see G. Calchi Novati, 'Italy in the Triangle of the Horn: Too Many Corners for a Half Power', *Journal of Modern African Studies*, 32 (3), 1994, pp. 369–85; the historic Italian ambivalence between a *politica tigrana* (encouraging Tigrayan separatism) and a *politica scioana* (encouraging Ethiopian centralism) is examined in Haggai Ehrlich, *Ethiopia and the Challenge of Independence* (Boulder: Lynne Rienner, 1986), pp. 140–1.
9 The clearest indication was that British relations with the former British Somaliland were handled through the embassy in Addis Ababa, whereas those with the former Italian Somalia were handled through the High Commission in Nairobi.
10 See F.-X. Verschave and C. Vidal, *France–Rwanda: l'engrenage d'un genocide* (Paris: Observatoire permanent de la Coopération française, September 1994).
11 See Arnold Hughes, 'The Attempted Gambian Coup d'état of 27 July 1981', in Hughes (ed.), *The Gambia: Studies in Society and Politics* (Birmingham: CWAS, 1991), ch. 9.
12 See James Mayall, 'Britain and Anglophone Africa', in Amadu Sesay, *Africa and Europe: From Partition to Interdependence or Dependence?* ch. 4; for the aid relationship between Western Europe and Africa, see John Ravenhill, 'Africa and Europe: The Dilution of a "special relationship"', in John W. Harbeson and Donald Rothchild, *Africa in World Politics* (Boulder: Westview, 1991), ch. 9.
13 See Rolf Hofmeier, 'Aid from the Federal Republic of Germany to Africa', *Journal of Modern African Studies*, 24 (4), 1986, pp. 577–601; a small white German-speaking community remains in Namibia.
14 See Carol Cosgrove Twitchett, *Europe and Africa: From Association to Partnership* (Farnborough: Saxon House, 1978), pp. 9–11.
15 'La Belgique et l'Afrique', *Marchés tropicaux et mediterranéens*, 48 (2436), 1991, pp. 1873–90.
16 Norman MacQueen, 'Portugal and Africa: The Politics of Re-engagement', *Journal of Modern African Studies*, 23 (1), 1985, pp. 31–51.
17 See Mayall, 'Britain and Anglophone Africa'.

18 Ravenhill, 'Africa and Europe'.
19 Ravenhill, 'Africa and Europe', pp. 182–3.
20 The senior Conservative Party politician Duncan Sandys did, however, serve as chairman of LonRho. For LonRho's role in Africa up to the mid-1970s, see Suzanne Cronje, Margaret Ling and Gillian Cronje, *LonRho: Portrait of a Multinational* (London: Friedmann, 1976).
21 World Bank, *World Development Report 1980* (New York: Oxford University Press, 1980), table 1; the other three were Ethiopia, Zaïre and Mozambique.
22 World Bank, *World Development Report 1993* (New York: Oxford University Press, 1993), table 1.
23 The flavour of these relationships is superbly conveyed by Stephen Smith and Antoine Glaser, *Ces Messieurs Afrique: Le Paris-Village du continent noir* (Paris: Calmann-Levy, 1992).
24 See Claude Wauthier, 'France in Africa: President Giscard d'Estaing's Ambitious Diplomacy', *Africa Contemporary Record*, 12, 1979–80 (New York: Africana, 1981), pp. A120–7.
25 See Jean-François Bayart, *La politique africaine de François Mitterrand* (Paris: Karthala, 1984); Bach, 'France's Involvement in sub-Saharan Africa'.
26 See Stremlau, *The International Politics of the Nigerian Civil War*, pp. 224–33.
27 The flavour of the occasion is well conveyed in Tamar Golan, 'A Certain Mystery: How can France do everything that it does in Africa – and get away with it?', *African Affairs*, 80 (318), 1981, pp. 3–11.
28 Smith and Glaser, *Ces Messieurs Afrique*.
29 For the French role in Gabon, see Pierre Péan, *Affaires Africaines* (Paris: Fayard, 1983).
30 See Kaye Whiteman, *Chad* (London: Minority Rights Group, Report no. 80, 1988), pp. 8–9.
31 See Robert B. Charlick, *Niger: Personal Rule and Survival in the Sahel* (Boulder: Westview, 1991), pp. 53–62.
32 See Eliphas G. Mukonoweshuro, 'The Politics of Squalor and Dependency: Chronic Political Instability and Economic Collapse in the Comoro Islands', *African Affairs*, 89 (357), 1990, pp. 555–77.
33 See Smith and Glaser, *Ces Messieurs Afrique*, pp. 63–82.
34 See Crawford Young and Thomas Turner, *The Rise and Decline of the Zaïrean State* (Madison: University of Wisconsin Press, 1985), ch. 12, for a discussion of Mobutu's foreign policy up to the mid-1980s; Edward Bustin, 'The Foreign Policy of the Republic of Zaïre', *Annals of the American Academy of Political and Social Science*, 489, 1987, pp. 63–75; and *Africa Confidential*, 35 (25), 16 December 1994.
35 See Andreas Mehler, *Kamerun in der Aera Biya: Bedingungen, erste Schritte und Blackaden einer demokratischen Transition* (Hamburg: Institut für Afrika-Kunde, 1993), p. 372.
36 See Verschave and Vidal, *France–Rwanda*; and *Rearming with Impunity* (Washington: Human Rights Arms Project, 1995).

37 See the analysis in Nicolas van der Walle, 'The Decline of the Franc Zone: Monetary Politics in Francophone Africa', *African Affairs*, 90 (360), 1991, pp. 383–405, from which much of this account is taken.
38 Van der Walle, 'The Decline of the Franc Zone'.
39 Van der Walle, 'The Decline of the Franc Zone'. There were two principal regional banks, the Union Monetaire Ouest-Africain (UMOA) for West Africa, and the Banque des Etats de l'Afrique Centrale (BEAC) for Central Africa.
40 Van der Walle, 'The Decline of the Franc Zone'; Smith and Glaser, *Ces Messieurs Afrique*, pp. 63–82; Péan, *Affaires Africaines*, pp. 21–2.
41 See Ravenhill. 'Africa and Europe'.
42 Smith and Glaser, *Ces Messieurs Afrique*, pp. 185–208.
43 Alain Rouvez, 'French, British and Belgian Military Involvement', in David R. Smock (ed.), *Making War and Waging Peace: Foreign Intervention in Africa* (Washington: United States Institute of Peace, 1993), ch. 2.
44 John Chipman, *French Power in Africa* (Oxford: Blackwell, 1989), p. 118.
45 Smith and Glaser, *Ces Messieurs Afrique*, p. 104; the *pré carré* (or 'square meadow') is a phrase commonly used to refer to francophone Africa; the DGSE is the French security service.
46 See Smith and Glaser, *Ces Messieurs Afrique*, pp. 83–104; Péan, *Affaires Africaines*, p. 22.
47 Smith and Glaser, *Ces Messieurs Afrique*, p. 92.
48 Chipman, *French Power in Africa*, pp. 130, 132.
49 See, for example, Smith and Glaser, *Ces Messieurs Afrique*, p. ii; Verschave and Vidal, *France–Rwanda*, p. 28.
50 Quoted from A. Chafer, 'French African Policy: Towards Change', *African Affairs*, 91 (362), 1992, pp. 37–51; see also Roy May, Roger Charlton and Tony Cleobury, 'France and Africa: Policy or Bad Habits', Boston University, Conference on Francophone Africa, October 1994.
51 The term 'European Community' (or EC) is used throughout this section, for an institution which has successively been known as the European Common Market, the European Economic Community, the European Community, and most recently the European Union.
52 See, for example, Michael Davenport, 'Africa and the Unimportance of Being Preferred', *Journal of Common Market Studies*, 30 (2), 1992, pp. 233–51.
53 These comprised fourteen former French colonies and trust territories, including Madagascar (but excluding Djibouti, which was still a colony), the three former Belgian colonies, and Somalia, most of which had been under Italian trusteeship; Guinea is sometimes included as a nineteenth associate, but was effectively excluded by French hostility, and by its own reluctance to participate in an arrangement which it regarded as neocolonial.
54 For analysis of the Yaoundé Conventions and other EC–African relations preceding the Lomé Conventions, see Twitchett, *Europe and Africa*; and I. William Zartman, *The Politics of Trade Negotiations between Africa and the*

European Economic Community (Princeton: Princeton University Press, 1971).

55 For the negotiation of the Lomé I Convention, see John Ravenhill, *Collective Clientelism: The Lomé Conventions and North–South Relations* (New York: Columbia University Press, 1985), pp. 77–97.

56 Tony Hill, 'Africa and the European Community: The Third Lomé Convention', *Africa South of the Sahara 1986* (London: Europa, 1986), pp. 60–7; for a more general discussion of the changing EC–ACP relationship, see Aderemi Oyewumi, 'The Lomé Convention: From Partnership to Paternalism', *Round Table*, 318, 1991, pp. 129–37.

57 See Kevin Watkins, 'Africa and the European Community: The Lome Conventions', *Africa South of the Sahara 1991* (London: Europa, 1991), pp. 39–51. There are useful summaries in *Keesings Record of World Events* of Lomé II (1981, pp. 30700–2), Lomé III (1985, pp. 33485–7), and Lomé IV (1989, p. 37133).

58 See the discussion of 'political conditionality' in chapter 8.

59 The EC provided between 6.3 per cent and 10.1 per cent of Western bilateral and multilateral aid to sub-Saharan Africa between 1984 and 1988; see OECD, Development Assistance Committee, *1989 Report: Development Cooperation in the 1990s* (Paris: OECD, 1989), table 35, p. 242.

60 In 1987–8, for example, Ethiopia was the largest ACP recipient of EC aid, at 5.7 per cent of the total, followed by Côte d'Ivoire with 5.3 per cent and Senegal with 3.2 per cent (OECD-DAC, *1989 Report*, table 40, p. 256).

61 See Trevor Parfitt and Sandy Bullock, 'The Prospects for a New Lomé Convention', *Review of African Political Economy*, 47, 1990, pp. 104–16.

62 Though Pisani's phrase is much quoted, I have been unable to trace the original source; see Christopher Stevens, 'The Renegotiation of the Convention', in Robert Boardman, Timothy M. Shaw and Panayotis Soldatos (eds.), *Europe, Africa and Lomé III* (London: University Press of America, 1985), p. 78.

63 These were Robert Lemagnen (1958–61), Henri Rochereau (1962–9), Jean-François Deniau (1969–73), Claude Cheysson (1973–81), and Edgard Pisani (1981–5); Lorenzo Natali (Italy) became the first non-French Commissioner (1985–9), followed by Manuel Marin (Spain, 1989–95), and João de Deus Pinheiro (Portugal, from 1995).

64 See Twitchett, *Europe and Africa*, pp. 25–8, for the founding and early staffing of DG VIII.

65 See Paul Bowles, 'Recipient Needs and Donor Interests in the Allocation of EEC Aid to Developing Countries', *Canadian Journal of Development Studies*, 10 (1), 1989, pp. 7–20; and also M. K. and M. N. Anyadike-Danes, 'The Geographic Allocation of the European Development Fund under the Lomé Conventions', *World Development*, 10 (11), 1992, pp. 1647–61.

66 It was, at any rate, during the Natali commissionership that Ethiopia became the largest single ACP recipient of EC aid.

67 Accusations made privately to the author; for illegal fishing in Namibian

waters, see Reginald H. Green, 'Namibia: From Blood and Iron to Reconciliation', in Oliver Furley, (ed.), *Conflict in Africa* (London: I. B. Tauris, 1995), p. 218.

68 One of the most remarkable instances was Kwame Nkrumah's evident pleasure at being privately entertained by Queen Elizabeth; see David Rooney, *Kwame Nkrumah: The Political Kingdom in the Third World* (London: I. B. Tauris, 1988), p. 152. Nkrumah also retained an English personal secretary. President Mobutu modelled his palace at Gbadolite after that of the king of the Belgians; see Colette Braeckman, *Le dinosaure: le Zaïre de Mobutu* (Paris: Fayard, 1992), p. 150.

69 *Sunday Times* (London), 30 October 1994.

5 The politics of solidarity

1 Ali A. Mazrui, 'On the Concept of "We are all Africans"', *Towards a Pax Africana: A Study of Ideology and Ambition* (London: Weidenfeld and Nicolson, 1967), ch. 3.

2 See Amadu Sesay, 'International Politics in Africa: A Comparative Study of the Foreign Policies of Liberia and Sierra Leone, 1957–73', Ph.D. thesis, University of London, 1978, e.g. p. 184.

3 See, for example, Brendan Seery, 'Africa's Reluctant New Policeman Twirls His Truncheon: the Lesotho Experience and South Africa's Role in Peacekeeping', in Mark Shaw and Jakkie Cilliers (eds.), *South Africa and Peacekeeping in Africa* (Johannesburg: Institute for Defence Policy, 1995), pp. 87–97.

4 For the viewpoint of Nkrumah's Ghana, the main opponent of the kind of organisation established at Addis Ababa, see W. Scott Thompson, *Ghana's Foreign Policy 1957–1966* (Princeton: Princeton University Press, 1969), pp. 316–23.

5 See G. J. Naldi, *Documents of the Organization of African Unity* (London: Mansell, 1992), for the text of the Charter.

6 There was some, of course, but apart from the perennial problem of Chad, this was largely restricted to the year or two immediately after the OAU's formation, when a number of European states continued to intervene in a 'post-colonial' mode: the French in Gabon, the Belgians in Zaïre, and the British in East Africa, all in 1964; compared either with the much more numerous cases up to 1963, and from 1975 onwards, it was relatively slight.

7 These were Côte d'Ivoire and Gabon; the other two recognisers were Tanzania and Zambia; see John J. Stremlau, *The International Politics of the Nigerian Civil War, 1967–1970* (Princeton: Princeton University Press, 1977) pp. 136–9.

8 Both the recognition of Biafra in 1968, and the breach with West Germany in 1965 over its establishment of diplomatic relations with East Germany, could likewise be regarded as principled if quixotic decisions from which Tanzania had more to lose than to gain. For Nyerere's defence of his

actions over Rhodesia, see Julius K. Nyerere, 'The Honour of Africa', *Freedom and Socialism* (Dar es Salaam: Oxford University Press, 1968), pp. 115–33; and over the refusal of West German aid, 'Principles and Development', *ibid*, pp. 187–206. See also Christos A. Frangonikolopoulos, 'Tanzanian Foreign Policy: The Proportions of Autonomy', *Round Table*, 307, 1988, pp. 276–92.

9 The most detailed study of African–Israeli relations is Joel Peters, *Israel and Africa: The Problematic Friendship* (London: British Academic Press, 1992).

10 See, for example, A. O. Adeoye, 'The OAU and the Namibian Crisis, 1963–1988', *African Review*, 16 (1–2), 1989, pp. 98–112.

11 See Anthony G. Pazzanita, 'The Proposed Referendum in the Western Sahara: Background, Developments, and Prospects', in Yahia H. Zoubir and Daniel Volman (eds.), *International Dimensions of the Western Sahara Conflict* (London: Praeger, 1993), pp. 187–225.

12 See Amadu Sesay, 'The Limits of Peace-Keeping by a Regional Organisation: The OAU Peace-Keeping Force in Chad', *Conflict Quarterly*, 11 (1), 1991, pp. 7–26.

13 For the text of the OAU Convention Concerning the Specific Aspects of Refugee Problems in Africa, see G. J. Naldi, *The Organization of African Unity: An Analysis of its Role* (London: Mansell, 1989).

14 *Keesings Record of World Events*, June 1993, p. 39500.

15 Organisation of African Unity, *Declaration of the Assembly of Heads of State and Government on the Establishment within the OAU of a Mechanism for Conflict Prevention, Management and Resolution* (AHG/DECL.3 (XXIX), 1993); interview with the Director of the Political Department, OAU Secretariat, Addis Ababa, January 1995.

16 See S. K. B. Asante, 'ECOWAS/CEAO: Conflict and Cooperation in West Africa', in Ralph I. Onwuka and Amadu Sesay, *The Future of Regionalism in Africa* (London: Macmillan, 1985), ch. 5; Daniel C. Bach, 'The Politics of West African Economic Cooperation: C.E.A.O. and E.C.O.W.A.S.', *Journal of Modern African Studies*, 21 (4), 1983, pp. 605–23.

17 See, for example, Carol Lancaster, 'The Lagos Three: Economic Regionalism in sub-Saharan Africa', in John W. Harbeson and Donald Rothchild (eds.), *Africa in World Politics* (Boulder: Westview, 1991), pp. 249–67; Omotunde E. G. Johnson, 'Economic Integration in Africa: Enhancing Prospects for Success', *Journal of Modern African Studies*, 29 (1), 1991, pp. 1–26; Elliot Berg, 'Reappraising Export Prospects and Regional Trade Arrangements', in Douglas Rimmer (ed.), *Action in Africa: The Experience of People Involved in Government, Business and Aid* (London: Currey, 1993), ch. 6; Rolf J. Langhammer, 'The Developing Countries and Regionalism', *Journal of Common Market Studies*, 30 (2), 1992, pp. 211–31. For two useful collections of papers on African regional organisations, see Onwuka and Sesay, *The Future of Regionalism in Africa*, and Domenico Mazzeo (ed.), *African Regional Organizations* (Cambridge: Cambridge University Press, 1984). A case could be made that the most effective regional organisation

in terms of economic integration was the Southern African Customs Union (SACU), which was, however, debarred from serving as an instrument of regional security owing to its domination by South Africa; see Robert D. A. Henderson, 'The Southern African Customs Union: Politics of Dependence', in Onwuka and Sesay, *The Future of Regionalism*, ch. 13.

18 The classic analysis is Arthur Hazlewood, 'The Economics of Federation and Dissolution in Central Africa', in Hazlewood (ed.), *African Integration and Disintegration: Case Studies in Economic and Political Union* (Oxford: Oxford University Press, 1967).

19 An excellent general survey of the problems of African regional integration is John Ravenhill, 'The Future of Regionalism in Africa', in Onwuka and Sesay, *The Future of Regionalism in Africa*, ch. 12.

20 Michael Davenport, 'Africa and the Unimportance of Being Preferred', *Journal of Common Market Studies*, 30 (2), 1992, pp. 233–51, citing R. J. Langhammer and U. Hiemenz, *Regional Integration among Developing Countries: Opportunities, Obstacles and Options* (Tübingen: Mohr, 1990).

21 Barry Buzan, *People States and Fear: The National Security Problem in International Relations* (Brighton: Wheatsheaf, 1983), p. 106.

22 See Arnold Hughes, 'The Collapse of the Senegambian Confederation', *Journal of Commonwealth and Comparative Politics*, 30 (2), 1992, pp. 200–22; Peter Robson, 'The Mano River Union', *Journal of Modern African Studies*, 20 (4), 1982, pp. 613–28.

23 For a statement of aspirations, see Joseph Wayas, *Nigeria's Leadership Role in Africa* (London: Macmillan, 1979); for an appraisal, see Julius O. Ihonvbere, 'Nigeria as Africa's Great Power: Constraints and Prospects for the 1990s', *International Journal*, 46 (3), 1991, pp. 510–35; see also Ibrahim A. Gambari, *Theory and Reality in Foreign Policy Making: Nigeria after the Second Republic* (Atlantic Heights: Humanities Press, 1989).

24 For a systematic survey of interventions during the first twenty-five years of African independence, see Arnold Hughes and Roy May, 'Armies on Loan: Toward an Explanation of Transnational Intervention among African States: 1960–85', in Simon Baynham (ed.), *Military Power and Politics in Black Africa* (Beckenham: Croom Helm, 1986), ch. 7.

25 Hughes, 'The Collapse of the Senegambian Confederation'; Arnold Hughes and Janet Lewis, 'Beyond *Francophonie*? The Senegambia Confederation in Retrospect', in Anthony Kirk-Greene and Daniel Bach (eds.), *State and Society in Francophone Africa since Independence* (London: Macmillan, 1995), ch. 15.

26 For Uganda after Amin, see two volumes edited by Holger Bernt Hansen and Michael Twaddle, *Uganda Now* (London: Currey, 1988); and *Changing Uganda* (London: Currey, 1991); see also Phares Mutibwa, *Uganda since Independence: A Story of Unfulfilled Hopes* (London: Hurst, 1992).

27 For the origins of the Mozambique–Zimbabwe relationship in the Zimbabwe independence war, see W. Cyrus Reed, 'International Politics and

National Liberation: ZANU and the Politics of Contested Sovereignty in Zimbabwe', *African Studies Review*, 36 (2), 1993, pp. 31–59.

28 See Sesay, 'The Limits of Peace-Keeping'; Dean Pittman, 'The OAU and Chad', in Yassin El-Ayouty and William Zartman (eds.), *The OAU after Twenty Years* (New York: Praeger, 1984), pp. 297–325.

29 These have been examined in Aderemi I. Ajibewa, 'Regional Security in West Africa: A Comparative Study with Special Reference to the OAU Peacekeeping Force in Chad and the ECOMOG in Liberia', Ph.D. thesis, Lancaster University, 1994; see also Margaret A. Vogt (ed.), *The Liberian Crisis and ECOMOG: A Bold Attempt at Regional Peace-Keeping* (Lagos: Gabumo, 1992).

30 See Yekutiel Gershoni, 'From ECOWAS to ECOMOG: The Liberian Crisis and the Struggle for Political Hegemony in West Africa', *Liberian Studies Journal*, 18 (1), 1993, pp. 21–43; William Reno, 'Foreign Firms and the Financing of Charles Taylor's NPFL', *Liberian Studies Journal*, 18 (2), 1993, pp. 175–88.

31 See Naomi Chazan and Victor T. Levine, 'Africa and the Middle East: Patterns of Convergence and Divergence', in John W. Harbeson and Donald Rothchild (eds.), *Africa in World Politics*, ch. 10; and Dunstan M. Wai, 'African–Arab Relations: Interdependence or Misplaced Optimism?', *Journal of Modern African Studies*, 21 (2), 1983, pp. 187–213.

32 See for example World Bank, *World Development Report 1993* (New York: Oxford University Press, 1993), tables 1, 3, 31.

33 See Peters, *Israel and Africa*, pp. 29–39.

34 See E. C. Chibwe, *Arab Dollars for Africa* (London: Croom Helm, 1976); Shireen Hunter, *OPEC and the Third World: The Politics of Aid* (London: Croom Helm, 1984).

35 A summary of allocations and other information appears in *Africa South of the Sahara 1986* (London: Europa, 1985), pp. 182–3, and in other annual issues of the same publication.

36 See Jeff Haynes, *Religion in Third World Politics* (Buckingham: Open University Press, 1993), esp. ch. 5.

37 See René Lemarchand, 'Libyan Adventurism', in Harbeson and Rothchild, *Africa in World Politics*, ch. 7; and for a fuller account, *The Green and the Black: Quadhafi's Policies in Africa* (Bloomington: Indiana University Press, 1988); see also Oye Ogunbadejo, 'Qaddafi and Africa's International Relations', *Journal of Modern African Studies*, 24 (1), 1986, pp. 33–68.

6 The resort to the superpowers

1 The classic example must be an article written by an academic at Georgetown University, Washington, Chester A. Crocker, 'South Africa: Strategy for Change', *Foreign Affairs*, 59 (2), 1980, pp. 323–51, which has often been ascribed a significant influence in securing his appointment as Assistant Secretary of State for African Affairs in the Reagan Administration, 1981–9; other examples include Steven R. David, *Third World*

Coups d'Etat and International Security (Baltimore: Johns Hopkins University Press, 1987); Bruce D. Porter, *The USSR in Third World Conflicts: Soviet Arms and Diplomacy in Local Wars, 1945–1980* (Cambridge: Cambridge University Press, 1984); and I. William Zartman, *Ripe for Resolution: Conflict and Intervention in Africa* (Oxford: Oxford University Press, 1985).

2 See Arthur Gavshon, *Crisis in Africa: Battleground of East and West* (Harmondsworth: Penguin, 1981), front cover; see also Gerard Chaliand, *The Struggle for Africa: Conflict of the Great Powers* (London: Macmillan, 1982).

3 I am drawing here on Alexander R. Thomson, 'Incomplete Engagement: An Examination of US Foreign Policy towards the Republic of South Africa, 1981–1988', Ph.D. thesis, Lancaster University, 1994.

4 On Soviet policy in the Horn, see Robert G. Patman, *The Soviet Union in the Horn of Africa: The Diplomacy of Intervention and Disengagement* (Cambridge: Cambridge University Press, 1990).

5 Zbigniew Brzezinski, *Power and Principle: Memoirs of the National Security Adviser 1977–1981* (New York: Farrar Straus Giroux, 1983), p. 189.

6 John J. Stremlau, *The International Politics of the Nigerian Civil War, 1967–1970* (Princeton: Princeton University Press, 1977), p. 65.

7 See Larry W. Bowman, 'The Strategic Importance of South Africa to the United States: An Appraisal and Policy Analysis', *African Affairs*, 81 (323), 1982, pp. 169–91; Christopher Coker, 'The Western Alliance and Africa, 1949–1981', *African Affairs*, 81 (324), 1982, pp. 319–35; for an account which emphasises the potential vulnerability of Western access to southern African minerals, see Hanns W. Maull, 'South Africa's Minerals: The Achilles Heel of Western Economic Security?', *International Affairs*, 68 (4), 1986, pp. 619–26; for one which discounts it, see Oye Ogunbadejo, *The International Politics of Africa's Strategic Minerals* (London: Pinter, 1985), esp. p. 195.

8 See Richard J. Payne and Eddie Ganaway, 'The Influence of Black Americans on US Policy towards Southern Africa', *African Affairs*, 79 (317), 1980, pp. 585–98; Masipula Sithole, 'Black Americans and United States Policy towards Africa', *African Affairs*, 85 (340), 1986, pp. 325–50.

9 See for example, John W. Harbeson, 'The International Politics of Identity in the Horn of Africa', in John W. Harbeson and Donald Rothchild (eds.), *Africa in World Politics* (Boulder: Westview, 1991), ch. 6.

10 See William Attwood, *The Reds and the Blacks* (New York: Harper and Row, 1967), for an account by the first US ambassador to Guinea; and for an academic account of the same period, Robert Legvold, *Soviet Policy in West Africa* (New Haven: Harvard University Press, 1970).

11 Steven R. David, *Choosing Sides: Alignment and Realignment in the Third World* (Baltimore: Johns Hopkins University Press, 1991), ch. 1.

12 For a comparative appraisal of destabilisation in these two countries, see William Minter, *Apartheid's Contras: An Enquiry into the Roots of War in Angola and Mozambique* (London: Zed, 1994); see also Mario J. Azevedo, 'A

Sober Commitment to Liberation? Mozambique and South Africa, 1974–79', *African Affairs*, 79 (317), 1980, pp. 567–84.

13 See Christopher Coker, 'The Soviet Union and Eastern Europe', in R. Craig Nation and Mark V. Kauppi (eds.), *The Soviet Impact in Africa* (Lexington: Lexington Books, 1984), pp. 68–70.

14 See also David, *Choosing Sides*, chs. 4 and 5.

15 See Thomas J. Redden, 'The US Comprehensive Anti-Apartheid Act of 1986: Anti-Apartheid or Anti-African National Congress?', *African Affairs*, 87 (349), 1988, pp. 595–605.

16 There is a substantial literature on Soviet involvement in Africa, most of it written by Americans; see David E. Albright (ed.), *Africa and International Communism* (London: Macmillan, 1980); Nation and Kauppi, *The Soviet Impact in Africa*; Richard B. Remnek, 'Soviet Military Interests in Africa', *Orbis*, 28 (1), 1984, pp. 123–43; Marina Ottaway, 'The Soviet Union and Africa', in Harbeson and Rothchild, *Africa in World Politics*, ch. 11; and Mark Webber, 'Soviet Policy in Sub-Saharan Africa: The Final Phase', *Journal of Modern African Studies*, 30 (1), 1992, pp. 1–30.

17 See Stephen Ellis and Tsepo Sechaba, *Comrades against Apartheid: The ANC and the South African Communist Party in Exile* (London: Currey, 1992), p. 74.

18 On Chinese policy in Africa, see Gerald Segal, 'China and Africa', *Annals of the American Academy of Political and Social Science*, 519, 1992; Bruce D. Larkin, *China and Africa 1949–1970: The Foreign Policy of the People's Republic of China* (Berkeley: California University Press, 1971); Philip Snow, *The Star Raft: China's Encounter with Africa* (London: Weidenfeld and Nicolson, 1988).

19 Ethiopia under the Mengistu Haile-Mariam regime between 1977 and 1991 probably made the most determined effort of any African state to institute a Soviet-style system, an endeavour which I have examined in Christopher Clapham, *Transformation and Continuity in Revolutionary Ethiopia* (Cambridge: Cambridge University Press, 1988).

20 This was made clear to me by Soviet academics in Addis Ababa under the Mengistu regime; see, however, Robert F. Gorman, 'Soviet Perspectives on the Prospects for Political and Economic Development in Africa', *African Affairs*, 83 (331), 1984, pp. 163–87, which presents a rather more optimistic Soviet view about 'socialist' development in Africa.

21 The Stalinist theory of nationalities was particularly influential in Ethiopia, where it was adopted both by the Mengistu government and – with very different implications – by the EPRDF regime that ousted it.

22 For the East German role in Africa, see Gareth M. Winrow, 'East Germany in sub-Saharan Africa: A Reassessment', *World Today*, 44 (12), 1988, pp. 205–8; and Winrow, *The Foreign Policy of the GDR in Africa* (Cambridge: Cambridge University Press, 1990); Jude Howell, 'The End of an Era: The Rise and Fall of GDR Aid', *Journal of Modern African Studies*, 32 (4), 1994, pp. 305–28, concentrates on GDR development aid to Mozambique.

23 On the Cuban role in Africa, see Pamela S. Falk, 'Cuba in Africa', *Foreign Affairs*, 65 (5), 1987, pp. 1077–96; and Sergio Diaz-Briquets, (ed.), *Cuban Internationalism in Sub-Saharan Africa* (Pittsburg: Duquesne University Press, 1989).

24 I have seen no analysis of North Korean involvement in Africa; for a vignette of the incongruous encounter between the *juche* idea and the Somali revolution, see I. M. Lewis, 'Kim Il Sung in Somalia: The End of Tribalism?', in P. Cohen and W. Shack (eds.), *The Politics of Office* (Oxford: Oxford University Press, 1979).

25 I regarded this famous tale as mere Western misinformation, until in the late 1960s I landed in Conakry, and saw the fabled snow ploughs rusting near the end of the runway.

26 For the career backgrounds of Soviet ambassadors in Ethiopia under the Mengistu regime, see Clapham, *Transformation and Continuity*, p. 232.

27 This awkward circumlocution was required because no African state came close to the level of economic development which was needed in Soviet Marxist theory for it to be designated as 'socialist'; see Margot Light, *The Soviet Theory of International Relations* (Brighton: Wheatsheaf, 1988), pp. 300–5.

28 See David, *Third World Coups d'Etat*, pp. 94–6 (Angola) and 124–6 (Sudan); and David Birmingham, 'The Twenty-Seventh of May: An Historical Note on the Abortive 1977 *coup* in Angola', *African Affairs*, 77 (309), 1978, pp. 554–64.

29 See Christopher Coker, *NATO, the Warsaw Pact and Africa* (Basingstoke: Macmillan, 1985), ch. 7.

30 See Mette Skak, 'CMEA Relations with Africa: A Case of Disparity in Foreign Policy Instruments', *Cooperation and Conflict*, 21 (1), 1986, pp. 3–23; and Ralph I. Onwuka, 'CMEA–African Economic Relations', in Ralph I. Onwuka and Timothy M. Shaw (eds.), *Africa in World Politics* (London: Macmillan, 1989), ch. 4.

31 See Coker, 'The Soviet Union and Eastern Europe', pp. 68–70.

32 See Clapham, *Transformation and Continuity*, pp. 120–1.

33 This was implicit in the recommendations of a Soviet team attached to the Ethiopian National Council for Central Planning in 1985; see Paul B. Henze, *Ethiopia: Crisis of a Marxist Economy: Analysis and Text of a Soviet Report* (Santa Monica: RAND, 1989).

34 See Paul B. Henze, 'Arming the Horn 1960–1980: Military Expenditures, Arms Imports and Military Aid in Ethiopia, Kenya, Somalia and Sudan, with Statistics on Economic Growth and Governmental Expenditures', in Sven Rubenson (ed.), *Proceedings of the Seventh International Conference of Ethiopian Studies* (Lund: Scandinavian Institute of African Studies, 1984), pp. 637–56.

35 See Sharif Harir and Terje Tvedt, *Short-Cut to Decay: The Case of the Sudan* (Uppsala: Nordiska Afrikainstitutet, 1994).

36 See the list of interventions in Arnold Hughes and Roy May, 'Armies on

Loan: Toward an Explanation of Trans-national Military Intervention among Black African States: 1960–85', in Simon Baynham (ed.), *Military Power and Politics in Black Africa* (London: Croom Helm, 1986), ch. 7; the number of interventions increases dramatically from the mid-1970s onwards.

37 These figures are taken from 'Aggregate tables of the value of the trade in major weapons with the Third World, 1968–87', *SIPRI Yearbook 1988* (Oxford: Oxford University Press, 1988), appendix 7A, pp. 202–3; and 'Tables of the volume of trade in major conventional weapons, 1984–93', *SIPRI Yearbook 1994* (Oxford: Oxford University Press, 1994), appendix 13B, p. 510; since the figures in the 1988 volume are given in constant 1985 US$, and those in the 1994 volume at constant 1990 US$, the 1990 figures have been deflated by a constant of 0.67, reached by dividing the 1988 totals for 1984–6, which are given in both volumes, by those in the 1994 volume. It should be noted that the SIPRI figures are only for 'major weapons', and thus exclude weapons such as small arms and landmines which have been especially important in many African conflicts. Figures for the arms trade are also published by the United States Arms Control and Disarmament Agency.

38 For the role of the USSR as a weapons supplier, see Jonathan Alford, 'The New Military Instruments', in E. J. Feuchtwanger and Peter Nailor (eds.), *The Soviet Union and the Third World* (London: Macmillan, 1981), ch. 2.

39 See Henze, 'Arming the Horn'.

40 See Coker, *NATO, the Warsaw Pact and Africa*, ch. 5; for the idea of *Eurafrique* in French strategic thought, see John Chipman, *French Power in Africa* (Oxford: Blackwell, 1989), ch. 3.

41 See Michael P. Kelley, *A State in Disarray: Conditions of Chad's Survival* (Boulder: Westview, 1986), pp. 121–2; Roy May and Roger Charlton, 'Chad: France's Fortuitous Success', *Review of the Association for the Study of Modern and Contemporary France*, 37, 1987, pp. 1–14; David, *Choosing Sides*, pp. 140–1 (Somalia) and 180–2 (Sudan).

42 For a critical view, see George K. Kieh, 'Merchants of Repression: An Assessment of United States Military Assistance to Liberia', *Liberia-Forum*, 5 (9), 1989, pp. 50–61.

43 See I. M. Lewis, *A Modern History of Somalia: Nation and State in the Horn of Africa* (Harlow: Longman, 1980), ch. 8.

44 See Christopher Clapham, *Liberia and Sierra Leone: An Essay in Comparative Politics* (Cambridge: Cambridge University Press, 1976).

45 The disastrous effect of local militias on security was equally evident in Sudan; see M. A. Mohamed Salih and Sharif Harir, 'Tribal Militias: The Genesis of National Disintegration', in Harir and Tvedt, *Short-Cut to Decay*, pp. 186–203.

46 Margot Light, 'Moscow's Retreat from Africa', in Arnold Hughes (ed.), *Marxism's Retreat from Africa* (London: Cass, 1992), pp. 21–40; see also Webber, 'Soviet Policy in Sub-Saharan Africa'.

47 See Abbashar Jamal, 'Funding Fundamentalism: Sudan', *Review of African Political Economy*, 52, 1991, pp. 103–9.

48 David Pool, 'Eritrean Independence', *African Affairs*, 32 (368), 1993, pp. 389–402.

49 See Charles W. Freeman, 'The Angola/Namibia Accords', *Foreign Affairs*, 68 (3), 1989, pp. 126–41; Geoffrey Berridge, 'Diplomacy and the Angola/Namibia Accords', *International Affairs*, 65 (3), 1989, pp. 463–79.

50 See Margaret J. Anstee, 'Angola: The Forgotten Tragedy: A Test Case for UN Peacekeeping', *International Relations*, 11 (6), 1993, pp. 495–511; Anthony W. Pereira, 'The Neglected Tragedy: The Return to War in Angola, 1992–3', *Journal of Modern African Studies*, 32 (1), 1994, pp. 1–28.

51 See Christopher Clapham, 'International Relations in Africa after the End of the Cold War', in Eberhard Kienle and William Hale (eds.), *The End of the Cold War: Effects and Prospects for Asia and Africa*, forthcoming; for an expression of regret for the Soviet Union's withdrawal of support for former clients, see Mohamed M. El-Doufani, 'Regional Revisionist Client States under Unipolarity', *Third World Quarterly*, 13 (2), 1992, pp. 255–65.

7 The international politics of economic failure

1 For an overview of Africa's economic malaise, see Thomas M Callaghy, 'Africa and the World Economy: Caught Between a Rock and a Hard Place', in John W. Harbeson and Donald Rothchild (eds.), *Africa in World Politics* (Boulder: Westview, 1991), ch. 3; two useful edited volumes on the same theme are Thomas M. Callaghy and John Ravenhill (eds.), *Hemmed In: Responses to Africa's Economic Decline* (New York: Columbia University Press, 1993), and Jennifer A. Widner (ed.), *Economic Change and Political Liberalization in Sub-Saharan Africa* (Baltimore: Johns Hopkins University Press, 1994).

2 World Bank, *World Development Report 1994* (New York: Oxford University Press, 1994).

3 *Ibid.*, table 1.

4 *Ibid.*, table 4.

5 See Reginald H. Green, 'Food Policy, Food Production and Hunger in sub-Saharan Africa: Retrospect and Prospect', *International Journal*, 42 (4), 1986, pp. 768–801, for an overview which includes tables showing the decline in per capita food production in Africa. Again, it should be noted that statistics for peasant agriculture are especially liable to error.

6 Callaghy, 'Africa and the World Economy'.

7 World Bank, *World Development Report 1994*, table 21, pp. 202–3.

8 Calculated from *ibid.*, table 3; the African total excludes a number of states for which data were not available; if South Africa is excluded, the sub-Saharan Africa total sinks to about half that of the Netherlands.

9 See Maria Louisa Cesoni, 'Les routes des drogues: explorations en Afrique subsaharienne', *Revue Tiers-Monde*, 33 (131), 1992, pp. 645–71; and also

Observatoire Geopolitique des Drogues, *Etat des Drogues; Drogue des Etats* (Paris: Hachette, 1994).

10 World Bank, *World Development Report 1993* records exports as 28 per cent of gross domestic product for sub-Saharan states in 1991 (table 9); it does not record imports as a percentage of consumption expenditure, but combined current account deficits equivalent to 6.7 per cent of GDP (table 18) indicate imports equivalent to about 35 per cent of GDP.

11 See René Lemarchand, 'The State, the Parallel Economy, and the Changing Structure of Patronage Systems', in Donald Rothchild and Naomi Chazan (eds.), *The Precarious Balance: State and Society in Africa* (Boulder: Westview, 1988), ch. 6; for further examples in the same genre, see Mark Duffield, 'The Political Economy of Internal War: Asset Transfer, Complex Emergencies, and International Aid', in Joanna Macrae and Anthony Zwi (eds.), *War and Hunger: Rethinking International Responses to Complex Emergencies* (London: Zed, 1994), ch. 3.

12 See Jurgen Wolf, 'Zambia under the IMF Regime', *African Affairs*, 87 (349), 1988, pp. 579–94; and Crawford Young and Thomas Turner, *The Rise and Decline of the Zaïrean State* (Madison: University of Wisconsin Press, 1985), p. 307.

13 See Julius O. Ihonvbere, *Nigeria: The Politics of Adjustment and Democracy* (London: Transaction, 1994), pp. 132–3; and Axel Klein, 'Trapped in the Traffick: Growing Problems of Drug Consumption in Lagos', *Journal of Modern African Studies*, 32 (4), 1994, pp. 657–77. By 1994, Nigeria had become one of the world's major drug trafficking countries; see Observatoire Geopolitique des Drogues, *Etat des Drogues*, pp. 68–78.

14 Like other statistics, debt figures need to be treated with caution; these are taken from *World Development Report 1985* (table 16) for 1970, and from *World Development Report 1993* (table 21) for 1980 and 1991; it is not clear whether the 1970 figures are strictly comparable with those for 1980 and 1991, but they none the less reflect the general level of magnitude.

15 World Bank, *World Development Report 1994*, table 23.

16 See David F. Gordon, 'Debt, Conditionality and Reform: The International Relations of Economic Policy Restructuring in sub-Saharan Africa', in Callaghy and Ravenhill, *Hemmed In*, pp. 90–129.

17 For an approach sympathetic to the viewpoint of African states, see Bade Onimode (ed.), *The IMF, the World Bank and the African Debt* (2 vols., London: Zed, 1989); and Adebayo Adedeji, (ed.), *Africa within the World: Beyond Dispossession and Dependence* (London: Zed, 1993). For useful reviews of the literature, see Douglas Rimmer, 'External Debt and Structural Adjustment in Tropical Africa', *African Affairs*, 89 (355), 1990, pp. 283–91; and 'Adjustment Blues', *African Affairs*, 94 (374), 1995, pp. 109–13.

18 This viewpoint is reflected in the work of Robert H. Bates, *Markets and States in Tropical Africa: The Political Basis of Agricultural Policies* (Berkeley:

California University Press, 1981), and in the World Bank publications noted below.

19 Willi Wapenhans, 'The Political Economy of Structural Adjustment: An External View', in Rolph van der Hoeven and Fred van der Kraaij (eds.), *Structural Adjustment and Beyond in Sub-Saharan Africa* (London: Currey, 1994), ch. 4.

20 John Toye, 'Structural Adjustment: Context, Assumptions, Origin and Diversity', in Hoeven and Kraaij, *Structural Adjustment and Beyond*, ch. 3.

21 World Bank, *Accelerated Development in Sub-Saharan Africa: An Agenda for Action* (Washington: World Bank, 1981).

22 World Bank, *Africa's Adjustment and Growth in the 1980s* (Washington: World Bank, 1989); for a critique, see Trevor Parfitt, 'Lies, Damned Lies and Statistics: World Bank and ECA Structural Adjustment Controversy', *Review of African Political Economy*, 47, 1990, pp. 128–43; see also UN Economic Commission for Africa, *African Alternative Framework to Structural Adjustment Programmes for Socio-Economic Recovery and Transformation* (Addis Ababa: ECA, 1989).

23 World Bank, *Sub-Saharan Africa: From Crisis to Sustainable Growth* (Washington: World Bank, 1989); for discussions of these reports, see John Ravenhill, 'A Second Decade of Adjustment: Greater Complexity, Greater Uncertainty', in Callaghy and Ravenhill, *Hemmed In*, ch. 1.

24 World Bank, *Governance and Development* (Washington: World Bank, 1992).

25 World Bank, *Adjustment in Africa: Reforms, Results, and the Road Ahead* (New York: Oxford University Press, 1994).

26 Toye, 'Structural Adjustment'.

27 N. N. Susungi, resident representative in Europe of the African Development Bank, at a conference organised by the Royal African Society, St Catherine's College, Oxford, 1992; the paper derived from this talk has been published as 'The Origins of the Debt Crisis and its Aftermath in Africa', in Douglas Rimmer (ed.), *Action in Africa: The Experience of People Involved in Government, Business and Aid* (London: Currey, 1993), ch. 8, but this splendid analogy does not appear in the published text.

28 See Andrew Buckoke, *Fishing in Africa: A Guide to War and Corruption* (London: Picador, 1991), ch. 5, for a journalist's account.

29 Michael Hodd, 'Africa, the IMF and the World Bank', *African Affairs*, 86 (344), 1987, pp. 331–42.

30 Van der Hoeven and van der Kraaij, *Structural Adjustment*, p. xx, and Fred van der Kraaij, 'Background Notes on Sub-Saharan Africa', pp. 240–57 of the same volume; the only other exceptions were Cape Verde, Djibouti, Eritrea (which became independent only in 1993), Liberia (which had no government), and Seychelles.

31 There have been many summaries of the characteristic ingredients of structural adjustment programmes; see, for example, Toye, 'Structural Adjustment', pp. 18–35.

32 See Jeffrey Herbst, *The Politics of Reform in Ghana, 1982–1991* (Berkeley:

California University Press, 1993), ch. 3; for a view of the devaluation by the Ghanaian finance minister, see Kwesi Botchwey, 'Deregulating the Foreign-Exchange Market in Ghana', in Rimmer, *Action in Africa*, ch. 4.

33 Calculated from data cited in Ihonvbere, *Nigeria*, p. 136.

34 For an account of the politics of the devaluation, see Antoine Glaser and Stephen Smith, *L'Afrique sans Africains: Le Rêve Blanc du Continent Noir* (Paris: Stock, 1994), pp. 200–24.

35 See, for example, Nicolas van der Walle, 'The Politics of Nonreform in Cameroon', in Callaghy and Ravenhill, *Hemmed In*, ch. 10, esp. pp. 261–2; the Cameroonian experience could be replicated from virtually any other African state.

36 Amongst this literature, Paul Mosley, J. Harrigan and John Toye, *Aid and Power: The World Bank and Policy-based Lending* (2 vols. London: Routledge, 1991) is especially worth noting, in addition to the volumes edited by Callaghy and Ravenhill and by van der Hoeven and van der Kraaij noted above.

37 See, for example, Pamela Spass (ed.), *Mortgaging Women's Lives: Feminist Critiques of Structural Adjustment* (London: Zed, 1994).

38 However, see Herbst, *The Politics of Reform in Ghana*, and Gordon, 'Debt, Conditionality and Reform', in Callaghy and Ravenhill, *Hemmed In*.

39 See Nicolas van der Walle, 'The Decline of the Franc Zone: Monetary Politics in Francophone Africa', *African Affairs*, 90 (360), 1991, pp. 383–405.

40 Zambia was especially prone to such riots; see Michael Bratton, 'Economic Crisis and Political Realignment in Zambia', in Widner, *Economic Change*, ch. 5.

41 This argument is put forward in Mosley et al., *Aid and Power*; see also Gordon, 'Debt, Conditionality and Reform'.

42 Young and Turner, *The Zairean State*, pp. 378–86.

43 Frank B. Kimble, 'The United States–Liberia Operational Experts Project', *Liberian Studies Journal*, 15 (1), 1990, pp. 1–12.

44 The most coherent attempt that I have seen to articulate the proper functions of the state in terms of the requirements imposed by structural adjustment is that by Herbst in *The Politics of Reform in Ghana*, ch. 6.

45 World Bank, *Sub-Saharan Africa*; see Callaghy, 'Africa and the World Economy'.

46 Douglas Rimmer, 'Structural Adjustment in Africa', *International Update* (Johannesburg: SAIIA) April 1995.

47 For changes over time in the IMF and World Bank agenda, see Ravenhill, 'A Second Decade of Adjustment', and Reginald H. Green, 'The IMF and the World Bank in Africa: How Much Learning?', both in Callaghy and Ravenhill, *Hemmed In*.

48 See Callaghy, 'Africa and the World Economy'; and Herbst, *The Politics of Reform in Ghana*, ch. 8.

49 See Jurgen Wolf, 'Zambia under the IMF Regime'; Matthew Martin,

'Neither Phoenix nor Icarus: Negotiating Economic Reform in Ghana and Zambia', in Callaghy and Ravenhill, *Hemmed In*, ch. 4.

50 Rimmer, 'Structural Adjustment in Africa'.

51 See Winsome J. Leslie, *Zaïre: Continuity and Political Change in an Oppressive State* (Boulder: Westview, 1993), pp. 113–25.

52 See van der Walle, 'The Politics of Nonreform in Cameroon'.

53 See Jean-Paul Azam, 'The Uncertain Distributional Impact of Structural Adjustment in Sub-Saharan Africa', in Hoeven and Kraaij, *Structural Adjustment and Beyond*, ch. 7.

54 See Jeffrey Herbst, 'The Politics of Sustained Agricultural Reform in Africa', in Callaghy and Ravenhill, *Hemmed In*, ch. 9; John Toye, 'Interest Group Politics and the Implementation of Adjustment Policies in Sub-Saharan Africa', *Journal of International Development*, 4 (2), 1992, pp. 183–97.

55 See van der Walle, 'The Politics of Nonreform in Cameroon'.

56 See Stephen Smith and Antoine Glaser, *Ces Messieurs Afrique: Le Paris-Village du continent noir* (Paris: Calmann-Levy, 1992), esp. chapters on Bolloré and Bouyges.

57 See William Reno, *Corruption and State Politics in Sierra Leone* (Cambridge: Cambridge University Press, 1995), ch. 6.

58 William Reno, 'Old Brigades, Money Bags, New Breeds, and the Ironies of Reform in Nigeria', *Canadian Journal of African Studies*, 27 (1), 1993, pp. 66–87.

59 See Herbst, *The Politics of Reform in Ghana*, ch. 2; for an assessment of Rawlings, see James C. W. Akiakpor, 'Rawlings, Economic Policy Reform and the Poor: Consistency or Betrayal?', *Journal of Modern African Studies*, 29 (4), 1991, pp. 583–600.

60 See Herbst, *The Politics of Reform in Ghana*, ch. 1.

61 See, for example, Kwame Nkrumah, *Neo-Colonialism: The Last Stage of Imperialism* (London: Nelson, 1965).

62 Herbst, *The Politics of Reform in Ghana*, p. 129.

63 *World Development Report 1994*, table 19; these figures exclude some states for which statistics were not available, but which were likely to be exceptionally aid dependent, including Somalia, Zaïre and Zambia.

64 *World Development Report 1994*, table 19; Uganda at 20.5 per cent and Ethiopia at 16.5 per cent were the only other states with ODA at over 15 per cent of GNP. OECD figures (*Development Assistance Committee 1993 Report*, table 49, p. 236) report ODA as a percentage of GNP in 1991/92 of 12.6 per cent for sub-Saharan Africa as a whole, with individual country figures of 96.2 per cent for Tanzania and 93.4 per cent for Mozambique, followed by Uganda at 42.7 per cent and Burkina Faso at 31.3 per cent; the figures for other areas of the developing world are not widely out of line with those given by the World Bank, but the totals for Tanzania and Mozambique stretch the bounds of credibility.

65 For analyses of the developmental effectiveness of aid, see Robert Cassen, *Does Aid Work? Report of the Independent Consultants' Study of Aid-Effective-*

ness (Oxford: Oxford University Press, 1986); and Paul Mosley, *Overseas Aid: Its Defence and Reform* (Brighton: Wheatsheaf, 1987); for an analysis of aid as a foreign policy tool of donor states, see Robert D. McKinlay, 'The Aid Relationship: A Foreign Policy Model and Interpretation of the Distribution of Official Bilateral Economic Aid of the US, UK, France and Germany, 1960–70', *Comparative Political Studies*, 11 (4), 1979, pp. 411–63; for a vituperative attack on the morality and management of official bilateral and multilateral aid agencies, see Graham Hancock, *Lords of Poverty* (London: Macmillan, 1989).

66 Otwin Marenin, 'United States Aid to African Police Forces', *African Affairs*, 85 (341), pp. 509–44, none the less indicates that such aid did not always achieve its purposes: the major sub-Saharan recipients, in descending order of numbers of police officers trained in the United States, were Zaïre, Liberia, Ethiopia and the Somali Republic.

67 These programmes, too, were problematic; see John M. Cohen, 'Foreign Advisers and Capacity-building: The case of Kenya', *Public Administration and Development*, 12 (5), 1992, pp. 493–510.

68 For an account of this project, see Paolo Dieci and Claudio Viezzoli (eds.), *Resettlement and Rural Development in Ethiopia: Social and Economic Research, Training and Technical Assistance in the Beles Valley* (Milan: FrancoAngeli, 1992).

69 See Christopher Clapham, *Transformation and Continuity in Revolutionary Ethiopia* (Cambridge: Cambridge University Press, 1990), pp. 167–68, 251.

70 *World Development Report 1994*, tables 1, 19.

71 See notably Joseph Hanlon, *Mozambique: Who Calls the Shots?* (London: Currey, 1991); this is a polemical work, and makes a number of assertions, notably that Mozambique was destabilised with the connivance of Western powers because the success of its socialist policies presented a threat to Western interests in the Third World (pp. 1–2), which appear to me to be very doubtful indeed; much of the material that it provides on the co-optation of policy-making by aid donors is, however, uncontestable; see the review by Mike Powell in *Review of African Political Economy*, 53, 1992, pp. 117–19. See also David N. Plank, 'Aid, Debt and the End of Sovereignty: Mozambique and its Donors', *Journal of Modern African Studies*, 31 (3), 1993, pp. 407–30; and Julie Cliff, 'Donor-dependence or Donor Control? The case of Mozambique', *Community Development Journal*, 28 (3), 1993, pp. 237–44.

72 See, for example, Terje Tvedt, 'The Collapse of the State in Southern Sudan after the Addis Ababa Agreement: A Study of Internal Causes and the Role of the NGOs', in Sharif Harir and Terje Tvedt (eds.), *Short-Cut to Decay: The Case of the Sudan* (Uppsala: Nordiska Afrikainstitutet, 1994), pp. 61–105.

73 See Alan Fowler, 'Distant Obligations: Speculations on NGO Funding and the Global Market', *Review of African Political Economy*, No. 55, 1992, pp. 9–29; and David Himbara and Dawood Sultan, 'Reconstructing the

Ugandan State and Economy: The Challenge of an International Bantustan', *Review of African Political Economy*, No. 63, 1995, pp. 85–93.

8 The externalisation of political accountability

1 President Nyerere of Tanzania was almost alone in raising the issue; see Christos A. Frangonikolopoulos, 'Tanzanian Foreign Policy: The Proportions of Autonomy', *Round Table*, 307, 1988, pp. 276–92.

2 Novelists were generally faster than political scientists to recognise the abuse of power, and to describe it from the viewpoint of those who suffered from it. See, for example, Chinua Achebe, *A Man of the People* (London: Heinemann, 1966), Ayi Kwei Armah, *The Beautyful Ones Are Not Yet Born* (London: Heinemann, 1968), or T. M. Aluko, *Chief the Honourable Minister* (London: Heinemann, 1970). See also Achille Mbembe, 'Provisional Notes on the Postcolony', *Africa*, 62 (1), 1992, pp. 3–37.

3 See Phares Mutibwa, *Uganda since Independence: A Story of Unfulfilled Hopes* (London: Hurst, 1992).

4 See Pierre Péan, *Bokassa 1er* (Paris: Alain Moreau, 1977); Thomas O'Toole, *The Central African Republic: The Continent's Hidden Heart* (Boulder: Westview, 1986), pp. 48–56; Claude Wauthier, 'France in Africa: President Giscard d'Estaing's Ambitious Diplomacy', *Africa Contemporary Record*, 12, 1979–80 (New York: Africana, 1981), pp. A120–7.

5 Randall Fegley, *Equatorial Guinea: An African Tragedy* (New York: Peter Lang, 1989).

6 See Oliver Furley, 'Britain and Uganda from Amin to Museveni: Blind Eye Diplomacy', in Kumar Rupesinghe (ed.), *Conflict Resolution in Uganda* (London: Currey, 1989), pp. 275–94.

7 See Linus C. Okere, 'The Press and Foreign Policy in Nigeria', *Round Table*, 321, 1992, pp. 61–71; Fegley, *Equatorial Guinea*, p. 122.

8 Fegley, *Equatorial Guinea*, p. 164.

9 There is a photograph of the occasion on the cover of *West Africa* magazine, no. 3284, 30 June 1980, which also, in no. 3281, 9 June 1980, published photographs of the executions.

10 Claude E. Welch, 'The Organisation of African Unity and the Promotion of Human Rights', *Journal of Modern African Studies*, 29 (4), 1991, pp. 535–55; the text of the Charter has been published by the Secretariat of the African Commission on Human and Peoples' Rights, Banjul, n.d.

11 Robert H. Jackson, *Quasi-states: Sovereignty, International Relations and the Third World* (Cambridge: Cambridge University Press, 1990), pp. 154–9; see also K. O. Kufuor, 'Safeguarding Human Rights: A Critique of the African Commission on Human and Peoples' Rights', *Africa Development*, 18 (2), 1993; and Peter Takirambudde, 'Six Years of the African Charter on Human and Peoples' Rights: An Assessment', *Lesotho Law Journal*, 7 (2), 1991.

12 See David A. Korn, *Ethiopia, the United States and the Soviet Union, 1974–1985* (London: Croom Helm, 1986), esp. ch. 2, for the tangled US diplomacy of this transition.

13 See Crawford Young and Thomas Turner, *The Rise and Decline of the Zaïrean State* (Madison: University of Wisconsin Press, 1985), pp. 388–9.

14 Carol Cosgrove Twitchett, *A Framework for Development: The EEC and the ACP* (London: Allen and Unwin, 1981), pp. 126–7.

15 *Keesings Record of World Events*, 1985, pp. 33485–7.

16 *Amnesty International Report 1981* (London: Amnesty, 1981), p. 55.

17 For a general study of human rights in international relations, including the role of NGOs and the development of a 'world society', see R. J. Vincent, *Human Rights and International Relations* (Cambridge: Cambridge University Press, 1986), esp. chs. 5 and 6.

18 Organisation of African Unity, *Declaration of the Assembly of Heads of State and Government of the Organisation of African Unity on the Political and Socio-Economic Situation in Africa and the Fundamental Changes taking place in the World* (AHG/Decl.1 (XXVI), Addis Ababa, July 1990).

19 From Deepak Lal, *The Poverty of 'Development Economics'* (London: IEA, 1983), cited in John Toye, 'Structural Adjustment: Context, Assumptions, Origin and Diversity', in Rolph van der Hoeven and Fred van der Kraaij (eds.), *Structural Adjustment and Beyond in Sub-Saharan Africa* (London: Currey, 1994), pp. 18–35.

20 See Comi Toulabor, '"Paristroika" and the One-Party System', in Anthony Kirk-Greene and Daniel Bach (eds.), *State and Society in Francophone Africa since Independence* (London: Macmillan, 1995), ch. 8.

21 See *African Voices: A Newsletter on Democracy and Governance in Africa* (Washington: USAID, 1992 onwards).

22 Douglas Hurd, UK Foreign Secretary, quoted in John Johnson, 'Aid and Good Governance in Africa', *Round Table*, 320, 1991, pp. 395–400.

23 'Resolution of the Council and of the Member States meeting in the Council on human rights, democracy and development', *Bulletin of the European Communities*, 24 (11), November 1991, pp. 122–3.

24 United States Department of State, *Country Reports on Human Rights Practices* (Washington: US Government Printing Office, February 1978); this first report covers only countries receiving (or proposed for) US aid; from 1979, it included all member states of the United Nations, with non-members including North Korea and Taiwan; see United States, *Country Reports on Human Rights Practices for 1979* (Washington: US Government Printing Office, February 1980).

25 *Amnesty International Report* (London: Amnesty, annual).

26 See, for example, Pierre Landell-Mills, 'Governance, Cultural Change, and Empowerment', *Journal of Modern African Studies*, 30 (4), 1992, pp. 543–67; though writing formally in a personal capacity, Landell-Mills was Senior Policy Adviser for Africa at the World Bank.

27 The UK Overseas Development Administration, for example, prepared a paper entitled 'Taking Account of Good Government' (ODA, Government and Institutions Department, Technical Note No. 10, London, October 1993), designed to guide the British aid programme. See also Robert B.

Charlick, *The Concept of Governance and its Implications for A.I.D.'s Development Assistance Program in Africa* (Washington: USAID Africa Bureau, June 1992).

28 See Peter Gibbon, 'The World Bank and the New Politics of Aid', *European Journal of Development Research*, 5 (1), 1993, pp. 35–62; the World Bank Vice-President for Africa, Edward Jaycox, specified five fundamental elements in 'good governance': accountability, transparency, predictability, openness, and the rule of law; from a speech in Nairobi reported in *Sunday Nation* (Nairobi), 29 January 1995.

29 See *International Herald Tribune*, 13 January 1993, for a report marking US ambassador Smith Hempstone's departure from Kenya.

30 *The Times* (London), 25 November 1994; *Keesings*, p. 40265, November 1994.

31 Interview, Nairobi, January 1995.

32 Interview, Addis Ababa, January 1995.

33 See Human Rights Watch/Africa, 'Multipartyism Betrayed in Kenya: Continuing Rural Violence and Restrictions on Freedom of Speech and Assembly', 6 (4), July 1994.

34 The 'spirit of La Baule' was cited to me in exactly this context by a French diplomat interviewed in Kigali in February 1995.

35 For an account from the viewpoint of the Commonwealth Secretariat, see Patsy Robertson, 'Monitoring African Elections', in Douglas Rimmer (ed.), *Action in Africa: The Experience of People Involved in Government, Business and Aid* (London: Currey, 1993), ch. 13.

36 See Gisela Geisler, 'Fair? What Has Fairness Got to Do with It? Vagaries of Election Observations and Democratic Standards', *Journal of Modern African Studies*, 31 (4), 1993, pp. 613–37; see also Eric Bjornlund, Michael Bratton and Clark Gibson, 'Observing Multiparty Elections in Africa: Lessons from Zambia', *African Affairs*, 91 (364), 1992, pp. 405–31.

37 For Benin, see Chris Allen, 'Restructuring an Authoritarian State: "Democratic Renewal" in Benin', *Review of African Political Economy*, 54, 1992, pp. 43–58; for Zambia, see Jan Kees van Donge, 'Zambia: Kaunda and Chiluba: Enduring Patterns of Political Culture', in John Wiseman (ed.), *Democracy and Political Change in Sub-Saharan Africa* (London: Routledge, 1995), ch. 9; and Carolyn Baylies and Morris Szeftel, 'The Fall and Rise of Multi-party Politics in Zambia', *Review of African Political Economy*, 54, 1992, pp. 75–91. All of these authors are sceptical about long-term prospects for democracy.

38 See Jan Kees van Donge, 'Kamuzu's Legacy: The Democratization of Malawi', *African Affairs*, 94 (375), 1995, pp. 227–57; Denis Venter, 'Malawi: The Transition to Multi-party Politics', in Wiseman, *Democracy and Political Change*, ch. 8.

39 See Richard C. Crook, 'Côte d'Ivoire: Multi-party Democracy and Political Change: Surviving the Crisis', in Wiseman, *Democracy and Political Change*, ch. 2.

40 See *Keesings Record of World Events 1991*, p. 38563.

41 See *Keesings Record of World Events 1993*, p. 39254.
42 See Nicolas van der Walle, 'The Politics of Nonreform in Cameroon', in Thomas M. Callaghy and John Ravenhill, (eds.), *Hemmed In: Responses to Africa's Economic Decline* (New York: Columbia University Press, 1993), ch. 10.
43 See Kathryn Nwajiaku, 'The National Conferences in Benin and Togo Revisited', *Journal of Modern African Studies*, 32 (3), 1994, pp. 429–47.
44 See Emeka Nwokedi, 'Nigeria's Democratic Transition: Explaining the Annulled 1993 Presidential Election', *Round Table*, 330, 1994, pp. 189–204; Julius O. Ihonvbere and Olufemi Vaughan, 'Nigeria: Democracy and Civil Society: the Nigerian Transition Programme, 1985–1993', in Wiseman, *Democracy and Political Change*, ch. 4.
45 See 'Mobutu Ascendant', *Africa Report*, May–June 1994; *Africa Confidential*, 35 (25), December 1994.
46 See Richard Hodder-Williams, 'Conflict in Zimbabwe: The Matabeleland Problem', *Conflict Studies*, 151 (London: Institute for the Study of Conflict, 1983); and for a local-level viewpoint, Richard Werbner, *Tears of the Dead: The Social Biography of an African Family* (Edinburgh: Edinburgh University Press, 1991).
47 Interviews, Harare, February 1995; see also 'Frightened Zimbabwe to cast its lacklustre vote', *Sunday Times* (Johannesburg), 2 April 1995.
48 See *Keesings Record of World Events*, March, April and May 1994 pp. 39900, 39949 and 39994.
49 This was evident from comparison of newspapers in Nairobi and Harare in early 1995; see also 'Zim press bids to break free', *The Star* (Johannesburg), 1 April 1995.
50 See Holger Bernt Hansen and Michael Twaddle, 'Uganda: The Advent of No-party Democracy', and Christopher Clapham, 'Ethiopia and Eritrea: The Politics of Post-insurgency', both in Wiseman, *Democracy and Political Change*, chs. 7 and 6.
51 For two contrasting views of the elections in Ghana, see Richard Jeffries and Clare Thomas, 'The Ghanaian Elections of 1992', *African Affairs*, 92 (368), 1993, pp. 331–66; and Mike Oquaye, 'The Ghanaian Elections of 1992 – a Dissenting View', *African Affairs*, 94 (375), 1995, pp. 259–75.
52 See Margaret J. Anstee, 'Angola: The Forgotten Tragedy: A Test Case for UN Peacekeeping', *International Relations*, 11 (6), 1993, pp. 495–511; A. W. Pereira, 'The Neglected Tragedy: The Return to War in Angola, 1992–3', *Journal of Modern African Studies*, 32 (1), 1994, pp. 1–28.
53 See Eduardo Serpa, 'The Mozambican Elections', *Africa Institute Bulletin* (Pretoria), 34 (5), 1994.
54 See Samuel M. Makinda, 'Iran, Sudan and Islam', *The World Today*, 49 (6), 1993, pp. 108–11.
55 *The Independent* (London), 3 May 1995; see also A. B. Zack-Williams and Stephen Riley, 'Sierra Leone: The Coup and its Consequences', *Review of African Political Economy*, 56, 1993, pp. 91–8.

56 John A. Wiseman, pers. comm.; for the background, see John A. Wiseman and Elizabeth Vidler, 'The July 1994 Coup d'Etat in The Gambia: The End of an Era', *Round Table*, 333, 1995, pp. 53–65.

57 See Peter M. Lewis, 'Endgame in Nigeria? The Politics of a Failed Democratic Transition', *African Affairs*, 93 (372), 1994, pp. 323–40.

9 The international politics of insurgency

1 The origins of Renamo have often been described. Even though the policies of the Frelimo government created sources of rural discontent from which Renamo could benefit, as argued for instance in Tom Young, 'The MNR/RENAMO: External and Internal Dynamics', *African Affairs*, 89 (357), 1990, pp. 491–509, I see no reason to disagree with the conclusion in William Minter, *Apartheid's Contras: An Enquiry into the Roots of War in Angola and Mozambique* (London: Zed, 1994) that Renamo was in all essentials an external creation.

2 The insurgencies of Southern Africa have as a whole attracted vastly more intensive study than those of other regions, doubtless because of their close association with the politics of liberation and destabilisation – or in other words, because they fit into the categories which dominate the image of the continent, both internally and externally. See in particular Stephen Ellis and Tsepo Sechaba, *Comrades against Apartheid: The ANC and the South African Communist Party in Exile* (London: Currey, 1992); Colin Leys and John S. Saul, *Namibia's Liberation Struggle: The Two-Edged Sword* (London: Currey, 1995); Norma J. Kriger, *Zimbabwe's Guerrilla War: Peasant Voices* (Cambridge: Cambridge University Press, 1992); and W. C. Reed, 'International Politics and National Liberation: ZANU and the Politics of Contested Sovereignty in Zimbabwe', *African Studies Review*, 36 (2), 1993, pp. 31–59. The insurgencies of the Horn, and notably the Eritrean People's Liberation Front (EPLF), which has some claim to be regarded as the most effectively organised insurgency that the world has yet seen, have by contrast been little studied; the major exception is an excellent study of the TPLF, John Young, 'Peasants and Revolution in Ethiopia: Tigray 1975–1989', Ph.D. thesis, Simon Fraser University, 1994, which, however, concentrates on internal dynamics. There is likewise very little material available on Uganda and Rwanda, or on Liberia and Sierra Leone, but see Paul Richards, 'Rebellion in Liberia and Sierra Leone: A Crisis of Youth?', in Oliver Furley (ed.), *Conflict in Africa* (London: I. B. Tauris, 1995), ch. 7; and Stephen Ellis, 'Liberia 1989–1994: A Study of Ethnic and Spiritual Violence', *African Affairs*, 94 (375), 1995, pp. 165–97.

3 United Nations General Assembly Resolution 1514(XV), 15 December 1960; see Dusan J. Djonovich, *United Nations Resolutions, Vol. VIII 1960–1962* (New York: Oceana, 1974), pp. 188–9.

4 See, for example, Reed, 'International Politics and National Liberation', for the connections between ZANU and China.

5 On the Ewe movements, see David Brown, 'Borderline Politics in Ghana:

The National Liberation Movement of Western Togoland', *Journal of Modern African Studies*, 18 (4), 1980, pp. 575–609.

6 The term 'warlord', which was commonly applied to China in the 1920s, was to the best of my knowledge first applied to Africa by Roy May, 'Political Authority in Chad: The Relevance of the "warlord" model', Birmingham, PSA Conference, 1985; see also Roger Charlton and Roy May, 'Warlords and Militarism in Chad', *Review of African Political Economy*, 45/46, 1989, pp. 12–25; it has since acquired universal currency, especially in Somalia.

7 The roles of coercion and popular support in the Zimbabwe liberation war have been assessed in Kriger, *Zimbabwe's Guerrilla War*.

8 See Leys and Saul, *Namibia's Liberation Struggle*, for an analysis of this issue and its effects.

9 See Fred Bridgland, *Jonas Savimbi: A Key to Africa* (Edinburgh: Mainstream, 1986), pp. 256–76.

10 See Minter, *Apartheid's Contras*, ch. 6.

11 See the analysis in Reed, 'International Politics and National Liberation'.

12 The number of refugees in Africa provides one of the clearest indicators of the failure of many African states to provide tolerable conditions of life for many of their people, and this failure in turn has had a significant impact on the international relations of the continent. A book which – like most books on international relations – is essentially concerned with people doing things, necessarily tends to ignore those (including those killed and maimed in Africa's numerous wars) who enter the sphere of politics by having things done to them. I can only note that an account of Africa's international relations from the viewpoint of its victims has yet to be written, and regret that I cannot provide it here.

13 See Jeffrey Herbst, 'Migration, the Politics of Protest, and State Consolidation in Africa', *African Affairs*, 89 (355), 1990, pp. 183–203.

14 See *The Economist*, 1 April 1995, pp. 42–3.

15 The 'chimurenga' or liberation war in Zimbabwe, in particular, was accompanied by the systematic killing of local notables who were regarded as representatives of the central government; see Kriger, *Zimbabwe's Guerrilla War*, pp. 104–5, and for a more general discussion of coercion and guerrilla warfare, pp. 121–33; for examples of the ill-treatment of southern Sudanese civilians by the SPLA, see Andrew Buckoke, *Fishing in Africa: A Guide to War and Corruption* (London: Picador, 1991), pp. 55–6.

16 Renamo atrocities have often been described; see for example, Alex Vines, *Renamo: Terrorism in Mozambique* (York: CSAS, 1991); for a regional breakdown of the 1995 election results, see Eduardo Serpa, 'The Mozambican Elections', *Africa Institute Bulletin* (Pretoria), 34 (5), 1994.

17 See Minter, *Apartheid's Contras*, ch. 8, for a discussion of this point.

18 See the *Independent* (London), 3 May 1995.

19 See Ellis and Sechaba, *Comrades against Apartheid*, pp. 191–6.

20 See Roland Marchal, 'Le Sud-Soudan à l'aube d'un nouveau drame

humanitaire', Ministère des Affaires etrangères (Paris), *Bulletin du Centre d'Analyse et de prévision*, no. 61, 1994/95, pp. 111–25.

21 See Reed, 'International Politics and National Liberation'.

22 See Lauren Dobell, 'SWAPO in Office', in Leys and Saul, *Namibia's Liberation Struggle*, ch. 9.

23 Interview, Asmara, January 1995.

24 For a remarkable (and indeed horrifying) participant account of illicit South African operations in Angola, see Jannie Breytenbach, *They Live By The Sword* (Johannesburg: Lemur, 1990); for a fuller account, see Fred Bridgland, *The War for Africa* (Gibraltar: Ashanti, 1990).

25 For an account of the Liberia–Sierra Leone borderland, see Richards, 'Rebellion in Liberia and Sierra Leone'.

26 See Bridgland, *Jonas Savimbi*, p. 256.

27 See W. W. Schneidman, 'Conflict Resolution in Mozambique', in David R. Smock (ed.), *Making War and Waging Peace: Foreign Intervention in Africa* (Washington: US Institute of Peace, 1993), ch. 9.

28 According to informants in Kampala in February 1995, this was the case with the NRA in Uganda, who had contacts in the government able to supply them with ordinary Ugandan passports.

29 Information provided by former EPLF and TPLF representatives, Asmara and Addis Ababa, January 1995.

30 Bridgland, *Jonas Savimbi*, p. 462.

31 A point acknowledged by Amnesty International; see Richards, 'Rebellion in Liberia and Sierra Leone', fn.19. At times, differences in treatment of human rights abuses by governments and insurgents appeared to reflect either sympathy for the insurgents, or a feeling on the part of human rights monitors that higher standards ought to be expected of governments; see for example, AfricaWatch, *Evil Days in Ethiopia: Thirty Years of War and Famine in Ethiopia* (New York: Human Rights Watch, 1991).

32 See John J. Stremlau, *The International Politics of the Nigerian Civil War 1967–1970* (Princeton: Princeton University Press, 1977), pp. 238–52.

33 Much of this section draws on the superb account in William DeMars, 'Tactics of Protection: International Human Rights Organizations in the Ethiopian Conflict, 1980–1986', in Eileen McCarthy-Arnolds et al. (eds.), *Africa, Human Rights, and the Global System* (Westport: Greenwood Press, 1994), ch. 5. For an account of the relief operation in neighbouring Tigray, see Barbara Hendrie, 'Relief behind the Lines: The Cross-Border Operation in Tigray', in Joanna Macrae and Anthony Zwi (eds.), *War and Hunger: Rethinking International Responses to Complex Emergencies* (London: Zed, 1994), ch. 7.

34 DeMars, 'Tactics of Protection', p. 82.

35 James Firebrace and Gail Smith, *The Hidden Revolution* (London: War on Want, 1982).

36 *Sunday Times* (London), 27 March 1983.

37 For the EC investigation, see *Keesings Record of World Events 1983*, p. 32240.
38 DeMars, 'Tactics of Protection'.
39 See *Humanitarianism Unbound? Current Dilemmas facing Multi-Mandate Relief Operations in Political Emergencies* (London: African Rights, Discussion Paper no. 5, November 1994).
40 See Mark Duffield, 'The Political Economy of Internal War: Asset Transfer, Complex Emergencies and International Aid', in Macrae and Zwi, *War and Hunger*, ch. 3.
41 *Agence France Presse* despatch, 22 June 1994.
42 For SWAPO, see Lauren Dobell, 'SWAPO in Office', in Leys and Saul, *Namibia's Liberation Struggle*, ch. 9.
43 Ellis and Sechaba, *Comrades against Apartheid*, pp. 156–7.
44 For a general assessment of Qadhafi's policies, see René Lemarchand (ed.), *The Green and the Black: Qadhafi's Policies in Africa* (Bloomington: Indiana University Press, 1988); for material on Libyan support for the NPFL and RUF, see Richards, 'Rebellion in Liberia and Sierra Leone'.
45 Dobell, 'SWAPO in Office'; the figure of $75m, converted from rand at the then rate of exchange, appears, however, to be of South African origin and may well be unreliable.
46 See Duffield, 'The Political Economy of Internal War'.
47 See The *Economist*, 1 April 1995; African Rights, *Humanitarianism Unbound?*, pp. 28–36.
48 This allegation is taken seriously in a confidential UN report on the Somali operation, *Report of the Commission of Enquiry established pursuant to Security Council Resolution 885 (1993) to investigate armed attacks on UNOSOM II personnel which led to casualties among them* (New York: United Nations, 24 February 1994).
49 *The Times* (London), 28 February 1995.
50 Eritrean informants, Asmara, January 1995.
51 See *The Star* (Johannesburg), 7 April 1994; F. De Boeck (Catholic University of Leuven) has written a detailed account of the Angola/Zaïre diamond trade in an unpublished paper, 'The Zaïrean Crisis: Local and Global Perspectives', Conference on the Criminalisation of Politics, Paris, December 1994.
52 Stephen Ellis, 'Of Elephants and Men: Politics and Nature Conservation in South Africa', *Journal of Southern African Studies*, 20 (1), 1994, pp. 53–69; see also Minter, *Apartheid's Contras*, p. 127.
53 William Reno, 'Foreign Firms and the Financing of Charles Taylor's NPFL', *Liberian Studies Journal*, 18 (2), 1993, pp. 175–88.
54 Paul Richards (University College, London), talk at African Studies Association of the UK conference, Lancaster, September 1994; see Richards, 'Rebellion in Liberia and Sierra Leone', p. 150.
55 Stephen Smith and Antoine Glaser, *Ces Messieurs Afrique: Le Paris-Village du continent noir* (Paris: Calmann-Levy, 1991), ch. 5.
56 See Mark Duffield, 'NGOs, Disaster Relief and Asset Transfer in the Horn:

Political Survival in a Permanent Emergency', *Development and Change*, 24 (1), 1993 pp. 131–57.

57 See Stremlau, *Nigerian Civil War*, ch. 4.

58 See Ruth Iyob, 'Regional Hegemony: Domination and Resistance in the Horn of Africa', *Journal of Modern African Studies*, 31 (2), 1993, pp. 257–76.

59 See Guillermo O'Donnell, Philippe C. Schmitter and Laurence Whitehead (eds.), *Transitions from Authoritarian Rule: Comparative Perspectives* (Baltimore: Johns Hopkins University Press, 1986); the nature of the 'pact' in the Latin American cases was rather different from that suggested here, but the idea that the transition from authoritarian rule required precisely negotiated conditions which reflected the interests of different social groups was common to both cases.

60 There is a large literature on the Zimbabwean and Namibian settlements, including, for Zimbabwe: Robert O. Matthews, 'From Rhodesia to Zimbabwe: Prerequisites of a Settlement', *International Journal*, 45 (2), 1990, pp. 292–333; and for Namibia, Charles W. Freeman, 'The Angola/Namibia Accords', *Foreign Affairs*, 68 (3), 1989, pp. 126–41.

61 For a survey of external mediation in Sudan, see Ann Mosley Lesch, 'External Involvement in the Sudanese Civil War', and 'Negotiations in Sudan', in Smock, *Making War and Waging Peace*, pp. 79–138.

62 Interviews with RPF officials, Kigali, February 1995.

63 For an account of the complex balance of internal and external factors involved in Nimairi's shift in international alignment, see Steven R. David, *Choosing Sides: Alignment and Realignment in the Third World* (Baltimore: Johns Hopkins University Press, 1991), ch. 5.

64 For a collection of papers on the breakdown of the Addis Ababa agreement and the return to civil war in Sudan, see Sharif Harir and Terje Tvedt (eds.), *Short-Cut to Decay: The Case of the Sudan* (Uppsala: Nordiska Afrikainstitutet, 1994).

65 See the chapters by Daniel S. Papp, Abiodun Williams and Witney W. Schneidman in Smock, *Making War and Waging Peace*; and Anthony W. Pereira, 'The Neglected Tragedy: The Return to War in Angola, 1992–3', *Journal of Modern African Studies*, 32 (1), 1994, pp. 1–28.

66 A Congolese force had been sent to Chad under OAU auspices in 1980.

67 See Amadu Sesay, 'The Limits of Peace-keeping by a Regional Organisation: The OAU Peace-keeping Force in Chad', *Conflict Quarterly*, 11 (1), 1991, pp. 7–26.

68 See Christopher Clapham, 'Problems of Peace Enforcement: Lessons to be drawn from Multi-National Peace-Keeping Operations in On-Going Conflicts in Africa', in Jakkie Cilliers (ed.), *South Africa and Peacekeeping in Africa* (Johannesburg: Institute for Defence Policy, 1995).

69 Isaias Afewerki described the OAU to its assembled heads of state in June 1993 as 'an utter failure for thirty years'. *Keesings Record of World Events*, June 1993, p. 39500.

70 Whether Museveni knew about the RPF invasion in advance, or even

encouraged it, remains a disputed issue; he was in Washington at that moment, and certainly sought to discourage Western states from aiding the Habyarimana government against the RPF.

71 See, for example, *Sunday Nation* (Nairobi), 5 February 1995.

72 See F.-X. Verschave and C. Vidal, *France-Rwanda: l'engrenage d'un genocide* (Paris: Observatoire permanent de la Coopération française, September 1994); Mitterrand's comments appeared in a series of interviews published in *Le Figuro* (Paris), August 1994.

73 See Solomon M. Nkiwane, 'Development of Zimbabwe's Foreign Relations 1980–90', *Round Table*, 326, 1993, pp. 199–216.

74 Interview, Asmara, January 1995; see also *The Economist* (London), 14 October 1995.

75 Dobell, 'SWAPO in Office'.

10 The privatisation of diplomacy

1 See Fred Halliday, *Rethinking International Relations* (Basingstoke: Macmillan, 1994) for an exploration of the development of international relations theory in the light of the end of the Cold War.

2 The study of 'social administration', and its incestuous relationship with the interests and institutions of the welfare state, provides the extreme example; the study of law has likewise been historically associated with the interests of the legal profession. Students of international relations have no need to feel any special sense of guilt.

3 See Halliday, *Rethinking International Relations*, chs. 8–10.

4 See Robert H. Jackson, *Quasi-states: Sovereignty, International Relations and the Third World* (Cambridge: Cambridge University Press, 1990), p. 11; for a study which carries this detatchment into the sensitive area of liberation movements, see Colin Leys and John S. Saul, *Namibia's Liberation Struggle: The Two-Edged Sword* (London: Currey, 1995).

5 See Jean-François Bayart, Achille Mbembe and Comi Toulabor, *La politique par le bas en Afrique noire: contributions à une problematique de la democratie* (Paris: Karthala, 1992).

6 Goran Hyden, *Beyond Ujamaa in Tanzania: Underdevelopment and an Uncaptured Peasantry* (London: Heinemann, 1980).

7 Translated as Jean-François Bayart, 'Civil Society in Africa', in Patrick Chabal (ed.), *Political Domination in Africa: Reflections on the Limits of Power* (Cambridge: Cambridge University Press, 1986), ch. 6.

8 On *kalabule* in Ghana, see Naomi Chazan, *An Anatomy of Ghanaian Politics: Managing Political Recession, 1969–1982* (Boulder: Westview, 1983), ch. 6, and Douglas Rimmer, *Staying Poor: Ghana's Political Economy, 1950–1990* (Oxford: Pergamon, 1992); on *magendo* in Uganda, see Holger Bernt Hansen and Michael Twaddle (eds.), *Uganda Now* (London: Currey, 1988), and *Changing Uganda* (London: Currey, 1991), notably the copious index references.

9 See Janet MacGaffey, 'How to Survive and Become Rich amidst Devasta-

tion: The Second Economy in Zaïre', *African Affairs*, 82 (328), 1983, pp. 351–66; and *The Real Economy of Zaïre: The Contribution of Smuggling and Other Unofficial Activities to National Wealth* (London: Currey, 1991).

10 William Reno, *Corruption and State Politics in Sierra Leone* (Cambridge: Cambridge University Press, 1995).

11 Reno, *Corruption and State Politics*, p. 137.

12 Crawford Young and Thomas Turner, *The Rise and Decline of the Zaïrean State* (Madison: University of Wisconsin Press, 1985), pp. 387–8.

13 Reno, *Corruption and State Politics*, pp. 137–8.

14 See Phil O'Keefe, 'Toxic Terrorism', *Review of African Political Economy*, 42, 1988, pp. 84–90; Samuel O. Atteh, 'Political Economy of Environmental Degradation: The Dumping of Toxic Waste in Africa', *International Studies* (New Delhi), 30 (3), 1993, pp. 277–98.

15 See Observatoire Geopolitique des Drogues, *Etat des Drogues, Drogue des Etats* (Paris: Hachette, 1994); United States Department of State, Bureau for International Narcotics and Law Enforcement Affairs, *International Narcotics Control Strategy Report* (Washington, 1995).

16 For drug production in south-west Rwanda, see *The Geopolitical Drug Dispatch*, no. 27, January 1994; though allegations of official French involvement, derived from interviews in Rwanda in February 1995, must obviously be treated with caution, the reports of drug production in the area concerned date from before the genocide of mid-1994 and the subsequent Operation Turquoise, while the close relations between the Habyarimana and Mitterrand regimes are a matter of public record; see F.-X. Verschave and C. Vidal, *France-Rwanda: l'engrenage d'un genocide* (Paris: Observatoire permanent de la Coopération française, September 1994).

17 See chapters 4 and 9 above, and Stephen Smith and Antoine Glaser, *Ces Messieurs Afrique: le Paris-Village du continent noir* (Paris: Calmann-Levy, 1992).

18 'Zvogbo bemoans Tiny's departure', *The Herald* (Harare), 23 February 1995.

19 Suzanne Cronje, Margaret Ling and Gillian Cronje, *LonRho: Portrait of a Multinational* (London: Friedmann, 1976), pp. 179–81.

20 Interview, Nairobi, January 1995.

21 See, for example, Young and Turner, *The Rise and Decline of the Zaïrean State*; Michael G. Schatzberg, *The Dialectics of Oppression in Zaïre* (Bloomington: Indiana University Press, 1988); MacGaffey, *The Real Economy of Zaïre*; Steve Askin and Carole Collins, 'External Collusion with Kleptocracy: Can Zaïre Recapture its Stolen Wealth?', *Review of African Political Economy*, 57, 1993, pp. 72–85.

22 'Any sensible man keeps his money in Switzerland'; Antoine Glaser and Stephen Smith, *L'Afrique sans Africains: Le Rêve Blanc du Continent Noir* (Paris: Stock, 1994), p. 170.

23 Reno, *Corruption and State Politics*, p. 180.

24 *Ibid.*, pp. 180–2.

25 William Minter, *Apartheid's Contras: An Enquiry into the Roots of War in Angola and Mozambique* (London: Zed, 1994), p. 127.
26 In 1992/93, the UNDP allocated 55 per cent of its resources to 45 of the world's poorest states, most of which were in Africa; about a quarter of UNHCR expenditure likewise went to Africa, along with the largest share of WFP funding, and 18.7 per cent of the WHO budget; see *Africa South of the Sahara 1995* (London: Europa, 1994), pp. 75–93.
27 See Peter Gill, *A Year in the Death of Africa* (London: Paladin, 1986), ch. 7, for an account of the influence of Edouard Saouma's campaign for re-election as Director-General of the FAO on the allocation of its resources in Africa.
28 See Andrew Buckoke, *Fishing in Africa: A Guide to War and Corruption* (London: Picador, 1991), p. 46.
29 List of NGOs supplied by the United Nations Rwanda Emergency Office, Kigali, February 1995; other material is derived from interviews and personal observation in Rwanda at the same time.
30 Interview, Kigali, February 1995.
31 See African Rights, *Humanitarianism Unbound? Current Dilemmas Facing Multi-Mandate Relief Operations in Political Emergencies* (London: African Rights, 1994), pp. 6–9.
32 See African Rights, *Humanitarianism Unbound?*, pp. 28–36; *The Economist* (London), 1 April 1995, pp. 42–3.
33 See Witney W. Schneidman, 'Conflict Resolution in Mozambique', in David R. Smock (ed.), *Making War and Waging Peace: Foreign Intervention in Africa* (Washington: US Institute of Peace, 1993), ch. 9.
34 See Ann Mosely Lesch, 'Negotiations in Sudan', in Smock, *Making War and Waging Peace*, ch. 5.
35 African Rights, *Humanitarianism Unbound?*, pp. 28–36, supplemented by interviews in Rwanda, February 1995.
36 See John M. Mackenzie, *The Empire of Nature: Hunting, Conservation and British Imperialism* (Manchester: Manchester University Press, 1988).
37 Stephen Ellis, 'Of Elephants and Men: Politics and Nature Conservation in South Africa', *Journal of Southern African Studies*, 20 (1), 1994, pp. 53–69.
38 This section draws on research by Rosaleen Duffy, Lancaster University, for a forthcoming Ph.D. on the international politics of nature conservation in Africa.
39 Terence Ranger, pers. comm.
40 Ellis, 'Of Elephants and Men'.
41 Cardinal Arinze of Nigeria was most often mentioned in this context; see *The Times* (London), 1 November 1994.
42 See, for example, 'A Visit with a Difference: Archbishop Carey in Southern Sudan', *Sudan Democratic Gazette*, no. 45, February 1994.
43 See Paul Gifford, 'Some Recent Developments in African Christianity', *African Affairs*, 93 (373), 1994, pp. 513–34; the most horrifying example of the association of churches with incumbent regimes, however, was pro-

vided by the association of the Catholic Church with the Rwandan genocide; see *The Economist* (London), 14 January 1995, p. 53; *The Times* (London), 28 February 1995.

44 See Gifford, 'Some Recent Developments'.

Conclusion

1 The Treaty of Westphalia in 1648 is conventionally taken as marking the establishment of the modern European sovereign state system.

2 See Stephen Ellis, 'Tuning in to Pavement Radio', *African Affairs*, 88 (352), 1989, pp. 321–30.

Bibliography

Achebe, Chinua, *A Man of the People* (London: Heinemann, 1966).

Adedeji, Adebayo, 'The Case for Remaking Africa', in Douglas Rimmer (ed.), *Action in Africa: the Experience of People Involved in Government, Business and Aid* (London: Currey, 1993), pp. 43–57.

Adedeji, Adebayo (ed.), *Africa within the World: Beyond Dispossession and Dependence* (London: Zed, 1993).

Adeoye, A. O., 'The OAU and the Namibian Crisis, 1963–1988', *African Review*, 16 (1–2), 1989, pp. 98–112.

African Rights, *Humanitarianism Unbound? Current Dilemmas facing Multi-Mandate Relief Operations in Political Emergencies* (London: African Rights, Discussion Paper no. 5, November 1994).

AfricaWatch, *Evil Days: Thirty Years of War and Famine in Ethiopia* (New York: Human Rights Watch, 1991).

Afrifa, A. A., *The Ghana Coup* (London: Cass, 1966).

Ajibewa, Aderemi I., 'Regional Security in West Africa: a Comparative Study with Special Reference to the OAU Peacekeeping Force in Chad and the ECOMOG in Liberia', Ph.D. thesis, Lancaster University, 1994.

Akiakpor, James C. W., 'Rawlings, Economic Policy Reform and the Poor: Consistency or Betrayal?' *Journal of Modern African Studies*, 29 (4), 1991, pp. 583–600.

Albright, David E. (ed.), *Africa and International Communism* (London: Macmillan, 1980).

Alford, Jonathan, 'The New Military Instruments', in E. J. Feuchtwanger and Peter Nailor (eds.), *The Soviet Union and the Third World* (London: Macmillan, 1981), ch. 2.

Allen, Chris, 'Restructuring an Authoritarian State: "Democratic Renewal" in Benin', *Review of African Political Economy*, 54, 1992, pp. 43–58.

Aluko, Olajide, 'Nigeria and Britain since Gowon', *African Affairs*, 76 (304), 1977, pp. 303–20.

'The Expulsion of Illegal Aliens from Nigeria: A Study in Nigeria's Decision-making', *African Affairs*, 84 (337), 1985, pp. 539–60.

'Oil at Concessionary Prices for Africa: a Case Study in Nigerian Decision-making', *African Affairs*, 75 (301), 1987, pp. 425–43.

Aluko, T. M., *Chief the Honourable Minister* (London: Heinemann, 1970).

Amnesty International Report (London: Amnesty, annual).

Anstee, Margaret J., 'Angola: the Forgotten Tragedy: a Test Case for UN Peacekeeping', *International Relations*, 11 (6), 1993, pp. 495–511.

Anyadike-Danes, M. K. and M. N., 'The Geographic Allocation of the European Development Fund under the Lomé Conventions', *World Development*, 10 (11), 1992, pp. 1647–61.

Anyang' Nyong'o, Peter (ed.), *Arms and Daggers in the Heart of Africa: Studies on Internal Conflicts* (Nairobi: Academy Science Publishers, 1993).

Armah, Ayi Kwei, *The Beautyful Ones Are Not Yet Born* (London: Heinemann, 1968).

Asante, S. K. B., 'ECOWAS/CEAO: Conflict and Cooperation in West Africa', in Ralph I. Onwuka and Amadu Sesay (eds.), *The Future of Regionalism in Africa* (London: Macmillan, 1985), ch. 5.

Askin, Steve and Collins, Carole, 'External Collusion with Kleptocracy: Can Zaïre Recapture its Stolen Wealth?', *Review of African Political Economy*, 57, 1993, pp. 72–85.

Atteh, Samuel O., 'Political Economy of Environmental Degradation: The Dumping of Toxic Waste in Africa', *International Studies* (New Delhi), 30 (3), 1993, pp. 277–98.

Attwood, William, *The Reds and the Blacks* (New York: Harper & Row, 1967).

Awolowo, Obafemi, *AWO: The Autobiography of Chief Obafemi Awolowo* (Cambridge: Cambridge University Press, 1960).

Azam, Jean-Paul, 'The Uncertain Distributional Impact of Structural Adjustment in Sub-Saharan Africa', in Rolph van der Hoeven and Fred van der Kraaij (eds.), *Structural Adjustment and Beyond in Sub-Saharan Africa* (London: Currey, 1994), ch. 7.

Azevedo, Mario J., 'A Sober Commitment to Liberation? Mozambique and South Africa, 1974–79', *African Affairs*, 79 (317), 1980, pp. 567–84.

Bach, Daniel C., 'The Politics of West African Economic Cooperation: CEAO and ECOWAS', *Journal of Modern African Studies*, 21 (4), 1983, pp. 605–23.

'France's Involvement in sub-Saharan Africa: a Necessary Condition to Middle Power Status in the International System', in Amadu Sesay (ed.), *Africa and Europe: from Partition to Interdependence or Dependence?* (London: Croom Helm, 1986), ch. 5.

Baissa, Lemmu, 'United States Military Assistance to Ethiopia, 1953–1974: a Reappraisal of a Difficult Patron–Client Relationship', *Northeast African Studies*, 11 (3), 1989, pp. 51–70.

Bates, Robert H., *Markets and States in Tropical Africa: the Political Basis of Agricultural Policies* (Berkeley: California University Press, 1981).

Bayart, Jean-François, *La politique africaine de François Mitterrand* (Paris: Karthala, 1984).

'Civil Society in Africa', in Patrick Chabal (ed.), *Political Domination in Africa:*

Reflections on the Limits of Power (Cambridge: Cambridge University Press, 1986), ch. 6.

The State in Africa: the Politics of the Belly (London: Longman, 1993).

Bayart, Jean-François, Mbembe, Achille and Toulabor, Comi, *La politique par le bas en Afrique noire: contributions à une problematique de la democratie* (Paris: Karthala, 1992).

Baylies, Carolyn and Szeftel, Morris, 'The Fall and Rise of Multi-party Politics in Zambia', *Review of African Political Economy*, 54, 1992, pp. 75–91.

Baynham, Simon (ed.), *Military Power and Politics in Black Africa* (London: Croom Helm, 1986).

Beblawi, Hazem and Luciani, Giacomo (eds.), *The Rentier State* (London: Croom Helm, 1987).

Berg Report, see World Bank, *Accelerated Development in Sub-Saharan Africa*.

Berg, Elliot, 'Reappraising Export Prospects and Regional Trade Arrangements', in Douglas Rimmer (ed.), *Action in Africa: the Experience of People Involved in Government, Business and Aid* (London: Currey, 1993), ch. 6.

Berridge, Geoffrey, 'Diplomacy and the Angola/Namibia Accords', *International Affairs*, 65 (3), 1989, pp. 463–79.

Birmingham, David, 'The Twenty-Seventh of May: an Historical Note on the Abortive 1977 *coup* in Angola', *African Affairs*, 77 (309), 1978, pp. 554–64.

Bjornlund, Eric, Bratton, Michael and Gibson, Clark, 'Observing Multiparty Elections in Africa: Lessons from Zambia', *African Affairs*, 91 (364), 1992, pp. 405–31.

Boardman, Robert, Shaw, Timothy M. and Soldatos, Panayotis (eds.), *Europe, Africa and Lomé III* (London: University Press of America, 1985).

Botchwey, Kwesi, 'Deregulating the Foreign-Exchange Market in Ghana', in Douglas Rimmer (ed.), *Action in Africa: the Experience of People Involved in Government, Business and Aid* (London: Currey, 1993), ch. 4.

Bowles, Paul, 'Recipient Needs and Donor Interests in the Allocation of EEC Aid to Developing Countries', *Canadian Journal of Development Studies*, 10 (1), 1989, pp. 7–20.

Bowman, Larry W., 'The Strategic Importance of South Africa to the United States: an Appraisal and Policy Analysis', *African Affairs*, 81 (323), 1982, pp. 169–91.

Braeckman, Colette, *Le dinosaure: le Zaïre de Mobutu* (Paris: Fayard, 1992).

Bratton, Michael, 'Economic Crisis and Political Realignment in Zambia', in Jennifer A. Widner (ed.), *Economic Change and Political Liberalization in Sub-Saharan Africa* (Baltimore: Johns Hopkins University Press, 1994), ch. 5.

Breytenbach, Jannie, *They Live By The Sword* (Johannesburg: Lemur, 1990).

Bridgland, Fred, *Jonas Savimbi: a Key to Africa* (Edinburgh: Mainstream, 1986).

The War for Africa (Gibraltar: Ashanti, 1990).

Brown, David, 'Borderline Politics in Ghana: The National Liberation Movement of Western Togoland', *Journal of Modern African Studies*, 18 (4), 1980, pp. 575–609.

Brzezinski, Zbigniew, *Power and Principle: Memoirs of the National Security Adviser 1977–1981* (New York: Farrar Straus Giroux, 1983).

Buckoke, Andrew, *Fishing in Africa: A Guide to War and Corruption* (London: Picador, 1991).

Bustin, Edward, 'The Foreign Policy of the Republic of Zaïre', *Annals of the American Academy of Political and Social Science*, 489, 1987, pp. 63–75.

Buzan, Barry, *People States and Fear: The National Security Problem in International Relations* (Brighton: Wheatsheaf, 1983).

Callaghy, Thomas M. 'Africa and the World Economy: Caught Between a Rock and a Hard Place', in John W. Harbeson and Donald Rothchild (eds.), *Africa in World Politics* (Boulder: Westview, 1991), ch. 3.

Callaghy, Thomas M. and Ravenhill, John (eds.), *Hemmed In: Responses to Africa's Economic Decline* (New York: Columbia University Press, 1993).

Cassen, Robert, *Does Aid Work? Report of the Independent Consultants' Study of Aid-Effectiveness* (Oxford: Oxford University Press, 1986).

Cesoni, Maria Louisa, 'Les routes des drogues: explorations en Afrique subsaharienne', *Revue Tiers-Monde*, 33 (131), 1992, pp. 645–71.

Chabal, Patrick (ed.), *Political Domination in Africa: Reflections on the Limits of Power* (Cambridge: Cambridge University Press, 1986).

Chafer, Anthony, 'French African Policy: Towards Change', *African Affairs*, 91 (362), 1992, pp. 37–51.

Chaliand, Gerard, *The Struggle for Africa: Conflict of the Great Powers* (London: Macmillan, 1982).

Charlick, Robert B., *Niger: Personal Rule and Survival in the Sahel* (Boulder: Westview, 1991).

The Concept of Governance and its Implications for AID's Development Assistance Program in Africa (Washington: USAID, June 1992).

Charlton, Roger and May, Roy, 'Warlords and Militarism in Chad', *Review of African Political Economy*, 45/46, 1989, pp. 12–25.

Chazan, Naomi, *An Anatomy of Ghanaian Politics: Managing Political Recession, 1969–1982* (Boulder: Westview, 1983).

Chazan, Naomi and Levine, Victor T., 'Africa and the Middle East: Patterns of Convergence and Divergence', in John W. Harbeson and Donald Rothchild (eds.), *Africa in World Politics* (Boulder: Westview, 1991), ch. 10.

Chibwe, E. C., *Arab Dollars for Africa* (London: Croom Helm, 1976).

Chipman, John, *French Power in Africa* (Oxford: Blackwell, 1989).

Clapham, Christopher, *Liberia and Sierra Leone: An Essay in Comparative Politics* (Cambridge: Cambridge University Press, 1976).

'The Politics of Failure: Clientelism, Political Instability and National Integration in Liberia and Sierra Leone', in Christopher Clapham (ed.), *Private Patronage and Public Power* (London: Pinter, 1982), pp. 76–92.

Transformation and Continuity in Revolutionary Ethiopia (Cambridge: Cambridge University Press, 1988).

'Liberia', in Donal B. Cruise O'Brien et al. (eds.), *Contemporary West African States* (Cambridge: Cambridge University Press, 1989), pp. 99–111.

'Ethiopia and Eritrea: The Politics of Post-insurgency', in John Wiseman (ed.), *Democracy and Political Change in Sub-Saharan Africa* (London: Routledge, 1995), ch. 6.

'Problems of Peace Enforcement: Lessons to be drawn from Multi-National Peace-Keeping Operations in On-Going Conflicts in Africa', in Jakkie Cilliers (ed.), *South Africa and Peacekeeping in Africa* (Johannesburg: Institute for Defence Policy, 1995).

'International Relations in Africa after the End of the Cold War', in Eberhard Kienle and William Hale (eds.), *The End of the Cold War: Effects and Prospects for Asia and Africa*, forthcoming.

Cliff, Julie, 'Donor-dependence or Donor Control? The case of Mozambique', *Community Development Journal*, 28 (3), 1993, pp. 237–44.

Cohen, John M., 'Foreign Advisers and Capacity-building: The Case of Kenya', *Public Administration and Development*, 12 (5), 1992, pp. 493–510.

Coker, Christopher, 'The Western Alliance and Africa, 1949–1981', *African Affairs*, 81 (324), 1982, pp. 319–35.

'The Soviet Union and Eastern Europe', in R. Craig Nation and Mark V. Kauppi (eds.), *The Soviet Impact in Africa* (Lexington: Lexington Books, 1984).

NATO, the Warsaw Pact and Africa (Basingstoke: Macmillan, 1985).

Colley, Linda, *Britons: Forging the Nation 1707–1837* (London: Pimlico, 1994).

Crocker, Chester A., 'South Africa: Strategy for Change', *Foreign Affairs*, 59 (2), 1980, pp. 323–51.

Cronje, Suzanne, Ling, Margaret and Cronje, Gillian, *LonRho: Portrait of a Multinational* (London: Friedmann, 1976).

Crook, Richard C., 'Côte d'Ivoire: Multi-party Democracy and Political Change', in John Wiseman (ed.), *Democracy and Political Change in Sub-Saharan Africa* (London: Routledge, 1995), ch. 2.

Cruise O'Brien, Donal B. et al. (eds.), *Contemporary West African States* (Cambridge: Cambridge University Press, 1989).

Davenport, Michael, 'Africa and the Unimportance of Being Preferred', *Journal of Common Market Studies*, 30 (2), 1992, pp. 233–51.

David, Steven R., *Third World Coups d'Etat and International Security* (Baltimore: Johns Hopkins University Press, 1987).

Choosing Sides: Alignment and Realignment in the Third World (Baltimore: Johns Hopkins University Press, 1991).

Davidson, Basil, *The Black Man's Burden: Africa and the Curse of the Nation-State* (London: Currey, 1992).

De Boeck, F., 'The Zaïrean Crisis: Local and Global Perspectives', conference on the Criminalisation of Politics, Paris, December 1994.

Decalo, Samuel, 'The Process, Prospects and Constraints of Democratization in Africa', *African Affairs*, 91 (362), 1992, pp. 7–35.

Delancey, Mark et al., *African International Relations: An Annotated Bibliography* (2nd edn, Boulder: Westview, 1994).

DeMars, William, 'Tactics of Protection: International Human Rights Organizations in the Ethiopian conflict, 1980–1986', in Eileen McCarthy-Arnolds et al. (eds.), *Africa, Human Rights, and the Global System* (Westport: Greenwood Press, 1994), ch. 5.

Diaz-Briquets, Sergio (ed.), *Cuban Internationalism in Sub-Saharan Africa* (Pittsburg: Duquesne University Press, 1989).

Dieci, Paolo and Viezzoli, Claudio (eds.), *Resettlement and Rural Development in Ethiopia: Social and Economic Research, Training and Technical Assistance in the Beles Valley* (Milan: FrancoAngeli, 1992).

Djonovich, Dusan J., *United Nations Resolutions, Vol. VIII 1960–1962* (New York: Oceana, 1974).

Dobell, Lauren, 'SWAPO in Office', in Colin Leys and John S. Saul (eds.), *Namibia's Liberation Struggle: The Two-Edged Sword* (London: Currey, 1995), ch. 9.

Duffield, Mark, 'NGOs, Disaster Relief and Asset Transfer in the Horn: Political Survival in a Permanent Emergency', *Development and Change*, 24 (1), 1993 pp. 131–57.

'The Political Economy of Internal War: Asset Transfer, Complex Emergencies, and International Aid', in Joanna Macrae and Anthony Zwi (eds.), *War and Hunger: Rethinking International Responses to Complex Emergencies* (London: Zed, 1994), ch. 3.

Dunn, John (ed.), *West African States: Failure and Promise* (Cambridge: Cambridge University Press, 1978).

Ehrlich, Haggai, *Ethiopia and the Challenge of Independence* (Boulder: Lynne Rienner, 1986).

Ekwe-Ekwe, Herbert, *Conflict and Intervention in Africa: Nigeria, Angola, Zaïre* (London: Macmillan, 1990).

El-Doufani, Mohamed M., 'Regional Revisionist Client States under Unipolarity', *Third World Quarterly*, 13 (2), 1992, pp. 255–65.

Ellis, Stephen, 'Tuning in to Pavement Radio', *African Affairs*, 88 (352), 1989, pp. 321–30.

'Of Elephants and Men: Politics and Nature Conservation in South Africa', *Journal of Southern African Studies*, 20 (1), 1994, pp. 53–69.

'Liberia 1989–1994: A Study of Ethnic and Spiritual Violence', *African Affairs*, 94 (375), 1995, pp. 165–97.

Ellis, Stephen and Sechaba, Tsepo, *Comrades against Apartheid: The ANC and the South African Communist Party in Exile* (London: Currey, 1992).

Falk, Pamela S., 'Cuba in Africa', *Foreign Affairs*, 65 (5), 1987, pp. 1077–96.

Fegley, Randall, *Equatorial Guinea: An African Tragedy* (New York: Peter Lang, 1989).

Feuchtwanger, E. J. and Nailor, Peter (eds.), *The Soviet Union and the Third World* (London: Macmillan, 1981).

Firebrace, James and Smith, Gail, *The Hidden Revolution* (London: War on Want, 1982).

Foltz, William J. and Bienen, Henry S., *Arms and the African: Military Influences on Africa's International Relations* (New Haven: Yale University Press, 1985).

Forde, Daryll and Kaberry, P. M. (eds.), *West African Kingdoms in the Nineteenth Century* (Oxford: Oxford University Press, 1967).

Fowler, Alan, 'Distant Obligations: Speculations on NGO Funding and the Global Market', *Review of African Political Economy*, 55, 1992, pp. 9–29.

Frangonikolopoulos, Christos A., 'Tanzanian Foreign Policy: The Proportions of Autonomy', *Round Table*, 307, 1988, pp. 276–92.

Freeman, Charles W., 'The Angola/Namibia Accords', *Foreign Affairs*, 68 (3), 1989, pp. 126–41.

Furley, Oliver, 'Britain and Uganda from Amin to Museveni: Blind Eye Diplomacy', in Kumar Rupesinghe (ed.), *Conflict Resolution in Uganda* (London: Currey, 1989), pp. 275–94.

Furley, Oliver (ed.), *Conflict in Africa* (London: I. B.Tauris, 1995).

Galloway, Colin, 'The Dikko Affair and British–Nigerian Relations', *Round Table*, 311, 1989, pp. 323–36.

Gambari, Ibrahim A., *Theory and Reality in Foreign Policy Making: Nigeria after the Second Republic* (Atlantic Heights: Humanities Press, 1989).

Gann, L. H. and Duignan, Peter, *Burden of Empire: an Appraisal of Western Colonialism in Africa South of the Sahara* (London: Pall Mall, 1968).

Gavshon, Arthur, *Crisis in Africa: Battleground of East and West* (Harmondsworth: Penguin, 1981).

Geisler, Gisela, 'Fair? What Has Fairness Got to Do with It? Vagaries of Election Observations and Democratic Standards', *Journal of Modern African Studies*, 31 (4), 1993, pp. 613–37.

Gershoni, Yekutiel, 'From ECOWAS to ECOMOG: the Liberian Crisis and the Struggle for Political Hegemony in West Africa', *Liberian Studies Journal*, 18 (1), 1993, pp. 21–43.

Gibbon, Peter, 'The World Bank and the New Politics of Aid', *European Journal of Development Research*, 5 (1), 1993, pp. 35–62.

Gifford, Paul, 'Some Recent Developments in African Christianity', *African Affairs*, 93 (373), 1994, pp. 513–34.

Gill, Peter, *A Year in the Death of Africa* (London: Paladin, 1986).

Glaser, Antoine and Smith, Stephen, *L'Afrique sans Africains: Le Rêve Blanc du Continent Noir* (Paris: Stock, 1994).

Golan, Tamar, 'A Certain Mystery: How can France do everything that it does in Africa – and get away with it?', *African Affairs*, 80 (318), 1981, pp. 3–11.

Gordon, David F., 'Debt, Conditionality and Reform: The International Relations of Economic Policy Restructuring in Sub-Saharan Africa', in Thomas M. Callaghy and John Ravenhill (eds.), *Hemmed In: Responses to Africa's Economic Decline* (New York: Columbia University Press, 1993), pp. 90–129.

Gorman, Robert F., 'Soviet Perspectives on the Prospects for Political and Economic Development in Africa', *African Affairs*, 83 (331), 1984, pp. 163–87.

Green, Reginald H., 'Food Policy, Food Production and Hunger in sub-Saharan Africa: Retrospect and Prospect', *International Journal*, 42 (4), 1986, pp. 768–801.

'The IMF and the World Bank in Africa: How Much Learning?', in Thomas M. Callaghy and John Ravenhill (eds.), *Hemmed In: Responses to Africa's Economic Decline* (New York: Columbia University Press, 1993), ch. 2.

'Namibia: From Blood and Iron to Reconciliation', in Oliver Furley (ed.), *Conflict in Africa* (London: I. B. Tauris, 1995), ch. 10.

Hale, William and Kienle, Eberhard (eds.), *Africa and Asia after the Cold War* (London: I. B. Tauris, forthcoming).

Halliday, Fred, *Rethinking International Relations* (Basingstoke: Macmillan, 1994).

Hancock, Graham, *Lords of Poverty* (London: Macmillan, 1989).

Hanlon, Joseph, *Mozambique: Who Calls the Shots?* (London: Currey, 1991).

Hansen, Holger Bernt and Twaddle, Michael (eds.), *Uganda Now* (London: Currey, 1988).

Changing Uganda (London: Currey, 1991).

'Uganda: The Advent of No-party Democracy', in John Wiseman (ed.), *Democracy and Political Change in Sub-Saharan Africa* (London: Routledge, 1995), ch. 7.

Harbeson, John W., 'The International Politics of Identity in the Horn of Africa', in John W. Harbeson and Donald Rothchild (eds.), *Africa in World Politics* (Boulder: Westview, 1991), ch. 6.

Harbeson, John W. and Rothchild, Donald (eds.), *Africa in World Politics* (Boulder: Westview, 1991).

Harir, Sharif, and Tvedt, Terje (eds.), *Short-Cut to Decay: The Case of the Sudan* (Uppsala: Nordiska Afrikainstitutet, 1994).

Hassen, Mohammed, *The Oromo of Ethiopia: A History 1570–1860* (Cambridge: Cambridge University Press, 1990).

Haynes, Jeff, *Religion in Third World Politics* (Buckingham: Open University Press, 1993).

'Ghana: From Personalities to Democratic Rule', in John A. Wiseman (ed.), *Democracy and Political Change in Sub-Saharan Africa* (London: Routledge, 1995), ch. 5.

Hazlewood, Arthur, 'The Economics of Federation and Dissolution in Central Africa', in Arthur Hazlewood (ed.), *African Integration and Disintegration: Case Studies in Economic and Political Union* (Oxford: Oxford University Press, 1967).

Henderson, Robert D. A., 'The Southern African Customs Union: Politics of Dependence', in Ralph I. Onwuka and Amadu Sesay (ed.), *The Future of Regionalism in Africa* (London: Macmillan, 1985), ch. 13.

Hendrie, Barbara, 'Cross-Border Relief Operations in Eritrea and Tigray', *Disasters*, 13 (4), 1990, pp. 351–60.

'Relief behind the Lines: the Cross-Border Operation in Tigray', in Joanna Macrae and Anthony Zwi (eds.), *War & Hunger: Rethinking International Responses to Complex Emergencies* (London: Zed, 1994), ch. 7.

Henze, Paul B., 'Arming the Horn 1960–1980: Military Expenditures, Arms Imports and Military Aid in Ethiopia, Kenya, Somalia and Sudan, with

Statistics on Economic Growth and Governmental Expenditures', in Sven Rubenson (ed.), *Proceedings of the Seventh International Conference of Ethiopian Studies* (Lund: Scandinavian Institute of African Studies, 1984), pp. 637–56.

Ethiopia: Crisis of a Marxist Economy: Analysis and Text of a Soviet Report (Santa Monica: RAND, 1989).

Herbst, Jeffrey, 'Migration, the Politics of Protest, and State Consolidation in Africa', *African Affairs*, 89 (355), 1990, pp. 183–203.

The Politics of Reform in Ghana, 1982–1991 (Berkeley: California University Press, 1993).

'The Politics of Sustained Agricultural Reform in Africa', in Thomas M. Callaghy and John Ravenhill (eds.), *Hemmed In: Responses to Africa's Economic Decline* (New York: Columbia University Press, 1993), ch. 9.

Hill, Tony, 'Africa and the European Community: The Third Lomé Convention', *Africa South of the Sahara 1986* (London: Europa, 1986), pp. 60–7.

Himbara, David and Sultan, Dawood 'Reconstructing the Ugandan State and Economy: the Challenge of an International Bantustan', *Review of African Political Economy*, 63, 1995, pp. 85–93.

Hodd, Michael, 'Africa, the IMF and the World Bank', *African Affairs*, 86 (344), 1987, pp. 331–42.

Hodder-Williams, Richard, 'Conflict in Zimbabwe: the Matabeleland Problem', *Conflict Studies*, 151 (London: Institute for the Study of Conflict, 1983).

Hofmeier, Rolf, 'Aid from the Federal Republic of Germany to Africa', *Journal of Modern African Studies*, 24 (4), 1986, pp. 577–601.

Howell, Jude, 'The End of an Era: the Rise and Fall of GDR Aid', *Journal of Modern African Studies*, 32 (4), 1994, pp. 305–28.

Hughes, Arnold, 'The Attempted Gambian Coup d'état of 27 July 1981', in Arnold Hughes (ed.), *The Gambia: Studies in Society and Politics* (Birmingham: Centre of West African Studies, 1991), ch. 9.

'The Collapse of the Senegambian Confederation', *Journal of Commonwealth and Comparative Politics*, 30 (2), 1992, pp. 200–22.

Hughes, Arnold and Lewis, Janet, 'Beyond *Francophonie*? The Senegambia Confederation in Retrospect', in Anthony Kirk-Greene and Daniel Bach (eds.), *State and Society in Francophone Africa since Independence* (London: Macmillan, 1995), ch. 15.

Hughes, Arnold and May, Roy, 'Armies on Loan: toward an Explanation of Transnational Intervention among African States: 1960–85', in Simon Baynham (ed.), *Military Power and Politics in Black Africa* (Beckenham: Croom Helm, 1986), ch. 7.

Human Rights Watch/Africa, *Divide and Rule: State Sponsored Ethnic Violence in Kenya* (New York: Human Rights Watch, November 1993).

Hunter, Shireen, *OPEC and the Third World: the Politics of Aid* (London: Croom Helm, 1984).

Hyden, Goran, *Beyond Ujamaa in Tanzania: Underdevelopment and an Uncaptured Peasantry* (London: Heinemann, 1980).

Ihonvbere, Julius O., 'Nigeria as Africa's Great Power: Constraints and Prospects for the 1990s', *International Journal*, 46 (3), 1991, pp. 510–35.

Nigeria: The Politics of Adjustment and Democracy (New Brunswick: Transaction, 1994).

Ihonvbere, Julius O. and Vaughan, Olufemi, 'Nigeria: Democracy and Civil Society: the Nigerian Transition Programme, 1985–1993', in John Wiseman (ed.), *Democracy and Political Change in Sub-Saharan Africa* (London: Routledge, 1995), ch. 4.

Iliffe, John, *Africans: the History of a Continent* (Cambridge: Cambridge University Press, 1995).

Iyob, Ruth, 'Regional Hegemony: Domination and Resistance in the Horn of Africa', *Journal of Modern African Studies*, 31 (2), 1993, pp. 257–76.

Jackson, Robert H., *Quasi-states: Sovereignty, International Relations and the Third World* (Cambridge: Cambridge University Press, 1990).

Jackson, Robert H. and Rosberg, Carl G., *Personal Rule in Black Africa: Prince, Autocrat, Prophet, Tyrant* (Berkeley: California University Press, 1982).

'Sovereignty and Underdevelopment: Juridical Statehood in the African Crisis', *Journal of Modern African Studies*, 24 (1), 1986, pp. 1–31.

Jamal, Abbashar, 'Funding Fundamentalism: Sudan', *Review of African Political Economy*, (52), 1991, pp. 103–9.

Jeffries, Richard and Thomas, Clare, 'The Ghanaian Elections of 1992', *African Affairs*, 92 (368), 1993, pp. 331–66.

Johnson, John, 'Aid and Good Governance in Africa', *Round Table*, 320, 1991, pp. 395–400.

Johnson, Omotunde E. G., 'Economic Integration in Africa: Enhancing Prospects for Success', *Journal of Modern African Studies*, 29 (1), 1991, pp. 1–26.

Johnson, R. W., 'Guinea', in John Dunn (ed.), *West African States: Failure and Promise* (Cambridge: Cambridge University Press, 1978), ch. 3.

Kasfir, Nelson, *The Shrinking Political Arena: Participation and Ethnicity in African Politics, with a Case Study of Uganda* (Berkeley: California University Press, 1976).

Kelley, Michael P., 'Weak States and Captured Patrons: French Desire to Disengage from Chad', *Round Table*, 296, 1985, pp. 328–38.

A State in Disarray: Conditions of Chad's Survival (Boulder: Westview, 1986).

Kieh, George K., 'Merchants of Repression: An Assessment of United States Military Assistance to Liberia', *Liberia-Forum*, 5 (9), 1989, pp. 50–61.

Kimble, Frank B., 'The United States–Liberia Operational Experts Project', *Liberian Studies Journal*, 15 (1), 1990, pp. 1–12.

Kinder, Hermann and Hilgemann, Werner, *The Penguin Atlas of World History*, Vol. 2 (London: Penguin, 1978).

Kirk-Greene, A. H. M., 'The Thin White Line: the Size of the British Colonial Service in Africa', *African Affairs*, 79 (314), 1980, pp. 25–44.

Kirk-Greene, A. H. M. and Bach, Daniel (eds.), *State and Society in Francophone Africa since Independence* (London: Macmillan, 1995).

Klein, Axel, 'Trapped in the Traffick: Growing Problems of Drug Consumption in Lagos', *Journal of Modern African Studies*, 32 (4), 1994, pp. 657–77.

Korn, David A., *Ethiopia, the United States and the Soviet Union, 1974–1985* (London: Croom Helm, 1986).

Kriger, Norma J., *Zimbabwe's Guerrilla War: Peasant Voices* (Cambridge: Cambridge University Press, 1992).

Kufuor, K. O., 'Safeguarding Human Rights: a Critique of the African Commission on Human and Peoples' Rights', *Africa Development*, 18 (2), 1993.

Laidi, Zaki, *The Superpowers and Africa: the Constraints of a Rivalry, 1960–1990* (Chicago: Chicago University Press, 1990).

Lal, Deepak, *The Poverty of 'Development Economics'* (London: IEA, 1983).

Lancaster, Carol, 'The Lagos Three: Economic Regionalism in sub-Saharan Africa', in John W. Harbeson and Donald Rothchild (eds.), *Africa in World Politics* (Boulder: Westview, 1991), pp. 249–67.

Landell-Mills, Pierre, 'Governance, Cultural Change, and Empowerment', *Journal of Modern African Studies*, 30 (4), 1992, pp. 543–67.

Langhammer, Rolf J., 'The Developing Countries and Regionalism', *Journal of Common Market Studies*, 30 (2), 1992, pp. 211–31.

Langhammer, Rolf J. and Hiemenz, U., *Regional Integration among Developing Countries: Opportunities, Obstacles and Options* (Tübingen: Mohr, 1990).

Lanne, Bernard, 'Histoire d'une frontière ou la "bande d'Aouzou"', *Afrique et Asie modernes*, 154, 1987, pp. 3–15.

LaPalombara, Joseph and Weiner, Myron (eds.), *Political Parties and Political Development* (Princeton: Princeton University Press, 1968).

Larkin, Bruce D., *China and Africa 1949–1970: the Foreign Policy of the People's Republic of China* (Berkeley: California University Press, 1971).

Lawson, Colin W., 'Soviet Economic Aid to Africa', *African Affairs*, 87 (349), 1988, pp. 501–18.

Lefebvre, Jeffrey A., 'Donor Dependency and American Arms Transfers to the Horn of Africa: the F-5 Legacy', *Journal of Modern African Studies*, 25 (3), 1987, pp. 465–88.

Legvold, Robert, *Soviet Policy in West Africa* (New Haven: Harvard University Press, 1970).

Lemarchand, René, *The Green and the Black: Quadhafi's Policies in Africa* (Bloomington: Indiana University Press, 1988).

'The State, the Parallel Economy, and the Changing Structure of Patronage Systems', in Donald Rothchild and Naomi Chazan (eds.), *The Precarious Balance: State and Society in Africa* (Boulder: Westview, 1988), ch. 6.

'Libyan Adventurism', in John W. Harbeson and Donald Rothchild (eds.), *Africa in World Politics* (Boulder: Westview, 1991), ch. 7.

Lesch, Ann Mosely, 'External Involvement in the Sudanese Civil War', and 'Negotiations in Sudan', in David R. Smock (ed.), *Making War and Waging Peace* (Washington: US Institute of Peace, 1993), chs. 4 and 5.

Leslie, Winsome J., *Zaïre: Continuity and Political Change in an Oppressive State* (Boulder: Westview, 1993).

Lewis, I. M., 'Kim Il Sung in Somalia: the End of Tribalism?', in P. Cohen and

W. Shack (eds.), *The Politics of Office* (Oxford: Oxford University Press, 1979).

A Modern History of Somalia: Nation and State in the Horn of Africa (Harlow: Longman, 1980).

Lewis, Peter M., 'Endgame in Nigeria? The Politics of a Failed Democratic Transition', *African Affairs*, 93 (372), 1994, pp. 323–40.

Leys, Colin and Saul, John S. (eds.), *Namibia's Liberation Struggle: the Two-Edged Sword* (London: Currey, 1995).

Light, Margot, *The Soviet Theory of International Relations* (Brighton: Wheatsheaf, 1988).

'Moscow's Retreat from Africa', in Arnold Hughes (ed.), *Marxism's Retreat from Africa* (London: Cass, 1992), pp. 21–40.

Lofchie, Michael F. (ed.), *The State of the Nations* (Berkeley: California University Press, 1971).

MacGaffey, Janet, 'How to Survive and Become Rich amidst Devastation: the Second Economy in Zaïre', *African Affairs*, 82 (328), 1983, pp. 351–66.

The Real Economy of Zaïre: the Contribution of Smuggling and Other Unofficial Activities to National Wealth (London: Currey, 1991).

Mackenzie, John M., *The Empire of Nature: Hunting, Conservation and British Imperialism* (Manchester: Manchester University Press, 1988).

MacQueen, Norman, 'Portugal and Africa: The Politics of Re-engagement', *Journal of Modern African Studies*, 23 (1), 1985, pp. 31–51.

Macrae, Joanna and Zwi, Anthony (eds.), *War & Hunger: Rethinking International Responses to Complex Emergencies* (London: Zed, 1994).

Mair, Lucy, *Primitive Government* (Harmondsworth: Penguin, 1962).

Makinda, Samuel M., 'Iran, Sudan and Islam', *The World Today*, 49 (6), 1993, pp. 108–11.

Marchal, Roland, 'Le Sud-Soudan à l'aube d'un nouveau drame humanitaire', Ministère des Affaires etrangères (Paris), *Bulletin du Centre d'Analyse et de prévision*, no. 61, 1994/95, pp. 111–25.

Marenin, Otwin, 'United States Aid to African Police Forces', *African Affairs*, 85 (341), pp. 509–44.

Martin, Matthew, 'Neither Phoenix nor Icarus: Negotiating Economic Reform in Ghana and Zambia', in Thomas M. Callaghy and John Ravenhill (eds.), *Hemmed In: Responses to Africa's Economic Decline* (New York: Columbia University Press, 1993), ch. 4.

Matthews, Robert O., 'From Rhodesia to Zimbabwe: prerequisites of a Settlement', *International Journal*, 45 (2), 1990, pp. 292–333.

Maull, Hanns W. 'South Africa's Minerals: the Achilles Heel of Western Economic Security?', *International Affairs*, 68 (4), 1986, pp. 619–26.

May, Roy, 'Political Authority in Chad: the Relevance of the "Warlord" model', Birmingham University, PSA conference, 1985.

May, Roy and Charlton, Roger, 'Chad: France's Fortuitous Success', *Review of the Association for the Study of Modern and Contemporary France*, 37, 1987, pp. 1–14.

May, Roy, Charlton, Roger and Cleobury, Tony, 'France and Africa: Policy or Bad Habits?', Boston University, Conference on Francophone Africa, 1994.

Mayall, James, 'Britain and Anglophone Africa', in Amadu Sesay (ed.), *Africa and Europe: From Partition to Interdependence or Dependence?* (London: Croom Helm, 1986), ch. 4.

Nationalism and International Society (Cambridge: Cambridge University Press, 1990).

Mazrui, Ali A., *Towards a Pax Africana: a Study of Ideology and Ambition* (London: Weidenfeld and Nicolson, 1967).

'Africa and Other Civilizations: Conquest and Counterconquest', in John W. Harbeson and Donald Rothchild (eds.), *Africa in World Politics* (Boulder: Westview, 1991), ch. 4.

Mazzeo, Domenico (ed.), *African Regional Organizations* (Cambridge: Cambridge University Press, 1984).

Mbembe, Achille, 'Provisional Notes on the Postcolony', *Africa*, 62 (1), 1992, pp. 3–37.

McKinlay, Robert D., 'The Aid Relationship: A Foreign Policy Model and Interpretation of the Distribution of Official Bilateral Economic Aid of the US, UK, France and Germany, 1960–70', *Comparative Political Studies*, 11 (4), 1979, pp. 411–63.

Mehler, Andreas, *Kamerun in der Aera Biya: Bedingungen, erste Schritte und Blackaden einer demokratischen Transition* (Hamburg: Institut für Afrika-Kunde, 1993).

Middleton, John and Tait, David (eds.), *Tribes without Rulers: Studies in African Segmentary Systems* (London: Routledge, 1958).

Minter, William, *Apartheid's Contras: an Enquiry into the Roots of War in Angola and Mozambique* (London: Zed, 1994).

Mosley, Paul, *Overseas Aid: its Defence and Reform* (Brighton: Wheatsheaf, 1987).

Mosley, Paul, Harrigan, J. and Toye, John, *Aid and Power: the World Bank and Policy-based Lending* (2 vols. London: Routledge, 1991).

Mukonoweshuro, Eliphas G., 'The Politics of Squalor and Dependency: Chronic Political Instability and Economic Collapse in the Comoro Islands', *African Affairs*, 89 (357), 1990, pp. 555–77.

Mutibwa, Phares, *Uganda since Independence: a Story of Unfulfilled Hopes* (London: Hurst, 1992).

Naldi, G. J., *The Organization of African Unity: an Analysis of its Role* (London: Mansell, 1989).

Documents of the Organization of African Unity (London: Mansell, 1992).

Nation, R. Craig and Kauppi, Mark V. (eds.), *The Soviet Impact in Africa* (Lexington: Lexington Books, 1984).

Nkiwane, Solomon M., 'Development of Zimbabwe's Foreign Relations 1980–90', *Round Table*, 326, 1993, pp. 199–216.

Nkrumah, Kwame, *Neo-Colonialism: The Last Stage of Imperialism* (London: Nelson, 1965).

Novati, G. Calchi, 'Italy in the Triangle of the Horn: Too Many Corners for a Half Power', *Journal of Modern African Studies*, 32 (3), 1994, pp. 369–85.

Nwajiaku, Kathryn, 'The National Conferences in Benin and Togo Revisited', *Journal of Modern African Studies*, 32 (3), 1994, pp. 429–47.

Nwokedi, Emeka, 'Nigeria's Democratic Transition: Explaining the Annulled 1993 Presidential Election', *Round Table*, no. 330, 1994, pp. 189–204.

Nyerere, Julius K., 'The Honour of Africa', *Freedom and Socialism* (Dar es Salaam: Oxford University Press, 1968), pp. 115–33.

O'Brien, D. B. Cruise, *The Mourides of Senegal: The Political and Economic Organization of an Islamic Brotherhood* (Oxford: Oxford University Press, 1971).

Observatoire Geopolitique des Drogues, *Etat des Drogues; Drogue des Etats* (Paris: Hachette, 1994).

O'Donnell, Guillermo, Schmitter, Philippe C. and Whitehead, Laurence (eds.), *Transitions from Authoritarian Rule: Comparative Perspectives* (Baltimore: Johns Hopkins University Press, 1986).

Ogunbadejo, Oye, *The International Politics of Africa's Strategic Minerals* (London: Pinter, 1985).

'Qaddafi and Africa's International Relations', *Journal of Modern African Studies*, 24 (1), 1986, pp. 33–68.

O'Keefe, Phil, 'Toxic Terrorism', *Review of African Political Economy*, 42, 1988, pp. 84–90.

Okere, Linus C., 'The Press and Foreign Policy in Nigeria', *Round Table*, 321, 1992, pp. 61–71.

Onimode, Bade (ed.), *The IMF, the World Bank and the African Debt* (2 vols. London: Zed, 1989).

Onwuka, Ralph I., 'CMEA–African Economic Relations', in Ralph I. Onwuka and Timothy M. Shaw (eds.), *Africa in World Politics* (London: Macmillan, 1989), ch. 4.

Onwuka, Ralph I. and Sesay, Amadu (eds.), *The Future of Regionalism in Africa* (London: Macmillan, 1985).

Oquaye, Mike, 'The Ghanaian Elections of 1992 – a Dissenting View', *African Affairs*, 94 (375), 1995, pp. 259–75.

Organisation for Economic Cooperation and Development, *Development Assistance Committee 1993 Report* (Paris: OECD, 1994).

Organisation of African Unity, *African Charter on Human and Peoples' Rights* (Banjul: African Commission on Human and Peoples' Rights, n.d.).

Declaration of the Assembly of Heads of State and Government of the Organisation of African Unity on the Political and Socio-Economic Situation in Africa and the Fundamental Changes taking place in the World (AHG/Decl.1 (XXVI), Addis Ababa, July 1990).

Declaration of the Assembly of Heads of State and Government on the Establishment within the OAU of a Mechanism for Conflict Prevention, Management and Resolution (AHG/Decl.3 (XXIX), Cairo, June 1993).

O'Toole, Thomas, *The Central African Republic: The Continent's Hidden Heart* (Boulder: Westview, 1986).

Ottaway, Marina, 'The Soviet Union and Africa', in John W. Harbeson and Donald Rothchild (eds.), *Africa in World Politics* (Boulder: Westview, 1991), ch. 11.

Overseas Development Administration, 'Taking Account of Good Government' (ODA, Government and Institutions Department, Technical Note no. 10, London, October 1993).

Oyewumi, Aderemi, 'The Lomé Convention: From Partnership to Paternalism', *Round Table*, 318, 1991, pp. 129–37.

Papp, Daniel S., 'The Angolan Civil War and Namibia: The Role of External Intervention', in David R. Smock (ed.), *Making War and Waging Peace: Foreign Intervention in Africa* (Washington: US Institute of Peace, 1993), ch. 7.

Parfitt, Trevor, 'Lies, Damned Lies and Statistics: World Bank and ECA Structural Adjustment Controversy', *Review of African Political Economy*, 47, 1990, pp. 128–43.

Parfitt, Trevor and Bullock, Sandy, 'The Prospects for a New Lomé Convention', *Review of African Political Economy*, 47, 1990, pp. 104–16.

Patman, Robert G., *The Soviet Union in the Horn of Africa: the Diplomacy of Intervention and Disengagement* (Cambridge: Cambridge University Press, 1990).

Payne, Richard J. and Ganaway, Eddie, 'The Influence of Black Americans on US Policy towards Southern Africa', *African Affairs*, 79 (317), 1980, pp. 585–98.

Payton, Gary D., 'The Somali Coup of 1969: The Case for Soviet Complicity', *Journal of Modern African Studies*, 18 (3), 1980, pp. 493–508.

Pazzanita, Anthony G., 'The Proposed Referendum in the Western Sahara: Background, Developments, and Prospects', in Yahia H. Zoubir and Daniel Volman (eds.), *International Dimensions of the Western Sahara Conflict* (London: Praeger, 1993), pp. 187–225.

Péan, Pierre, *Bokassa 1er* (Paris: Alain Moreau, 1977).

Affaires Africaines (Paris: Fayard, 1983).

Pereira, Anthony W., 'The Neglected Tragedy: The Return to War in Angola, 1992–3', *Journal of Modern African Studies*, 32 (1), 1994, pp. 1–28.

Peters, Joel, *Israel and Africa: the Problematic Friendship* (London: British Academic Press, 1992).

Pittman, Dean, 'The OAU and Chad', in Yassin El-Ayouty and William Zartman (eds.), *The OAU after Twenty Years* (New York: Praeger, 1984), pp. 297–325.

Plank, David N., 'Aid, Debt and the End of Sovereignty: Mozambique and its Donors', *Journal of Modern African Studies*, 31 (3), 1993, pp. 407–30.

Pool, David, 'Eritrean Independence', *African Affairs*, 32 (368), 1993, pp. 389–402.

Porter, Bruce D., *The USSR in Third World Conflicts: Soviet Arms and Diplomacy in Local Wars, 1945–1980* (Cambridge: Cambridge University Press, 1984).

Ramsis, Christine A., 'France and the Parti Democratique de Guinée', Ph.D. thesis, University of London, 1993.

Ravenhill, John, *Collective Clientelism: The Lomé Conventions and North–South Relations* (New York: Columbia University Press, 1985).

'The Future of Regionalism in Africa', in Ralph I. Onwuka and Amadu Sesay (eds.), *The Future of Regionalism in Africa* (London: Macmillan, 1985), ch. 12.

'Africa and Europe: the Dilution of a "Special relationship"', in John W. Harbeson and Donald Rothchild (eds.), *Africa in World Politics* (Boulder: Westview, 1991), ch. 9.

'A Second Decade of Adjustment: Greater Complexity, Greater Uncertainty', in Thomas M. Callaghy and John Ravenhill (eds.), *Hemmed In: Responses to Africa's Economic Decline* (New York: Columbia University Press, 1993), ch. 1.

Redden, Thomas J., 'The US Comprehensive Anti-Apartheid Act of 1986: Anti-Apartheid or Anti-African National Congress?', *African Affairs*, 87 (349), 1988, pp. 595–605.

Reed, W. Cyrus, 'International Politics and National Liberation: ZANU and the Politics of Contested Sovereignty in Zimbabwe', *African Studies Review*, 36 (2), 1993, pp. 31–59.

Remnek, Richard B., 'Soviet Military Interests in Africa', *Orbis*, 28 (1), 1984, pp. 123–43.

Reno, William, 'Economic Reform and the Strange Case of "Liberalization" in Sierra Leone', *Governance*, 6 (1), 1993, pp. 23–42.

'Foreign Firms and the Financing of Charles Taylor's NPFL', *Liberian Studies Journal*, 18 (2), 1993, pp. 175–88.

'Old Brigades, Money Bags, New Breeds, and the Ironies of Reform in Nigeria', *Canadian Journal of African Studies*, 27 (1), 1993, pp. 66–87.

Corruption and State Politics in Sierra Leone (Cambridge: Cambridge University Press, 1995).

Richards, Paul, 'Rebellion in Liberia and Sierra Leone: A Crisis of Youth?', in Oliver Furley (ed.), *Conflict in Africa* (London: I. B.Tauris, 1995), ch. 7.

Rimmer, Douglas, *The Economies of West Africa* (London: Weidenfeld and Nicolson, 1984).

'External Debt and Structural Adjustment in Tropical Africa', *African Affairs*, 89 (355), 1990, pp. 283–91.

Staying Poor: Ghana's Political Economy, 1950–1990 (Oxford: Pergamon, 1992).

'Adjustment Blues', *African Affairs*, 94 (374), 1995, pp. 109–13.

'Structural Adjustment in Africa', *International Update* (Johannesburg: SAIIA) April 1995.

Rimmer, Douglas (ed.), *Action in Africa: the Experience of People Involved in Government, Business and Aid* (London: Currey, 1993).

Robertson, Patsy, 'Monitoring African Elections', in Douglas Rimmer (ed.), *Action in Africa: the Experience of People Involved in Government, Business and Aid* (London: Currey, 1993), ch. 13.

Robson, Peter, 'The Mano River Union', *Journal of Modern African Studies*, 20 (4), 1982, pp. 613–28.

Rooney, David, *Kwame Nkrumah: the Political Kingdom in the Third World* (London: I. B. Tauris, 1988).

Rothchild, Donald and Chazan, Naomi (eds.), *The Precarious Balance: State and Society in Africa* (Boulder: Westview, 1988).

Rouvez, Alain, 'French, British and Belgian Military Involvement', in David R. Smock (ed.), *Making War and Waging Peace: Foreign Intervention in Africa* (Washington: United States Institute of Peace, 1993), ch. 2.

St. Jorre, John de, *The Nigerian Civil War* (London: Hodder and Stoughton, 1972).

Salih, M. A. Mohamed and Harir, Sharif, 'Tribal Militias: The Genesis of National Disintegration', in Sharif Harir and Terje Tvedt (eds.), *Short-Cut to Decay: the Case of the Sudan* (Uppsala: Nordiska Afrikainstitutet, 1994), pp. 186–203.

Schatzberg, Michael G., *The Dialectics of Oppression in Zaïre* (Bloomington: Indiana University Press, 1988).

Schneidman, Witney W., 'Conflict Resolution in Mozambique', in David R. Smock (ed.), *Making War and Waging Peace: Foreign Intervention in Africa* (Washington: US Institute of Peace, 1993), ch. 9.

Seery, Brendan, 'Africa's Reluctant New Policeman Twirls His Truncheon: The Lesotho Experience and South Africa's Role in Peacekeeping', in Mark Shaw and Jakkie Cilliers (eds.), *South Africa and Peacekeeping in Africa* (Johannesburg: Institute for Defence Policy, 1995), pp. 87–97.

Segal, Gerald, 'China and Africa', *Annals of the American Academy of Political and Social Science*, 519, 1992.

Serpa, Eduardo, 'The Mozambican Elections', *Africa Institute Bulletin* (Pretoria), 34 (5), 1994.

Sesay, Amadu, 'International Politics in Africa: a Comparative Study of the Foreign Policies of Liberia and Sierra Leone, 1957–73', Ph.D. thesis, University of London, 1978.

'The Limits of Peace-keeping by a Regional Organisation: The OAU Peace-keeping Force in Chad', *Conflict Quarterly*, 11 (1), 1991, pp. 7–26.

Sesay, Amadu (ed.), *Africa and Europe: From Partition To Interdependence Or Dependence?* (London: Croom Helm, 1986).

Shaw, Mark and Cilliers, Jakkie (eds.), *South Africa and Peacekeeping in Africa* (Johannesburg: Institute for Defence Policy, 1995).

Sithole, Masipula, 'Black Americans and United States Policy towards Africa', *African Affairs*, 85 (340), 1986, pp. 325–50.

Skak, Mette, 'CMEA Relations with Africa: A Case of Disparity in Foreign Policy Instruments', *Cooperation and Conflict*, 21 (1), 1986, pp. 3–23.

Skalnik, Peter, 'Why Ghana is not a Nation-State', *Africa Insight*, 22 (1), 1992, pp. 66–72.

Smith, Stephen and Glaser, Antoine, *Ces Messieurs Afrique: Le Paris-Village du continent noir* (Paris: Calmann-Levy, 1992).

Smock, David R. (ed.), *Making War and Waging Peace: Foreign Intervention in Africa* (Washington: United States Institute of Peace, 1993).

Snow, Philip, *The Star Raft: China's Encounter with Africa* (London: Weidenfeld and Nicolson, 1988).

Somerville, Keith, *Foreign Military Intervention in Africa* (London: Pinter, 1990).

Spass, Pamela (ed.), *Mortgaging Women's Lives: Feminist Critiques of Structural Adjustment* (London: Zed, 1994).

Stevens, Christopher, 'The Renegotiation of the Convention', in Robert Boardman, Timothy M. Shaw and Panayotis Soldatos (eds.), *Europe, Africa and Lomé III* (London: University Press of America, 1985), ch. 4.

Stockholm International Peace Research Institute, *SIPRI Yearbook* (Oxford: Oxford University Press, annual).

Stremlau, John J., *The International Politics of the Nigerian Civil War, 1967–1970* (Princeton: Princeton University Press, 1977).

Susungi, N. N., 'The Origins of the Debt Crisis and its Aftermath in Africa', in Douglas Rimmer (ed.), *Action in Africa: the Experience of People Involved in Government, Business and Aid* (London: Currey, 1993), ch. 8.

Takirambudde, Peter, 'Six Years of the African Charter on Human and Peoples' Rights: an Assessment', *Lesotho Law Journal*, 7 (2), 1991.

Thompson, W. Scott, *Ghana's Foreign Policy 1957–1966* (Princeton: Princeton University Press, 1969).

Thomson, Alexander R., 'Incomplete Engagement: an Examination of US Foreign Policy towards the Republic of South Africa, 1981–1988', Ph.D. thesis, Lancaster University, 1994.

Toulabor, Comi, '"Paristroika" and the One-Party System', in Anthony Kirk-Greene and Daniel Bach (eds.), *State and Society in Francophone Africa since Independence* (London: Macmillan, 1995), ch. 8.

Touval, Saadia, *The Boundary Politics of Independent Africa* (New Haven: Harvard University Press, 1972).

Toye, John, 'Interest Group Politics and the Implementation of Adjustment Policies in Sub-Saharan Africa', *Journal of International Development*, 4 (2), 1992, pp. 183–97.

'Structural Adjustment: Context, Assumptions, Origin and Diversity', in Rolph van der Hoeven and Fred van der Kraaij (eds.), *Structural Adjustment and Beyond in Sub-Saharan Africa* (London: Currey, 1994), ch. 3.

Tvedt, Terje, 'The Collapse of the State in Southern Sudan after the Addis Ababa Agreement: A Study of Internal Causes and the Role of the NGOs', in Sharif Harir and Terje Tvedt (eds.), *Short-Cut to Decay: The Case of the Sudan* (Uppsala: Nordiska Afrikainstitutet, 1994), pp. 61–105.

Twitchett, Carol Cosgrove, *Europe and Africa: From Association to Partnership* (Farnborough: Saxon House, 1978).

A Framework for Development: the EEC and the ACP (London: Allen and Unwin, 1981).

United Nations, *Report of the Commission of Enquiry established pursuant to Security Council Resolution 885 (1993) to investigate armed attacks on UNOSOM II personnel which led to casualties among them* (New York: United Nations, 24 February 1994).

United Nations Economic Commission for Africa, *African Alternative Framework to Structural Adjustment Programmes for Socio-Economic Recovery and Transformation* (Addis Ababa: ECA, 1989).

United States Department of State, *Country Reports on Human Rights Practices* (Washington: US Government Printing Office, February 1978), and later years.

United States Department of State, Bureau for International Narcotics and Law Enforcement Affairs, *International Narcotics Control Strategy Report* (Washington, 1995).

van der Hoeven, Rolph and van der Kraaij, Fred (eds.), *Structural Adjustment and Beyond in Sub-Saharan Africa* (London: Currey, 1994).

van der Walle, Nicolas, 'The Decline of the Franc Zone: Monetary Politics in Francophone Africa', *African Affairs*, 90 (360), 1991, pp. 383–405.

'The Politics of Nonreform in Cameroon', in Thomas M. Callaghy and John Ravenhill (eds.), *Hemmed In: Responses to Africa's Economic Decline* (New York: Columbia University Press, 1993) ch. 10.

van Donge, Jan Kees, 'Kamuzu's Legacy: The Democratization of Malawi', *African Affairs*, 94 (375), 1995, pp. 227–57.

'Zambia: Kaunda and Chiluba: Enduring Patterns of Political Culture', in John Wiseman (ed.), *Democracy and Political Change in Sub-Saharan Africa* (London: Routledge, 1995), ch. 9.

Venter, Denis, 'Malawi: The Transition to Multi-party Politics', in John Wiseman (ed.), *Democracy and Political Change in Sub-Saharan Africa* (London: Routledge, 1995), ch. 8.

Verschave, F.-X. and Vidal, C., *France–Rwanda: l'engrenage d'un genocide* (Paris: Observatoire permanent de la Coopération française, September 1994).

Vincent, R. J., *Human Rights and International Relations* (Cambridge: Cambridge University Press, 1986).

Vines, Alex, *Renamo: Terrorism in Mozambique* (York: CSAS, 1991).

Vogt, Margaret A. (ed.), *The Liberian Crisis and ECOMOG: A Bold Attempt at Regional Peace-Keeping* (Lagos: Gabumo, 1992).

Wai, Dunstan M., 'African–Arab Relations: Interdependence or Misplaced Optimism?', *Journal of Modern African Studies*, 21 (2), 1983, pp. 187–213.

Wallerstein, Immanuel, 'The Decline of the Party in Single-Party African States', in Joseph LaPalombara and Myron Weiner (eds.), *Political Parties and Political Development* (Princeton: Princeton University Press, 1968).

'The Range of Choice: Constraints on the Policies of Governments of Contemporary African Independent States', in Michael F. Lofchie (ed.), *The State of the Nations* (Berkeley: California University Press, 1971), ch. 2.

Wapenhans, Willi, 'The Political Economy of Structural Adjustment: An External View', in Rolph van der Hoeven and Fred van der Kraaij (eds.), *Structural Adjustment and Beyond in Sub-Saharan Africa* (London: Currey, 1994), ch. 4.

Watkins, Kevin, 'Africa and the European Community: The Lomé Conventions', *Africa South of the Sahara 1991* (London: Europa, 1991), pp. 39–51.

Wauthier, Claude, 'France in Africa: President Giscard d'Estaing's Ambitious Diplomacy', *Africa Contemporary Record*, 12, 1979–80 (New York: Africana, 1981), pp. A120–7.

Wayas, Joseph, *Nigeria's Leadership Role in Africa* (London: Macmillan, 1979).

Webber, Mark, 'Soviet Policy in Sub-Saharan Africa: The Final Phase', *Journal of Modern African Studies*, 30 (1), 1992, pp. 1–30.

Welch, Claude E., 'The Organisation of African Unity and the Promotion of Human Rights', *Journal of Modern African Studies*, 29 (4), 1991, pp. 535–55.

Werbner, Richard, *Tears of the Dead: The Social Biography of an African Family* (Edinburgh: Edinburgh University Press, 1991).

Whiteman, Kaye, *Chad* (London: Minority Rights Group, Report no. 80, 1988).

Widner, Jennifer A. (ed.), *Economic Change and Political Liberalization in Sub-Saharan Africa* (Baltimore: Johns Hopkins University Press, 1994).

Williams, Abiodun, 'Negotiations and the End of the Angolan Civil War', in David R. Smock (ed.), *Making War and Waging Peace: Foreign Intervention in Africa* (Washington: US Institute of Peace, 1993), ch. 8.

Wilson, Harold, *The Labour Government 1964–1970* (London: Weidenfeld and Nicolson, 1971).

Winrow, Gareth M., 'East Germany in sub-Saharan Africa: A Reassessment', *The World Today*, 44 (12), 1988, pp. 205–8.

The Foreign Policy of the GDR in Africa (Cambridge: Cambridge University Press, 1990).

Wiseman, John A. 'Leadership and Personal Danger in African Politics', *Journal of Modern African Politics*, 31 (4), 1993, pp. 657–60.

Wiseman, John A. (ed.), *Democracy and Political Change in Sub-Saharan Africa* (London: Routledge, 1995).

Wiseman, John A. and Vidler, Elizabeth, 'The July 1994 Coup d'Etat in The Gambia: The End of an Era', *Round Table*, 333, 1995, pp. 53–65.

Wolf, Jurgen, 'Zambia under the IMF Regime', *African Affairs*, 87 (349), 1988, pp. 579–94.

Woodward, Peter, 'Political Factors Contributing to the Generation of Refugees in the Horn of Africa', *International Relations*, 9 (2), 1987.

Sudan, 1898–1989: The Unstable State (London: Lester Crook, 1990).

'A New Map of Africa? Reflections on the Horn', *Africa Insight*, 23 (1), 1993, pp. 6–16.

World Bank, *Accelerated Development in Sub-Saharan Africa: An Agenda for Action* (Washington: World Bank, 1981).

Africa's Adjustment and Growth in the 1980s (Washington: World Bank, 1989).

Sub-Saharan Africa: From Crisis to Sustainable Growth (Washington: World Bank, 1989).

Governance and Development (Washington: World Bank, 1992).

Adjustment in Africa: Reforms, Results, and the Road Ahead (New York: Oxford University Press for World Bank, 1994).

World Development Report (New York: Oxford University Press, annual).

Wunsch, James S. and Oluwu, Dele (eds.), *The Failure of the Centralized State: Institutions and Self-governance in Africa* (Boulder: Westview, 1990).

Young, Crawford and Turner, Thomas, *The Rise and Decline of the Zaïrean State* (Madison: University of Wisconsin Press, 1985).

Young, John, 'Peasants and Revolution in Ethiopia: Tigray 1975–1989', Ph.D. thesis, Simon Fraser University, 1994.

Young, Tom, 'The MNR/RENAMO: External and Internal Dynamics', *African Affairs*, 89 (357), 1990, pp. 491–509.

Zack-Williams, A. B. and Riley, Stephen, 'Sierra Leone: The Coup and its Consequences', *Review of African Political Economy*, 56, 1993, pp. 91–8.

Zartman, I. William, *The Politics of Trade Negotiations between Africa and the European Economic Community* (Princeton: Princeton University Press, 1971).

Ripe for Resolution: Conflict and Intervention in Africa (Oxford: Oxford University Press, 1985).

Zoubir, Yahia H., 'The Western Sahara Conflict: Regional and International Dimensions', *Journal of Modern African Studies*, 28 (2), 1990, pp. 225–43.

Zoubir, Yahia H. and Volman, Daniel (eds.), *International Dimensions of the Western Sahara Conflict* (London: Praeger, 1993)

Index

Abacha, Sani, 203, 207
accountability, 187–207, 261, 266, 271–2
Accra, 1958 conference, 106
ACP group, 100–3, 126, 191
Addis Ababa
  1963 conference, 110
  1972 Agreement, 66, 151, 153, 237
Afghanistan, 83, 136, 150
African Charter of Human & Peoples' Rights, 116, 190–1
African Rights, 192
Ahidjo, Amadou, 53, 58, 94
aid, economic, 22, 43, 72, 104, 181–6, 197–8, 207
  see also military aid, individual donors
Aidid, Mohamed Farah, 223, 238, 255
Albania, 243
Algeria, 37, 39, 48, 71, 111, 130, 268
Amin, Idi, 101, 115, 123, 130, 153, 188–90, 213
Amnesty International, 192, 196
ANC, 143, 201, 216, 220, 224, 231
'Anglo-Saxons', 93
Angola
  attempted coup, 148
  economy, 140, 164, 171, 233–4
  external intervention, 112, 132, 145, 210, 231
  external relations, 89, 92, 109, 141–2, 146
  independence war, 20, 39, 85, 114–15, 136, 210, 243
  insurgency, 132, 140–1, 151, 155–6, 209, 212, 216, 224, 234, 255
  oil, 71, 141, 234
  peace settlements, 159, 205, 225–6, 237, 239
  regional relations, 117, 122, 132, 153, 184, 217, 221–2
Antarctica, 9
Aouzou Strip, 81
Arabs, Arab states, 66–7, 117, 125–33
Arab-Israeli war
  1967, 113, 128
  1973, 113, 128
Argentina, 69
arms, armaments, *see* militarisation, military aid
'asset transfer', 230
Australia, 69, 82
Austria, 17

Babangida, Ibrahim, 124, 203
BADEA, 128
Balladur, Edouard, 97
Baltic states, 16, 34
Banda, Hastings Kamuzu, 52, 65, 107, 202
Bandung, 1955 conference, 42
BBC World Service, 273
Belgium, 16, 249
  colonialism, 33, 270
  decolonisation, 38–9, 79
  military intervention, 39, 83
  post-colonial relations, 80–1, 84–5
Benin, 55, 82, 91, 130, 202
Berg Report, 71, 169
Bernhard, Prince, 262
Beshir, Omar al-, 66, 123, 206, 221, 239
Biafra , 14, 47, 49, 81, 90, 93, 112, 143, 210, 227, 235
Biarritz, 1994 conference, 93, 204
Biya, Paul, 93, 178
Bokassa, Jean-Bedel, 60–1, 90–2, 96, 115, 153, 188–90
Bolloré, Vincent, 91
Bongo, Ali-Ben, 97

Bongo, Omar, 97
Botswana, 34, 36, 55–6, 71, 164
boundaries, *see* frontiers
Bouyges, Martin, 91
Brazil, 69
Brazzaville group, 110
Bridgestone, 255
Britain, British, *see* United Kingdom
British Petroleum, 54
British Somaliland, *see* Somaliland
Burkina Faso, 125
Burma, 182
Burundi, 48, 51–2, 85

Cairo
  1964 conference, 112
  1993 conference, 117
Cambodia, 21, 46, 150, 182, 243
Cameroon, 52–3, 58, 91, 93–4, 96, 155, 178, 200, 203
Canada, 87, 198
Canterbury, Archbishop of, 263
Cape route, 138
Cape Verde, 117, 151, 202
Caritas, 227
Carter, Jimmy, 136
Casablanca group, 110, 130
Castro, Fidel, 145
Catholic Church, 127, 260, 263
CCCE, 95
Central African Federation, 119
Central African Republic, 60, 90–1, 96, 115, 153, 188
Chad
  domestic politics, 129, 132
  France, relations with, 65, 83, 89, 91–2, 96
  insurgency, state collapse, 20, 86, 114–15, 124, 132, 153, 155–6, 208, 212, 237–9
  Libya, relations with, 81, 92, 96, 115, 130, 155, 238
chat, 233, 255
Chiluba, Frederick, 177
China, 144, 210, 218, 231
Chissano, Joachim, 123
Christianity, 30, 32, 48, 66, 108, 127, 129, 192, 241, 263–5
'civil society', 194, 196, 248, 258, 260–1, 264
clientelism, 32, 36, 52, 59–60, 63–5, 88, 92, 146, 148–9, 180, 194, 247, 258, 269, 271
CMEA, 140, 148–9
cocoa, 68, 94
coffee, 69–70
Cold War, 3, 16–17, 41, 65, 122, 191, 245–6, 268
  end of, effects on Africa, 23–4, 51, 98, 153, 158–9, 164, 191–5, 225, 242, 244, 256
  on world politics, 15–16, 18, 24, 98, 105, 125–6, 158, 244, 248, 259
  'Second Cold War', 7, 100, 159, 217
colonialism, 4, 24, 30–3, 67, 245
  see also individual colonising states
Commonwealth, 79, 81–2, 84, 86–8, 90, 98–9, 126, 200, 205
Comoros, 92
Comprehensive Anti-Apartheid Act, 141
conflict resolution, *see* mediation
Congo-Leopoldville/Kinshasa, *see* Zaïre
copper, 69, 165, 177
corruption, 5, 72, 168, 198, 204, 249–255
Corsicans, 91, 97
Côte d'Ivoire
  decolonisation, 36
  democratisation, 202
  domestic politics, 47–8, 58, 127–8, 178
  economy, 72, 167, 255
  foreign relations, 38, 54, 64–5, 72, 129
  France, relations with, 84, 90, 92, 96
  regional relations, 81, 125, 131–2, 217, 234
coups d'état, *see* military aid
Cresson, Edith, 105
crops, cash, 68–70, 149
Cuba, 41, 114, 122, 140–1, 145, 148–9, 155, 189, 216–18
currencies, 68–9, 72, 93–4, 165–6, 171–3, 181, 222, 232, 272
Czechoslovakia, 16–17

Dahab, Abd al-Rahman al-, 221
Dahomey, *see* Benin
Dakar, 1992 conference, 117
debt, debt crisis, 166–70, 198, 202
decolonisation, 18, 33–41, 104, 268
  see also individual colonial powers
Decraene, Philippe, 91
de Gaulle, Charles, 38, 81, 89, 97
democracy, democratisation, 96, 105, 159, 192–207, 248, 263, 270
  see also 'political conditionalities'
Denard, Bob, 253
'dependency' theories, 67, 167, 179
DGSE, 96
Dhlakama, Alphonso, 253
diamonds, 90, 125, 141, 189, 233, 251, 254
Dikko, Umaru, 80
Djibouti, 48, 96, 129, 143
Doe, Samuel, 5–6, 222, 233, 249, 252–3

East African Community, 119

economies, African, 33, 44–5, 55, 67–72, 163–186
ECOWAS, 118–20, 124–5, 237
ECOMOG, 116, 122, 124–5, 131–2, 237–9
Edinburgh, Duke of, 262
education, western, 24, 32, 36, 38, 69, 78, 82, 146, 172, 186
Egypt, 113, 128, 130, 174
elections, 50, 200–6, 242
Elf-Aquitaine, 91–2, 234, 253
Emergency Relief Desk, 228
Enarea, 30
environment, African, 7, 25, 28, 30, 101, 116, 258, 261–2
EPLF, *see* Eritrea
EPRDF, 123, 205, 211, 220, 223, 241, 243
Equatorial Guinea, 86, 115, 118, 153
Eritrea
federation with Ethiopia, 85, 211
independence, 115–16, 158, 180, 205, 240–3, 256–7
insurgencies, 30, 123, 131, 145, 151–2, 158, 211–12, 215, 220–1, 223, 225, 227–8, 231, 233, 235, 243
regional relations, 131, 231, 241–2
separatism, 49, 55, 108
Eritrean Relief Ass., 228
Ethiopia
economy, 198, 233–4
EPRDF regime, 180, 205, 239, 241–3
famine, 101, 165, 184, 215, 227, 229–30, 232
Haile-Selassie regime, 40, 50–1, 58, 64–5, 108, 111, 113, 141
history, idea of the state, 30, 34, 40, 48–9, 51, 58, 142, 270
insurgencies, 30, 115, 122, 151–2, 156, 211–12, 223–5, 228–9, 238, 243
Italy, relations with, 82, 84, 103, 184–5
Mengistu regime, 58–60, 65–6, 102, 108, 123, 130, 154–8, 191, 228
regional relations, 48, 66, 111, 130–1, 143, 211, 217–18, 220–1
revolution, 1974, 55, 136, 138, 145, 151
superpowers, relations with, 64, 136–9, 141–2, 145, 153–5, 191, 217
ethnicity, 45, 51–3, 65–6, 180, 194
European Community, 84, 98–103, 104–5, 120, 126, 149, 191, 198, 229, 256
see also Lomé Conventions
Executive Outcomes, 254
'extraversion', 32, 139, 201
Eyadema, Gnassingbe, 60, 190, 203

famine, 108, 165, 184, 215, 227–30, 258
Fashoda, spirit of, 97
Fernando Po, 189
fisheries, 103
FNLA, 20, 114, 142, 210
Foccart, Jacques, 90, 97
Fonds d'Aide et de Coopération, 95
food, food production, 164, 172
foreign exchange, forex, 165–6, 170–1
foreign policy making, 37, 58–9, 62–7, 272
Franc Zone, Franc CFA, 93–4
France
aid, 84, 87, 93–5, 198
colonialism, 33, 35–7, 47, 85–6, 99, 143, 270
decolonisation, 37–9, 54, 181, 268
military aid, intervention, 60–1, 65, 81–4, 89–92, 95–7, 108–12, 190
post-colonial relations, 64, 79, 86, 88–98, 102, 104, 113, 120, 122, 141, 155, 178, 188, 194, 199–200, 203, 241, 254–5, 259
revolution, 16
francophonie, 78–9, 82, 86, 88–98, 120, 194
Frelimo, 123, 140, 243
front line states, 120, 210
frontiers, 4, 13, 28–9, 31–2, 34–5, 46–50, 73, 107, 112, 210, 213–22, 235, 245, 270

Gabon, 71, 81, 84, 91, 95–7, 200
Gambia, The, 43, 56, 84, 87, 116, 121–2, 125, 131, 190, 206–7
Garang, John, 220
Germany, 13, 16, 47, 84, 98–9, 102
GDR, 13, 145
Ghana
colonialism, 68
coups d'état, 112, 138, 143, 247
decolonisation, 36
democratisation, 58, 206
domestic politics, 47, 55, 64, 248
economy, 171, 180, 182, 248, 265
Ewe separatism, 49, 211
Nkrumah regime, 35, 38, 47, 52, 54, 65, 88, 106, 109–10
Rawlings regime, 61, 179–80, 205–6, 248
regional relations, 125
Giscard d'Estaing, Valéry, 89–90, 92, 96–7, 155, 188, 190
globalisation, 24–7, 195, 244, 256–8, 261–2
'godfather states', 224
Gold Coast, *see* Ghana
Gorbachev, Mikhail, 158, 199
Goukhouni Waddeye, 115, 237–8
'governance', 181, 197–8, 252
'governmentalities', 7, 271
guerrillas, *see* insurgents

Guinea-Bissau, 151, 167, 183, 210
Guinea, 38, 48, 54, 109–10, 118, 121, 123, 125, 131–2, 139, 146, 153, 181, 247
Gulf Oil, 141

Habre, Hissene, 65, 92–3, 96, 238
Habyarimana, Jean-Pierre, 97
Habyarimana, Juvenal, 83, 93, 240, 253, 261
Haile-Selassie, 40, 50, 58, 64–5, 108, 113, 138, 141
Hassan II, 48, 130, 224
Hempstone, Smith, 202
Heritage Foundation, 217
Horn of Africa, 42, 60, 64–5, 103, 108–9, 118, 120, 131, 133, 139–41, 157–8, 208, 212, 217, 227, 230
Houphouet-Boigny, Felix, 58, 64–5, 90, 94–5, 128, 132, 202, 255
human rights, 105, 115–16, 185, 189–98, 226–7, 229, 257–9, 261, 264
Human Rights Watch, 192

IBRD, IDA, *see* World Bank
'idea of the state', 9–12, 19, 44–56, 107, 129, 143, 189, 216, 223, 242, 270
IGADD, 118
IMF, 94, 170, 173, 178
India, 42, 82, 86
Indochina, 27, 86, 268
Indonesia, 42
informal economy, 72, 165, 247–52, 255
insurgents, insurgencies, 6, 23, 72, 123, 156–7, 179, 204–5, 207, 208–43, 244, 249, 259, 260, 273
  liberation, 113–14, 209–10, 212, 214–16, 235, 239
  reform, 211–12, 239–40
  separatist, 210–11, 240
  warlord, 212, 239, 255
intervention, *see* military aid
Iran, 46, 130–1, 206, 231
Iraq, 21, 131, 206
Isaias Afewerki, 116, 180, 205, 223, 240
Islam, 30, 32, 48, 66, 108, 126–9, 131, 206, 216, 231, 263, 265
Islamic fundamentalism, 127, 153, 158, 241
Israel, 113, 127–31
Italy
  aid, 84, 87, 184–5
  colonialism, 49, 81, 85, 270
  post-colonial relations, 82, 103, 232, 257
Ivory Coast, *see* Côte d'Ivoire

Japan, 69, 195, 255
Jawara, Dauda, 84, 116, 190, 206
Joint Church Aid, 227
'juridical statehood', 19, 82–3, 105, 107–9, 111, 114, 117, 122, 128–9, 133, 137, 142, 159, 225, 227, 235, 240, 247
  see also sovereignty

kalabule, 248
Katanga, attempted secession, 39, 47, 49, 81, 210, 235
Kaunda, Kenneth, 65, 120, 177, 202, 217
Keita, Modibo, 247
Kennedy, John F., 136
Kenya
  aid, 87
  democratisation, 197–9
  domestic politics, 49, 53
  economy, 72, 167, 170, 177–8
  foreign policy, 54
  Moi regime, 224, 240, 253
  mutiny, 1964, 84
  regional relations, 44, 48–9, 54, 119, 131, 143, 211, 216
  wildlife conservation, 263
Kenyatta, Jomo, 52–3
Kerekou, Mathieu, 202
Korea
  North, 145, 189
  South, 69
Kuwait, 21

La Baule, 1990 conference, 194, 199
Lagos Plan of Action, 116, 176
LAMCO, 255
language, role of, 24, 32, 49, 78, 150
Le Floch-Prigent, Loik, 91
Le Monde, 91
leaders, leadership, 35–7, 57–9, 62–4, 73, 77, 79, 87
  regional, 121–2
League of Arab States, 129
League of Nations, 17
legitimacy
  governmental, 9–13, 19–20, 45, 53, 173–4, 188, 206, 222, 224
  territorial, 10, 13, 18–20
Lesotho, 48, 87
liberation movements, *see* insurgencies
Liberia
  corruption, 252
  Doe coup and regime, 52, 58, 61, 131, 153, 155–7, 174, 190–1, 217, 238
  external intervention, 132, 237–9
  foreign policy, 129
  history and idea of the state, 34, 48, 270

Liberia (*cont.*)
IGNU, 226
insurgency and state collapse, 30, 92, 115, 122, 124–5, 132, 156, 164, 205, 208, 212, 222–6, 231, 233–4, 237–9, 255, 266
peace negotiations, 237
regional relations, 118, 121–3, 131, 217
True Whig Party regime, 40, 50, 113
Libya, 65, 81, 92, 96, 108, 115, 124, 129–30, 153, 189, 212–13, 216, 231, 238, 241
Lomé Conventions, 84–5, 98–103, 120, 149, 191, 257
LonRho, 87, 253
Lusaka, 1979 conference, 88

Maastricht Treaty, 198
Machel, Samora, 87, 123, 149, 241
Macias Nguema, Fernando, 115, 153, 189–90
Macnamara, Robert, 169
magendo, 248
Malawi, 52, 65, 82, 87, 107, 117, 119, 129, 170, 202
Mali, 47, 52, 125, 247
Malta, 16
Mandela, Nelson, 120
Mano River Union, 118, 121
Mao Zedong, 114, 213, 219, 231, 242
Marin, Manuel, 103
Marxism–Leninism, 58–9, 66, 108, 131, 144, 147, 150, 152, 180–1, 184, 191–242
Mauritania, 44, 48, 88, 96, 114
Mauritius, 170
Mba, Leon, 84, 91
Médecins sans Frontières, 227
media, 229, 273
mediation, 236–7, 260–1
Meles Zenawi, 180, 205, 243
Mengistu Haile-Mariam, 58–60, 65–6, 102, 108, 123, 130, 154, 156, 158, 184–5, 191, 217, 220, 228
militarisation, 40, 150–8, 168, 269
military aid
arms, 22, 43, 81, 104, 113, 138, 153, 155–6, 199, 269
coups d'état, 36, 50–1, 56–8, 60–1, 83, 130, 188, 190, 204, 237, 253
intervention, 83–4, 100, 105, 109, 111, 122–5, 130–3, 259
power, 32
regimes, 57, 60–2, 166, 203, 206–7
see also under individual Africa and external states
minerals, 28, 68–70, 135, 138, 148, 155, 164, 234
Mitterrand, François, 89–93, 96–7, 194, 204, 241, 253
Mitterrand, Jean-Christophe, 90, 95, 97
Mobutu Sese Soko, 61, 83, 89, 92–3, 138, 153, 155, 178, 191, 203–4, 225, 249, 252, 254, 262
Moi, Daniel arap, 199, 202–3, 224, 240, 253
Momoh, Joseph, 254
'monoeconomics', 169, 193
'monopoly state', 5, 56–62, 72, 78, 82, 153, 156, 158, 173, 193, 195–6, 235, 247, 273
Monrovia group, 110
Morocco, 14, 22, 44, 47, 111, 114, 130, 190, 216, 224
Moslem, Moslems, *see* Islam
Mozambique
aid, 72, 183–6
decolonisation, 85, 243
domestic politics, 126, 243
external intervention, 241, 253
foreign policy, 87, 149
insurgency, 132, 140, 151, 156, 209, 212, 217, 219
peace settlements, 205, 225, 237, 260–1
regional relations, 118, 122–3, 132, 184, 217, 220–1
MPLA, 20, 92, 114, 132, 155, 210, 218, 234, 243, 254
Mugabe, Robert, 120, 123, 145, 204, 241, 243
Murtala Mohamed, 61, 80
Museveni, Yoweri, 116, 123, 179–80, 205, 211, 240–1, 243, 248

Namibia, 22, 34, 37, 51, 84, 103, 114, 140, 159, 212, 214, 217, 234, 236, 241–2
Nasser, Gamal Abdel, 129
nationalism, nation-building, 35–8, 45, 53–4, 56–7, 68, 79, 194, 247–8
'nationalities', Stalinist doctrine of, 145, 194
NATO, 121, 135, 142, 151
neocolonialism, 52, 79, 85, 108, 181
Netherlands, 16, 164, 191
Nicaragua, 18, 150
Niger, 91, 130
Nigeria
civil war 1967–70, 47, 49, 80–1, 90, 93, 111–12, 137, 143, 151, 157, 210, 227, 235, 268
colonial government, 39
corruption, 252
decolonisation, 44
democratisation , 58, 71, 203, 206–7
domestic politics, 35, 49, 52–4, 56, 122, 129

economy, 165–7, 171, 179
foreign policy 87, 100, 108, 110
military regimes, 54, 61, 206–7
oil, 70–1, 80, 100, 166
regional relations, 64, 117–19, 121–2, 124–5, 238
Nimairi, Gaafar, 66, 153, 221, 237, 253
Nkomo, Joshua, 204, 241
Nkrumah, Kwame, 35, 38, 47, 65, 88, 106, 109–10, 112, 138, 247
Non-Aligned Movement, 45, 79, 126
non-alignment, 20, 63–5, 111, 113, 140
non-governmental organisations, NGOs, 183, 185–6, 192, 195–6, 226–30, 257–266, 273
African, 196, 264
Norway, 197
NPFL, 92, 124–5, 157, 223–4, 231, 234, 239
NRA, 30, 211, 213, 231, 241, 243
Nujoma, Sam, 223
Nyerere, Julius, 53, 58, 112, 170, 182, 190

OAU, 110–17, 130–3, 137, 146, 176, 189–92, 210, 215, 237–8, 251–2
Charter, 110–13, 240
Liberation Committee, 113, 209–10
Obote, Milton, 62, 110, 188–9
Ogaden, 1977–8 war, 60, 66, 102, 130, 136–7, 153–4, 220
oil, 70–1, 91–2, 128, 138, 140, 234
1970s price rise, 61, 70–2, 80, 99, 113, 128, 155, 165, 168, 269
Ojukwu, Chukwuemeka, 14
Olympio, Sylvanus, 190
'omnibalancing', 63, 65, 139
Operation Turquoise, 253
'opex', 174
OTRAG, 252
Oxfam, 227–8

PAC, 231
'pacted transitions', 236
Palestine, 127, 131
pan-Africanism, 47, 106, 120
parastatals, 171, 178, 180
Paris Club, 170
parties, political, 52–3, 56–7, 144, 196, 201, 242
Pasqua, Charles, 97
pastoralism, 28–9, 108
patron-client relations, *see* clientelism
peacekeeping, *see* United Nations
Pentecostalism, 263
personalism, 90–1
Philippines, 43
Pisani, Edgard, 102
Podgorny, Nicolai, 136
Polisario, 22, 96, 114
'political conditionalities', 24, 26, 101, 115, 126, 192–207, 225, 261
Politique Africaine, 247
Pompidou, Georges, 89
Portugal
colonialism, 32–3, 37, 142, 270
decolonisation, 20, 34, 38–9, 43, 85, 114, 151, 210
post-colonial relations, 85, 103, 112
post-colonialism, 77–105
see also individual colonial powers
'prebendal alliances', 62
primary production, 68–70, 100, 168, 171
privatisation
of diplomacy, 244–66
of parastatals, 171, 178–9, 250
PTA, 118

Qadhafi, Muammar, 65, 93, 108, 129, 155, 216, 231
'quasi-states', 15–16, 24, 222, 246, 271

radio trottoir, 273
Rawlings, Jerry, 61, 179–80, 206, 248
Reagan, Ronald, 141, 174, 225
refugees, 6, 116, 218–19, 224, 257, 273
regional organisations, 117–25
religion, 29, 32, 126
see also Christianity, Islam
Renamo, 123, 132, 140, 205, 209, 212, 217, 219, 224, 233, 237, 241, 253
'rentier states', 70–1
revenues, state, 33, 67–71, 79, 166–7, 187
revolutions, 55, 151
Rhodesia, 39, 51, 119, 132, 209, 214, 218
UDI, 1965–80, 14, 17, 54, 87–8, 112, 114, 144, 212, 216–17
see also Zimbabwe
Rowland, Tiny, 253
RPF, 93, 204–5, 211, 219, 232, 237, 240, 259, 261
RUF, 219, 222, 231
rulers, *see* leaders, leadership
Rusk, Dean, 137
Russia, *see* USSR
Rwanda, 34, 48, 51, 83, 85, 93, 96–7, 199, 208, 225, 239, 253, 261, 270
1994 genocide, 93, 203–5, 219, 232, 259–60

SACU, 171, 176
SADC, SADCC, 118

Sadiq al-Mahdi, 221
SADR, *see* Western Sahara
Salim Salim, 117, 192
São Tomé and Principe, 151, 202
Saudi Arabia, 131, 231, 257
Save the Children Fund, 227
Savimbi, Jonas, 92, 205, 224–5, 234, 255
Sawyer, Amos, 124
security, 4–5, 80–4, 108, 256
  complexes, 120–1, 212
  personal, 4–5, 120, 147
  regime, 83–4
  regional, 120–5
  state, 82–3, 120, 147, 151
  territorial, 80–2
Sekou Touré, Ahmad, 38, 54, 110, 121, 139, 247
Senegal, 54, 58, 84, 91, 96, 117, 122–3, 125, 131–2, 170
Senegambian Confederation, 121, 123
Senghor, Leopold Sedar, 58
settlers, white, 39–40, 51, 112
Shaba, 1977–8 invasions, 83, 89, 92, 153, 217
'shadow state', 249–56, 266
Sierra Leone
  colonial rule, 48, 68
  corruption, 249, 251–2, 254
  domestic politics, 56, 129
  external intervention, 131, 254
  foreign policy, 107
  insurgency, 125, 208, 212, 219, 222, 231, 233–4
  military regime, 206
  regional relations, 118, 121, 123, 125, 217
  Stevens regime, 58, 153, 179, 254
Singapore, 42, 69
Siyad Barre, Mohammed, 60–1, 156–7, 191, 220, 254–5
slavery, 30, 127, 192, 246
smuggling, 6, 187, 222, 272–3
'sobels', 219
socialism, 55, 144, 170, 179, 182, 201, 268
  see also Marxism–Leninism
'socialist orientation', 147
Somalia, Somali Republic
  external intervention, 125, 230, 232–3, 237–9, 259
  foreign policy, 65–6, 129, 136, 139, 225
  idea of the state, 34–5, 108, 216, 270
  insurgency, state collapse, 14, 30, 86, 115, 156, 164, 205, 208, 211–13, 223, 232–4, 237–9, 255, 258, 266
  irredentism, 44, 47–50, 111, 130–1, 154, 211, 216
  Italy, relations with, 35, 84, 103, 232
  Siyad Barre regime, 60–1, 155–7, 191, 220, 254–5
  Somaliland, 35, 50, 82, 158, 220
  Somali National Alliance, 223
  Somali National Movement, 220
  superpower relations, 143, 146, 152, 154–5, 217
South Africa
  apartheid foreign policy, 14, 45, 138, 224
  apartheid regime, 39–40, 48
  destabilisation, 122–3, 132, 140, 184–5, 209, 216, 220, 269
  domestic history and politics, 30, 34, 122
  external policies towards *apartheid*, 17, 51, 88, 99, 115, 127, 141, 143, 189
  France, relations with, 92
  majority rule, 1994, 34, 38–9, 159, 201, 236, 253–4, 257
  Namibia, control over, 22, 37, 214–15
  regional relations, 108–9, 118–22, 222, 233
  wildlife conservation, 233, 263
sovereignty, 8, 16–19, 23, 27, 41–3, 103, 107, 187–92, 259, 267–9, 272
  juridical/negative, 15–18, 25, 50, 81–3, 109, 115, 137, 195, 199, 247, 256, 258
  'letterbox', 20
Soviet Union, *see* USSR
Spain
  colonialism, 85, 114, 270
  post-colonial relations, 85, 103
Spanish Sahara, *see* Western Sahara
Stabex, 100
statehood, 8–15, 22–3, 244–9, 265–6, 267–74
  see also 'idea of the state', juridical, monopoly, quasi-, & rentier states
Stevens, Siaka, 58, 121, 153, 179, 251–2, 254
Strasser, Valentine, 206
structural adjustment, 7, 26, 67, 71, 168, 169–81, 193, 197–8, 226, 246, 250–1, 270
Sudan
  Beshir regime, 206, 239
  civil war, 49, 150–3, 156, 211–12, 217–21, 224–5, 232, 235
  colonial government, 39
  domestic politics, 44, 122
  economy, 164
  foreign policy, 66–7, 108, 139
  idea of the state, 48, 66–7, 241, 270
  independence, 34
  mediation, 236–7
  military coups, 61, 130–1, 148, 253
  regional relations, 123–4, 153, 155, 158, 220–1, 241

religion, 127, 129, 131–2, 158, 206, 263
SPLA, 150, 212, 217, 219–20, 224, 235
superpower relations, 66–7, 141, 148, 217
Sullivan Code, 141
superpowers, 3, 18, 40–2, 55, 74, 77, 134–59, 215, 269
see also USA, USSR
SWAPO, 22, 212, 215–17, 221, 223–4, 231–2, 234
Swaziland, 48, 87
Sweden, 87, 197
Switzerland, 254–5
Syria, 131
Sysmin, 101

TanZam Railway, 144
Tanzania, Tanganyika
aid, 183–4, 197–8
domestic politics, 58
economy, 170, 176
Germany, relations with, 84
mutiny, 1964, 84
Nyerere, foreign policy of, 53–4, 112–13
regional relations, 119–20
Zanzibar, union with, 50
Taylor, Charles, 62, 92, 124, 157, 223–4, 234, 238–9, 255
terms of trade, 69, 71
territoriality, 10–11, 44, 46–50, 216
Thatcher, Margaret, 87
Timbuktu, 30
Togo, 47–9, 54, 60, 96, 190, 203
Tolbert, William, 113, 121, 153, 155, 190
Tombalbaye, François, 91
toxic waste trade, 252, 255
TPLF, 30, 152, 211–12, 225, 228–9
Tripoli, 1982 conference, 115
Tshombe, Moise, 81

UDEAC, 118
Uganda
Amin regime, 101, 115, 123, 130, 153, 188–90, 213
colonial rule, 39
decolonisation, 44
democratisation, 199
economy, 180, 198, 248
insurgency, 30, 208, 211, 213, 231, 239
Museveni regime, 116, 123, 179–80, 205, 239–43, 248
mutiny, 1964, 84
Obote regimes, 62, 110, 188–9
regional relations, 93, 119
state collapse, 86, 248, 265
Unita, 20, 92, 114, 130, 140–1, 159, 205, 212, 217, 224, 231, 233–4, 237, 239
United Kingdom, UK, 12, 16, 61, 98–9, 141, 143, 174, 198
aid, 82–4, 87, 194–5
colonialism, 26, 32, 36, 48, 85, 270
decolonisation, 37–40, 42
military aid, intervention, 80–1, 83–4, 112
post-colonial relations, 52, 54, 80–4, 86–8, 89, 104, 112, 188–9, 191, 241
United Nations, UN, 20–2, 39, 137, 222, 267–8
Charter, 17, 25, 41, 111, 268, 272
ECA, 176
General Assembly, 17, 209, 215
peacekeeping, 123–4, 205
Security Council, 86, 111
UNDP, 257
UNHCR, 257
UNICEF, 257
UNITAF, 116, 125, 230, 232, 237–8
UNOSOM, 116, 124–5, 232, 237–9, 255
United States of America, USA
aid, 198, 229
democracy and rights, 191, 197–9, 202–3, 248
domestic politics, 16, 43, 168, 246
foreign policy, 55, 60, 86, 191, 194, 196, 243, 254, 256
military aid, intervention, 64–5, 116, 140, 154–5, 191–2, 210, 217, 230–1, 237–8
relations with Africa, 38, 52, 61, 88, 92–3, 108, 114, 130, 132, 134–42, 151–9, 174, 191, 217, 224–5
unity, African, 5, 106, 110–11, 120, 132
Universal Declaration of Human Rights, 196
Upper Volta, *see* Burkina Faso
USSR, Soviet Union
aid, 145, 218, 231
collapse of, 7, 13, 18, 134, 194, 256, 270
domestic politics, 16–17, 35, 122, 146–7, 199
foreign policy, 55, 79, 83
military aid and intervention, 60–1, 65, 108–9, 112, 140–1, 145, 149, 152–5, 209–10, 216, 241
relations with Africa, 38, 52, 64–6, 88–9, 102, 108, 114, 122, 134–42, 142–50, 151–9, 174, 184, 189, 191, 217, 227, 229, 237

Varsano, Serge, 91

Venetian Republic, 16
Vietnam, 21, 46, 136, 149–50, 243

War on Want, 227, 229
'warlords', 212, 232, 238, 273
  see also insurgency
Warsaw Pact, 121, 135, 154, 164
weapons, *see* militarisation
Western Sahara, 14, 22, 48, 86, 96, 114–15, 130
wildlife conservation, 261–3
Wilson, Harold, 81
World Bank, 71, 86, 95, 102, 164, 168–70, 174–5, 177–9, 181, 193, 197–8, 200
World Food Programme, 257
World Health Organisation, 257
World Vision, 227
World War
  First, 84
  Second, 41
World Wide Fund for Nature, 262–3

Yamoussoukro Basilica, 127–8
  conferences, 132
Yaoundé Conventions, 84, 99
Yugoslavia, 14, 35, 125, 194

Zaïre
  colonial rule, 31, 38
  corruption, 252–4
  crisis, 1960, 79, 85, 123, 139, 268
  domestic politics, 44
  economy, 164–5, 174, 178, 233
  external intervention, 112, 155
  external relations, 80, 93, 129–30
  France, role of, 92–3, 96, 203–4
  insurgency, 155, 208
  Katanga secession, 47, 81, 210, 235
  Mobutu regime, 61, 92, 138, 153, 155, 178, 191, 203–4, 225, 249, 262
  regional relations, 132, 219, 222, 232–3, 240
  Shaba invasions, 83, 89, 217
Zambia, 31, 38, 65, 87, 117, 119–20, 144, 164–5, 177, 202, 217, 221, 241
Zanzibar, 50
Zimbabwe, 34, 87, 114, 119–20, 123, 132, 145–6, 178, 206, 236, 241–3, 253, 263
  ZANU, ZANU-PF, 204, 210, 212, 214, 217–18, 221, 243, 253
  ZAPU, 145, 204, 210, 214, 217, 221, 241
Zvogbo, Edison, 253

CAMBRIDGE STUDIES IN INTERNATIONAL RELATIONS 50

38 *Mark Rupert*
Producing hegemony
The politics of mass production and American global power

37 *Cynthia Weber*
Simulating sovereignty
Intervention, the state and symbolic exchange

36 *Gary Goertz*
Contexts of international politics

35 *James L. Richardson*
Crisis diplomacy
The Great Powers since the mid-nineteenth century

34 *Bradley S. Klein*
Strategic studies and world order
The global politics of deterrence

33 *T. V. Paul*
Asymmetric conflicts: war initiation by weaker powers

32 *Christine Sylvester*
Feminist theory and international relations in a postmodern era

31 *Peter J. Schraeder*
US foreign policy toward Africa
Incrementalism, crisis and change

30 *Graham Spinardi*
From Polaris to Trident: The development of US Fleet Ballistic Missile technology

29 *David A. Welch*
Justice and the genesis of war

28 *Russell J. Leng*
Interstate crisis behavior, 1816–1980: realism versus reciprocity

27 *John A. Vasquez*
The war puzzle

26 *Stephen Gill (ed.)*
Gramsci, historical materialism and international relations

25 *Mike Bowker and Robin Brown (eds.)*
From Cold War to collapse: theory and world politics in the 1980s

24 *R. B. J. Walker*
Inside/outside: international relations as political theory

23 *Edward Reis*
The Strategic Defense Initiative

22 *Keith Krause*
Arms and the state: patterns of military production and trade

21 *Roger Buckley*
US–Japan alliance diplomacy 1945–1990

20 *James N. Rosenau and Ernst-Otto Czempiel (eds.)*
Governance without government: order and change in world politics

19 *Michael Nicholson*
Rationality and the analysis of international conflict

18 *John Stopford and Susan Strange*
Rival states, rival firms
Competition for world market shares

17 *Terry Nardin and David R. Mapel (eds.)*
Traditions of international ethics

16 *Charles F. Doran*
Systems in crisis
New imperatives of high politics at century's end

15 *Deon Geldenhuys*
Isolated states: a comparative analysis

14 *Kalevi J. Holsti*
Peace and war: armed conflicts and international order 1648–1989

13 *Saki Dockrill*
Britain's policy for West German rearmament 1950–1955

12 *Robert H. Jackson*
Quasi-states: sovereignty, international relations and the Third World

11 *James Barber and John Barratt*
South Africa's foreign policy
The search for status and security 1945–1988

10 *James Mayall*
Nationalism and international society

9 *William Bloom*
Personal identity, national identity and international relations

8 *Zeev Maoz*
National choices and international processes

7 *Ian Clark*
The hierarchy of states
Reform and resistance in the international order

6 *Hidemi Suganami*
The domestic analogy and world order proposals

5 *Stephen Gill*
American hegemony and the Trilateral Commission

4 *Michael C. Pugh*
The ANZUS crisis, nuclear visiting and deterrence

3 *Michael Nicholson*
Formal theories in international relations

2 *Friedrich V. Kratochwil*
Rules, norms, and decisions
On the conditions of practical and legal reasoning in international relations and domestic affairs

1 *Myles L. C. Robertson*
Soviet policy towards Japan
An analysis of trends in the 1970s and 1980s